BER

DISCOVER
ISRAEL

Edited and designed by
D & N Publishing,
Lambourn, Berkshire.

Cartography by Hardlines, Charlbury, Oxfordshire.

Our thanks to Chaim Rockman for his valuable assistance in updating this guide.

Although we have made every effort to ensure the accuracy of all the information in this book, changes do occur. We cannot therefore take responsibility for facts, addresses and circumstances in general that are constantly subject to alteration.

If you have any new information, suggestions or corrections to contribute to this guide, we would like to hear from you. Please write to Berlitz Publishing at the above address.

Photographic Acknowledgements

Copyright © Baha'i Centre 202, 204; Colorific 148, 150, 151, 153, 158, 159, 196, 203, 209, 211, 253; ER Fairbeard 205; Peter Goodfellow 47, 51, 53, 72/3, 183, 220, 223 (upper), 235, 245, 281; Tim Hill 10, 13, 15, 16, 18, 21, 26, 28, 30/1, 32 (lower), 35, 36, 40/1, 42, 43, 50, 64, 65, 67, 69, 71, 74, 75, 78, 98, 101, 103, 104, 107, 108, 112, 114, 115, 117, 119, 120, 121, 123, 124/5, 126, 127, 128/9, 130, 132, 133, 135, 137, 141, 142, 164, 168/9, 170, 172/3, 175, 176, 178, 179 (upper and lower), 186, 223 (lower), 229, 230, 241, 243, 244, 250, 254, 255, 256, 258, 273, 277, 278, 279, 282, 284, 286; Hulton Deutsch Collection 253 (upper and lower); Carlton Reid 1, 6, 11, 17, 23, 29, 32 (upper), 37, 38, 44, 56, 110, 137/8, 139, 146, 156, 180, 184, 188/9, 192, 194, 195, 210, 214, 217, 225, 226, 227, 238, 247, 248, 261, 262, 264/5, 266, 269, 270, 275, 288; Israel Government Tourist Office 155, 218; Telegraph Colour Library 251.

Front cover photograph: Roman baths at Tiberius (© Telegraph Colour Library)

Back cover photograph: Camel Sculpture (Carlton Reid/Berlitz Publishing)

Photograph previous page: Italian church on the Mount of the Beatitudes.

 The Berlitz tick is used to indicate places or events of particular interest.

Phototypeset, originated and printed by C.S. Graphics, Singapore.

BERLITZ®

DISCOVER
ISRAEL

Carlton Reid

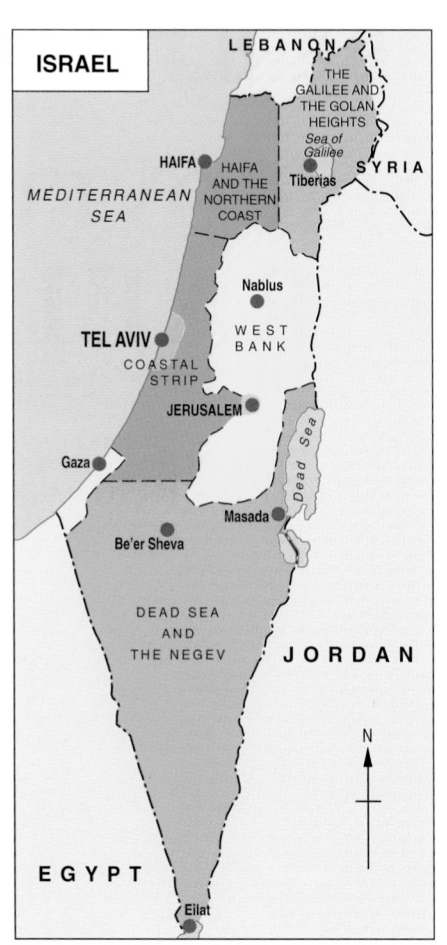

Contents

ISRAEL: FACTS AND
FIGURES 7

THE COUNTRY, ITS HISTORY
AND ITS PEOPLE 44

A CRASH COURSE IN ISRAELI
HISTORY 52

A YEAR IN ISRAEL 72

ON THE SHORTLIST 76

LEISURE ROUTES
AND THEMES 78

JERUSALEM 98

THE WEST BANK 142

TEL AVIV AND JAFFA 164

THE COASTAL STRIP 180

HAIFA AND THE
NORTHERN COAST 196

THE BAHA'I SHRINE
AND GARDENS 202

THE GALILEE 214

THE SEA OF GALILEE: A
CIRCUMNAVIGATION BY ROAD 224

SAFED 229

THE DEAD SEA AND
THE NEGEV 238

THE DEAD SEA SCROLLS
AND QUMRAN 251

WHAT TO DO 272

USEFUL NUMBERS AND
ADDRESSES 294

HOTELS AND
RESTAURANTS 304

Index 313

MAPS

Israel 8; Palestine in the Time of Jesus 49; Twelve Tribes 52; West Bank 144; Coastal Strip 182; Haifa and the Northern Coast 198; the Galilee and the Golan Heights 216; Dead Sea 240; Negev Desert 260.

Town plans: Be'er Sheva 259; Bethlehem 149; Eilat 267; Haifa 199; Jerusalem: 100, Ancient Walls 105, Old City 106, Jewish Quarter 109, Herod's Temple 113; Tel Aviv 166.

A Few Practical Matters

Israel has more tourist attractions, especially pilgrim attractions, per square kilometre than any other country on earth. For a country so small, this is quite some boast. A visit to Israel is a must for Christians, Jews, Muslims, birdwatchers, sun-seekers, archaeologists, sociologists and scuba-divers. Basically everybody will find something to interest them in this tiny country.

Israel has high mountains, expanses of desert, lush fields and exotic seas. Certainly other parts of the world have wonders that are higher, more barren, lusher and more exotic, but Israel has all of these within borders 418km (260 miles) from north to south and 112km (70 miles) at its maximum width. These other parts of the world may sometimes be on a grand scale but none can compare with the compactness of Israel. Good things come in small bundles.

*T*he blue-domed Monastery of St George clings precariously to the cliff of Wadi Qelt.

Israel has a quality and a "feeling" unlike anywhere else in the world. Israel is special to the Jews because they believe in their God-given covenant over the actual land, the land of their fathers; to the Christians because this is where their Saviour, Jesus Christ, lived, worked and, eventually, died; and to Muslims for its associations with Abraham and the dream-visit of the prophet Mohammed.

"Unbelievers" have strictly non-religious claims for the specialness of Israel: it's the light, so clear and sharp and bright; it's the people, cosmopolitan and confident; or it's a host of a million and one other secular reasons.

Nobody could come to Israel without being moved by its mystical, spiritual, and yet at the same time, very physical,

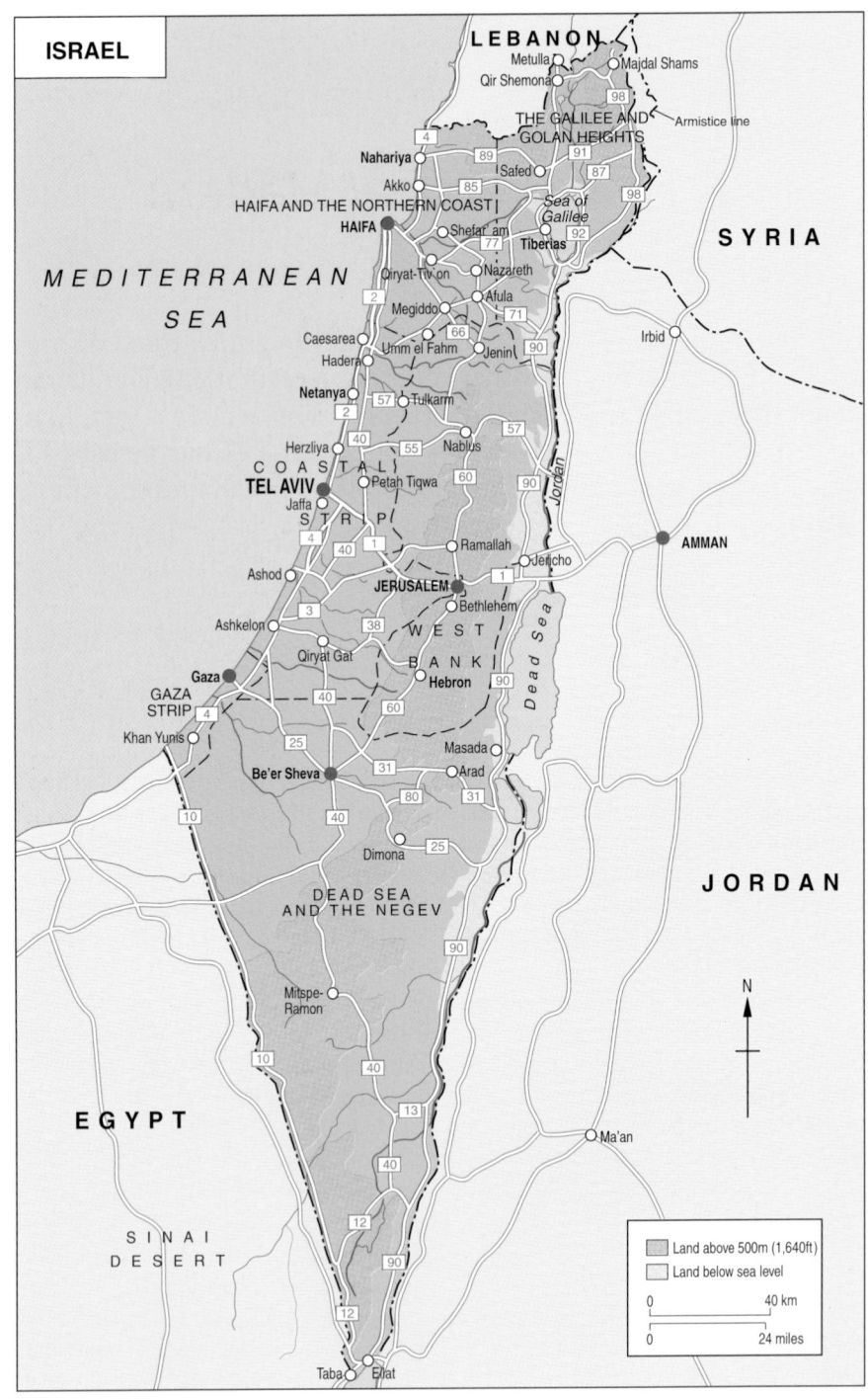

ISRAEL

LEBANON

Metulla
Majdal Shams
Qir Shemona
98
THE GALILEE AND
GOLAN HEIGHTS
Armistice line
Nahariya
89
Safed
91
87
Akko
85
98
Sea of
Galilee
HAIFA AND THE NORTHERN COAST
HAIFA
Shefar'am
77
92
Tiberias
MEDITERRANEAN
Qiryat-Tiv'on
Nazareth
SEA
Megiddo
Afula
71
66
Caesarea
Umm el Fahm
Jenin
90
Hadera
Irbid
Netanya
57
Tulkarm
2
Herzliya
55
Nablus
57
C O A S T A L
Petah Tiqwa
60
90
TEL AVIV
Jaffa
Jordan
S T R I P
4
40
1
Ramallah
AMMAN
Ashod
Jericho
JERUSALEM
1
Ashkelon
Bethlehem
3
38
W E S T
Qiryat Gat
B A N K
Gaza
Hebron
90
GAZA
60
Dead Sea
STRIP
40
4
Khan Yunis
25
Masada
Be'er Sheva
31
Arad
80
31
10
40
Dimona
25
J O R D A N
DEAD SEA
AND THE NEGEV
90
Mitspe-
Ramon
N
10
40
E G Y P T
13
Ma'an
40
12
S I N A I
90
D E S E R T
Land above 500m (1,640ft)
Land below sea level
12
0   40 km
0   24 miles
Taba Eilat

8

Average Temperatures in Degrees Fahrenheit and Centigrade

		Jan	Feb	Mar	Apr	May	June	July	Aug	Sept	Oct	Nov	Dec
Jerusalem													
	°F	53	57	61	69	77	81	83	85	82	78	66	56
	°C	11	14	16	20	25	27	28	30	28	25	19	14
Tel Aviv													
	°F	65	66	68	72	77	83	86	86	89	84	76	66
	°C	18	19	20	22	25	28	30	30	31	29	24	19
Eilat													
	°F	70	73	79	87	95	99	103	103	97	92	83	74
	°C	21	22	26	31	35	37	40	40	36	33	28	23

qualities. No wonder, then, that people have fought long and hard over this land—and continue to do so.

Yet Israel is not one big Beirut. Death and destruction do not stalk the streets. It is as safe to walk the streets in Tel Aviv as it is in a small town in Britain or America. And, in actual fact, it is much safer than walking the streets in a large metropolis such as New York. The muggings, murders and rapes that are becoming almost commonplace in the Western world do not affect Israel to anywhere near the same degree. Conflict is present, but it is a rarely seen conflict. Israel proper, that is, within the pre-1967 borders, is safe.

Whether you're a pilgrim, a sun-seeker, an archaeology buff, a hiker or just a plain hedonist, Israel will have something to offer you. Israel is a land of contrasts: fertile plains versus seemingly barren deserts; Jew versus Palestinian; soldier versus civilian; piety versus the "sins-of-the-flesh"; simple shrines ver-sus emporiums of religious kitsch; political doves versus political hawks; and five-star hotels versus flea-bitten hostels.

Climate

Israel is an all-year round holiday destination. Every season has its merits and even when the weather is below par in one place, it is likely to be fine somewhere else. So, for instance, in winter if the skies are grey and chilly in Jerusalem, head down to the Dead Sea, where it may well be balmy and pleasant. Or, in summer, if the weather is hot and humid in Tel Aviv, go up to Jerusalem where it will be cooler and more breezy.

The weather in Israel is reasonably predictable and is very seasonal. It will be blisteringly hot in the summer, especially in the southern desert areas, and reasonably chilly in the winter, particularly in the northern hills. Snow can fall on the hills—indeed, Mount Hermon is surprisingly a ski resort in the depths of winter.

Generally speaking, rain falls only during the winter, and even then it's

*I*srael, showing the main towns, roads and geographical features.

A banana seller plies his trade at the Damascus Gate in Jerusalem.

more often sunny than not. Days will be clear, bright and crisp. In the summer (and sometimes in early spring or late autumn) much of Israel can suffer for days at a time the hot desert winds known by the Arabic name *hamseen* (meaning "fifty," as in fifty days long).

Time

Israel is two hours ahead of Greenwich Mean Time. The recently introduced Summer Time in Israel is one hour ahead of the regular clock, but its permanent annual dates have not yet been fixed by law.

When To Go

The cheapest time to go, as long as you avoid the inevitable Christmas rush, is during the months of December, January and February. Because of the heat, Tiberias and Eilat drop their prices in summer rather than winter. Spring and autumn are particularly good times, as then the weather is fine, warm and dry. However, expect to pay more at these times.

Passport Requirements

Citizens of the UK, USA, Australia, New Zealand and most countries in the European Community need a valid passport for entry into Israel. A visa will be stamped into it when you enter the country. If you intend to travel to Arab countries any time in the future you should ask for this visa not to be stamped into your passport. Instead a slip of paper, the AL17, can be provided.

Visitors are given a three-month visa. Extensions can be processed by any district office of the Ministry of the Interior. The main offices are:

Shalom Meyer Tower
Visa Department
9 Rehov Ahad Ha'am
Tel Aviv
Tel. 03-5193333

Generali Building
Rehov Shlomzion
Hamalka
Jerusalem
Tel. 02-290222.

Getting There

By Air

Ben-Gurion International Airport is situated in Lod, 20km (12 miles) south east of Tel Aviv, 50km (31 miles) west of Jerusalem. Its facilities include an Israeli Government Tourist Office (IGTO) that is open around the clock to provide information and to help arrange accommodation. It also has a bank and post office, both of which are open 24-hours a day except for holidays and Shabbat. The El Al Lost and Found department, also open 24-hours a day, can be reached on tel. 03-9716934. Flight information can be gleaned from a recording on tel. 03-9731111.

Transport from the Airport

An El Al Airport bus leaves Ben-Gurion Airport Terminal in Tel Aviv approximately every hour, from 6 a.m. to 10 p.m. Egged buses leave for Tel Aviv every 15 minutes from 5 a.m. to 11.10 p.m. The United Tours Bus number 222 travels between the airport and the Railway Station, Rehov Arlosoroff, Tel Aviv, every hour all the year round. The service operates from 4.00 a.m. to 12.00 p.m. The bus stops at the Palace, Diplomat, Sheraton and Dan Hotels. For further details contact 03-5614444. Buses no longer operate between the airport and Jerusalem, but taxi fares are very reasonable.

Sherut (or Shared) Taxis

These are available around the clock. Fares are standardized—look to see what everybody else is paying (*see also* page 19).

*T*ime out in a game of matzkot *for an early-morning discussion on Tel Aviv beach.*

Ordinary taxis are also available. The fare is officially fixed, although there are different rates for different times of day.

By Sea

Israel's main ports are on the Mediterranean coast at Haifa and Ashdod. Cruising into Haifa is easily the best way to enter Israel. Lush, green Mount Carmel can be seen from far away, and when you get closer in the golden dome of the Baha'i Shrine comes into sharp focus. The Stability Line and Sol Line offer regular sailings from Europe to Haifa, and many Mediterranean cruises berth in Israel.

By Land

From Jordan

Allenby Bridge, near Jericho and the Dead Sea, some 40km (25 miles) from Jerusalem, is the crossing-point between Israel and Jordan. Visitors entering Israel via this route may re-enter Jordan by the same means. However, tourists crossing from Israel into Jordan via the Allenby Bridge are prohibited by the Jordanian Government from re-entering Israel.

The visa requirements are the same as any other point of entry into Israel. Those who need an Israeli visa in advance should make sure to obtain it before going to Jordan as it is not possible to obtain an Israeli visa in any Arab country, except Egypt.

Any tourist crossing to Jordan needs a Jordanian visa and a Jordanian permit to cross the bridge, and will have to pay a transit tax. This is levied in the form of a revenue stamp which can be purchased at any post office in Israel as well as at the bridge. Private vehicles, including bicycles, may not cross the bridge, although the rule against bicycles has been waived in special circumstances. Cameras must be empty of film.

The bridge is open only in the mornings. It is closed on Saturdays and Jewish holidays. Transit buses take you from Jordan to Israel (and vice versa) and once past all the frontier posts you will have to catch a taxi to your next destination—probably either Jerusalem or Amman.

From Egypt

The points of entry are Nizzana, Rafiah and Taba, open 363 days a year (exceptions are Yom Kippur and the first day of Muslim Idel Adha).

Nizzana, which is the main point of entry, is about 60km (37 miles) south west of Be'er Sheva, and is open between 8.00 a.m. and 4.00 p.m. Rafiah, located 50km (31 miles) south west of Ashkelon, is open between 8.30 a.m. and 5.00 p.m. Taba, the most-used point of entry from Egypt, and just south of Eilat, is open from 7.00 a.m. to 9.00 p.m. Tourists who cross from Taba to Egypt do *not* need a visa in advance, but can obtain one on presentation of a passport.

The Egyptian visa, which is valid for up to 7 days, is free of charge, but a small tax is levied. Travel is permitted to the tourist sites in southern Sinai only and visitors must return to Israel via Taba. The AL17 entry form into Israel is required. Bear in mind that most Arab countries will take any Egyptian visa from the above points to be evidence of travel to Israel and will therefore prevent your entry to their country. Ask for your stamp to be on the AL17 form rather than in your passport.

Rented cars are not permitted to cross into Egypt. United Tours has regular buses from Tel Aviv to Cairo (tel. 03-7543404).

Customs

Travellers over 17 may import duty free into Israel 250 cigarettes or 250g of tobacco products; two litres of wine and one litre of spirits; plus, a quarter of a litre of perfume.

Tourists may bring any amount of foreign currency and shekels into Israel but may take out no more foreign currency than was imported. Only during your stay can you reconvert foreign currency converted to shekels back to the original currency. You must keep the original bank receipts.

Money Matters

Israel changed its currency to the New Shekel (NIS) in 1986. Notes come in denominations of NIS 5, 10, 20, 50 and 100. One shekel is divided into 100 agorot.

When the Israeli economy was a bit shaky (in 1984, Israel had hyper-inflation of 450 per cent) it was the done thing to change money on the black market. Nowadays this is no longer necessary and banks will change money and accept credit cards with no huge loss on your part. Hotels will also be glad to change cash or travellers cheques but their rates are slightly less attractive, although undoubtably more convenient.

Banking hours are 8.30 a.m. to 12.30 a.m. (12 noon on Friday) and 4 a.m. to 5.30 p.m. Banks are usually closed Monday, Wednesday and Friday afternoons and all day Saturday. Watch out for holidays; banks close at the slightest provocation. Bank branches within international tourist hotels often have different and more convenient hours. The banks in Ben-Gurion Airport's departure area are always open.

US dollars can be exchanged just about everywhere for goods and services (even in hot-dog stands, although be prepared to forego any change). Sterling is not as widely recognized and only the larger shops and hotels will accept it. Shekels are needed for most small, everyday purchases but US dollars sometimes get you a discount on expensive items.

Tipping in dollars is appreciated. Exchange rates fluctuate in Israel so only change small amounts of hard currency at a time.

Chassidic Jewish children enjoying an ice-cream in the Jewish Quarter of Jerusalem. The birth rate of the Ultra-Orthodox Jews is much higher than the Israeli average.

Taking Money Abroad

Traveller's Cheques
Traveller's cheques are the best way to safeguard your money. American Express cheques are universally accepted but just about any banker's cheque will do—especially if it is in dollars. Once you arrive in Israel, try to think wholly in dollars; many shops only put dollar price-tags on their products and hotels use dollars for their tariff boards.

Credit Cards
Major credit cards are accepted at all the larger hotels, restaurants and shops. Smaller concerns usually take plastic but it is wise to ask first because a minority of businesses prefer cash.

Health and Medical Care

There are no vaccination requirements for tourists entering Israel, unless they arrive from infected areas. Tourists who are already in Israel and wish to obtain vaccination against cholera and yellow fever before they leave can do so at any district or sub-district office of the Ministry of Health.

Insurance

Travel insurance should cover everything from health and accident cost to lost baggage and trip cancellation. The cheapest way of covering yourself may be simply to extend your own house insurance.

Flight insurance is often included in the price of the ticket when the fare is paid with American Express, Visa or certain other major credit cards, and is also often included in package policies providing accident cover as an extra. These policies are available from most tour operators and insurance companies. Try and get a policy that is allied to Europ Assistance (in America, Travel Assistance International). This company provides medical and personal emergency services and offers immediate, on-the-spot medical, personal and financial help. Contact:

Europ Assistance Ltd
252 High Street
Croydon, Surrey
Tel. 081-680 1234

or
Europ Assistance Worldwide Services
1133 15th Street NW
Suite 400
Washington, DC 20005
Tel. 800 821-2828.

Student and Youth Travel

Student travellers should obtain an International Student Identity Card, essential for getting student discounts. Ask at your place of study for an application form.

The Israel Student Travel Association (ISSTA) offers a variety of low-priced tours and special programmes to student travellers. Contact them at:
109 Ben Yehuda Street
Tel Aviv
Tel. 03-5270111

or
5 Elissar Street
Jerusalem Tel. 02-257257.

Pilgrimages

Israel is the Holy Land. Christians go on pilgrimage, Jews don't. Jews return home; an important distinction.

The Ministry of Tourism's Pilgrimage Committee offers lectures, forums, fellowship sessions, maps and lists of religious sites. Their address is:

Box 1018
Jerusalem
Tel. 02-754863/754912/282295.

Another source of information is:
Christian Information Centre
Jaffa Gate
Jerusalem
Tel. 02-272692.

This is run by the Franciscans. They can supply tickets to Christmas midnight mass in Bethlehem. Bear in mind that numbers are often very restricted so request your tickets as far in advance as you can.

There are any number of reasons to visit Israel. Some come for the history, others just for the sun. These tourists on the Mount of Olives are on a trip retracing the steps of Jesus.

Jewish organizations, such as World Zionist Organisation (WIZO), United Synagogues, the United Jewish Appeal and, for Americans, the American Jewish Congress, offer tours geared to Jewish visitors. Any IGTO can also help arrange for services, or Bar Mitzvahs, at the Western Wall in Jerusalem or even on top of Masada. A useful address for further contacts and information is:

World Zionist Organization
Balfour House
741 High Road, Finchley
London N12
Tel. 081-446 1477.

Looking from Masada with the Dead Sea providing a scenic backdrop, the Roman siege camp is still visible.

Security

Israel is usually portrayed as one of the world's trouble spots and numerous wars over the years have harmed the Israeli tourist industry. Given the perpetual friction in the Middle East, mostly over the right of Israel to exist, the troubles are unlikely to go away. Yet as long as full-scale war is not about to erupt, then travelling to Israel is reasonably safe given that all human activities involve a certain amount of risk.

When flying to Israel on El Al, the national airline, you will experience your first taste of Israeli security. It's tight. You will be grilled, and so would any potential terrorist. Travelling with El Al has to be the safest way to fly anywhere and Israel proper is like this; there are risks but they are minimized.

Just as in many other countries, you sometimes have to be careful where and when you travel. If you plan to do a lot of independent touring, possibly to the West Bank and other such areas, then care is needed. Situations change rapidly in this part of the world and places that most people would want to avoid one day could very well be completely safe a fortnight later.

Getting Around

By Air
Israel's inland airline, Arkia, flies from Tel Aviv, Jerusalem, Haifa and Ben-Gurion airports to Eilat. There is also a Rosh Pinna flight. Its main office is at Sde Dov, Tel Aviv's local airport

(tel. 03-6902222). Services are brief and expensive, but breathtakingly beautiful.

Charter flights with other companies are also available but are even more expensive than Arkia. A group of ten passengers might make it worthwhile. Try: Ariel Azil (private operator, Jerusalem) Tel. 02-340354

Shahaf Airlines
228 Ben Yehuda Street
Tel Aviv
Tel. 09-501193

or
El-Rom Airlines
Sde Dov Airport
Tel Aviv
Tel. 03-410554.

By Train
Rail travel in Israel is more scenic than useful. Trains cover only a small part of a small country, but the service between Tel Aviv and Haifa is reasonably frequent and comfortable. The ride from Haifa to Jerusalem is deadly slow but goes in and out of some very picturesque valleys. The train from Jerusalem to Tel Aviv runs through the very pretty Sorek Valley. There is one class only, but seats may be reserved.

By Car
A car is a convenient and quick way of seeing a lot of the country. Walking and cycling would be better, more relaxing and healthier (and, of course, kinder to the environment) but few people have either the time or the inclination.

Distances are short in Israel and many sites are difficult to get to by

Hiring a car will give you the independence to see sights such as Maktesh Ramon in the Negev desert.

public transport, so a car is certainly useful. All the major car rental firms are represented and will have a car waiting for you at the airport if you wish. Local firms abound and tend to be cheaper.

Main roads in Israel are very good, but be warned: Israeli drivers are no shrinking violets. Most drive like maniacs! In the towns it can be a heart-stopping experience, until you get used to it. In the countryside, cars are few and far between.

There are many fly-drive packages available in your country of origin and they usually offer good value.

Car hire companies accept International driving licences. The minimum age for car rental is 21. Watch out for all the little extras added to the bill. If you plan to be travelling away from the most visited areas, one extra you will need is damage and accident insurance, just in case your vehicle is stoned. Although this is a rare occurrence in Israel proper, a yellow Israeli number plate is an invitation for attack in the West Bank or Gaza Strip.

The Israeli flag flies proudly on top of Masada where Army passing-out parades take place.

By Bus

Israel has a very extensive bus service. Egged, the Israeli bus cooperative, is fast, frequent, comfortable and reliable. Its services cover just about everywhere except certain parts of the Occupied Territories. Arab bus services make up the shortfall.

Egged buses are invariably air conditioned and will be fitted with sun-blinds. It is possible to reserve seats for long rides, a good idea on Friday or before a holiday, when the buses can be very crowded. There are no buses from late Friday afternoon to Saturday night, except in Haifa. Arab areas are exceptions to this rule but their services are less reliable.

For information about bus schedules ask at the information booth in the central bus station of any town or city or call 03-5375555 in Tel Aviv, 02-3045555 in Jerusalem, 04-535276 in Haifa, and 07-375161 in Eilat.

Egged Tours and a few other companies also offer special tourist trips. These vary from a half-day visit to a week-long tour, guide included. Brochures and other information can be picked up at travel agents or from bus stations. These trips offer very good value for money.

By Guide-Driven Limousine or Mini-Bus

Basically a luxury taxi service with a guide, these sorts of travel deal can work out to be very competitive for a small group of cost-sharing passengers, for instance a family. If you stay overnight anywhere, the guide's expenses will add to the overall cost. Companies specializing in guide/drivers services include:

Eshkolot-Yehuda Tours, 36 Keren Hayesod Street, Jerusalem, Tel. 02-635555

Tar Tours, 118 HaYarkon Street, Tel Aviv, Tel. 03-5101911.

Guide Mousine, Jerusalem, Tel: 02-341990

and
Twelve Tribes, Tel Aviv, Tel. 03-5229227

Taxis

All taxis are required to have meters and to use them in town. Complain to the IGTO if you get a particularly abusive driver. Remember to quote his number, which should be prominently displayed on a window or on the dashboard.

Sherut Taxis

These are shared taxis, accommodating about five or six people, who are all going in roughly the same direction. They are more expensive than buses but cheaper than normal taxis. If you see an extended Mercedes-Benz then that's a sherut (plural, *sherutim*). They run on set routes, but will not leave their stand until they are full. They are fast, frequent and popular—especially on Saturdays (there is a surcharge) when bus services do not exist. Set fares are paid to the driver whilst on the move and the interaction between passengers and driver is great fun—mass arguments can break out as loose change is passed between the occupants. Shout loud to get out when you're near your destination.

Getting to the Airport

From Tel Aviv

By United Tours Bus number 222 from the Railway Station, Rehov Arlosoroff to Ben-Gurion Airport every hour all the year round from 4.00 a.m. to 12.00 p.m. For further details, tel. 03-5614444.

By Egged Buses, every 15 minutes, from 6.00 a.m. to 11.30 p.m.

From Jerusalem

By Egged Buses, from 6.15 a.m. to 7.00 p.m., approximately every 20 minutes.

By sherut taxi: you'll usually get one when you need it, but for peace of mind book in advance at 21 Rehov Hamelech George, tel. 02-227227, or tel. 02-253233 for Nesher taxis.

Baggage Services

If flying El Al, you can check-in your luggage at their office in Haifa, Jerusalem or Tel Aviv the evening before departure (except on Friday, holy-days and the eve of holy-days). It will go straight to your plane and you need arrive at the airport only an hour before departure. However, given the security measures needed in Israel it is wise to be at the airport as early as possible.

The following El Al offices are open for check-in services:
Tel Aviv Railway Station
Arlosoroff Street
North Tel Aviv
Tel. 03-6917199.
Open from 4.00 p.m. to midnight.

12 Rehov Hillel
Jerusalem
Tel. 02-383166.
Open from 6.45 p.m. to 11.00 p.m.

6 Hanamel Street
Haifa
Tel. 04-5641100.
Open from 4.00 p.m. to 11 p.m.

Automobile Club

The Automobile and Touring Club of Israel (MEMS) is affiliated to the Federation Internationale de l'Automobile (FlA) and to the Alliance Internationale de Tourisme (AlT), and as such is linked to every Automobile and Touring Club in the world, providing reciprocal services for all tourists who are members of other clubs. Services include emergency help, towing, legal and technical advice and touring advice. They have an office at:
20Harakevet Street
Tel Aviv
Tel. 03-5641111.

Visiting Egypt

Egypt is the only Arab country to be officially at peace with Israel. Since the 1979 peace treaty, many visitors to Israel have taken the opportunity to visit Egypt (or just the Sinai desert). There is a daily air service to Cairo, and, at the time of writing, US and British nationals can still get a visa at Cairo Airport. There is also a bus service from Tel Aviv to Cairo which takes about ten hours but you must have a visa in advance, obtainable from the:
Egyptian Embassy
54 Basel Street
Tel Aviv
Tel. 03-5464151.

No visa is needed for the Sinai, as long as you are coming back to Israel. Israeli travel agents offer many package deals to Egypt and you can be back in Israel after just a day or two—enough time to see the Pyramids and visit the Cairo Museum.

Accommodation

Hotels
Hotels in Israel are as varied as you would imagine in a country geared for tourists. The large international hotels are well represented and their rooms are like similar hotel rooms anywhere in the world. Israel also has many independent hotels and these are often a little more lively than the international ones. Some are modestly priced, and although they may be run-down, they are full of personality.

The personality of a hotel is important. If you have the chance, try to visit a number of hotels before you decide where to stay. Price is absolutely no guide to personality. Except for one hotel, that is. The King David in Jerusalem, five-star and expensive, is plush, decadent and wonderful. It is easily the best hotel in Israel.

Some of the budget hotels are pretty rough but many others are clean, tidy and pleasant. However, they have no frills. The Tourism Ministry regulates and supervises all the hotels that it recommends. The standard star-system is used but expect huge differences between similar grades.

Most Israeli hotels serve kosher food (the exceptions are the Arab hotels in such places as Arab East Jerusalem) and some are so highly regulated by the Rabbinate (the head group of rabbis in Israel, who uphold religious laws) that they can call themselves *Glatt Kosher* (very kosher). A number of the international hotels are *Glatt Kosher*. This does not make them ultra-religious, it just means their kitchens are strictly regulated by the Rabbinate. Non-Jews would not be able to tell the difference.

Most hotels, even the smallest of the small, will include a buffet-style Israeli breakfast in with the price of a room. Also included will be service and the various taxes.

Kibbutz Guest Houses

Kibbutz guest houses are as modern and comfortable as any luxury hotel. The best of them are excellent and they are often situated in out-of-the-way places. Most have swimming pools and many offer lectures and tours to give guests a feel of kibbutz life. They are more akin to American motels than English farmhouse bed and breakfast places. They are cheaper than most city-centre hotels and the food on offer is wholesome and filling, but only rarely up to gourmet standards.

The swimming pool of the sumptuous King David Hotel in Jerusalem. This is easily the best hotel in Israel, but at a price.

Bed and Breakfast

A holiday in Israel usually entails being located in city hotels. But a recent phenomenon is the expansion of bed-and-breakfast places, a new concept to Israelis.

The best B & Bs in Israel are those on kibbutzim—for about £20 you get a simple room, bathroom included, and facilities for making coffee. Breakfast (and an evening meal if you pay extra) is taken with the kibbutzniks in their communal dining hall. An Israeli breakfast consists of salads and cheeses, and whereas in a hotel there will also be the choice of a cooked or continental breakfast, the kibbutz makes few concessions to tourists, aside from perhaps a box or two of cereal.

The rooms for tourists have become available mainly because there are no more separate children's houses on kibbutzim throughout Israel—unlike just a few years ago children now live with their parents. These accommodation blocks, or sometimes small apartments, have been converted into clean and simple B & B rooms.

As well as being an alternative and culturally enlightening way of getting a bed in Israel, the kibbutzim offering B & B are usually in peaceful, rural surroundings, very often with a farm on the site. Another advantage is that in the summer most kibbutzim have open-air swimming pools.

A book listing all the B & Bs in the country is available from IGTO offices in Israel. It is much better to book your accommodation in advance rather than just turning up on the off-chance. Countryside Accommodation (Yaron Eshkolot) in Tel Aviv offers a booking service for B & B accommodation and rooms in kibbutzim (tel. 03-5236541/6427430, fax 03-6425613). The same service is available in the UK only through Classic Tours in London (tel. 071 613 4441, fax 6134024). Also in the UK, you can try Israel Travel Service, tel. 061-839 1111.

Christian Houses

Located mainly in Jerusalem and Galilee, some 30 Christian hospices provide basic lodging and sometimes meals. Some hospices are real bargains, others are slightly over-priced for the sort of basic accommodation on offer. Non-Christians can get rooms, but on Christian holidays the places will be fully booked out.

Youth Hostels

The Israeli Youth Hostel Association operates over 30 youth hostels throughout Israel that are open to all. A youth hostel membership card (available in your country of origin or you can obtain one in Israel) will get you a small discount on accommodation, but not enough if you will only be staying a couple of nights. Accommodation is usually in single-sex dormitories although some hostels have family rooms that are available. Many of the hostels are in locations where very little other accommodation exists. For this reason they are often the places to stay if you don't have a car to get you quickly to the nearest hotel. More information can be obtained from:

Israeli Youth Hostel Association
Box 1075
3 Dorot Rishonim Street
Jerusalem
Tel. 03-252706.

A serene garden on kibbutz Yad HaNah, near Tulkarm. Just a 5-minute walk will get you to the not-so-serene West Bank.

Volunteer Work in Israel

Kibbutzim The kibbutz is an Israeli institution. The early kibbutzim helped to found and consolidate the state. Although greatly changed from the pioneering days of heady socialism, novel nationalism and back-breaking working conditions, the kibbutzim are still communally governed and most property is jointly owned. Work is organized on a co-operative basis. Members receive no salary, but in return for their work get housing, clothing, food, medical services, education for their children and other social amenities. Not all kibbutzim are agricultural; many are now involved in high-tech industries such as electronics and computers. There are over 200 kibbutzim in all parts of the country and the number of members ranges from 90 to over 2,000. Not all kibbutzim accept volunteers. Check with the contacts listed below.

There are four main kibbutz movements, loosely based around common views on politics and religious observance (usually lack of it and degrees in between).

Kibbutzim take in young volunteers who will be expected to work for around six hours a day in return for hearty food and basic accommodation. The age requirements are above 18 and below 32.

Hakibbutz Ha'Artzi	Hakibbutz Hadati	Ikhud Hakvutzot
13 Rehov Leonardo	(religiously observant)	Vehakibbutzim and
da Vinci	7 Rehov Dubnov	Hakibbutz Hemeyuhad
64733 Tel Aviv	Tel Aviv	10 Rehov Dubnov
Tel. 03-69252222	Tel. 03-6957231	Tel Aviv
		Tel. 03-5452555

Ha' Takam, United Kibbutz Movement
82 Rehov HaYarkon
Tel Aviv, tel. 03-5452555

The best bet to make sure of a kibbutz place is to volunteer before you leave for Israel. Contact either:

Kibbutz Representatives	or	The Jewish Agency
1a Accommodation Road		Kibbutz Aliyah Desk
London NW11		515 Park Avenue
Tel. 071-450 9235		New York, NY 10022
		Tel. 212-688-4134

Moshavim Moshavs are collective villages. Volunteer Moshav work is often a lot harder than volunteer kibbutz work—but as well as your board and lodging you will also receive a reasonably decent wage. There are two Moshavim movements—Moshav Ovdim and Moshav Shitufi. Moshav Ovdim is set up on principles of mutual aid and equality of opportunity, and Moshav Shitufi is based on co-operative economy and ownership, as in the kibbutz, but with each family owning its own house and accepting responsibility for its own domestic arrangements.

For further information contact:
19 Rehov Leonardo da Vinci
64733 Tel Aviv
Tel. 03-6958473

Camping

There are at least 15 official campsites spread throughout Israel that offer amenities such as electricity, hot showers, shops and restaurants. All campsites are guarded at night. At holiday times they can get very full with vacationing Israelis. For more information contact:

Israel Camping Union
Box 53
Nahariya
Tel. 04-925392.

Wild camping in Israel is possible and highly recommended. Away from civilization, for example if you are trekking through the Negev, it may be the only option. If you don't use a tent, some sort of covering would be a good idea for your sleeping bag because dew can be very heavy in the mornings. Wild animals such as the panthers in the Judean desert will not harm you. In the Carmel mountains wild dogs roam loose but their howling at night is more for show than anything else.

Public and Religious Holidays

On the major holidays, such as Rosh Hashanah, Yom Kippur, Simhat Torah, Yom Ha'Atzma'ut and Shavu'ot, Jewish businesses will close. On the first days of Sukkot and Pesach all businesses will close. Lesser holidays may be marked by an early closing day only.

In the Arab areas of Israel, the West Bank and the Gaza Strip, many restaurants close for the entire month of Ramadan. Arab shops will have different closing times but these are harder to pinpoint, especially with the disruption of the Intifada, when many shops have erratic hours or open only in the mornings. Many will be closed all day on Fridays.

Communications

Mail

The symbol of the Israeli post office is a white deer on a blue background. Post offices can be found in the commercial centres of all towns. The major ones will have Poste Restante facilities for any forwarded mail.

Mail in Israel is depressingly slow. Post offices are chaotic places, manned, it often seems, with staff especially trained in avoidance techniques and customer abuse. Do not expect many smiles. This is common to all Israeli officialdom. Don't let it upset you. Petty bureaucrats like being rude to you, it is a national institution and Israelis would have it no other way. Tourists may find this manner brusque, but it is as much a part of Israel as *falafel* and Uzi machine guns.

Telephones

The Israeli telephone system is usually reliable and works well. Public phones are available in most places, and they take phone cards which may be purchased at all post offices, and from news stands and book shops. Cards may also be purchased from the automatic machines next to the public phones. Most public phones also take Visa and Master Card.

Information (dial 144) has listings in English and most operators speak English. Direct dialling is available to most Western countries. For special overseas calls, the international operator is obtained by dialling 188. Overseas calls can be made from special booths in all the major tourist centres. These are often located in or near the Central Post Office, which also offers telex and fax facilities. You can dial from your hotel but charges will be astronomical.

Tipping

Because of tourism, especially North American tourism, tipping is now standard in Israel. A 10 per cent tip is the norm. In medium- and high-priced restaurants, a service charge is already added but tourists usually leave more. Hotel rates include a service charge, but porters and chambermaids usually expect a little extra, depending on the service. Sherut taxi drivers do not need to be tipped. Taxi drivers have to operate their meters as required by law. If a taxi driver does not use his meter, the chances are he has already built a healthy tip into his suggested fee.

It does work both ways though: if you're travelling a long distance, for example from Tel Aviv to Jerusalem, you may be able to agree to a price that would be far lower than the meter rate. Hotels usually have a board in the foyer with recommended prices to certain destinations and you can haggle down from this if you wish. No matter how badly they may have treated you, taxi drivers will still expect a tip.

Special Telephone Numbers
Information 144
Time 155
Telephone Repairs 166
Overseas Operator 188
Overseas (reverse charges or collect calls) (03) 622881
Direct Dialling
Information 195
Telegrams 171
Auto Alarm (wake-up calls) 174/175
Ambulance (Magen David Adom) 101
Police 100
Fire 102

Toilets
Public toilets, when they can be found, are identified by a *00* sign. Unfortunately, amenities in these places are often pretty basic. Other than in hotels and restaurants, the best facilities are usually at national parks and nature reserves, and the worst are those located at petrol stations.

*I*srael is full of public art, and sculpture gardens are especially popular. This fountain is in the Liberty Bell Park in Jerusalem.

Children

Taking a child (or multiples thereof) to Israel is a sure way to strike up conversations with the natives. Israelis—

An Arab baby takes a nap while Daddy does the shopping in the shuq *of the Old City in Jerusalem.*

Arabs and Jews alike—adore children. For the locals, in some ways, having children is a political statement: it ensures the continuation of the Israelis and therefore makes them feel secure. If one side of the political, national and racial divide has more babies than another then that side will be the winner by dint of demography.

The Victorian ethic that children should be seen but not heard would be an alien one to most Israelis: children are the lifeblood and are seen as mini-citizens rather than mere youngsters. Many members of the next generation tend to be boisterous. Because of this emphasis on youth, children are welcome everywhere and unlike some countries, they are not a handicap to a successful holiday. Israel is geared to looking after children. Most hotels will have special offers for accompanied children such as discounted rates or more usually free accommodation if sharing the parents' room. Museums and other attractions offer special rates for children. Baby-sitting will not be a problem at the larger hotels. Car seats are available from rental firms (book in advance to make sure) and most restaurants can provide high chairs.

Entertaining children is always a problem—a child's attention span can often be very short. Israel's many beaches, swimming pools and water-parks will keep them happy for a while but even these joys can be short-lived if you offer them to the children every day. So, when an extra ice-cream is simply not enough there are a number of alternatives.Try the Biblical Zoo in Jerusalem, the Dolphinarium in Tel Aviv, the Hai Bar Wildlife Reserve in Eilat and the Hula Nature Reserve in Qiryat Shermona.

If you really do need some space there are a number of Summer Camps that will look after your children for much of the duration of your holiday. General information is available from:
Neve Hanofesh
44 Hibat Zion Street
Ramat Gan
Tel. 03-6194883/5701621.

Camps, many of which have English-speaking helpers, can be found in community centres throughout the country. Any IGTO can point you in the right direction.

A captured Russian-built tank at Latrun Fort Artillery Museum provides an interesting play area for some children.

Food and Drink

Israel has a wide selection of eateries, ranging from nouvelle cuisine to back-street *hummous* joints. Prices vary but the expensive restaurants can be very costly indeed. Alcohol is expensive, especially the imported beers. Israeli wine is extremely palatable and cheaper than the imports. For a nice, cold drink on a hot day try Nesher Malt, a malt beer quite unlike normal malt beer because it's sweeter and less tangy.

There is no shortage of eating places in Israel. Jerusalem, Tel Aviv and some of the larger towns produce regularly updated eating guides with menu listings and prices. These guides are free from hotels or the IGTO. Bear in mind that these publications are often paid for by restaurant advertisements so take any favourable comments with a pinch of salt. Hotel food is often reasonable but not particularly adventurous. There is no such thing as Israeli cuisine (apart from the ubiquitous *falafel*—fried chick-pea balls served in pitta bread) but Israel has a tremendous selection of restaurants from around the world. Traditional Diaspora food can be found, as well as food typical of New York, French food, Vietnamese food and food from many other countries. Ethnic restaurants abound. Oriental restaurants are very popular in Israel. But Oriental does not mean Chinese,

In a hot country such as Israel, eating at open-air cafés is the norm rather than a treat. This is Ben Yehuda Street in Jerusalem.

*T*ypical Middle Eastern fare: a hummous *lunch*.

rather it means Middle Eastern: shish kebabs, *shwarma*, *hummous*, *tehina* and other such delicacies. Bon appetit, or in Hebrew, *Be'tayavon*.

Less Able Visitors

Israel is a modern country and facilities for the disabled are very good. Specially designed tours for the handicapped are available. They are almost identical to tours for non-handicapped tourists but are generally more leisurely. Numerous Israeli companies cater to the disabled traveller. Special buses are provided for the wheelchair-bound and hotels are chosen for easy wheelchair access.

*M*ahane *Yehuda market in Jerusalem is a lively* shtetl-*type produce market where you can buy fruit, pastries and* bagali *like these.*

Special tours for the blind and deaf are also available.

For general travel advice contact one of the following organizations:

Royal Association for Disability and Rehabilitation (RADAR)
25 Mortimer Street
London W1

Mobility International
43 Dorset Street
London W1

The National Society for Mentally Handicapped Children
117 Golden Lane
London EC1.

Kosher and Vegetarian Meals

Meat eaters will find plenty to excite their palates in the Holy Land. Pork and shellfish may be forbidden in most Jewish restaurants (Israeli restaurants that do serve pork will euphemistically call it "white steak") but Arab districts will be in no short supply—indeed they do a roaring trade to Israelis keen to flaunt the Jewish dietary laws.

For non-meat eaters the choice is also very wide. Many Middle Eastern dishes are based around pulses and even in meat-orientated restaurants it would be possible to order a varied and interesting meal without having recourse to meat. Middle Eastern staples such as *hummous*, *tehina* and *falafel* (respectively: chick-pea paste, sesame seed paste, and deep-fried balls of ground chick-peas) are available everywhere and become the basis for most Israeli meals, especially meals on the run. Thanks to street-side cafés and corner vendors, the *falafel* and pitta bread sandwich has become the national dish; it's totally vegetarian and very nutritious.

Falafel has to be the most wholesome fast-food snack in the world and it is also very cheap. Add one of the *harif* side-dishes for an extra "bite"—*harif* is a hot pepper mixture, which, depending on the vendor, can either be mildly spicy or mouth-searingly hot. You have been warned.

Thanks to Kashrut (the Jewish dietary regulations) there are two basic types of Israeli restaurant. The first is the "meat" restaurant which will have various animal cuts on the menu but which will not be able to serve any milk with these cuts. This is because of the Biblical injunction not to seethe a kid in its mother's milk. Cheese-and-meat dishes such as lasagne are ruled out but this also means that ice-cream is not served and coffee will have to be taken black. As a way of by-passing these restrictions there are many Israeli products that mimic milk, or its derivatives, very well. Non-dairy ice cream and non-dairy creamers for coffee are the most common.

The second type of restaurant is the "dairy" one. Such a restaurant will be largely vegetarian, although fish may be on the menu. As long as meat is not served then milk products are allowed. Dairy restaurants tend to be light-weight cafés rather than full-blown restaurants—although there are many fine exceptions to this rule.

So even if a café doesn't explicitly state it is vegetarian, if it claims to be dairy this amounts to virtually the same thing. Of course vegans will find little they can eat in a dairy restaurant, so they should search out a stated vegetarian/vegan alternative.

Vegetarianism is quite popular amongst Jews (especially non-Israeli Jews) because not eating meat means you can be safe in the knowledge you are not transgressing any of the dietary laws. Many Orthodox Jews will go vegetarian in meat restaurants rather than take the risk that the proprietors are not quite as kosher as they claim.

MAM (a Hebrew acronym for "Welfare Manpower Pool") will provide medical professionals to assist and escort disabled visitors.

MAM
35 Ben Zvi Boulevard
94555 Jerusalem
Tel. 02-223251.

Israel Government Tourist Offices worldwide, and in Israel, have pamphlets giving more specific details for handicapped travellers.

Shops

Shopping in Israel can be very varied: exclusive jewellery and diamonds; oriental carpets and Middle Eastern antiques; women's fashions and furs; leather goods; paintings and sculptures; ceramics and pottery; silverware (including ritual Jewish artefacts, known as Judaica) and copperware; embroidery and batiks; in-laid woodwork; and religious mementoes such as olive wood statuettes. Several hundred shops are approved by the Ministry of Tourism. These shops display a sign stating "Listed by the Ministry of Tourism".

For more colourful shopping, where you can haggle to your heart's content, there are many oriental markets, or *shuqs*. They can be found in the narrow alleyways of the old parts of town: notable *shuqs* can be found in Jerusalem, Bethlehem, Akko, Nazareth, Hebron and the Druse villages. These sell handmade arts and crafts—including olive wood, mother-of-pearl, leather and bamboo items, hand-blown glass and clothing. The standard "I've been to..." cotton T-shirts are also available in the *shuqs* at knockdown prices. *Shuqs* are not just there for the tourist, however, so sections will be set aside for general goods and food. If you want a broom handle or a bunch of bananas, the *shuq* will provide—it's just a matter of looking for what you want.

Shops are generally open from 8.30 a.m. to 1 p.m. and then again from 4 to 7 p.m., but department stores, restaurants and many tourist shops stay open all day.

Costs in Israel

Israel has had its fair share of economic problems, most of them stemming from the immense cost of maintaining the Israeli Defence Forces. Events do change, but at the time of writing Israel's economy is stable, with prices remaining constant.

Compared to the rest of the Middle East, Israel is not a cheap country for the tourist. Food in supermarkets and in restaurants is expensive and hotels do not come cheap. At certain times of the year you can get special deals on accommodation but food will always remain expensive. Shopping at the many markets can reduce your grocery bill—and be colourful at the same time.

If you enjoy *falafel* and *hummous* (staple snack food in Israel) then you can live quite cheaply in Israel, but if your tastes are not quite this basic then Israel can stretch the purse. Gourmet

The Arab Quarter in the Old City of Jerusalem is a treasure trove of bargains.

restaurants can work out to be very costly.

Fancy goods can be quite cheap (and if you're buying from an Arab market then you will haggle down to a very attractive price) but tourist basics such as camera film can cost a fortune.

Newspapers, Television and Radio

Israelis are voracious readers. Daily newspapers and international periodicals such as *Time* and *Newsweek* are very popular. News-stands are plentiful and well stocked with periodicals from all over the world. *The International Herald Tribune* and many British papers are flown in daily.

There are more than two dozen daily newspapers, the majority of which are printed in Hebrew. The Hebrew press is independent, often critical of the Government and always entertaining—if you can read Hebrew. The English-language daily is the *Jerusalem Post*, and this is widely available in all cities. On Fridays, this paper comes with a weekend supplement which contains listings for all major events, including film, theatre, concerts, radio and television. There is no publication on Saturdays.

There are many free periodicals given away to tourists, many of them glossy and full of advertisements for fur coats, diamonds and items of Judaica (*see* page 34). Nuggets of information can often be gleaned from them but it can be a tough search.

*I*sraelis are avid *newspaper-readers. Hebrew newspapers can be bought all over the place, including from the pavement.*

The magazine *The Jerusalem Report* is worth a look, as is *Eretz*—for the photographs alone. It's a sort of Israeli *National Geographic*, with fascinating articles on a wide range of topics. It's available in the larger news-stands or bookstores, or subscriptions are available from PO Box 565, Givatayim.

Kol Israel (Voice of Israel) operates five radio stations, which are on the air some 18 hours a day. Their offerings vary from pop music and rock 'n' roll to talk shows, commentary and news broadcasts. There are also Arabic language and classical music stations.

Israel Television broadcasts educational programmes during the day, and news and entertainment in the evenings. News is usually in Hebrew and Arabic, but is broadcast in English at 6.15 p.m. daily except for Saturdays. Many movies and programmes are imports from the US or Britain. Jordan Television offers competing entertainment.

Many of the better hotels have televisions tuned in to satellite TV—especially CNN. Israelis are obsessed by news and a 24-hour news channel is their idea of bliss.

Israel and the Arts

Israel has the most vibrant arts scene in the Middle East and would certainly put most of the Western world to shame for the sheer breadth of home-grown talent, and this from a population of only 4 million.

As well as the musical arts (Israel Philharmonic Orchestra and others) Israel also excels at dance and a number of troupes have achieved international

Holocaust sculpture at the Yad Vashem Memorial and Museum in Jerusalem.

status. Theatre is very popular and Israel has the highest per capita theatre attendance in the world. Ha-bimah and Cameri Theatres in Tel Aviv are two of the best.

In the pliable and visual arts Diaspora Jews have long had a disadvantage over their gentile neighbours. The Bible associated the making of images with idolatry and this attitude carried over into rabbinical and mediaeval Judaism. Some communities both in Israel and in the Diaspora used representational forms of art but they steered well clear of images of God. If pictures were used at all, this would be in the form of abstract designs or non-human subjects such as animals (the lion of Judah was a popular motif).

Traditional Jewish craftsmen devoted their creative energies to calligraphy, illustrated manuscripts, and to fashioning ceremonial objects in silver and gold (called Judaica). Jewish metal-workers were highly respected in the Arab world. On the whole, Jewish culture has influenced Jews to express themselves through instrumental music, song, literature and poetry.

It is only in the twentieth century that Jewish artists have been able to express themselves freely. Artists such as Chagall and Kitaj are now world famous. Examples of Chagall's work can be seen throughout Israel; for instance the twelve stained glass windows at the Hadassah hospital, just outside Jerusalem. These depict

*P*osters such as these in Be'er Sheva advertise who's new in the world of pop music.

Jacob's blessings on his sons, and those of Moses on the tribes of Israel (public tours in the morning only). Also worth going out of your way for are the Gobelin Tapestries hanging in the Great Hall of the Knesset building.

Whilst contemporary Jewish painting and sculpture reflects modern trends, it is also influenced by the Israeli temperament. Much Israeli art is stark, brutal and mind-grabbing; there is little room for subtlety. Their lines are bold and brash rather than mellow and meek. Much of this art is on show in museums throughout the country. A good selection can be seen at the Bezalel National Art Museum, 10 Shmuel Ha-Nagid Street, Jerusalem. There are also many sculpture gardens. Israel's fine weather means outdoor displays are possible all the year round. Every town will have at least one major sculpture—usually in a traditional design (for instance, the bronze immigrants at Karmiel). A well-known sculpture garden, which displays an exotic and eclectic group of weird and wonderful exhibits, overlooks the sea at Jaffa, near Tel Aviv.

Much Israeli art is available to buy. Avant-garde works are available in the more exclusive galleries in Tel Aviv and Jerusalem but the biggest seller is Judaica. The Frank Meisler Galleries (the best is next to the King David Hotel in Jerusalem) hold some wonderful, dynamic sculptures in brass and silver. Most are items of Judaica but make a detour to see the moveable Freud. Meisler's works are very, very expensive but a browse is well worth while.

Clusters of galleries and art shops can be found in the old parts of Safed (Jaffa) and Yafo (Tel Aviv). In

Jerusalem there is an artists' colony at Mishkenot Shaananim at Yemin Moshe, which is outside the city walls and down from Jaffa Gate; aim for the windmill. Also in Jerusalem is the Jerusalem Artists' House at 12 Shmuel Ha-Nagid Street which is especially strong on sculpture. There is also an artists' village in the Carmel mountains. Called Ein Hod, this village is reasonably close to Haifa and is perfect for anyone seeking art in a rustic setting.

Islamic art is just as impressive as Israeli art. Most of it is religiously orientated and again no representations of God are used. Instead the Arabic script is employed as a patterning device. Examples of this sort of work abound but the most beautiful is that on the exterior of the Dome of the Rock in Jerusalem. The Arab *shuqs* will have much Arabic art on sale, including many fine Persian paintings. The best museum for Islamic art is undoubtably the LA Mayer Memorial Institute for Islamic Art at 2 Rehov HaPalmah in Jerusalem.

Clothing Requirements

What to wear in Israel is generally not a problem. The uniform for men is based around a loose, open-necked shirt, a pair of cotton slacks (or shorts)

The view is of Tel Aviv from Jaffa. The sculpture is of steel and is unnamed. It is only one of many such dramatic objects in the Jaffa Sculpture Garden.

Cotton will keep you cool and protected from the sun, vital when walking in the Judean desert.

and brown leather sandals. None of the plush hotels would mind if you turned up for dinner dressed like this.

In summer everybody in Israel wears sandals. Unless male tourists are used to them, it may be inadvisable to wear them on holiday as they take a few days to get used to. The straps and buckles make the skin sore and tender, and until this skin toughens up you can expect to hobble for a week or so. But as sandals are so comfortable once they have been broken in, it may be worth buying a pair in your home country and road-testing them before the holiday. Trainers or dress shoes are fine for the winter but the heat generated by the average tourist walkabout (hours of walking round sites, museums and gardens) means feet can get uncomfortable very quickly.

Most women will have no problem wearing sandals. If you like unusual designs then you can buy very cheaply after a wander round an Israeli shoe-shop or an Arab market. The thong-type sandals are especially exotic, and widely available.

Covering up

No matter what you wear on your feet or on your back, there is one very important thing to realize about travelling around Israel: as it has so many sites of religious significance there are strict rules concerning appropriate clothing. When entering a mosque, church or synagogue (or any site considered Holy) you must be modestly dressed. For men this means long trousers and a shirt (short sleeves are acceptable). In synagogues men also have to wear some form of head covering. This can be a hat, although more normally it will be a skull cap, or *kipah* (plural *kippot*). These are usually available at the entrance. At the Western Wall in Jerusalem there is a large box containing cardboard *kippot* next to the low railings just before the Wall itself.

Clothing requirements for women can be very strict. Bare arms and bare legs are deemed immodest in the extreme. Some form of head-covering, such as a scarf, would be prudent, although not compulsory. In Mea Shear'im, an area of Jerusalem populated with Ultra-Orthodox Jews, the stipulations against bare flesh must be taken seriously. Large notices call for female modesty and running the gauntlet by walking through Mea Shear'im in a T-shirt and shorts is not to be recommended. You could expect abuse—both verbal and physical.

For this reason, it is usually wise to carry some form of light clothing as an alternative to shorts and a T-shirt. At places such as the Al-Aqsa mosque in Jerusalem both men and women will be asked to wear a dress-type garment if they are showing too much skin.

At many secular sites it is also best to dress modestly. At Yad Vashem, the Holocaust museum and memorial, it would be distasteful to walk around looking as if you have just stepped off the beach. But do not think all these restrictions mean sombre clothing is needed. As long as most of the body is covered, anything goes.

Covering up is not only important for religious reasons. The Middle Eastern sun can burn skin very easily. Pure cotton garments which cover the whole body will protect the skin much better than the best of the sun creams. Avoid man-made fibres as, in general, they do not absorb moisture. Instead they transmit it away from the wearer

at great speed. Cotton feels best next to the skin in hot, humid conditions. Garments should be semi-reflective so white is preferable to black. Clothing should always be loose fitting. Air circulates within such garments and skin temperature can be regulated. Bare, unprotected skin gets hot and burnt.

Remember also to wear a hat whenever the sun is likely to be fierce, for instance whilst climbing Masada or touring exposed archaeological sites.

Electrical Appliances

The electric current in Israel is 220 volts AC, single phase, 50 cycles. Israeli sockets are usually three-pronged; any other type and you will need a plug-adaptor for the plug. Electric shavers, travelling irons and so on should be equipped with adaptors to the local current or transformers. These can be purchased in Israel, although not cheaply.

*S*treet *vendors in the* Old Port *area of Jaffa.*

THE COUNTRY, ITS HISTORY AND ITS PEOPLE

A Kaleidoscope of Sights, Sounds and Echoes from the Past

There is so much to see and do in Israel that your visit will be memorable both for its variety and its quality. Few other places in the world can offer the same contrasts, and all within the space of such a small country. You will find history all around you, in a landscape moulded by civilization upon civilization for thousands of years. Today the religions and customs of Israelis are as varied as they have ever been.

Five thousand years ago Israel was a small but important part of the Fertile Crescent, the area of the Middle East where civilization began. This area was situated between the Arabian desert and Egypt to the south and the Armenian mountains and the great river valleys of Mesopotamia (modern Iraq) to the north.

The great empires of the past, Sumer, Accad, Egypt, Babylon, and Assyria, all from the Fertile Crescent,

*A*vdat was a Nabatean town, originally founded as a way-station for caravans. This is a millstone dating from the Byzantine period.

clashed with each other with a tenacious regularity. Often their mutual battlefield was the land of Canaan. This was because the "land flowing with milk and honey" was a crossroads between empires and continents. Israel formed a land bridge between Africa, Asia and Europe. It lay along the great trade highways. The Syrian desert prevented any natural routes to the east so everybody and everything was channelled through Canaan, the narrowest part of the Fertile Crescent.

Being at a continental crossroads Canaan was frequently ravaged. First one side would cross and plunder; then the other. Before the great empires this land may have been reasonably peaceful (and there are many rich prehistoric remains to attest to man's existence here) but once the power-plays started, tranquillity would have been an alien concept. Cities were frequently razed to the ground, but then rebuilt on the debris of the same site until the next imperial army came through. Each successive rebuilding and destruction added more layers of debris. These layers gradually formed large mounds, or *tels*, on which the cities grew and grew. It was only when the Greeks and Romans needed much bigger sites for their great urban developments that these *tel*-built cities were abandoned. Today Israel abounds in *tels*. Most have been excavated but many have not. They can be dissected to reveal layer upon layer re-telling the history of a bloody and turbulent past.

Israel's topography is also an important factor in defining the course of history. There are deserts to the east and south, fertile coastal plains to the west and mountains through the middle. These mountains were vital to control of the plains and many of the passes and valleys became critical strategic footholds. Capture an important topographical feature and you were half-way to winning your battle. Cities such as Megiddo and Hatzor, which guarded strategic passes, became synonymous with never-ending battles. Indeed, the word Armageddon, the battle of last things in the *Revelation to John* (*16:16*), is the Greek form of Har-Megiddo, Hill of Megiddo.

Cities were often autonomous mini-states, ruled by powerful overlords or kings. Tribal and regional loyalties grew out of these city-states. Furthermore, the mountainous nature of the land created pockets of isolated peoples. The result was often fierce local loyalties that prevented the sort of unification necessary to empire-building. This, along with the fact that these tribal peoples were constantly being invaded by very large armies, meant that throughout its history, Israel has only been united three times under native rule: under David and Solomon in the 10th century BC; by the Jewish Maccabees and later Herod the Great in the 2nd and 1st centuries BC and in the modern State of Israel since 1948. At all other times the country has been either politically fragmented (the period of the Tribes of Israel under the Judges, for instance), or under the foreign dominion of the Egyptians, Assyrians, Babylonians, Persians, Greeks, Romans, Byzantines, Arabs, Crusaders, Mamelukes, Turks and Britons.

How to Impress an Israeli

In cafés and restaurants throughout Israel you generally get two choices of coffee—either instant, which the Israelis called *Nes* (from Nescafé), or Turki, sweet Arabic coffee. *Nes* is by far the most common but to shock your host, waitress or waiter ask for *botz* coffee. This is made from ground Turkish coffee, but instead of allowing the grounds to settle, the cup of coffee is stirred vigorously so the bits become part of the drink. *Botz* means mud in Hebrew!

Geography

Israel is bordered by the Mediterranean Sea to the west, the Great Syro-African Rift to the east and the Red Sea to the south. Israel's immediate neighbours are Lebanon, Syria, Jordan and Egypt. The West Bank and the Gaza Strip

*S*pring flowers in the hills near Tiberias, overlooking the Sea of Galilee. In the foreground are thistles such as Jesus might have seen and which "shot up and choked the corn" in the parable of the sower (St Matthew 13).

form the Occupied Territories and have not been formally annexed. They have been under Israeli rule since the end of the 1967 war. The Golan Heights, on the border with Syria, were formally annexed in 1981.

Israel is a surprisingly small country, with a total area (including the Occupied Territories) of 21,000km² (8,108 square miles). It measures 418km (260 miles) from north to south and 115km (70 miles) at its maximum width. It is no larger than Wales or New Jersey.

The northern and central segment of Israel, where most of the population lives, is divided into three distinct strips: to the west, the coastal plain with the large cities of Tel Aviv and Haifa; to the east, the Jordan and Arava Valleys with the River Jordan linking the two inland seas, the Sea of Galilee and the Dead Sea; and in the centre, the mountain range that includes the hills of Galilee, and the West Bank. Jerusalem, the capital of Israel, lies among some of the small valleys of these hills.

To the east of Jerusalem lies the Judean desert. The Golan Heights and the snow-capped Mount Hermon rise in the north east. And in the south stretches the Negev Desert with Be'er Sheva as the capital and Eilat on the Gulf of Eilat. Altitudes vary from the 1,208m (3,962ft) of Mount Meron in the Upper Galilee, to the –392m (–1,286ft) of the Dead Sea, the lowest spot on earth.

History

In any historical study of Israel there are a multitude of names for the same land. Canaan, Israel, Israel and Judah, Palaestina, Kingdom of Jerusalem, the province of Palestine, The British Mandate of Palestine and Eretz Yisra'el: all of these names denote roughly the same place. At different times in history the borders of this land have been greater or smaller depending on the political situation at the time. But for our purposes this list of names describes what we now know simply as Israel.

Originally the land was called Canaan and was home to numerous tribes and peoples, including the Canaanites and other groupings familiar from the Bible, such as the Jebusites and the Midianites. With the invasion of the belligerent Hebrews it became the Land of Israel (Eretz Yisra'el). Later "Israel" meant just the Northern Israelite Kingdom, including Samaria and Galilee, while the south was called Judah. Judah became the Greek form "Judea", applying only to a small part of the country centred on Jerusalem, the Royal City of David.

In order to obscure the Jewish identification of the country, the Roman Emperor Hadrian changed Judea to Palaestina. Jews were forbidden to live in the new capital, Aelia Capitilina, built on the ruins of Jerusalem. The Jewish Dispersion, the Diaspora, dating from the time of the Babylonian expulsions, spread throughout the world.

After the Romans, the Byzantines, and the Seljuk Arabs came the European Crusaders. The Crusades started, in 1096, to defend the Holy Sepulchre in Jerusalem from the heathen Muslims,

> **Place Name Pronunciation**
> Because of the cultural diversity of Israel and the fact that both Hebrew and Arabic are difficult to transliterate into English, Israeli place names can be confusing. On maps, signs and tourist literature there seems to be no consensus on how to spell or pronounce certain towns and villages. So, is it Jaffa, Joppa, or Yafo? Acre, Acco or Akko? Nathanya, Natanya or Netanya? Elat, Elath or Eilat? Ashqelon or Ashkelon? Safed, Tzfat, S'fat, or Zefat? The permutations are endless but Yafo, Netanya, Eilat and Zefat seem to work best.
>
> Other problems occur when certain sites have competing names. For instance, Lake Tiberias, the Sea of Galilee and Kinneret Lake are one and the same place. The Sea of Galilee is used by Christians; Kinneret Lake by Israelis; and some people prefer Lake Tiberias.
>
> Political, racial and religious factors also come into play: the capital of Israel is called Jerusalem by Christians; Yerushalayim by Israelis and al-Quds ash-sharif by Muslims. Similarly, modern Nablus is often called by its biblical name of Shechem by Israelis and many Israeli villages are still called by their Arabic names by the Palestinians.

but greed, boredom and straightforward hooliganism soon became more important motives. A number of anti-Muslim wars ensued, but by the 15th century, the Crusades were a spent force and the Crusader Kingdom of Jerusalem became Palestine again, a

*T*he first guidebook to Israel was the Bible. This map of Judea shows the province in the time of Jesus.

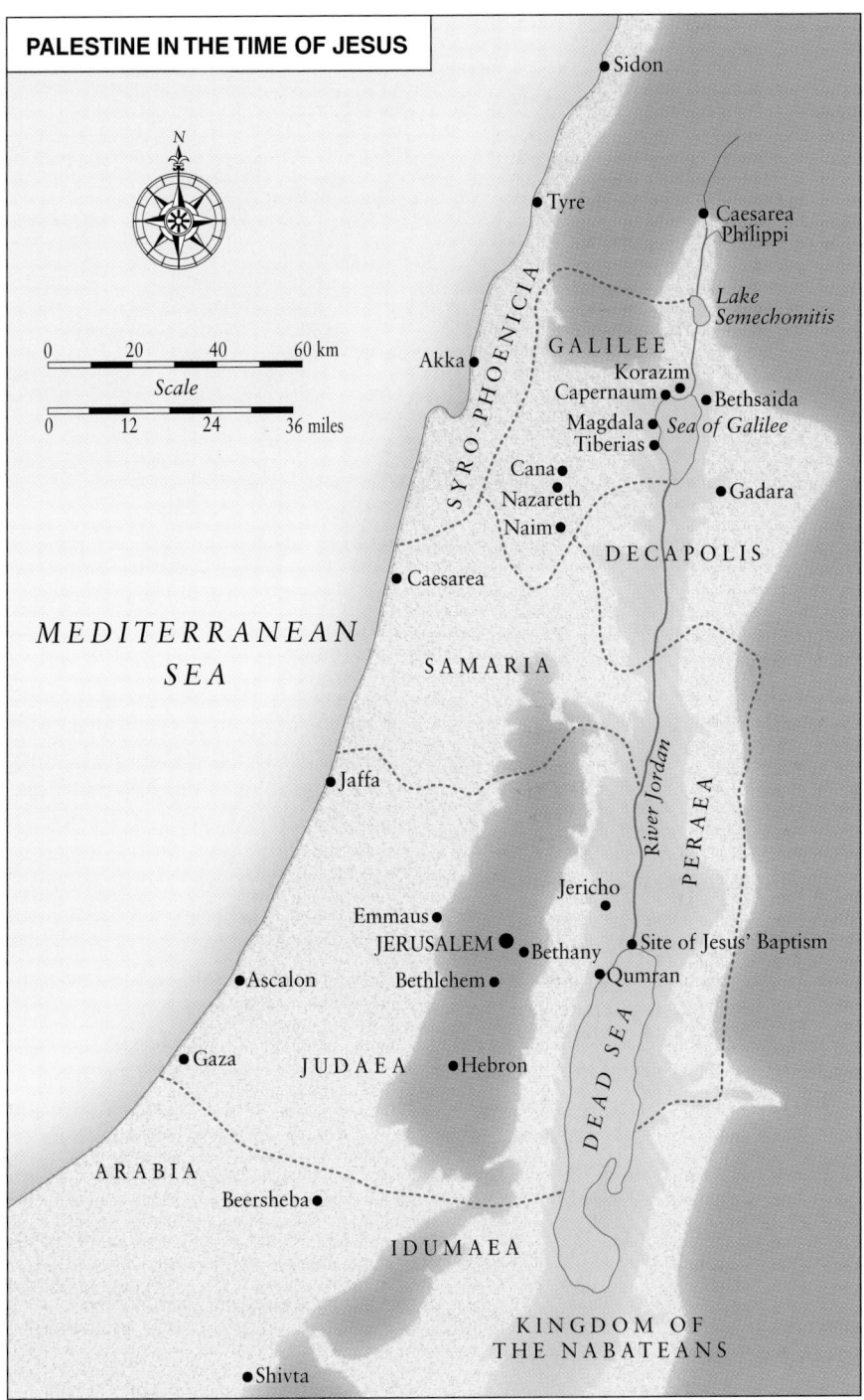

PALESTINE IN THE TIME OF JESUS

Sidon

N

Tyre

Caesarea
Philippi

SYRO-PHOENICIA

*Lake
Semechomitis*

GALILEE

Korazim

Akka

Capernaum   Bethsaida

Magdala   *Sea of Galilee*

Tiberias

Cana

Nazareth

Naim   Gadara

DECAPOLIS

0   20   40   60 km

Scale

0   12   24   36 miles

Caesarea

MEDITERRANEAN
SEA

SAMARIA

Jaffa

River Jordan

PERAEA

Jericho

Emmaus

JERUSALEM   Site of Jesus' Baptism
Bethany

Ascalon   Bethlehem   Qumran

Gaza   DEAD SEA

JUDAEA   Hebron

ARABIA

Beersheba

IDUMAEA

KINGDOM OF
THE NABATEANS

Shivta

King David's Tower, near Jerusalem's Jaffa Gate, is an Ottoman structure built over the ruins of a stronghold built to protect King Herod.

mere province in a huge Muslim empire, later to be ruled by the Ottoman Turks.

It was a country that had seen better days. The land was badly husbanded; much of what is now fertile was then barren; malarial swamps existed in the north; living conditions were primitive and many villages were no better than hovels. In the 18th and 19th centuries, travellers were shocked to see the Holy Land as a provincial backwater, neglected and run-down. Mark Twain, who visited Palestine in 1867, described it as: "...[a] desolate country whose soil is rich enough, but is given over wholly to weeds—a silent mournful expanse..." (From *The Innocents Abroad*).

After the First World War, Palestine came under the control of the British. Until 1948 this was the Mandate period. The Jewish presence in the land had never totally been eradicated but it wasn't until the end of the 19th century and the beginning of the 20th that large-scale Jewish immigration started to worry the Arab population. Much of Palestine was owned by absentee landlords living in Damascus and Cairo. These landlords sold huge tracts of (often worthless) land to the Jews and distinctly Jewish settlements started to appear and prosper. Slowly the land came back to life as the Jews worked to re-create their biblical State. Kibbutzim, or communal settlements, were founded by idealistic Zionist settlers. Agriculture in the Holy Land was improved and modernized; the malarial swamps were drained and made fertile; and the coastal plains started to produce hyper-crops again. Extra work was created and an influx of migrant Arab labourers flooded into the country eager to work for the Jews. As well as work, the revitalized Palestine had better educational opportunities and better health facilities than the rest of the Arab world. But Jewish numbers continued to rise too and Palestinian Arabs were opposed to this parallel growth—frequent anti-Jewish pogroms resulted in many deaths.

After the Second World War and the horrors of the Holocaust, mass immigration and a desperate need for sanctuary forced the Jews to re-create their ancient homeland. They called it Eretz Yisra'el, the Land of Israel. But to the Arab world the Jews were a Dhimmi ("protected") people who, like the Christians, should remain inferior to Muslims. They could not comprehend a nation-state of Jews.

Consequently, six Arab states invaded the new country in an attempt to destroy it at birth. A vicious war ensued. Many Palestinian Arabs fled for fear of their lives, others were ousted by Jewish soldiers. The war ended with victory for the new Zionist State. Israel had secured its borders. But Arab armies continued to harass Israel. The 1967 Six-Day War finally taught the Arab world that this small country was no push-over; Israel would fight, and fight to the bloody end if necessary. New terror-tactics were employed by the Arab world—the Palestinian Liberation Organisation (PLO) was formed and terrorist atrocities were committed in Israel and around the world. Israel wanted the right to exist. The Arab world had a different message—"we'll throw the Jews into the sea." This fear of a new Holocaust coloured (and still colours) the Israeli response to attacks on its right to exist.

Christian Crusader meets Muslim: statues near the Dung Gate, Jerusalem, commemorating the mediaeval Crusades.

A Crash Course in Israeli History

Old Stone Age (600,000 to 12,000 BC): cavemen, hunting, discovery and use of fire. Time of the cave-dwellers of the Carmel.

Middle Stone Age (12,000 to 7500 BC): man begins to gather and cultivate grain; more sophisticated tools are developed.

Late Stone Age (7500 to 4000 BC): first real settlements are founded, including Jericho; animal husbandry, irrigation, and pottery begin.

Copper (Chalcolithic) Age (4000 to 3200 BC): settlements grow into small towns; copper used in tools; patterns appear on pottery; a culture develops at Be'er Sheva.

Early Bronze (Canaanite) Age (3200 to 2200 BC): towns are fortified, beginning of city-states; temples and palaces built.

Middle Bronze (Canaanite) Age (2200 to 1550 BC): trade develops; the Hyksos invade Canaan and Egypt; the Age of the Patriarchs; Abraham leaves Ur of the Chaldees and heads to Canaan, in the process spawning a people, the Hebrews. Whilst Abraham may only be an imaginary figure, a mythic-progenitor of a "race", the story of a migration from Mesopotamia rings true and a leader such as Abraham, who united a number of clans into a "people", may indeed have existed. Likewise this "father-figure" may be pure myth, an epic explanation for the ancient Near Eastern origin of the Hebrew traditions, gods and rituals. It must also be pointed out that Muslims see Abraham as their father-figure too: as well as begetting

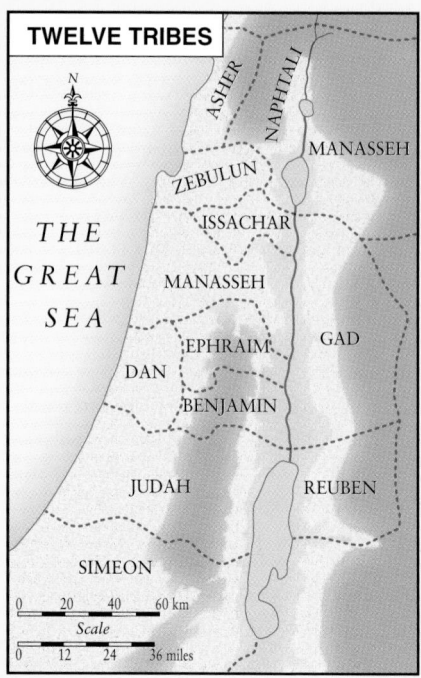

The twelve tribes of Israel.

Isaac and the Hebrews, Muslims believe he begat Ishma'el and the Arabs.

Late Bronze Age (1550 to 1200 BC): children of Israel captive in Egypt; the alphabet develops; the Exodus from Egypt; Moses unites the Hebrews; the Ten Commandments delivered on Mount Sinai; Israel invades Canaan and conquers its Promised Land.

Early Iron Age (1200 to 1020 BC): period of the Judges (Deborah, Gideon and Samson, for example); Philistines invade from the Aegean across the Mediterranean and establish a league of city-states on the coastal plain.

Middle Iron Age (1020 to 842 BC): the united monarchy under King Saul and King David (1000 BC); David transfers

The walls of Jericho, part of the oldest known town in the world, dating back to c.9000 BC.

the Ark of the Covenant (containing the Ten Commandments) to Jerusalem as a political device to unite the tribes; his ploy succeeds and Jerusalem becomes the capital of the kingdom; in c.950 BC King Solomon builds the First Temple on Mount Moriah; the golden age of Israelite culture and power. But in 928 BC Solomon dies and the monarchy is divided. The Northern Tribes under Jeroboam break away to form the Kingdom of Israel. The Southern Tribes, now known as the Kingdom of Judah, with their capital at Jerusalem, are ruled by Rehoboam, Solomon's weak son.

Late Iron Age (842 to 586 BC): period of the later kings and prophets; in 586, destruction of the First Temple by the Babylonians.

Babylonian and Persian Periods (587 to 332 BC): Israel captive in Babylon, followed by Persian domination; the Second Temple is built; times of Ezra and Nehemiah.

Hellenistic and Maccabean Periods (332 to 37 BC): domination by Alexander the Great, by the Ptolomies and Seleucids; the successful Maccabean revolt; time of the Hasmonean dynasty; period of Jewish Renaissance; civil war by the last Hasmonean princes allows the Roman general Pompey to enter Israel and he annexes it as a Roman province; time of the Sadducees and the Pharisees. The Sadducee version of "Judaism" was Temple-based, upper-class and power was derived from the priesthood. Sadducees tended to accommodate themselves to the Hellenistic world in order to keep power and placate their various overlords. Pharisees were anti-pagan, religiously radical and more biased towards the synagogue (a concept developed in exile in Babylon) than the Temple. Pharisees cultivate the "Oral Law". The concept of rabbi, or teacher, is developed. Their religion becomes more portable as the dependence on the Temple is lessened.

Roman Period (37 BC to AD 324): Herodian dynasty; birth of Jesus (5 BC, the dating discrepancy came about because of calendar changes by the church), his ministry and crucifixion by the Romans; Jewish wars against Rome; Second Temple and all of Jerusalem razed to the ground (AD 70); Sadducees disappear from history because of the loss of the Temple; the Pharisee movement, with a portable religion, survives. The Sanhedrin (Jewish High Court) decamps to Yavne; fall of Masada (73); Bar Kokhba's revolt against Rome (132–135); Judah ha-Nasi (c. 200) collates the Mishnah (the summary of the Oral Law), beginning of modern-day Judaism based on Rabbinical authority.

Byzantine Period (AD 324 to AD 640): Jewish revolt, Byzantine domination. in about AD 400 the various commentaries on the Mishnah are compiled and codified into the Jerusalem Talmud. A century later a more authoritative version of the Talmud is completed in Babylon.

Persian invasion and sack of Jerusalem (AD 614): in AD 622 Islam is born with Mohammed's flight from Mecca to Medina; Islam grows very quickly and Muslim Arabs conquer the entire Middle East.

Arab Period (AD 637 to 1096): Jerusalem surrenders (AD 637); Arab capital first at Damascus, later Baghdad; joint Christian-Muslim protectorate of Holy Places; many Christian pilgrimages.

The Crusades (1096 to 1291): First Crusade (1096–1099), sack of Jerusalem, Crusader kingdom under Godfrey de Bouillon; Jews massacred and expelled; Second Crusade (1147–1149); Saladin captures Jerusalem (1187), but does not sack it; Jews let back into Jerusalem; Third Crusade (1189–1192); Fourth Crusade (1202– 1204). The Crusaders killed all in their way but were especially careful to massacre as many Jews as possible. The Jews were seen as "God-killers", despite the fact that Jesus was crucified by the Romans.

Ottoman Turkish Period (1291 to 1917): Mongols, Mamelukes, and Seljuks replace Arabs and Byzantines as overlords of the Holy Land; Ottomans conquer Palestine; Suleiman the Magnificent rebuilds Jerusalem (mid-1500s); Jews who are expelled from the Iberian Peninsula, welcomed into the Ottoman Empire; Napoleon's campaign in Egypt and Palestine (1799); Zionism begins with Herzl (1860–1904), publication in 1896 of Judenstaat, The Jewish State; First Zionist Congress (1897) in Basle; First World War (1914–18); Ottoman Turks support the Germans; the British promise both the Jews and Arabs that they will get eventual control of a Palestine severed from the Ottoman Empire.

British Mandate (1917 to 1948): League of Nations grants Great Britain the "mandate" to govern Palestine (1920); Sir Herbert Samuel becomes first High Commissioner; Jordan becomes a separate kingdom (1923), ruled by a Saudi-Arabian monarchy installed by the British; many Arab attacks on Jews (1929); Jewish immigration restricted, Arab immigration unrestricted; Pan-Arab Congress (1937) in Syria; Second

World War—many Jews fight for the Allies; Holocaust, six million European Jews are systematically slaughtered at a time when Jewish immigration to Israel was still restricted; end of war sees mass attempted immigration to Israel by many Jewish survivors of the Holocaust; immigration heavily restricted by the British; Arab and Jewish terrorism; King David Hotel, site of British military headquarters blown up (1946) by the Irgun, a radical Jewish terrorist group led by a reclusive Menahem Begin.

Proclamation of State of Israel (1948): British Mandate ends on 14 May 1948, and the State of Israel proclaimed on same day. Six Arab armies invade the new state. Israel, the underdog, fights back and wins; many Palestinians flee at beginning of war (some out of fear of a repeat of the massacre at Deir Yassin on 9 April 1948, committed by the Irgun and the Stern Gang, an attack condemned by the Jewish Agency), many others are forcibly ejected as the course of the war forced strong-arm tactics against a possible "fifth column".

Suez Campaign (1956): joint British, French and Israeli action is taken to counteract increased terrorist activity, to remove Egyptian blockade of Gulf of Aqaba and reclaim Suez canal.

Six-Day War (June 1967): Israeli Defence Forces launch a pre-emptive strike against the Arab armies massing on its borders, ready to invade. In a lightning campaign Israel defeats the Arab armies yet again, despite still being the underdog. This label is now redundant. Israel controls the West Bank, the Gaza Strip, the Golan Heights and the Sinai Peninsula. Jerusalem is officially annexed and becomes the capital of Israel; rest of the world does not recognize Jerusalem as such.

Yom Kippur War (1973): the Sinai and the Golan Heights are attacked by Egypt and Syria in a co-ordinated attempt to oust Israel.

Peace with Egypt (1977): Anwar Sadat of Egypt and Menahem Begin of Israel sign Camp David peace accords.

Invasion of Lebanon (1982): to protect its northern border Israel invades Lebanon to mop up PLO terrorist positions. However, under the leadership of Ariel Sharon, the army goes deeply into Lebanon proper in an attempt to eradicate the PLO totally. Beirut is shelled and the PLO ousted. Christian Arabs fight Shi'ite Arabs for control (a long-running feud exacerbated, but not started, by the Israelis). Lebanese society is further destabilized and Israel eventually withdraws. Much disquiet in Israel over the invasion.

Intifada (1987 to present): after a road accident in the Gaza Strip in December 1987, the Palestinian Uprising (the so-called "war of stones"), or Intifada, erupts. Tactics in the early days are stone-throwing and boycotting Israeli goods. Three years of the Intifada leads to no concessions so new tactics are adopted—increased use of arms. Jews are stabbed and gunned down. Civilian targets, such as crowded market-places full of Orthodox Jews, are bombed. Increased Palestinian violence leads to reciprocal measures by West Bank Jewish settlers. The Intifada starts as a spontaneous reaction to Israeli domination, but becomes increasingly led by Muslim fundamentalists who wish to see the total destruction of Israel.

Gulf War (1990 to 1991): Saddam Hussein of Iraq invades Kuwait; PLO backs Iraq; American-led international blockade of Iraq; Saddam Hussein links Kuwait invasion with Israeli occupation of West Bank and Gaza Strip; Gulf War breaks out; Western Allies launch fiercest military campaign since the end of the Second World War; Iraq is forced to back down; peace process starts.

Latrun Fort Artillery Museum.

The Intifada, the popular Palestinian uprising, divided the camps ever more deeply—the doves were weary of fighting an unjust battle, a battle that could never be won; the hawks became even more adamant that the Occupied Territories should be annexed and any opposition quelled by force or mass expulsions.

The Gulf War opened up wounds and reminded Israelis that they alone were the masters of their survival. Palestinian support for Iraqi aggression muddied the waters, and prospects of peace—tenuous at the best of times—were very dim in the aftermath.

The PLO now states in public Israel's right to exist, within secure borders. In return Palestinians want a state of their own and a right to self-determination. An important step towards this was taken in September 1993, when Israel signed a historic peace accord with the PLO in Washington DC, giving the Dead Sea town of Jericho and the Gaza Strip a limited form of self-government. In time, such autonomy may lead to lasting peace, though it will take time to heal the memories of past transgressions on both sides. In the short term, much of the security advice in this book, and especially in the chapter on the West Bank, holds true.

Both sides in this historical drama are playing with a script as old as time, a script penned in blood, suffering and misery. The land of Israel has always been fought over and true peace has usually been a short-lived phenomenon. The moral dilemma of subjecting an indigenous population, the Palestinians, to unpopular rule may one day rip the young state apart—the widespread anti-war response after the invasion of Lebanon opened up deep rivalries between Israeli doves and hawks—or it could go some way in forging a new understanding, a fresh approach.

The Israeli Year

There are so many festivals and holidays in Israel that it's a wonder any work gets done at all. Jews have a packed ritual year aside from the Jewish secular festivals. Christians have three Christmasses, depending on their persuasion. Muslims have set religious holidays and then an immense number of "days", mostly commemorating some glorious (or infamous) period of recent history. With three great faiths, there are three separate New Years. If you like celebrations, holidays and non-stop festivities, then Israel is the place to go.

Pre-planning is difficult and tourists will have to keep a number of calendars in mind when trying to figure out which festivity is coming next. The first is the regular calendar used in most of the world, the Gregorian calendar. Then there is the Jewish lunar-solar calendar, which has 12 lunar months of 29 or 30 days each, with a complicated system of leap years during which there is an extra month. 1994–5 corresponds to 5754–5. The Muslim calendar also has 12 lunar months, but has no leap years, so holidays move backwards from season to season. The Eastern Orthodox Christian churches follow the old Julian calendar, which is 12 days behind Western calculations. If you work to the Gregorian calendar most of the time and check with the IGTO to clarify the dates of forthcoming holidays and festivals, you won't go far wrong.

Shabbat

For tourists and natives alike the most important "holiday" occurs every week: the Jewish Sabbath. This begins on Friday at sunset and ends on Saturday night. The Sabbath, or *Shabbat*, Hebrew for "rest" is central to a proper understanding of Jewish ritual; it is regarded as a gift from God to the Jewish people. Shabbat is not just a Jewish Sunday. It is far more important than simply a day of rest; for a start it is mentioned as a central rule of the Ten Commandments. Various traditions ascribe to it special powers and Shabbat is rife with symbolism: the Shabbat as bride, the Shabbat as an honoured guest, the Shabbat as a remembrance of the Jew's Exodus from Egypt.

Nowadays everybody has to respect the Sabbath because almost everything stops. Shops will close early, buses will have severely truncated services and people will rush out of matinée showings at cinemas. On Shabbat, Orthodox Jews do no work at all. Lighting fires, cooking food and turning on electricity are all forbidden. Many restaurants and cafés will also close. Most hotels serve food cooked in advance and kept warm. Non-observant tourists can either stock up with supplies earlier in the day or, alternatively, visit the Christian or Arab parts of town (if there are any).

The observance of Shabbat varies throughout the country. In Tel Aviv the cafés do their best business on Friday night, and in Haifa there are some inter-urban bus services. This is largely because Haifa is a stronghold of the powerful Israeli trade union, *Histradrut*, and compromises have been made with the religious authorities. In Ultra-Orthodox Jewish areas, especially in Mea Shea'rim in Jerusalem and Tel Aviv's Orthodox suburb of Bnei Brak, no traffic is allowed at all; transgressors can expect a hail of stones. This often leads to friction between Ultra-Orthodox Jews and secular Jews.

The end of Shabbat is marked with Havdalah. To separate the holy day of Shabbat from the profane rest of the week the Jewish family will gather around a special Havdalah candle and listen in silence as the blessing is read. A glass of wine is lifted and then a container of sweet-smelling spices is passed around the room for each person present to inhale; this is to remember the sweetness of the passing Shabbat.

Mimouna

As well as the traditional Pesach celebrations Israel is also getting used to the Moroccan Mimouna festivities. This was imported by Moroccan Jews in the mid-1960s and has now become part of the Israeli psyche. According to tradition, this day is the anniversary of the death of Maimon ben Joseph, the father of the highly esteemed mediaeval scholar and physician Maimonides, who lived for a time in Fez, Morocco. Mimouna is a time of outdoor picnics and expeditions. It is also a time when Israeli families, especially Sephardic ones, openly invite strangers into their homes. On offer will be heavily sweetened foods and drinks. Many "host" families advertise their generosity in the Israeli newspapers; tourists can get a real taste of Israeli home life this way. The IGTO will be able to put you in touch with "host" families.

The Christian Sabbath is, as per normal, Sunday. Churches will fill out and many people will take this as their rest day, but, for Jews, Sunday is just an ordinary day which marks the beginning of their week.

The Muslim "Sabbath" (more rightly called "a day of assembly", and not strictly speaking a day of rest) is Friday, when many Arab stores and holy sites will close. Arab stores also close at fairly erratic times because of the Intifada.

The number of rest-days means that Israel has a staggered weekend, and as there is no consensus, there will always be something open throughout this "weekend". When the Jewish Shabbat comes in, you can go along to the non-Jewish neighbourhoods if you want food, entertainment or other services—and vice versa for the other sabbaths. So, unless all your touring makes you desperate for a rest-day you can enjoy a seven-day week.

Religious Holidays

Most Jewish religious holidays are bound by rules that are similar to those pertaining to Shabbat. Although, except for Yom Kippur, food may be cooked as normal. Bear in mind that all these apparent restrictions will be mostly confined to the Ultra-Orthodox Jews, and except for a lack of public transport, the Shabbat regulations will not impinge that much on your holiday—unless, of course, you are observant yourself.

In some hotels religious etiquette is followed very closely, and so on festivals such as Passover (Pesach) you may have to eat *matzot* (unleavened bread crackers) instead of bread.

Festivals

Israel is blessed with many cultural secular events. **The Festival of Music and Drama**, centred in Jerusalem, Tel Aviv and the restored Roman Theatres in Caesarea and Beit Shean, takes place in September of each year, with the participation of the country's leading musical and dramatic talent and world-famous visiting companies and artists. A similar event, **The International Music Festival** (first one held in July 1990) is held in Netanya.

The annual **Ein Gev Music Festival**, with a varied programme of classical and folk music, is held during Pesach at Kibbutz Ein Gev on the shores of the Sea of Galilee. You can drive round from Tiberias or there are special boat trips.

In July each year there is the **Karmiel Dance Festival** held in the very attractive Galilee mountains. Dance companies from around the world come here, although it is Israeli and Chassidic dancing that is to the fore.

Cinema fans can feast their eyes on a variety of films offered at the **Jerusalem International Film Festival** (usually held in June or July) at the Cinematheque, just underneath Mount Zion.

Other festivals include the **Eilat Water Festival**, where watersports and moonlight pageants take place. An **International Harp Contest** is held every three years, drawing young musicians from all around the world, while the **Zimriya**, an international choir festival, is another well-established triennial event. Spring in Jerusalem and Spring in Tel Aviv, two annual festivals, include music, drama and dance.

The Sigd

One festival which gets scant mention elsewhere, and that is almost unheard of in the Diaspora, is the **Sigd**. This is a fast day of the Ethiopian Jews, and is one of their most important festivals. Held in November, the Sigd was traditionally a day of longing for the return to Israel. Ethiopian Jews would climb to the highest peaks in their isolated villages and celebrate the giving of the Law at Sinai, and pine for a lost homeland. Now held at points throughout Israel, but mostly on Mount Zion, the Sigd has come to be a demonstration of solidarity between the so-called Falasha (Ethiopian) Jews and their co-religionists (*falasha*, which means stranger, is a derogatory word and is now used as sparingly as possible).

Political Structures

The State of Israel was proclaimed on 14 May 1948. It is a parliamentary democracy, the only true one in the Middle East (in other words, Israel is unique in this part of the world for not being a feudal kingdom, a military dictatorship or a totalitarian "socialist" state). This democracy has a President elected by the 120-member single chamber Knesset (parliament), which itself is elected by universal suffrage. The head of the Government is the Prime Minister.

Voting is by Proportional Representation. This means that very small minority parties can wield a certain amount of power because of their floating loyalty. Racist parties, such as the Kach movement, or Ultra-Orthodox religious parties, such as Agudat Yisra'el, use their few Knesset seats to influence policy (Kach is now outlawed). On the whole their influence is overrated but on certain divisive issues, such as the imposition of Halakah (Jewish religious law), the minority parties can "blackmail" the Knesset to pass unpopular laws. There are some Palestinian Members of Knesset, although there have been boycotts since the start of the Intifada (Palestinian Uprising).

People

Israel is a country of immense variety; the whole world in a nation-state. It is no exaggeration to say that in terms of

*B*en *Yehuda Street in Jerusalem is a stroller's paradise—street cafés line this pedestrianized road, long since empty of cars.*

Shesh-besh (backgammon) players in Jaffa. This game is played all over Israel and is taken very seriously.

people, Israel is one of the most cosmopolitan countries in the world. Every race, creed and colour is represented on the streets—Jews from all over the globe have made their home here. The non-Jewish population is just as diverse—ranging from Armenian monks to Scottish priests, and from Christian Arabs to the Druse mountain dwellers. But it isn't, as many people would have you believe, one big melting pot. Nationalities and ethnic groupings do not fuse in Israel, they remain distinct—and therefore such groupings keep their vibrancy, their spirit and their identity. Where would be the interest in one amorphous mass of humanity?

Israel demands participation. The immense human effort put into creating this country is evident everywhere—people are proud of this and will tell

you so. In taxis, in shops, in hotel lobbies, at sporting events, at archeological digs, at public beaches—basically, everywhere, you will be coerced into discussions. Don't look upon this as an intrusion but as a vital indicator of how important this land is to the people who live here.

The population of Israel, including the territories of Judea, Samaria and Gaza Strip, is more than 5 million, of whom more than 4 million are Jews, ¾ million Muslims, and the rest Christians, Druse

---

An Israeli Defence Force

Israelis are known for being curt in public. You are unlikely to get a "please" or a "thank you" in conversation with them, but this is just a gruff exterior, and beating beneath it is a heart of gold. Or so says the popular myth anyway. Native-born Israelis, who have these sorts of attitudes imbibed with their mothers' milk, are nicknamed "sabras". A sabra is a prickly pear, a fruit of the cactus family—prickly on the outside, sweet on the inside.

Language

The official languages in Israel are Hebrew and Arabic, although English-speakers can be found just about everywhere. English is taught in schools and most people understand the basics.

With Israel being such a cosmopolitan country, there are many other languages to be heard on the streets, including Russian, Yiddish and German. Because of the huge influx of Jews from Russia many public signs now include the Russian Cyrillic script.

Hebrew came back to life with the rise of Zionism at the end of the 19th century. Whilst it has always been the language of liturgy and ritual, it ceased to be the vernacular over 1,700 years ago. Today's Hebrew is similar to Biblical Hebrew but with many new words added and new uses given to ancient Hebrew words. So, for instance the modern Hebrew word for "battle-tank" is the Biblical Hebrew word for "chariot".

English words such as "television" are used, but often new constructions are invented or developed and then made popular by usage in the media. Hebrew has grown from the 8,000 word vocabulary of the Bible to the 120,000 words that are in use today. And all this from just 200 "root" combinations of three letters. Hebrew is a guttural language and so can appear to be brusque and abrupt. It is harsher than Arabic but has a melody all of its own. It is a comparatively simple language to learn, with the strangely scripted alphabet being the highest stumbling block for most people. Once the fear of a new alphabet is overcome—and the basic recognition takes just a few hours—the language itself is straightforward and logical.

It is a good idea to know some basic Hebrew words and phrases before coming to the country. A language guide appears at the back of this book.

---

and other peoples. A few years ago more Israelis were emigrating than there were immigrants arriving. Since late 1989, tens of thousands of Russian Jews have been arriving. There were more than 500,000 new immigrants by the end of 1992. This is like America absorbing the population of France overnight—a huge task and one that is causing much trouble. The Russian Jews are highly educated but there are few jobs for them. Israel, however, is a past expert at absorbing masses of immigrants, and chances are that within four or five years the Russian immigrants will be fully integrated.

The 200,000th new immigrant when asked what he wanted to do now he had arrived in the Promised Land, said, "I want to marry an Israeli." The integration shouldn't be too tough!

Religion

Israel contains Jews, Muslims, Samaritans, Christians (including Protestants, Armenian Orthodox, Catholics, Copts, and Eastern Orthodox), Druse, Baha'is, and various other sects. Jews make up approximately 80 per cent of the population. All denominations are free to worship in their own ways, maintain their religious and charitable institutions and administer their internal affairs. The inviolability of Holy Places and centres of worship of all faiths is guaranteed by law.

Judaism, Christianity and Islam (in that historical order) accord Israel with a status far and above the merely mundane. The Holy Land is supernaturally special—and has been for more than 3,000 years.

The Western world is partly based on thoughts, actions and beliefs that originated in this land. Much of our moral infrastructure comes from texts written on this soil. To wander around Israel with a guidebook in one hand and the Bible in the other is a religious act (although non-believers can use the Bible as a guidebook too)—it is a recognition that Israel has an importance in our greater consciousness far outweighing its tiny size.

Praying at the Western Wall. Written prayers are folded up small and placed in the cracks of the Wall.

Judaism

Some might say that Judaism is not just a faith, but a people. Whilst it is possible to convert to Judaism you do not embrace a faith but actually become one of the people. Many commentators have accused the "Chosen People" of racism. However, if you convert by the strict rules of Halakah (religious and legal precepts of Judaism) then you are 100 per cent Jewish. This is not to say that Judaism, for Jews, does not inculcate a feeling of being "a people apart" but this belief of being special is not racism, it is clannism.

So, Judaism is the religion of the Jewish people, the Jewish clan. It is not the religion of the Hebrews of the Bible.

Normative Judaism (with rabbis and the institution of the synagogue) came about after the destruction of the Second Temple in AD 70. Without a temple, and a place for their animal sacrifices, the Jews had to rely on a portable religion away from their main cultic sanctuary. The synagogue (an institution dating from the Babylonian exile) replaced the Temple.

A short while before the destruction of the Second Temple, the Jews had been split into two movements: the Sadducees and the Pharisees. The Sadducees were a religious party linked to the Temple and mostly made up of aristocrats and "priests". They held a literal view of the Written Torah (or Pentateuch, the Five Books of Moses) and rejected the Oral Torah tradition, those rules and regulations given not by the Torah, but by sages down the centuries.

The Pharisees were more "liberal", more scholarly and more "for-the-people". They believed in both the Torahs, and also believed in bodily resurrection, angels, demons and the coming of the Messiah. Their reliance on teachers (rabbis) rather than Temple priests and on the synagogue and the home rather than the Temple meant they were much better prepared to survive after the fall of Jerusalem and the destruction of the Temple. They were, however, accused of pedantry and legalism because of their rigid adherence to the Halakah. The famous passages in the Christian New Testament, where Jesus is found criticizing the Pharisees, should not be seen as a fundamental disagreement between Jesus and the Pharisees, but as a quibble over how to far to interpret the Halakah. Jesus was closer to the mind-set of the Pharisees than most Christians imagine. It was the later authors of the gospels who created the severe antagonism between the two parties, mainly because the early Christians and the Jews parted company acrimoniously after the destruction of the Second Temple in AD 70.

It was in the post-Temple period that the religion and people of Judaism were developed. Halakah (or religious law) crystallized through the writing down of the Oral Tradition into the Mishnah. Judaism was an extremely scholarly religion and the rabbis debated many of the points in both the Mishnah and the Torah. The religion was not bound by time and newer interpretations could be formulated if the sages were authoritative enough. Discussions and commentaries on the Mishnah were collated into the Jerusalem Talmud (edited at the end of the 4th century, mostly in Tiberias) but this was later superseded by the Babylonian Talmud, a huge multi-authored work still authoritative today.

In the mediaeval period, rabbinical and ritual laws were clarified and codified in such works as the Mishneh Torah, of the great Spanish theologian Maimonides (1135–1204), and the Shulhan Arukh, of the Spanish mystic Joseph Caro (1488–1575). These works, along with the Talmud, defined the Jewish outlook on the world, but far from being simply adaptations of earlier religious texts, they were the condensed thoughts and beliefs of countless learned rabbis and commentators. There was no consensus of opinion with these works; the Jew had to come to his own conclusion over many matters, nothing was black and white. Judaism was a learned religion, taught from an early age.

Ever since the Babylonian exile, Jews had been a Diaspora (Dispersion) people. They had dispersed to virtually every corner of the world. The Arab world offered them the greatest sanctuary. At the time of the Crusades, when the Jews were being butchered throughout Europe and, of course, in Palestine, they had a comparatively peaceful life in the rest of the Middle East, North Africa and Spain. According to Islam, Jews and Christians were "People of the Book" (the Bible) and were higher in status than other peoples. They were still, however, a Dhimmi, or "protected" people and were considered second-class citizens. They had to wear distinctive clothes or badges, had to give way to Muslims in the street and could not build their synagogues higher than any mosque. Periodic persecutions were the exception rather than the rule.

A thriving intellectual life was especially prevalent in Muslim Spain where there was a Jewish community of about 100,000. After the Christian invasion of the country, the position of Jews became less tenable and the Spanish Inquisition led to the expulsion of the entire community in 1492. The Hebrew word for someone of Spanish origin is *Sephardi*. This term has also come to apply to the Jews of the Middle East, living under Muslim rule. Today over half the Jews of Israel are of Sephardi origin.

Jews living in Christian lands, especially in Eastern Europe, became known as *Ashkenazi* from the word for Germany. These two divisions are highly simplistic and there are many Jews who do fit into these two categories, but the definitions are now widely held. Jews in Christian Europe suffered greatly at the hands of their hosts. They were labelled God-killers and not allowed to follow any other occupation other than banking. Frequent persecutions, called pogroms, in eastern Europe, led to Ashkenazi Judaism becoming an insular, bookish society.

In the 18th and 19th centuries a flowering of Judaism occurred in eastern Europe with the spread of Chassidism.

*M*ea Shea'rim in *Jerusalem is home to many Ultra-Orthodox Jews.*

Based on the teaching of the Ba'al Shem Tov (the Master of the Good Name) the Chassidim, which literally means the "pious ones", placed great emphasis on piety, prayer and joy as opposed to the dull scholasticism of the Talmudic *yeshivot*.

Today the Chassidim are the most easily recognizable Jewish sect because of their dress, aloof manner and pale studious faces. The other Ashkenazi groupings were more in favour of integration, and today normative Judaism is basically made up of two opposing groups. The first, the Orthodox, stick rigidly to traditional teachings. The second, the, Reform Movement (born in 19th-century Germany but developed mostly in America), are more liberal and modernizing. So, for instance, Reform congregants can drive to synagogue on the sabbath whilst the Orthodox still disallow it. In America there are further sub-divisions between these two groupings. Basically, as the saying goes, take two Jews and you've got three opinions!

In Israel, it is the Orthodox who hold sway. The Reform Movement (in Israel called the *Mitkademet*, or Progressive) can hardly get a word in edgeways. The Ashkenazim and the Sephardim have their own Chief Rabbis (Orthodox) and the Chief Rabbinate gets to decide all matters of religious import.

Christianity

Jesus Christ was born in Bethlehem, Judea, of Jewish parents, in the last years of the reign of Herod the Great. He grew up in Nazareth, attended synagogue regularly and to all intents and purposes was a "good Jewish boy" no different from his contemporaries. But this was the man who changed world history. From his thoughts, parables and teachings has grown an immense world religion.

Yet he had simple beginnings, and for most of his life he worked as a simple carpenter. It was only the last three years of his life that saw his greatness revealed. He gathered around him twelve disciples and started a short period of ministry, mostly in the Galilee, an area known in New Testament times for its laxity in Jewish Law. The Galilee was more used to itinerant teachers and rabbis than High Priests and regular sacrifices. It was a good milieu for a Galilean Jewish teacher with unorthodox ideas. The Pharisees, often itinerant teachers themselves, argued with Jesus on points of Law. In the Galilee Jesus was harmless and his stories, which were steeped in the rural customs and practices of the time, completely apolitical.

It was when he went up to Jerusalem and challenged the Sadducees and the High Priests that Jesus started to get a reputation as a trouble-maker. In the eyes of the authorities he was a seditious spreader of unrest. And unrest among an expectant population waiting for the Messiah to overthrow the Romans was not a healthy thing. The Sadducees, ever compliant to their benefactors and protectors (and overlords) the Romans, conspired to dispose of this religious pretender. They turned him over to the Romans, who were only too happy to execute someone they thought was a rabble-rouser and a potential "king-of-the-Jews". They scourged him, and hanged him on a cross, the execution method not for criminals but for political seditionists.

*O*n the descent to the Dead Sea from Jerusalem, a signpost will direct you to the Inn of the Good Samaritan, once a busy staging post and refreshment stop.

Here religion takes over from history. To Christians, Jesus transcended this human existence and was resurrected, the True Son of God. From this event sprung Christianity.

For Jews, Jesus is a Jewish teacher, no different from similar rabbis of the period (such as Hillel and Shammai who used such ideas as "turn the other cheek" long before Jesus). For Muslims, Jesus is a great prophet, similar to Mohammed, but was not the Son of God and was not resurrected. For Christians, Jesus is the Christ (Greek for Messiah) and the Son of God.

Early Christianity (before the destruction of the Second Temple in AD 70) was largely Jewish in tone. Jesus was a Messiah figure, but he was not yet believed to be fully divine. Christian groups were still affiliated to the synagogue and many Jews believed Jesus to be their Messiah (although a non-supernatural figure). The earliest leader of the church was James, the brother of Jesus, the human son of the Virgin Mary.

After the destruction of the Temple, these early Christian communities were destroyed and Christianity was transplanted to the Gentile world, largely through the work of one man: Saul of Tarsus, an ex-Pharisee, later to be known as St Paul.

The teachings of the Apostles were popular and Christianity spread fast in the Gentile world of the Romans,

The Monastery of St George, 5km (3 miles) south west of Jericho, built into the north side of the cliffs of the Wadi Qelt. The first Christian hermitage here was established in the 5th century.

despite persecutions by the likes of Nero. With the conversion of Emperor Constantine in the 4th century Christianity's future was secure—it was now the state religion of the Roman Empire. However, Constantine's establishment of his new capital, Constantinople (Istanbul), led to the split between Eastern Orthodoxy and Roman Catholicism (a split started in the 4th century but not formally declared until 1054).

The Western Empire collapsed, but Christianity continued to spread and the Roman Catholic Church, with the institution of Papacy, became a dominant force. After centuries of rule and misrule, the Catholic Church was split apart by Martin Luther and the Protestant Movement.

Today just about every denomination imaginable is present in Israel, with especially strong Eastern Orthodox communities.

Islam

Islam, which in Arabic means "submission to Allah", is a monotheistic faith dating from AD 622. It was on this date that Mohammed, the Prophet of Allah, fled from Mecca, where he and his followers were being persecuted, to Medina. However, just seven years after this flight, Mohammed became the undisputed leader of a nascent religious and political force—a force that spread rapidly around the Fertile Crescent, Arabia and parts of North Africa.

Mohammed was said to be illiterate yet, miraculously, was able to write down the word of God on scraps of pottery, bones and other surfaces. These writings became known as the Koran (the Muslim Holy Book, divided into 114 Suras, or chapters).

Whilst being a worldly and astute leader, he did not think ahead on one very important point—he left no successor, and from the arguments that followed Mohammed's death came the two major splits in Islam. The breakaway group, and still in the minority, is the Shi'ite sect. The Sunni form of Islam is the most widespread.

Islam has no formal priesthood, but there are five basic duties incumbent on all Muslims: faith in the one God, Allah and his Prophet, Mohammed; daily prayer, facing Mecca; fasting at the time of Ramadan; the giving of alms; and at least one pilgrimage to Mecca during their lifetime.

Baha'i

The Baha'i faith is a worldwide faith, based mostly on Islamic teachings, and is said to be the newest of the world's major religions. It was founded by the

Y̶ou may not enter the Dome of the Rock with your shoes on, so shelves are provided outside this holy site.

Persian Baha'u'llah, who was a follower of the Bab, religious leader of the Babis, a sect of Shi'ite Islam. He was exiled from Persia and was brought, as a political prisoner, to Palestine in 1868. He was incarcerated by the Turks in the citadel at Akko. He remained here for two years. He was later given more freedom and lived in other places in Northern Palestine, but up to his death in 1892 he remained a political prisoner.

Baha'is believe Baha'u'llah to be the latest in a long line of prophets, or founders of religions. They offer a syncretist view of world history and world religions. All religions are essentially, they believe, the same, with spiritual similarities outweighing the differences. They believe their religion caps all religions because it encompasses them all (they would say succeeds them all). Divine revelation for them is continuous and progressive and whilst past religious leaders (such as Moses, Jesus and Mohammed) have differed in the "non-essential" aspects of their teachings, they "abide in the same Tabernacle, soar in the same heaven, are seated upon the same throne, utter the same speech, and proclaim the same Faith."

Jews, Christians and Muslims all would obviously dispute this, but Baha'is are profoundly serious in their optimistic vision of a single world religion—theirs.

Samaritans

The Samaritans of today, of whom there are only about 500 left, are the direct descendants of the Samaritans mentioned in the New Testament. The sect's origins are ancient, but the antipathy between Israelites and Samaritans as shown in the New Testament dates from the time of the return of the Jews from Babylon. The Samaritans had not been transported to Babylon with the Jews of Judea and had intermarried with their conquerors. They had, however, remained strict in their adherence to their version of the Torah. Their cultic site was at Mount Gerizim, where they were allowed to build a temple by the Persians. This temple was destroyed by the Hasmoneans, but Samaritans continue to worship on this mountain to this day.

Druse

A sectarian Muslim group, the Druse are today found in the mountainous regions of Lebanon, southern Syria, and various hill-towns in northern Israel. There are about 60,000 Druse in Israel, living mostly in the Carmel mountains. They stem from the Shi'ite Muslim sect of Isma'ilis; however, in belief and practice they are far different from the main body of Muslims, rejecting many of the prescriptions of the Islamic religious law and emphasizing such beliefs as the transmigration of the soul. Very little is known about the religious beliefs of the Druse because of the great secrecy they had to develop to escape from persecution by Muslims. What is known about them is that they draw heavily on the Bible and venerate such personages as Jethro (the idolatrous father-in-law of Moses) and the prophet Elijah.

The Druse speak Arabic but they are not Muslims and they share few allegiances with Palestinian Arabs. For this reason most Druse have been loyal to the State of Israel. Druse men serve in the Israeli Defence Forces, and many of the toughest border policemen are Druse. This loyalty was severely tested when Israel invaded Lebanon and there existed the potential for Israeli Druse to be fighting against Lebanese Druse.

Their most important holiday falls on 25 April, when Druse from all over the country gather in the holy village of Hittim, near Tiberias. On this date the Druse villages elsewhere in Israel are likely to be deserted.

The Dome of the Rock, viewed from the Mount of Olives.

A Year in Israel

Israel's many faiths, denominations and sects means it has a varied religious life. It often comes as a pleasant surprise to Jewish tourists that, in Israel, the year revolves around them. In the Diaspora their holidays are hidden. Christians may feel Christmas is the most important festival in the whole world, but for Jews it is just a normal day. So, when Israel comes to a standstill for a Jewish holiday it can take some getting used to. Christmas and Easter are important in Israel but not to the majority of people.

So, let's take a look at the cycles of time that will be imposed upon you once in Israel.

The Jewish Year

The Jewish calendar is very old. Its main details were developed by the Sumerians (the earliest Mesopotamian civilization) and originally formed an agricultural reckoner. The ancient Hebrews adapted it for their own use and their starting-point corresponds to our 3760 BC; this date is said to be when God created the earth.

The Jewish ritual year (or *chagim,* literally "festivals") begins on the first of Tishri (a Hebrew month which usually corresponds to September, or sometimes October). On this date falls **Rosh Hashanah**, literally "the head of the year". This is seen as a day of judgement on which the fortunes of the coming year depend. Ten days later comes the fast day of **Yom Kippur**, the Day of Atonement. This is the highpoint of the Jewish year, often known as "the Shabbat of Shabbats", and the country literally shuts down for twenty-five hours. Television and radio broadcasts are halted and solemnness rules. Many ultra-secular Jews will

deliberately be active on this day as a mark of disrespect.

Five days after Yom Kippur comes **Sukkot**, the Feast of Tabernacles, or "Tents". This is a week-long harvest festival, based around remembering the temporary dwellings of the Israelites during the Exodus. Sukkot is a joyous festival and is described in the liturgy as "the time of our rejoicing". Religious observant families build a small booth on their balconies or in the garden. This *sukkah*, covered with branches and leaves, is where they eat during the festival (*Leviticus 21:42–3*). The booths are usually festooned with multi-coloured streamers and other such decorations. Christians will see parallels with Christmas at this time and as there is a certain amount of gift-giving, the parallel is a neat one. On the fifth day of Sukkot is the secular-orientated "Walk around Jerusalem". This begins at about 6 a.m. but goes on most of the day as people walk the 11-, 22- or 27km (7-, 14- or 17-mile) routes. In the afternoon there is a parade down Jaffa Road to West Jerusalem. People travel from all over the country for this walk.

Throughout the year the Torah, or Pentateuch (Five Books of Moses) will have been read in stages during synagogue services. At the end of Sukkot the cycle of readings comes to an end and **Simhat Torah**, the "rejoicing of the Torah", marks this ritual completion with a bang. Worshippers sing and dance with the Torah scroll in public parks and streets. Alcohol consumption is allowed and if you wander around the right areas (Me'a Shearim is a good bet) you will catch sight of some tipsy Ultra-Orthodox Jews.

The holidays from Rosh Hashanah to the end of Sukkot, a period of about three weeks, are known as the "High Holidays" and Jewish tourists will be out in force in Israel.

Two months after the end of Sukkot comes the eight-day celebration of **Channukah**, the Feast of Lights. This usually falls in December and is sometimes given a Christmas-type feel by Jews in the Diaspora. In Israel the emphasis is more nationalistic. Channukah commemorates the victory of the militaristic Maccabees over the Seleucid rulers of Palestine, who outlawed Jewish religious practices in the 2nd century BC. As this is seen as a heroic rebellion against foreign rule, Israeli secularists celebrate Channukah just as much as the Orthodox.

The religious symbolism of Channukah comes from the fact that at the re-dedication of the temple by the victorious Maccabees, the last remaining jar of ritual olive oil, which should have ceased burning after only a day, lasted eight days, long enough for a new batch of oil to be ritually purified. This was seen as a miracle. Candles or oil lamps are lit for eight days out of recognition of this event. In towns around Israel you will see huge neon *menorahs*. These eight-branched candlesticks, also called *chanukiyot* (singular *chanukiah)* symbolically light the way, and "publicize the miracle". Hotels will hold candle-lighting ceremonies each evening and tourists are welcome to attend,whether they are Jewish or non-Jewish. You may be given small jelly doughnuts at these lightings. This is the traditional sweetmeat of Channukah and you will also find these *sufganiot* in shops throughout the country.

Tu bi'shvat, the New Year for Trees, in late January or February, is a happy time when schoolchildren all around the country plant trees. Tourists may also wish to make such a statement. It is customary to eat fruit on Tu bi'shvat, especially the fruits associated with the Bible: grapes, figs, pomegranates, olives and dates.

The month of Adar (February/March), on the 14th of which falls **Purim**, the Feast of Esther, is the most joyous month of the Jewish year. Purim celebrates the rescuing of the Jews of Persia by biblical Queen Esther. Both secular and religious Jews observe this festival. Children and adults alike dress up in costumes and there are sometimes parades and carnival-like events in the large cities. Men are encouraged to dress up as women, students can lampoon their teachers and religious Jews can concoct absurd interpretations of Biblical teachings. Alcohol consumption for the Orthodox is allowed (encouraged even) and frivolity is the order of the day.

Pesach, or Passover, in March or April, commemorates the exodus of the Israelites from Egypt. Orthodox Jews eat only unleavened bread, or *matza*, for a week. These are square wafers made from flour kept specially dry until minutes before they are made into a dough and cooked. Any product containing yeast (the so-called *chametz* products) is forbidden. Even possessing yeast products is prohibited. The first night of the holiday is marked by a festive meal and service, called a *seder*. Like Christmas or Thanksgiving for non-Jews, Pesach is a time when all the family is gathered together around one table. Many Jewish restaurants that have Kashrut licences close over Pesach because they couldn't hope to clean their kitchens as scrupulously as the Rabbinical authorities demand. Tourist hotels will kosher their kitchens so don't worry about starving for a week! In most Israeli hotels and restaurants, the menus will be very different from normal. Don't expect any bread for a start. If you can't last a week on *matzot*, then check out the freshly baked pitta bread in the Arab parts of town (if any).

The **Samaritan Passover** is held on Mount Gerizim, near Nablus, and is a colourful and somewhat bloodthirsty event. Unblemished lambs are sacrificed, cooked and eaten. Tourists can watch the procedure all the way through the night, but when the lambs are about to be eaten everybody apart from the Samaritans will be asked to leave. Special buses and tours can get you to the Samaritan Passover ceremonies, although it will be an all-nighter and you won't get back to your hotel rooms until about 9 or 10 the next morning.

In late April or early May, two days of mourning fall in close succession: **Holocaust Memorial Day** for the six million Jews murdered by the Nazis; and the Day of Remembrance, or Yom HaZikaron, for soldiers killed in Israel's wars. Restaurants, cinemas and other places of entertainment close. Be prepared to stop for a 2-minute silence when the sirens go off. Pedestrians will halt, cars and buses will pull to the side of the road and people sitting down will stand.

Israel Independence Day (Yom Ha'Atzma'ut), on the other hand, is a time of singing and dancing in the streets, picnics and bonfires. In the evening, Israeli children take great delight in bopping passers-by with plastic hammers which emit a squeak when they bounce off the head. This custom is relatively new and seems to be enjoyed by the locals. Tourists caught unawares would be deemed very bad sports if they reacted against such pseudo-violence. Your best bet is to carry a plastic hammer yourself and swat the little terrors back.

Lag Ba'Omer, between Passover and Shavu'ot, involves pilgrimages to ancient sages, bonfire lightings and ritual hair-cutting ceremonies for four year-olds. Its origins are biblical but the attendant celebrations surrounding it are not. The most popular explanation for the traditions of Lag Ba'Omer is that on this day Rabbi Simeon bar Yochai, the reputed author of the Zohar (the mystical religious textbook of the followers of the esoteric Jewish mysticism called Kabbalah), finally revealed his secret teachings to his disciples and then promptly died. Pilgrimages are made to the sage's tomb in Meron in the Galilee. Large bonfires are lit and there is a lot of singing and dancing (but this time no alcohol). Lag Ba'Omer is especially important to the Sephardic (Oriental Jewish) community; they camp out at Meron and there is a fair-like atmosphere.

Shavu'ot, or Pentecost, seven weeks after Passover, is a harvest festival (*see Exodus 23:16*), with the symbolic offering of first fruits by children and on kibbutzim. Secular Jews prefer to emphasize the land-based origin of the festival rather than the ritual one. Its main religious significance is in its association with the revelation of the Torah at Mount Sinai.

Tisha B'Av, a fast day which falls in mid-summer, marks the destruction of the First and Second Temples. It is the most sorrowful day of the Jewish year. Tradition associates it with other tragic events in Jewish history and the day has come to symbolize the bitterness of Jewish suffering throughout the course of history.

Christian Holidays

Christian holidays are quite complex in the Holy Land. They do not always agree; so **Christmas Day** for the Western churches is 25 December, but for the Eastern Orthodox churches (who use the Julian calendar) Christmas Day falls on 5 January. The Armenian church celebrates on 19 January. Thus there are three lots of processions and three lots of Masses. If you miss the first Christmas, at least you don't have long till the next one! Details of where, when, and how to celebrate Christmas in the Holy Land can be obtained from the Christian Information Centre, Jaffa Gate, Jerusalem (tel. 02-282621).

Most of the other Christian festival dates correspond, but different denominations have different festivals and different saint days. One of the most visually stunning Christian festivals is the Armenian **Happy Name Day**. This day of pomp, pageantry and mystery is held every year at the Holy Sepulchre in Jerusalem on 10 October. If you're in Israel in October try not to miss it.

Easter is important to Christians and Israel fills up at this time. Tourists and pilgrims should book hotel rooms well in advance. And if Pesach and Easter coincide, then you may well find standing room only. Easter festivities begin with processions on Palm Sunday from the Mount of Olives and continue throughout Holy Week, culminating in the Procession of the Cross along the Via Dolorosa on Good Friday.

Muslim Holidays

Whereas the Jewish calendar is lunar-solar, the Muslim calendar is purely lunar, so over the years Islamic holidays ease their way backwards from one season to another. The Muslim ritual year starts with **Muharram**. The tenth day of this month is celebrated as the anniversary of the First Creation, when Man and Woman, Paradise and Hell, life and death were all said to have been created.

Al-Hijra commemorates the flight of the prophet Mohammed from Mecca to Medina in the year AD 622.

Mawlid an-Nabi is the celebration of Mohammed's birthday. You may see processions of Arab Boy Scouts on this day.

The most important time for Muslims is the atoning month of **Ramadan**, when everybody fasts from dawn to dusk. A cannon blast marks the end of the fast and special foods are sold in the streets every evening. It is customary to break the fast with something sweet. The completion of the fast is a three-day festival, **Eid al-Fitr**.

On many of these Muslim holidays, especially the political and martyr-day ones, there will be large anti-Israeli demonstrations. In the West Bank and in East Jerusalem these demonstrations often lead to violent clashes and tourists should steer well clear. Neither Israelis nor Palestinians have any desire to harm tourists, but you may get caught up by accident, so if trouble looks to be brewing it would be wise to vacate the area.

In addition to the various religious and national holidays there are a number of other events. **Jerusalem Day**, held about two weeks after Lag Ba'Omer, marks the June 1967 reunification of the city (Muslims have a similar day, although for different reasons). **Armenian Remembrance Day** on 24 April commemorates the 1½ million Armenians murdered by the Turks in 1915. A procession is held in Jerusalem.

Just the Essentials

On a first-time visit to Israel you may be overwhelmed by the sheer wealth of choices you have wherever you start. The major landmarks and places to see are proposed here to help you establish priorities.

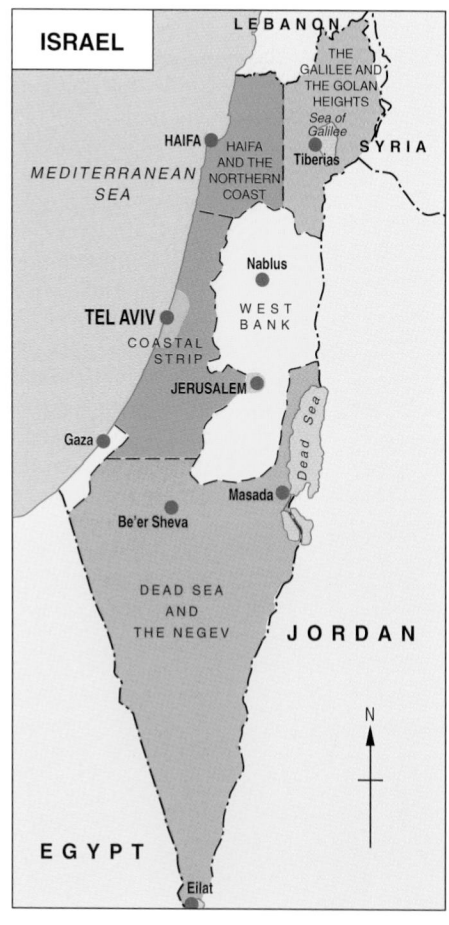

Jerusalem
Holy Sepulchre
Via Dolorosa
The Western Wall
Dome of the Rock
Kidron Valley tombs
King David Hotel
Garden of Gethsemane
Mount of Olives
Church of the Dormiton
Knesset
Israel Museum
Yemin Moshe

West Bank
Rachel's Tomb, Jerusalem–Bethlehem
  Road
Bethlehem: Grotto of the Nativity,
  Manger Square
Solomon's Pools
Herodian
Sebastya
Hebron: *shuq*, Tomb of the Patriarchs
Bethel
Valley of Dotan

Tel Aviv and Jaffa
Tel Aviv: the beach and marina
  Shalom Tower
  Yemenite Quarter and Carmel
    market
  Dizengoff Street cafés
  Yaacov Agam's water sculpture on
    Dizengoff Square
  Beth HaTefutsoth Museum
Jaffa: Flea Market, Old Port,
  House of Simon the Tanner

Coastal Strip
Ashkelon: beach, the Painted Roman
  Tomb
Rehovot: Weizmann Institute
Rishon-le-Zion
Herzliya: beach
Netanya: beach, diamond
  factories
Caeserea: ruined city
Greek and Roman aqueducts, outside
  ancient Caeserea
Zichron Yaakov wine tasteries

Haifa and the Northern Coast
Cape Carmel: Elijah's Cave
Haifa: *Af-Al-Pi* immigrant ship,
  Carmelite railway
Mount Carmel: Carmel Monastery,
  Baha'i Temple and Gardens
Akko: port area, *shuq*, Mosque of
  Ahmed Jezzar, subterranean
  Crusader city
Rosh Hanikra
Nahariya beach

The Galilee and the Golan
The Jezreel Valley
Megiddo
Montfort
Safed
Nazareth: Basilica of the Annunciation
Hula Nature Reserve
Sea of Galilee: circumnavigation,
  Mount of Beatitudes, Capernaum
Tiberias: hot springs and ruins of
  Hammat
Sea of Galilee beaches
Slopes of Mount Hermon
Banias
Vered Ha-Galil horse-riding ranch

Dead Sea and the Negev
Ruins of ancient Jericho
Qumran
Ein Gedi waterfalls
Makhtesh Ramon
Be'er Sheva: camel market (Thursdays)

Avdat
Shivta
Timna and King Solomon's Mines
Eilat: Coral Beach, Yellow Submarine
  and Underwater Observatory

Going Places with Somewhere Special in Mind

For a leisurely look at Israel, the following themed routes are much more worthwhile than a fast drive across this tiny country from north to south. The maps will help to show where each of the numbered sites can be found.

Crusader Ruins

The mediaeval Middle East was a place of almost non-stop religious warring. Crusaders built fortified towns and castles to protect themselves, and the Arab armies knocked them down again and built on top of the ruins. Today romantic Crusader outposts are thick on the ground—the best preserved are in Akko and the Galilee region.

*H*ave *jeep, will travel.*
You will find that there are many ways of getting around this beautiful, compact country.

1 CAESAREA
By starting on the coast at Caesarea, you will get to see some of the more extensive and best preserved Crusader ruins in the country (not to mention the best Roman and Greek ruins as well). The moat wall is particularly impressive here and the whole Crusader complex will give you a good idea of what a major Crusader town would have looked like.

2 AKKO
An hour's drive away is Akko, or Acre, once the Crusader capital of the country. The subterranean Crusader city is opposite the El-Jazzar mosque. From Caesarea drive north on the motorway (2) from Caesarea (outside rush hours, go via Haifa). Otherwise take the hilly

route (70) at the Zikron Ya'akov turn-off, taking you up and over the northern part of the Jezreel Valley. The second way is more scenic and can stop you getting caught up in some amazing traffic jams through metropolitan Haifa.

3 YEHI'AM CASTLE

A drive northwards from Akko on Route 4 will take you through the seaside resort of Nahariya. Take Route 89 out of town and climb for approximately 10 or 15 minutes until the turnoff for Yehi'am is marked. A narrow tarmac road brings you to the gates of the kibbutz; drive for a few more minutes and park in the gravel space on the right. The castle can be seen through the trees. Two hundred metres (220 yds) to the left is the office for Teva Yehi'am, where you can book kibbutz-style bed-and-breakfast apartments. In the summer months, there is a swimming pool only a stone's throw from the castle.

4 MONTFORT

Take the same small road out of Yehi'am and turn right towards the Arab-Jewish town of Ma'alot Tarshiha. At the village of Mi'ilya park the car and walk to the ruins of Montfort (on the way you could stop off at the third Crusader fortress in the area that used to protect Akko: King's Castle is not much to look at today but the position was, and still is, strategic). The trail is way-marked and it will take approximately 30 to 40 minutes to reach the ruins, the most dramatic of the three Crusader castles in Galilee. There are many places where you are able to picnic on the walk to the ruins themselves.

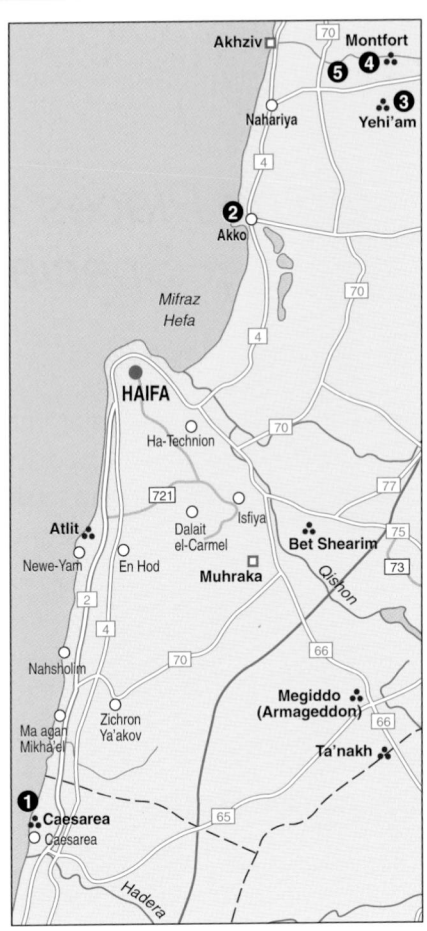

*P*laces to see the multitude of Crusader ruins.

5 KABRI SPRINGS

From Mi'ilya get back in the car and descend back down towards Nahariya on Route 89. Ten minutes from town, stop off at the Kabri Springs for a well-deserved drink. The waters here were once famous throughout the Middle East for their curative properties and their fine taste.

In the Footsteps of Christ: a Circuit of the Sea of Galilee

It is possible to walk, cycle or drive along this route.

The Galilee in New Testament times was a rural backwater, far from the power of the Temple authorities in Jerusalem. The Jerusalemites therefore considered the Galilee to be a hotbed of dissent and religious laxity, peopled with zealots and country folk. It was in this milieu that Jesus of Nazareth preached and converted his first followers. On a circuit of the Sea of Galilee many of the places familiar from the New Testament can be visited.

1 TIBERIAS
Most of the hotels are located in Tiberias and it is common to be based here for any Galilean circuit. With a car all of the following sights can be easily visited in a day.

2 MIGDAL
Northwards from Tiberias on a busy road (90) is Migdal, the biblical site of Magdala, the home town of Mary of Magdalene. There is not a great deal to see here apart from the general topography and the pleasant views over Lake Galilee.

3 GINNOSAR
On the right-hand side of the road, 2 minutes drive from Migdal, is Kibbutz Ginnosar, offset and hiding behind the banana groves. In the small museum here a 1st-century fishing boat can be seen, having been discovered in lakeside mud at low tide.

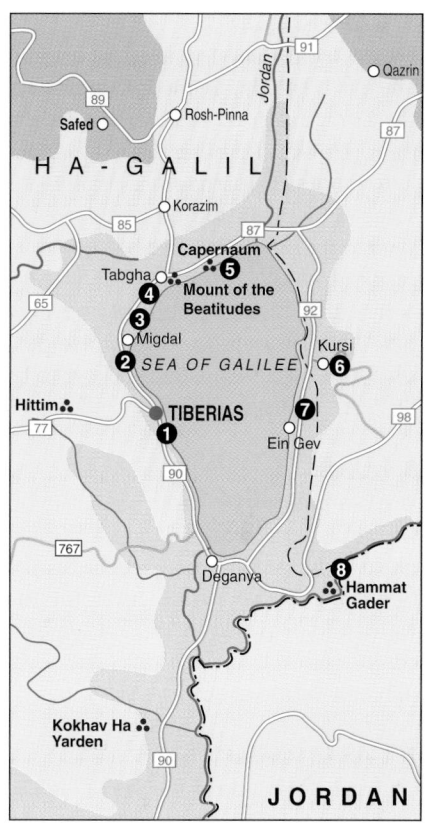

*F*ollowing Christ around the Sea of Galilee.

4 TABGHA
Distances between sights are very short and just minutes after Ginnosar you will come to Tabgha and the churches commemorating Jesus' well known multiplication of the loaves and the fishes. North of Tabgha, via the road that winds its way up the hill, is the Mount of the Beatitudes where the Sermon on the Mount was given. There are fine views from the church at the top of the Mount.

5 CAPERNAUM

Down from the Mount of Beatitudes and past Tabgha again is Capernaum the home town of St Peter the fisherman. Unlike the other Christian sites hereabouts, Capernaum actually has some ruins from the time of Jesus. A synagogue here may have been used by Jesus although this is archaeological conjecture because the building may possibly post-date Jesus. It is also possible to see what Christians believe to be St Peter's house.

6 KURSI

A 10-minute drive from Capernaum will bring you to Kursi, the traditional place where Christians believe the Gaderene Swine would have hit the water and drowned (*Mark 5:1*). A 5th-century church and a monastery complex marks the spot.

7 EASTERN SHORE

The rest of this side of the Sea of Galilee is relatively unspoilt compared with the Tiberias side and a drive here is pleasant. Christian sites are fewer and of more secular interest. Kibbutz Ein Gev has a fine restaurant serving, amongst other things, St Peter's Fish.

8 HAMMAT GADER

Known since Roman times, this spa location a few minutes off the main road is now a mix of mod-cons and ruins. Lazing by the pools is a good way to spend a hot afternoon, although the place can be crowded on holidays and weekends. The journey back to Tiberias will be via Kibbutz Deganya, the first such collective settlement in Israel. Near to here you can also visit the Jordan Baptismal site.

Ancient Monasteries

Monasticism was born in Israel—the pre-Christian Essenes lived a communal ascetic life centuries before Christians thought of the idea. The earliest monastery is therefore Qumran in the Judean desert by the Dead Sea. An even earlier example of Jewish asceticism (a rare occurrence) was the prophet Elijah who wandered the desert for 40 days and 40 nights.

The first Christian monks lived in Egypt. Within time, however, many were attracted to the *Midbar* or Wilderness of Judea. From the 4th-century onwards, ascetics started to live in caves to emulate Jesus' period in the wilderness. Later, communities developed, with the caves being kept on for especially ascetic individuals or for times of penitence. A few monasteries out of the many hundreds once in existence here have survived and can be visited today. But these are not museum pieces—most of the monasteries are still lived in by monks determined to live a simple Christian life.

*A*ncient monasteries.

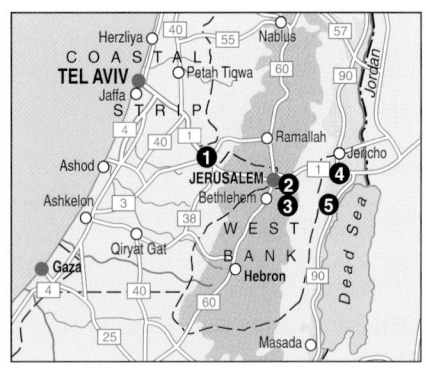

1 LATRUN

The most easily accessible of the modern living monasteries is the Latrun monastery, set up in 1861 by French Trappist monks. The present building dates from 1926 and whilst the monks are rarely seen, their work is famous throughout Israel—Latrun is worth a detour for the monastery-produced wines, brandies and olive oil. To get here, travel on the motorway from Tel Aviv to Jerusalem. Latrun has its own sign-posted interchange.

2 ST THEODOSIUS

From Jerusalem enter the West Bank and a drive of about 15 minutes eastwards from Bethlehem will bring you to the monastery of St Theodosius, a relatively modern building, built at the turn of the century on much older foundations. The original building used to house up to 700 monks, but was destroyed by invading Persians. The burial cave of the founder, St Theodosius, is inside the buildings, along with some fragments of a building from Crusader times. An ossuary of monk skulls, with crosses between their eye-sockets, can be visited.

3 MAR SABA

Far more dramatic than the two monasteries above is the one built into the Kidron gorge, Mar Saba, which is a narrow metalled 10-minute drive southwards from the monastery of St Theodosius. The monastery was built into the side of the gorge and is an amazing sight here in the middle of the wilderness. Once home to up to 7,000 monks, Mar Saba was an extremely important place in its heyday. Today there is still much to see, although this is a privilege reserved only for men—women have never been allowed into the monastery and this rule still applies. The so-called Women's Tower allows women to view the workings of the monastery from afar.

4 ST GEORGE

Drive back to Jerusalem and take the new road that bypasses Bethany (Route 1), and descend towards Jericho and the Dead Sea. Twenty minutes after leaving Jerusalem you'll come to a signpost pointing to Mitspe Jericho; take this and park the car on the gravel 2 minutes ahead. A 3-minute walk will take you to an observation platform that looks out over the blue-domed monastery of St George.

On the left, at most times of the year, will be the falling waters of Ain Qelt, an impressive sight. Once you've seen the monastery from this angle you can drive northwards for another few minutes until another car-park suggests itself. Like the first one, this parking spot is punctuated by fresh orange juice sellers and camel riders offering rides to tourists. A 15-minute walk downwards into Wadi Qelt will bring you to the monastery buildings. This is an idyllic and fascinating place, well worth taking some time to savour.

5 THE MONASTERY OF THE TEMPTATION

Continuing downwards on the same small road from the monastery of St George, you'll snake your way along Wadi Qelt and after just a few minutes Jericho will appear far below you. The whole town is visible and the *tel* especially so, with the ruins of the oldest city in the world being clearly defined even from this height. Continue down the steep road until it flattens out. After a stopover in Jericho, for lunch perhaps, return to Jerusalem on the wide, modern highway or travel southwards to the Dead Sea and Qumran, the world's first monastery.

A One-day Tour of the Old City of Jerusalem

Jerusalem the Golden is a city to savour. It can take years to get used to its small alleyways and shortcuts—much of the *shuq* looks so very alike. Yet a whistle-stop one-day orientation tour is more than possible. Of course, you'll miss out many of the smaller wonders but the main sights can all be visited briefly in a day.

1 JAFFA GATE

There are many gates to choose from to enter the Old City. In a car the Jaffa Gate has the advantage that you can take a brief look at some of the sights, yet still gain access almost to the heart of the *shuq*. Of course much of the Old City is impassable to cars. Just outside the wide gate is King David's Tower, an Ottoman-built citadel erected on ancient foundations.

2 DAVID STREET AND THE ARMENIAN QUARTER

Once through the Gate, the narrow entrance into the *shuq* is straight ahead, David Street. In a car you will be following the road around to the right, missing out on this first part of the Arab market. A few seconds after this first bend, you drive through part of the Armenian Quarter. Much is hidden behind high walls and you won't see a great deal from the road—an Armenian seminary is on the right, the Armenian Convent and St James' Church can be seen on the left.

3 ZION GATE

After the Armenian Convent, the road narrows and makes a sharp left turn (this is a one-way street, so no other vehicles will be coming the other way, but be careful to watch out for pedestrians). The Mount of Olives comes into sight beyond both the city walls and Ophel Archeological Park. On your right you will drive past the battle-scarred Zion Gate and on your left a row of souvenir and postcard shops. Around the corner is a large and orderly car-park.

4 JEWISH QUARTER

This is the start of the Jewish Quarter. The supermarket on the corner of the alleyway directly ahead is the place to aim for once you have parked your car. The narrow street here leads directly into the Old City. Five minutes further on and you come to the Cardo, the excavated main street of Aelio Capitolina, Roman Jerusalem. Go down into the Cardo for some high-class shops or turn right and come to the Burnt House and the Broad Wall. Ceramic signposts make sure you won't be lost for long in the Jewish Quarter.

It's possible to reach the Western Wall by walking through the Jewish Quarter although it is much more exciting to go via the Arab *shuq*. Turn back to the top of the Cardo and enter the more vibrant, less peaceful Arab Quarter. Zig-zag past the second-hand

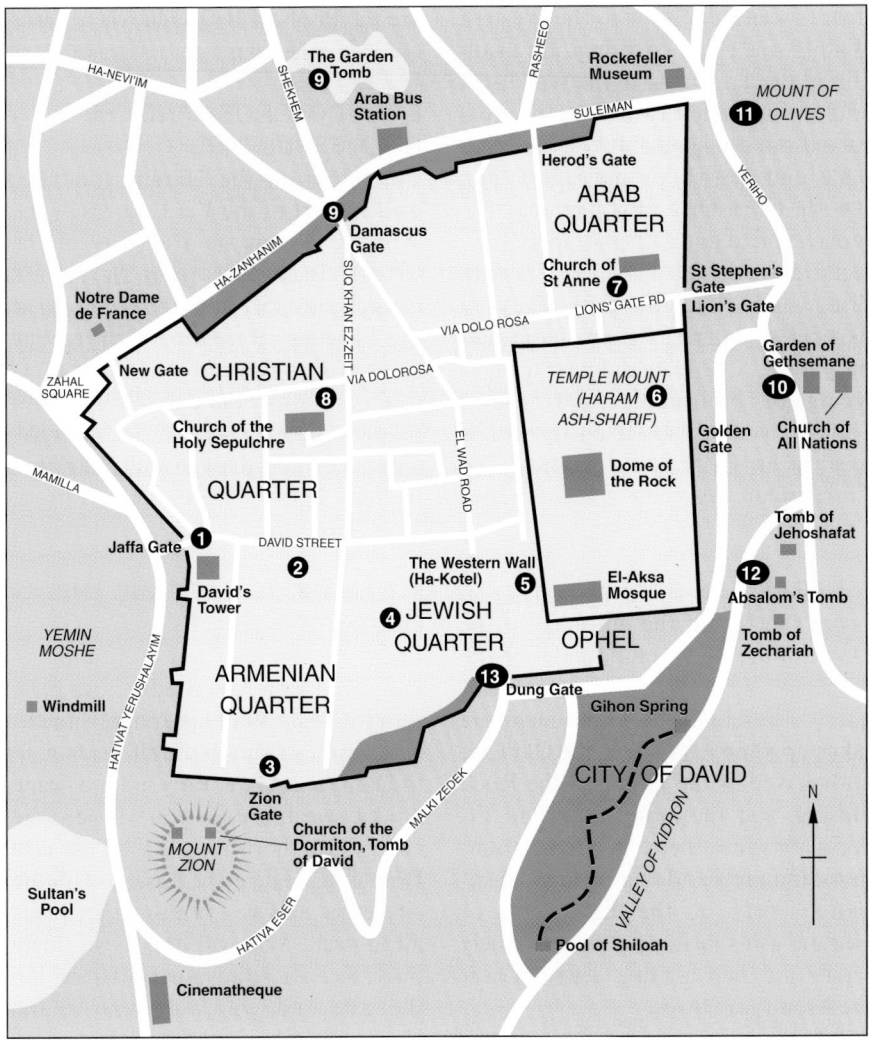

Don't miss these places in the Old City of Jerusalem.

clothes shops, past the grocery sellers and head downhill, bearing right as you go. The street you need to be on is Tariq Bab al-Silsileh, better known as Chain Gate Street—although finding a street-name sign is next to impossible.

Follow your nose downwards past the trinket sellers until you come to a major right-hand turn with a clearly visible street sign pointing the way to the Kotel, the Western Wall.

5 THE WESTERN WALL
The bustle of the *shuq* is replaced by a silent little side-street that has an army check-post at the end of it. Submit your belongings to a quick search and

then descend the steps to the Western Wall Plaza. Head-coverings are available at the fence close to the Wall itself, and on the far left is the entrance to a carved-out synagogue. If you are either male and Jewish or male and look Jewish, Ultra-Orthodox men may approach you to put leather-strapped phylactaries on. These men are looking to bring you back to your faith. They are particularly interested if you happen to be young, American and have a smattering of biblical Hebrew. On a Shabbat you will be fixed up with a meal in an Orthodox household. To short-circuit this route ask any Ultra-Orthodox Jew for Jeff Seidl.

6 HARAM ASH-SHARIF

From the Kotel, the entrance to the Dome of the Rock compound is on the far right. Visiting times are unfortunately restricted. The whole enclosure takes up almost a fifth of the Old City and as well as the Dome of the Rock mosque and the more important El-Aksa mosque, there are many fountains, minarets and secret places to explore. Parts of the Enclosure, or Haram ash-sharif, can be extremely serene and there are fine views out over the Mount of Olives.

7 CHURCH OF ST ANNE

There are a number of gates that will get you back into the Old City proper, but after resting in the Haram awhile the rude awakening of the *shuq* will jar. Whichever of the gates you come out of, bear right until you come to the Austrian Hospice. From here it is easy to find, first, the Monastery of the Flagellation and then further to the right, St Anne's Church. Close to here are the Pools of Bethsada where Jesus cured a lame man.

8 VIA DOLOROSA AND THE HOLY SEPULCHRE

Coming from the Haram you have walked part of the Via Dolorosa (The Way of Sorrow or The Way of the Cross). Backtrack from St Anne's Church and start from the beginning at the Pilgrims' Reception Centre. The route is sign-posted along most of its twists and turns but can be difficult to follow at times. There are 14 "stations" along the route, marked with faded wall plaques. The last five stations are in the Holy Sepulchre itself.

9 DAMASCUS GATE AND THE GARDEN TOMB

From the relative quiet around the Holy Sepulchre you need to dive back into the *shuq*. Walking roughly northwards will get you to the hill leading up to Damascus Gate. Why not buy some Arabic sweetmeats as you will need the energy for the walk back to the car. Damascus Gate is the busiest of all the city gates and is a mini-market place all to itself. You will find it extremely busy. Keep heading north after exiting the gate and you will come to the Garden Tomb, another haven of peace away from the hubbub. This is where Anglicans believe Golgotha, the tomb of Jesus, to be, not buried under the Holy Sepulchre.

10 CITY WALLS AND THE GARDEN OF GETHSEMANE

Retracing your steps from the Garden Tomb, cross the road towards Damascus Gate but turn left, sticking close to the city walls. At the road junction turn right, again keeping the walls close by. It is now possible to walk around the walls, with views over to the Mount of Olives, the City of David and the Kidron Valley to keep you company. Cross the road, aiming at the onion-shaped golden cupolas. Down below this is the Garden of Gethsemane.

11 MOUNT OF OLIVES
From the Garden of Gethsemane, visit the graves on the Mount of Olives and perhaps some of the various churches dotted about the hillside. If you're feeling fit, you could climb to the top of the Mount of Olives and view Jerusalem below—a fantastic sight, the "official" tourist view of the Old City.

12 ABSALOM'S TOMB
Down below Gethsemane, it is hard to miss the conically shaped Absalom's Tomb. Further down are the Bene Hezir Tomb and the tomb of Zechariah.

13 CITY WALLS
Walking back via the road hugging the city walls, a path climbs past the Ophel Archeological Gardens. This climb is a tough one but eventually you will come to the Dung Gate. Enter here or carry on around the city walls until you get to Mount Zion. A car-park will be the most obvious sign that you have arrived at your destination, but the imposing Dormiton is visible too. Enter via Zion Gate and either collect your car at the car-park around the corner or take a pleasant walk along the city walls, getting a higher vantage point on the places you have just been to, such as the Mount of Olives.

Nature Tour in the Galilee

The Galilee is blessed with green rolling hills (in winter and spring) and is a favourite place for trail-walking, horse-riding safaris and other outdoor pursuits. The area is dotted with nature reserves.

1 TIBERIAS
This is as good a place as any to start a nature tour of the Galilee—there are many fine hotels here and after your walks you could soothe your aching muscles in the hot spa water baths just outside town.

2 VERED HAGALIL
North of Tiberias, near to Tabgha, and well sign-posted, is Vered HaGalil, a riding stable and ranch. As well as offering very basic accommodation, this ranch is the Galilee base for off-the-beaten-track exploring on horseback. About 5km from Vered HaGalil is The Galilee Inn which offers trekking trips by donkey.

3 HULA VALLEY
Half an hour north from Vered HaGalil on a fast but relatively uninteresting road, Route 90 (apart from the switch-backs up the Mount of the Beatitudes) is a signpost for the Hula Valley Nature Reserve. Turn right at this sign and follow the road until the end—the tarmac peters out and after a reception area, water takes over. Much of this part of the Galilee was mosquito-infested swampland until the 1950s when the valley was drained to make excellent farmland. The Hula Valley Reserve, all 400 ha (1,000 acres) of it, is just a small part of this ancient swampland. The amount and range of animals living in this reserve is quite

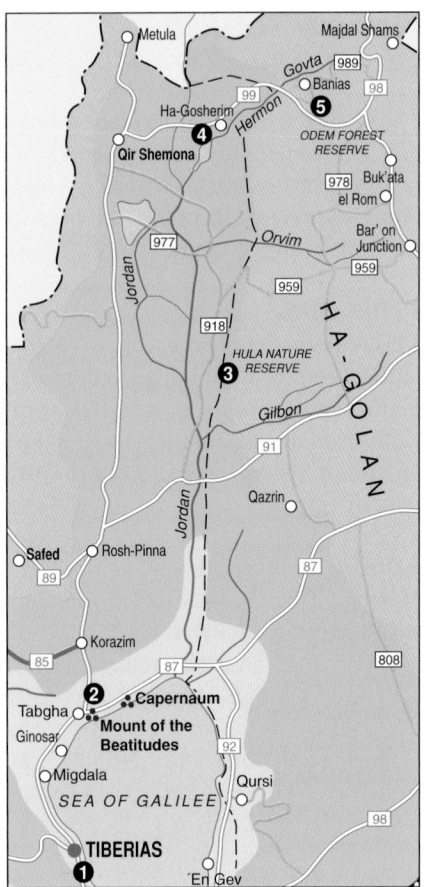

*W*here to see nature in the Galilee.

Dafna, where you can book in for motel-style bed and breakfast, is Hurshat Tal, an ancient oak wood on the banks of the Dan River. This is a good place for swimming. A few minutes further on from Hurshat Tal is Kibbutz Dan, which has its own small nature reserve, notable for its verdant location next to the Dan River.

5 BANIAS

Close to Kibbutz Dan, on the road to the Druse settlement of Majd al-Shams, is the nature reserve protecting the Banias waterfall, a wondrous sight in the springtime. It is possible to swim here. The site has been venerated for thousands of years: the rock-cut niches for statues of Pan, the nature god, are still clearly visible. These niches were carved by the Greeks who had a cave-temple here and the sanctuary became known as Paneas, which was corrupted over the years to Banias.

From Banias it is possible to climb a little further, getting into the foothills of the Golan Heights and eventually reaching the ski resort of Neve Ativ on the south side of Mount Hermon. The drive back to Tiberias should backtrack on the way you came—it is not normally safe to try to drive too close to the border with Syria, over the hill.

remarkable—a day spent here passes quickly.

4 HURSHAT TAL AND TEL DAN

North of Hula, again on Route 90, you pass through Kiryat Shmona, a nondescript town, and for the Dan Nature Reserves you need to take the right-hand turn as you leave towards Metulla (Route 99). Just after Kibbutz

Nature Tour by the Dead Sea

The Dead Sea, as its name suggests, is lifeless. Yet there are some small pockets around it that are teeming with natural flora and fauna—mainly because of the springs and water-courses which drain into it. Settlements are few and far

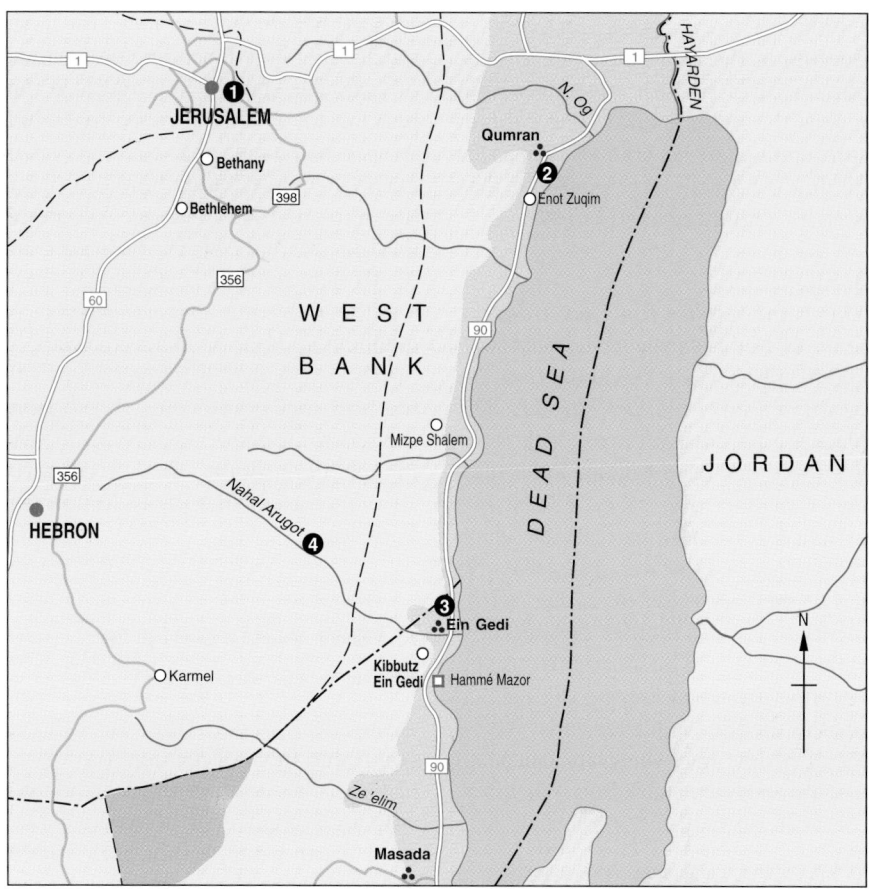

For the nature-lover in the Dead Sea area.

between, making those that you do find much appreciated.

1 JERUSALEM

The drive to the Dead Sea from Jerusalem takes only about an hour if you stop off briefly at places such as the Inn of the Good Samaritan and Mitspe Jericho. The gushing spring of Ain Qelt that is visible from an observation point is a dramatic example of a spring watering a slim part of the wilderness.

2 EN FASHKHA

At the valley floor, take a sharp right to get to the road running along beside the Dead Sea. If you were without a car, this is the point where the extreme heat and humidity of the Dead Sea area would hit you—in midsummer it can be like walking into a furnace after the relative coolness of lofty Jerusalem. A minute or two after the ruins of Qumran, on your right you will see the freshwater springs of En

Fashkha. There is a good beach here for floating in the Dead Sea, but it is the narrow strip of lush vegetation that makes the place special. The verdant surroundings attract animals such as the diminutive hyrax and goat-like ibex with its scimitar-shaped horns.

3 EIN GEDI

This is the famous Ein Gedi from the Song of Songs in the Old Testament, and the place where David hid from the wrath of Saul (*1 Samuel 24:1–11*). The place is a paradise on earth; little wonder there has been human habitation here ever since prehistory. The oasis is a fenced-off nature reserve which costs to get in. However, it is well worth it—as well as ruins of earlier settlements, there are a number of walks possible from here. The most obvious and the most travelled are the well-beaten ones to the Ein Gedi waterfalls. With a lot of people here the place can seem like a small theme park but, remember, this is all for real!

4 NAHAL ARUGOT

Hikes in the Judean Desert are way-marked by small painted stones at irregular intervals, although a large-scale map is still needed. Also very necessary is a water canteen of some sort and a sun hat, and be prepared for the shock of signposts warning you about the dangers of panther attacks. There have been none, and in fact you'll need to take just as much care not to fall down a ravine as to be on the look-out for panthers.

This particular route is a demanding but fascinating one. It is a 4- to 5-hour walk through a narrow, lush valley, following the course of a *nahal*, or

stream, which may or may not have much water in it depending on the time of year. The start of the route is at the parking lot at the entrance to Nahal Arugot, half a mile or so south of Nahal David, next to Kibbutz Ein Gedi. Take the narrow road between kilometre markers 243 and 244. The walk goes via the Roman ruins of Tel Goren, following the red route-marked stones. A highlight an hour or so into the walk is the Hidden Waterfall, a small detour off the trail, well sign-posted. From here the red route markings disappear, although it is a simple job to descend for 20 minutes to the Big Pools. Return the same way.

Israel with only a Week to Spare

A one-week whistle-stop tour can get you round most of the important sites of Israel. It's a punishing schedule involving a great deal of seeing Israel from a car window, but each varied stopover more than makes up for the discomfort.

1 DAY ONE—TEL AVIV

Flying to Tel Aviv is the most common way to get to Israel—El Al have night flights that get you into Israel early in the morning. Ben-Gurion Airport has many 24-hour car hire offices, with the Israeli firms, such as Eldan, being much the best value. It is just a 20-minute drive into Tel Aviv from the airport.

Stopping points on a week-long, whistle-stop tour of Israel.

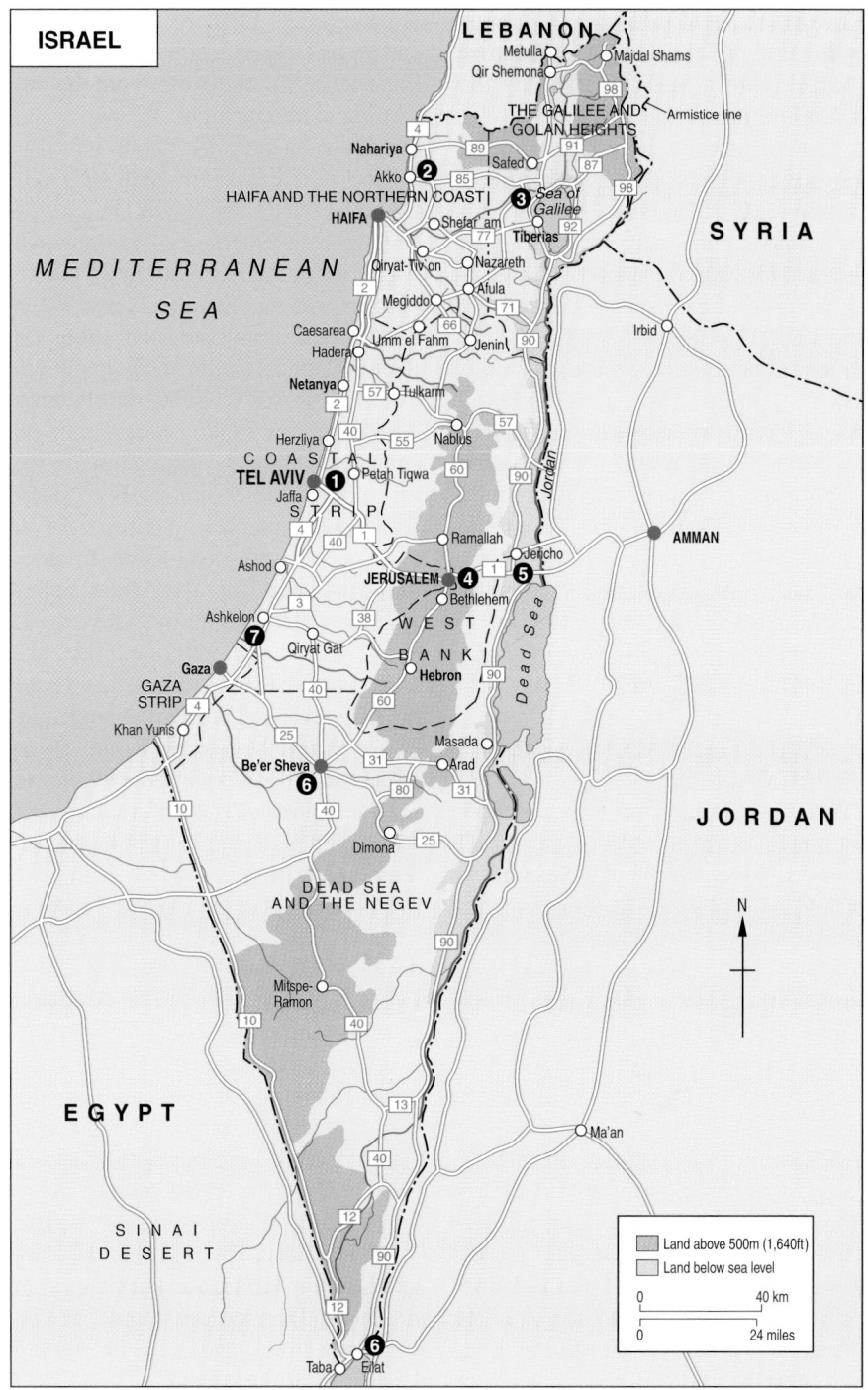

Have breakfast in Jaffa, change money in downtown Tel Aviv and acclimatize yourself with a quick walk along the sea-front promenade.

From Tel Aviv, drive north on the motorway (Route 2) towards Haifa, stopping off at Caesarea for a morning's ruin-spotting. After Caesarea, take the turn for Zichron Ya'akov at the interchange of the same name (Route 70) and stop off to take a quick look at the wine production process for which this town is famous. The Carmel-Oriental Wine Company exports its kosher wines all over the world and is situated on HaNadiv Street near the Rothschild family tomb. Drive north through the Carmel hills and take the main Haifa turn near Yokne'am (there are many fruit-sellers here, so you can stock up on fresh produce). Drop down into Haifa, and this is the end of the first day.

2 DAY TWO—AKKO AND THE UPPER GALILEE

Try to miss Haifa's rush hour and take the main road to Akko, very well sign-posted and very busy. Stop off at old Akko and view the subterranean Crusader city. Drive north on the main road to Nahariya, stopping off en route at the Holocaust museum of Lohemei HaGheta'ot, a kibbutz founded by survivors of the Warsaw Ghetto. Ten minutes on from here is the resort town of Nahariya, a good place for a quick swim. Further north are the sea caves of Rosh Hanikra; allow 2 hours for viewing them. Backtrack on yourself on Route 4 and take Route 89 out towards Safed. Stop off at the Kabri Springs, Kibbutz Yehi'am for its castle, and Mi'ilya for Montfort Castle, and then spend the afternoon walking

around Safed. Descend on Routes 89 and 90 to Tiberias, and visit the Galilee Experience on the waterfront before turning in for the night.

3 DAY THREE—THE SEA OF GALILEE AND THE NORTH

The sights of Tiberias can be done in a couple of hours—or you could take a boat trip on the Sea of Galilee. Then head north along the lake shore on Route 90 until Tabgha and Capernaum on Route 87. After visiting the churches here backtrack slightly onto Route 90 again and climb the twisting road to the turn off for the Mount of Beatitudes. Double back after here and turn right on to Route 90 and travel for 40 minutes until the sign for the Hula Valley Reserve. After an hour or so here, head back to Route 90 and turn left back the same way you came, to Tiberias. Drive through town and head uphill on Route 77 to Nazareth. Follow Route 60 to Afula and drop into the Jezreel Valley to see the impressive ruins of Megiddo, or Armageddon. By now it will be late afternoon or early evening—you can drive to a hotel in either Netanya or Tel Aviv.

4 DAY FOUR—JERUSALEM

From Netanya, drive to Tel Aviv and take the motorway (Route 1) to Jerusalem. After a rather dull drive through the coastal plain, you start to climb and the scenery changes dramatically. Stop off at Latrun monastery to buy some wine and view the Crusader ruins. Continue climbing to Jerusalem. Drive through modern West Jerusalem towards the Old City and head for Jaffa Gate. Park the car in the Jewish Quarter (see tour of the Old City on p. 84). At least a full day should be devoted to Jerusalem.

5 DAY FIVE—JERICHO AND THE DEAD SEA

Day five will involve a lot of mileage but the views from the car windows of first the Judean Desert and then the Negev Desert mean the journey will be a rewarding one. Leave Jerusalem early in the morning and follow the signposts for the Dead Sea. Descend to below sea level, stopping off briefly at the Inn of the Good Samaritan and Mitspe Jericho. The Mitspe Jericho turn-off is a minor left-hand turn that is easy to miss. Continue on this narrow minor road to the parking lot for the Monastery of St George. View the monastery from afar, then head on to Jericho. The views on the decent here are superb.

From Jericho take Route 90 to the Dead Sea. Stop off for an hour's break at the oasis of Ein Gedi, have a float in the Dead Sea and wash the salt away at the showers provided, then drive on for 10 minutes to Masada and take the cable car to the summit. An hour here is worthwhile for the views and the atmosphere. Drive from Masada to Eilat. This is a long journey made interesting by the dramatic scenery. If you have time before sunset, stop off at the Hai Bar Wildlife Reserve or the Timna Mines. Drive to Eilat for the night.

6 DAY SIX—EILAT, THE NEGEV AND BE'ER SHEVA

Spend part of the morning in Eilat, swimming at Coral Beach or visiting the Underwater Observatory and the Yellow Submarine. Drive out towards the Dead Sea on Route 90 but take the turn to Be'er Sheva and Makhtesh Ramon at either Route 40 or Route 13 half an hour further north. The ascent to the crater is a tough one, but the views are worth it. The crater itself is an amazing sight and if you stop along the route the silence is wonderful. There will probably be few other cars on this road. Traverse the crater and ascend to the Mitspe Ramon observatory. If you have enough time, stop here; if not continue onwards until you reach Route 40 and the city of Be'er Sheva. If you visit on a Thursday there will be a vibrant camel market on the southern edge of the town. Visit the Israeli Air Force Museum 8km from Be'er Sheva. Drive to Ashkelon on Route 34 for the night.

7 DAY SEVEN—ASHKELON AND THE SOUTHERN COASTAL STRIP

Ashkelon is worth a few hours of anybody's time; the variety of ruins here are particularly scenic and impressive. The drive northwards on Route 4 is short—spend some time in Tel Aviv and then return the hired car to the airport and take your flight home.

Jewish Sites

The whole of Israel, of course, is full of Jewish sites but to be technically correct the biblical ones are not strictly Jewish but Israelite. Judaism didn't really evolve until after the destruction of the Second Temple in AD 70 Rabbinical Jewish sites therefore are harder to join together in one themed route. However, the places mentioned below can be added to the other routes in this chapter as you see fit. Remember that Galilee is richest in Jewish sites.

The main places of note are:

- The tombs of Maimonides and other important rabbis in Tiberias;

- The synagogues and Jewish cemetery of Safed;
- Mount Meron;
- Bet Shearim near Haifa;
- The Western Wall and the Jewish Quarter in Jerusalem;
- Yavne—a site of Jewish learning after the destruction of the Second Temple.

Mount Meron Hikes

This hilly area near Safed is part of the largest nature reserve in Israel. Mount Meron is an imposing sight that dominates any car journey around it on the way to or from Safed. There are two way-marked routes on this mountain, each of which is graded for difficulty. The Meron Field School will provide information on expeditions in the region (tel. 06-989072).

THE MOUNTAIN TRAIL
This would take a fit, keen walker about four hours to complete. Park near the Field School on the lower parking lot a short way off Route 89. Close by will be the spring of Ein Hamama, a place that is lush with vegetation. Two and a half hours of ascending will bring you to the observation point at Mount Neria. Take in the fine views across to the Mediterranean and to the peaks of Lebanon. From here it is only approximately 40 minutes to the peak following the HaPisga path. You can either go back the way you came or for a change of scenery descend on the road.

THE PEAK TRAIL
This is an easier route to the peak starting from the upper car-park. It will take no more than 2 hours to get to the top and back. The views make it worth it, especially those from the Lebanon observation point half an hour from the peak. Descend to the car-park.

The Best Dusk Strolls in Israel

It is a Mediterranean custom to stroll around aimlessly come evening time. City-born Israelis have perfected this custom to a fine art. Jerusalem and Tel Aviv are the best places to wander aimlessly in the evenings, snacking on *falafel*, chocolate croissants and coffee.

MIDRAHOV MEANDERINGS — DIZENGOFF AND BEN YEHUDA
The place to be seen in Tel Aviv is Dizengoff Street. All the best cafés are located here and this with Dizengoff Square at its mid-point is the hub of Tel Aviv nightlife. There is no fixed route, so just wander from top to bottom stopping at open-air cafés, admiring the people and the view. For somewhere to eat, it's best to go down the side-streets off Dizengoff Street. Once you have had your fill of watching the world go by, a brief walk along the seaside promenade is a good way to end the evening (although of course Tel Aviv buzzes at night and there are plenty of late-opening clubs and night haunts to go to).

In Jerusalem, the same "watching the world go by" atmosphere can be had on the pedestrianized Ben Yehuda, the Midrahov, in downtown West Jerusalem. Here open air-cafés and *falafel* shops keep Jerusalemites and tourists alike fed and watered. It is customary (and also good fun) to have each course of your evening meal in a different establishment, finishing off with an ice-cream or a frozen yoghurt from one of the brightly lit outlets near Zion Square.

TEL AVIV TO JAFFA

It is possible to walk along the beach almost all the way to Jaffa, missing out on some very busy and smog-filled roads. Just as the sunset is starting is an ideal time to leave your Tel Aviv hotel and walk to Jaffa. There are no specific sights along the way except for the view of Old Jaffa getting closer and closer. Once at the end of the beach, clamber up through the sculpture garden and drop into the square of Old Jaffa. There are many fine fish restaurants here for your evening meal. Take a taxi back to Tel Aviv.

Prehistoric Man: A Ten-Hour Hike

The Carmel Hills and Mount Carmel itself are well known from the Bible. However, not so well known outside academic circles is how important Carmel is to the study of our distant ancestors. The hills hereabouts contain many caves where traces of early man have been found. Although there are no extant ruins, thanks to the dry climate the caves themselves have changed little from those distant days. The sea level has dropped since then and early man would not recognize today's topography, but his shelters and simple tools provide ample witness of how he lived, worked and foraged for food hereabouts. Artefacts from these caves are spread throughout Israel's museums, but a good selection can be seen in the Primordial Man Museum in Haifa. The Carmel Field School will provide information on expeditions in the region (tel. 06-399655).

THE CARMEL PARK

The Carmel Park is well sign-posted off Routes 2, 4 and 70 on the top of Mount Carmel. As well as traces of prehistoric man, this varied National Park contains monasteries, nature reserves, and Canaanite, Jewish and Samaritan ruins.

The Hatanur Cave was excavated in 1929–34 by the British archaeologist Dorothy Grod. The remains of early man were found accidentally in the late 1920s when a Haifa construction company was searching for stone suitable for quarrying. A test explosion uncovered prehistoric implements.

From Hatanur Cave walk eastwards down the cliff, passing a cave where no traces of early man were ever found, and carry on to the impressive and huge Nahal Cave. The rock-cut niches are examples of early man's first religious rituals, probably involving animistic deities resident in rocks, streams and the rest of nature. Such beliefs later formed the basis of the major religions known today.

After retreating from the Carmel Caves head north to the start of Nahal Oren, where you'll find the Oren Cave, a minute or so north of the junction leading up to Kibbutz Beit Oren. The inhabitants of the Oren Cave are believed to have been more permanently settled than the inhabitants of the caves above, suggesting the start of communal life and early forms of civilization, including formalized ritual practices. Vital evidence for the domestication of wheat—a major historical landmark—

has been found near the Oren Cave. Good news for dentists is that the Oren Cave area has the first human skulls to be found with teeth decay, suggesting a changed pattern of food preparation and eating—a hunter-gatherer society developing into a farming one, with cooked starches leading to the tooth-decay problem.

It's a simple matter to retrace some of your steps from here and return to the car. A visit to the Haifa Museum devoted to Primordial Man is very worthwhile.

A One Day Desert Car-Safari on Good Tarmac

As Israel is such a small country, you could leave virtually anywhere in the country and still be at the start of this tour with enough light to make it an unhurried affair. Providing you left early enough, of course.

From Be'er Sheva hustle your way through town (the traffic can be very congested and un-coordinated) southwards to Abraham's Well. This is the traditional site where Abraham sunk his first well and is now housed in a walled-off compound, and bricked up to look nothing like a biblical well. Never mind, it's the location that's important. Even when the gates are shut you can get a very good view from outside.

At Abraham's Well, you need to turn left and then shortly afterwards right onto a major highway (the 25 leading on to the 40). Five minutes out of town you will come to the Bet Eshel junction—bear right on to Route 40.

If you're expecting desert from this point, prepare to be disappointed as in its own way the area immediately south of Be'er Sheva is reasonably well vegetated for at least three quarters of an hour's driving. Slowly the colour of the countryside changes and well before Sde Boker you're into the real Negev.

Until you reach the Mitspe Ramon observation post, the journey has been unremarkable. All this changes after the crest of a hill on the climb past the observation centre—suddenly the whole vista opens out and you're looking into the Makhtesh Ramon (or Ramon Crater). This is unlike anywhere else you might have seen in the world. The descent into the crater, the undulating drive through a whole host of wadis and dirt tracks, along a bumpy tarmac road, is nothing short of amazing. You can see for miles ahead on the straight stretches, making it reasonably safe to let the car do the driving and you do some sightseeing. Stop the car a few times and walk around to feel the intensity of the desert and to savour its powerful beauty.

Slowly you climb out of the crater on twisting roads and then through the wilderness of Paran you'll descend into the baking Jordan Valley. From here you can turn left for the Dead Sea and Jerusalem or right for Eilat.

A Journey to the End of the World

1 TIBERIAS
After a late breakfast in your hotel, leave Tiberias and head west out of town climbing on the major highway (77) as you go.

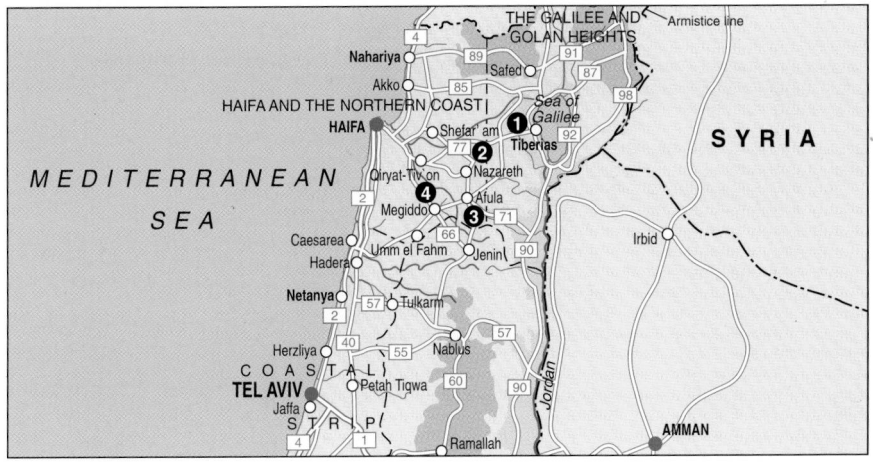

2 NAZARETH

After half an hours driving, descend through Kfar Kanna (traditional site of Cana, where Jesus performed his first miracle, turning water into wine) and then climb to the top of Nazareth before descending into the town centre. This road is often jam-packed with cars, no matter what the time of day. Expect delays and hold-ups.

3 AFULA

South out of Nazareth, take Route 60 and descend into the Jezreel Valley, a beautiful journey at any time of the year. After Afula, a 10-minute drive south from Nazareth, continue south to Megiddo Junction.

*T*o the Armageddon of John's Revelation.

4 MEGIDDO

In Biblical times, this crossroads was of vital strategic importance and was much fought over. In ancient times Megiddo was a byword for violent destruction, hence the use of its imagery by John in *The Revelation*. John's Armageddon, the battle of the end days, is a corruption of Har-Megiddo, meaning the mountain of Megiddo (*Revelation 16:16*).

JERUSALEM

A Golden City, Revered as Special Throughout the World

Modern Jerusalem is a heady mix of faith, power, dust and beauty— a city of contrasts, a microcosm of the country as a whole. Jerusalem is a mix of so many feelings, sights, sounds and contexts that tourists can be left reeling by the sheer intensity of the place. Jerusalem is not for the faint-hearted, but nor should it be missed. No visit to Israel would be complete without a stay in Jerusalem.

Because of its religious significance, Jerusalem is often portrayed as a magical place. Yet even non-believers find Jerusalem somehow special. Jerusalemites wonder why anybody would wish to live anywhere else in Israel. Jerusalem may not have the nightlife of Eilat or the cosmopolitan excesses of Tel Aviv, but it is far from being the provincial backwater that some Israelis would have you believe. The spiritual Jerusalem is important to one third of mankind. The earthly Jerusalem is home to 500,000 inhabitants and ranks as one of the most beautiful and inspiring cities in the world.

Jews, Christians and Muslims revere it as a Holy City. For prophets, poets and politicians, Jerusalem has always been a major theme, the most allegorical city ever. It might only be small, but its influence on religious and social history has been immense. People have died for Jerusalem—either by fighting to gain it or to defend it. In Jerusalem history repeats itself constantly as patriots on both sides continue to die for the city they feel is theirs and theirs alone.

The Dome of the Rock is Jerusalem's most notable landmark, and certainly one of the most beautiful buildings in Israel. See the loudspeaker that calls the devout in to pray five times a day.

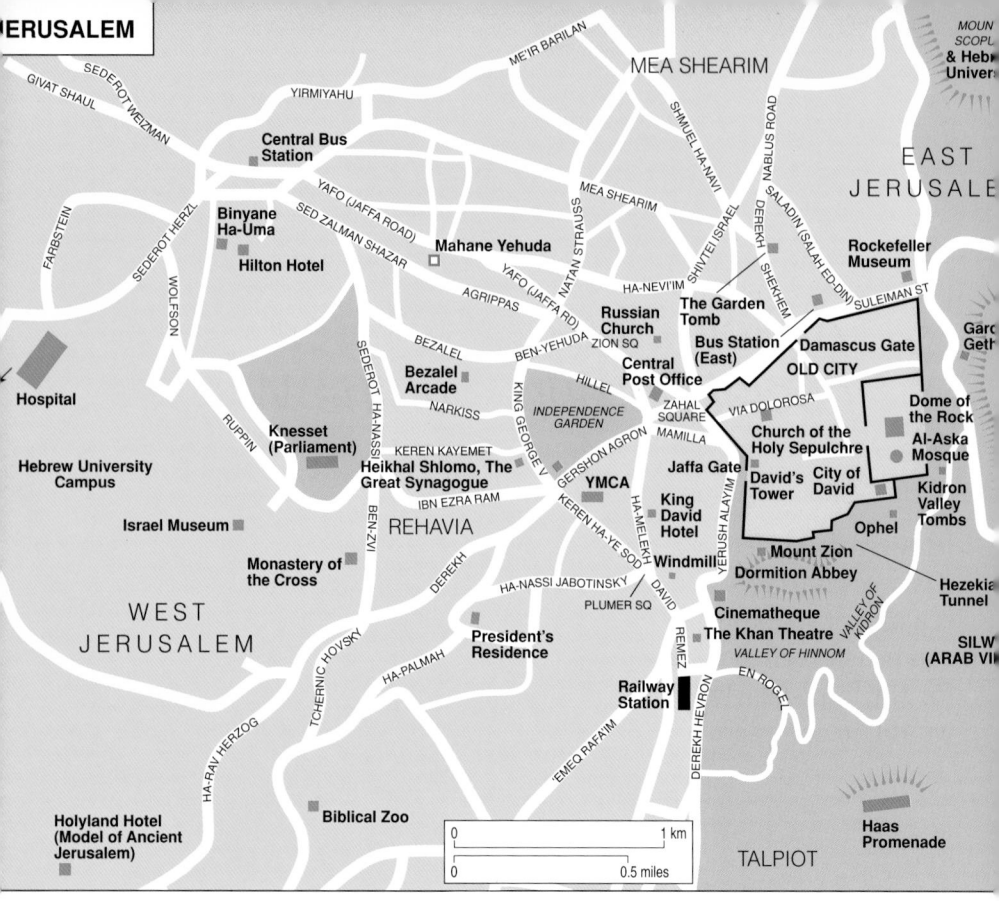

City plan of Jerusalem showing the main streets and places of interest.

Jerusalem can be divided in many ways but the most important modern division is that between **Israeli West Jerusalem** and **Arab East Jerusalem**. Before 1967, Jerusalem was physically divided between Israel and Jordan. Israel had the more modern half, while Jordan had the Old City and the older Arab areas. After the 1967 War and the capture of the whole of Jerusalem, the city has been officially one and was made the "eternal, united capital of Israel" (although many countries do not recognize this fact and many embassies and consulates are based in the old capital, Tel Aviv).

West Jerusalem covers 38km^2 (15 square miles). But if you include East Jerusalem, the whole city covers an area of 108km^2 (42 square miles). It has over 150 districts and separate residential quarters, many of which are modern developments on the edge of town, housing new immigrants and staking a claim to the land in the event of any future territorial disputes.

History

Archaeological excavations give Jerusalem an age of about 5,000 years, making it one of the oldest continuously inhabited cities in the world along with

Jericho down the road. Inhabited originally by the Canaanites and then the Jebusites, Jerusalem, already 2,000 years old, was conquered by King David. In a shrewd set of political and religious moves, David made Jerusalem the focal point of the Twelve tribes and, in about 1000 BC, the Jebusite city became the capital of the Kingdom of a united Israel. Solomon built the first stone temple on what was believed to be Mount Moriah, the place where Abraham was about to sacrifice his son, Isaac.

After King Solomon's death, the city remained the capital of the south, the Kingdom of Judah, for nearly four whole centuries. During this time it was home to a number of blood-and-thunder prophets, the likes of Isaiah and Jeremiah from the Old Testament, and, just as the prophets foretold, the city fell and was razed to the ground. In 586 BC it was sacked by the Babylonians

Golden Stone

Thanks to the first civil administrator of the British Mandate over Palestine, all new buildings in Jerusalem have to be constructed from the local golden stone. This makes even the most modern developments blend into the hillsides. Of course, rambling Arab houses are more pleasing to the eye, but blocks of flats in Jerusalem are not as stark as in many other countries.

Jerusalem straddles a much more physical border than that between political and racial East and West. The city perches high in the Judean hills 800m (2,625ft) above sea level with on the one side, the Judean desert, and on the other, the fertile plain leading down to Tel Aviv and the coast.

T he newest "official" viewing point over Jerusalem is from the Haas Promenade, on the Hill of Evil Council.

and the most influential people of Judah were carried off to Babylon.

"By the waters of Babylon, there we sat down and wept, when we remembered Zion." (*Psalm 137*). This faith in their lost land sustained the Jews throughout their captivity and those who returned from exile after 538 BC slowly rebuilt the Temple and recreated their city. A succession of empires came after the Babylonians and by the time of Jesus Jerusalem was a bustling and prosperous cosmopolitan city ruled by puppet leaders installed by the Romans.

Herod the Great, one such puppet king who ruled a generation before Jesus, beautified the Temple and the city and added palaces, fortresses, and Roman-style cultural institutions. He also expanded the city area though much hated taxes and the rule of force. Foreign rule was despised by the Jews and they rose up many times in bloody revolt against their oppressors, with the Great Revolt of AD 66–70 ending, yet again, in the destruction of both the Temple and the city. The Jews were scattered and became a Diaspora people.

Emperor Hadrian flattened the ruins, and in their place constructed a Roman city, free of Jews, a city pagan to the core. He called his creation Aelia Capitolina, and named the province Palaestina (after the Philistines). It is his urban plan for Jerusalem that shaped the Old City of today. His Cardo Maximus, the central thoroughfare spanning the city, was discovered after the 1967 recapture of Jerusalem.

Much of the modern-day Old City was built by the Christian Byzantines, especially many of the churches. The Arab Ummayads (late 7th and early 8th centuries AD) built many of the Muslim religious buildings, including the Dome of the Rock, but by this time Jerusalem was merely a provincial town in the vast Muslim empire of the early Middle Ages. For almost all the 12th century, the blood-thirsty Crusaders made it the capital of their Latin Kingdom, but until Allenby's conquest of the Holy City in 1917 both Jerusalem and the province of Palestine were considered to be nothing more than a backwater, forgotten, abused and uncared for.

City Quarters

The **Old City** is the historic heart of the city and is the Jerusalem of the imagination. It is divided into Armenian, Jewish, Arab and Christian quarters. The Christian Quarter is active and bustling, but is so badly over-populated that it cannot accept any more new residents. The Armenian Quarter is a walled enclave within the Old City itself and is home to a curious and quiet population of Armenians, the men being distinctively black-robed, black-bearded and aloof. The Jewish Quarter, tidy, quiet, and mellow, has been extensively rebuilt since the 1967 war, and vibrates with faith, longing and study. The Arab Quarter is loud, brash, bustling and smelly. Part active market, part tourist honey-pot, the Arab Quarter is the archetypal oriental *shuq*, or market.

Since the "reunification" of the city in 1967, Jerusalem has grown and grown. Modern developments have changed the face of the city almost overnight. Spacious neighbourhoods, luxury hotels, parks and gardens have appeared from nowhere. Jerusalem has rapidly grown into its historical role as the capital of the State of Israel.

Orientation

Today, Jerusalem is a small but thriving city. Unless you are staying at one of the outlying hotels, such as the Holy Land, or at one of the Kibbutz inns, just about everything in Jerusalem is within walking distance.

There are three points of focus—the first is the Old City with most of the tourist sites. Jaffa Gate and Damascus Gate are the two principal points of reference.

The second is the New City, centred around the triangle formed by Jaffa Road, Ben Yehuda Street and King George V Street. Zion Square is the main reference point. Here you will find modern amenities, restaurants and street cafés.

The third point of focus is Arab East Jerusalem, centred around the triangle formed by Sultan Suleiman Street, Nablus Road, and Saladin Street. Damascus Gate is the reference point.

The YMCA tower is an imposing sight, especially at sunset. The flags are on top of the King David Hotel.

Jerusalem may only be a small city by Western standards, but it is packed with interesting things to see, do, eat and smell. To get a real appreciation of the place at least three days should be pencilled in for sightseeing. A week is even better.

There are a number of walking tours on offer by commercial organizations that will speed you around all of the major sites in record time, but Jerusalem is better explored at random—wander from place to place and don't worry about getting lost. Jerusalem's basic shape means you're never far from a landmark.

Damascus Gate is one of the more important, and certainly the busiest, of the Old City gates.

To get a quick grasp of this basic shape there is no better way than taking the number 99 bus. This is a scheduled bus service that goes just about everywhere, penetrating deep into the New City and skirting the Old. The 99 stops at thirty-four of the most visited sights. If you buy an all-day ticket you can get on and off at will. Buy your ticket from Egged Tours offices in Zion Square, 44a Jaffa Road (tel. 02-224198), at the Central Bus Station (tel. 02-534596), or at the Jaffa Gate terminal building (tel. 02-247783). A free map showing the route is also available. The 99 bus operates on the hour every hour from 9 a.m. to 5 p.m. Sunday to Thursday, and 9 a.m. to 2 p.m. on Friday. There is no service on Shabbat.

Another tour which can give you a grasp of the lie of the land is the 4km (2½ mile) Ramparts Walk around the walls of the Old City. Enter at Damascus Gate (a good choice because of the 2nd-century Roman gate and museum), the Lions' Gate, Zion Gate, or Jaffa Gate. There is a small entrance fee, but you can exit and re-enter the Ramparts Walk as much as you like over the next 48 hours (72 hours if you buy on Friday).

The Old City

Jerusalem's **Old City** is surrounded by a huge wall, mostly built about 400 years ago by Suleiman the Magnificent, although some portions date back over 2,000 years. In the daytime the walls are golden and serene; at night they are floodlit and commanding. The wall's main gates are Jaffa Gate, entered from Mamilla-Agron Street or Jaffa Road, and Damascus Gate, entered from Ha-Nevi'im or Nablus Road.

The Old City quarters are easy to recognize, mainly by people-watching. The inhabitants are a colourful lot ranging from black-robed, grey-bearded Christians and black-robed, grey-bearded Jews to black-robed, grey-bearded Muslims. There are also nuns, monks, *keffiah*-wearing Arabs (the *keffiah* is the traditional Arab head-dress), and Ultra-Orthodox Jewish women. Not to mention children, some of them urchins. Jerusalem is packed with people and the place is certainly lively.

The best entrance for most tourists will be Jaffa Gate. The citadel tower at the entrance is called **King David's Tower**. It marks the place where once

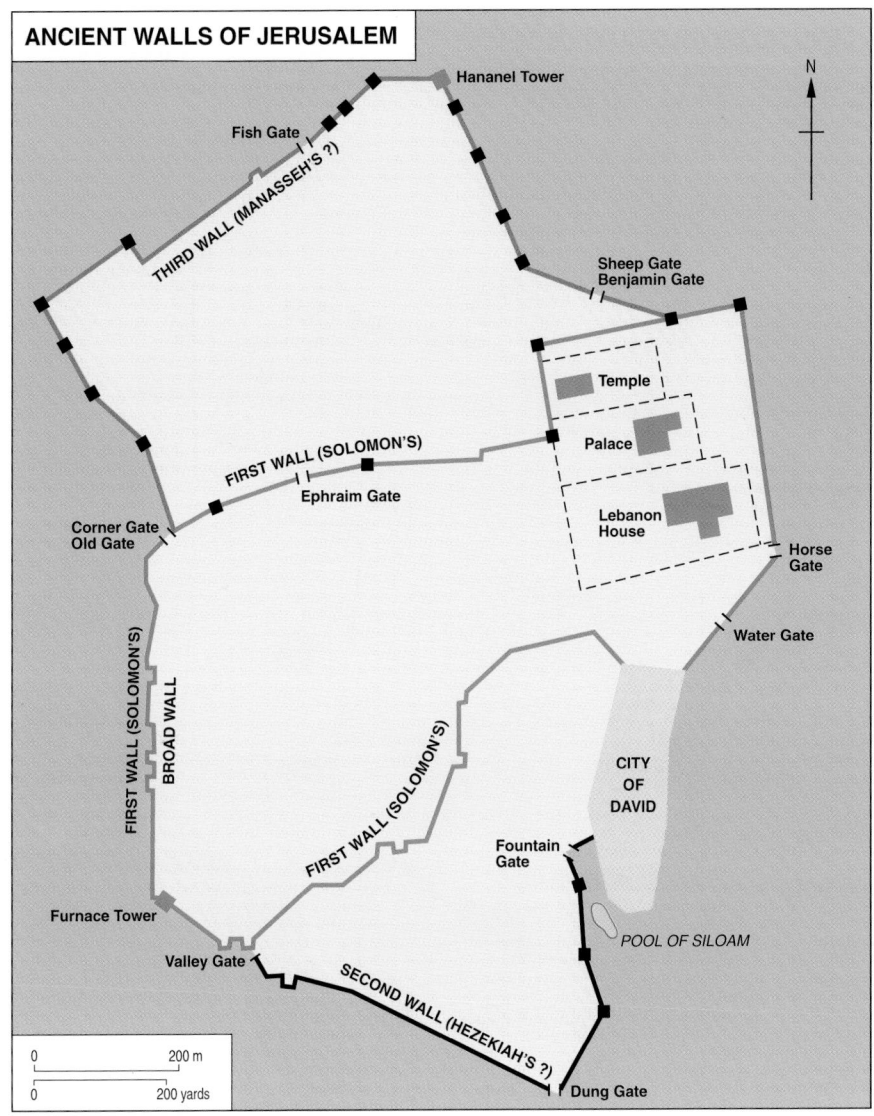

ANCIENT WALLS OF JERUSALEM

Hananel Tower

Fish Gate

THIRD WALL (MANASSEH'S ?)

N

Sheep Gate
Benjamin Gate

Temple

Palace

FIRST WALL (SOLOMON'S)

Ephraim Gate

Lebanon
House

Corner Gate
Old Gate

Horse
Gate

Water Gate

FIRST WALL (SOLOMON'S)

BROAD WALL

FIRST WALL (SOLOMON'S)

CITY
OF
DAVID

Fountain
Gate

Furnace Tower

POOL OF SILOAM

Valley Gate

SECOND WALL (HEZEKIAH'S ?)

0   200 m
0   200 yards

Dung Gate

stood three towers built by Herod near his palace. There is a daily tour of the tower in English at 11 a.m., and a **Sound and Light Show** is held nightly here from March to mid-November (except on Friday and holidays), the theme of which is the Old City's biblical history. Today the Tower is the **City**

The ancient walls of Jerusalem.

Museum (open 10 a.m.–5 p.m. daily, tel. 02-274111/283394), showing ancient maps of Jerusalem. It also houses an exhibition of dolls in the ethnic dress of the diverse population of this region.

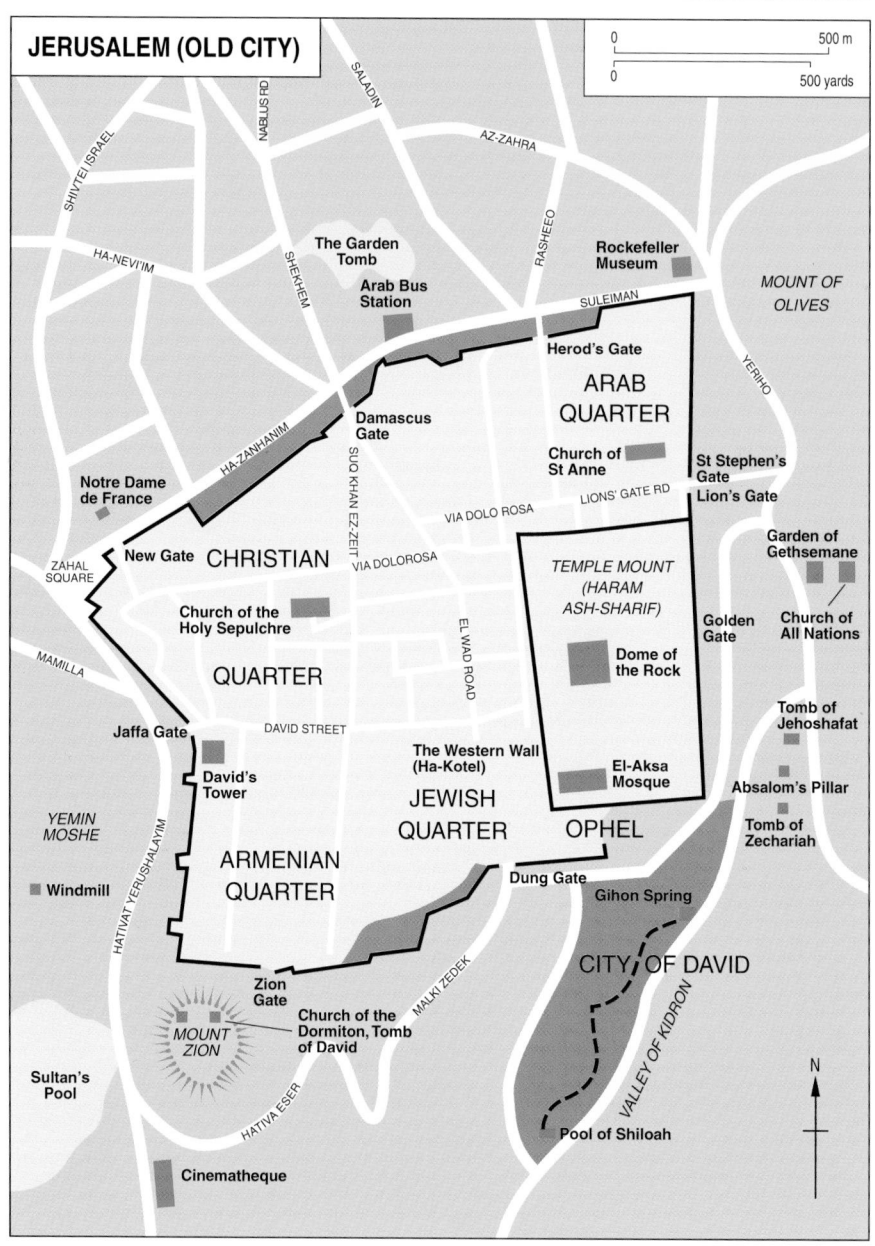

JERUSALEM (OLD CITY)

0   500 m
0   500 yards

SHIVTEI ISRAEL

NABLUS RD

SALADIN

AZ-ZAHRA

HA-NEVI'IM

SHEKHEM

RASHEED

The Garden Tomb

Rockefeller Museum

MOUNT OF OLIVES

Arab Bus Station

SULEIMAN

YERIHO

HA-ZANHANIM

Herod's Gate

ARAB QUARTER

Damascus Gate

SUQ KHAN EZ-ZEIT

Church of St Anne

St Stephen's Gate

Notre Dame de France

VIA DOLO ROSA

LIONS' GATE RD

Lion's Gate

ZAHAL SQUARE

New Gate

CHRISTIAN

VIA DOLOROSA

Garden of Gethsemane

TEMPLE MOUNT (HARAM ASH-SHARIF)

Church of the Holy Sepulchre

EL WAD ROAD

Dome of the Rock

Golden Gate

Church of All Nations

MAMILLA

QUARTER

Jaffa Gate

DAVID STREET

The Western Wall (Ha-Kotel)

El-Aksa Mosque

Tomb of Jehoshafat

David's Tower

JEWISH QUARTER

OPHEL

Absalom's Pillar

YEMIN MOSHE

HATIVAT YERUSHALAYIM

Tomb of Zechariah

Windmill

ARMENIAN QUARTER

Dung Gate

Gihon Spring

Zion Gate

CITY OF DAVID

MOUNT ZION

Church of the Dormiton, Tomb of David

MALKI ZEDEK

VALLEY OF KIDRON

Sultan's Pool

N

HATIVA ESER

Pool of Shiloah

Cinematheque

*T*he Old City of Jerusalem showing the four main quarters.

*K*ing David's Tower has nothing to do with King David. It is an Arab structure, built over the ruins of a Herodian stronghold.

City Gates

In all, there are eight gates in the Old City fortress-wall. Clockwise from the Western Wall they are: the Dung Gate, so-called because of the rubbish that was once being dumped here in biblical times; the Zion Gate, pock-marked with gunfire holes from 1948; the Jaffa Gate; the New Gate; the Damascus Gate; Herod's Gate; St Stephen's (or Lion's) Gate; and the blocked-up Golden Gate. This last gate, which you can see clearly from the Mount of Olives, has been sealed since 1530. An ancient Jewish belief has it that the Messiah will one day enter through the Golden Gate into Jerusalem. Possibly for this reason the gate was closed by the Muslims.

*J*erusalem has been fought over countless times, the last being in 1967. These are bullet holes in the Zion Gate.

The Armenian Quarter

As you come inside the wide courtyard, the Tourist Information Office is on your left, the *shuq* is straight ahead down the dark alleyway filled with people, and past the moat on the right is the road into the **Armenian Quarter**. This quarter is a quiet, residential area of small churches that parallels the wall. The road leads to the Western Wall and the Dome of the Rock, via the Jewish Quarter.

In the Armenian Quarter are many lush courtyards and ancient buildings, including the splendid **St James Cathedral** (within the Armenian monastery, built above the ruins of Herod's palace by the Crusaders), the **Church of the Holy Archangels**, the **Gulbenkian Public Library**, the **Library of Manuscripts**, and the **Edward Mardigian Museum of Armenian Art and History** (tel. 02-282331). There has been an Armenian community here since the 5th century and today there are over 3,500 people living, working and being educated in this quarter.

If you head straight into the *shuq* you'll enter **David Street**, the main thoroughfare into the Old City. Tourist goods abound here, and you'll be accosted by Arab shopkeepers eager for you to purchase their T-shirts, olivewood statuettes of Christian figures, mother-of-pearl rosary beads and much more. Don't be too offended by being pulled bodily into shops. If you really do not want to buy anything, simply stare straight ahead and act like the natives do: ignore the hustlers and carry on downhill. Any weakness on your part just to browse will be seen as good-as-a-commitment-to-buy by Arab shopkeepers. Do not haggle for something that you have no intention of buying: only start the bargaining process if you really want a certain item.

There are two routes you can choose from David Street. The **Church of the Holy Sepulchre** can be reached by taking the first left off David Street to Christian Quarter Road. For the Western Wall and Temple Mount continue straight along David Street until it becomes Chain Street and then follow the signs to "The Wall". You will pass lots of alleyways on the route downhill, but don't think you are lost in some sort of Middle-Eastern maze. Even taking the wrong turning is not disastrous, as the main routes are well-trodden and you won't be lost for too long.

Finally you arrive at the **Gate of the Chain**, the entrance to the Temple Mount. The Western Wall is off to your right, down a slightly cleaner alleyway. The Western Wall plaza opens up after just a few minutes walk. This is the **Jewish Quarter**.

The Jewish Quarter

This quarter has been razed to the ground many times in its history, but its most recent destruction came during the 1948 war, when it was all but flattened by Jordanian artillery. Since the 1967 recapture of the Old City, the quarter

The Jewish Quarter.

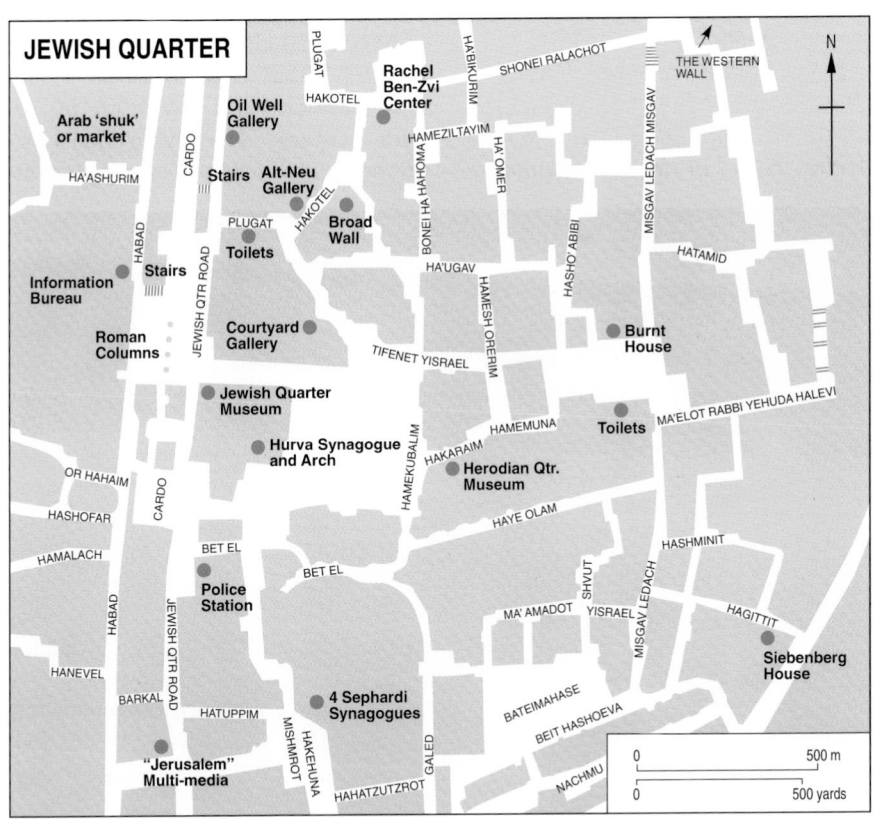

109

has been totally revamped, and now boasts a high concentration of synagogues, *yeshivas*, apartments, cafés and quality shops. Compared to the *shuq*, the Jewish quarter is an oasis of tranquillity and cleanliness. For this reason, it is a good escape from the rough-and-tumble of the other quarters. From David Street head into the **Cardo** and take refreshments from either of the two dairy cafés situated opposite each other.

The sights of the Jewish Quarter are well marked, and many signs and explanatory plaques are mounted at strategic points. Or you could join one of the daily walking seminar tours through the Old City that start in the Jewish Quarter (34 Habad Street, tel.

02-273515). The whole area is like an outdoor museum, and peaceful with it.

The **Cardo** is a recently excavated 6th-century street, the Cardo Maximus, and was Roman and Byzantine Jerusalem's main thoroughfare, although this street was originally the width of a six-lane highway. Today it is bordered by stately columns and lined with expensive shops. Much of the Cardo is still underground, with the Street of the Jews (Rehov Ha-Yehudim) being one level up from the Cardo and David Street. The southern portion of the Cardo is open to the sky. The Crusaders used this part of the Cardo as their market place and the arches beneath the Cardo cafés are remnants of the Crusader shops and stall-niches.

Above and along from the Cardo is the **Old Yishuv Court Museum** where you can experience Jewish life in the 19th century. The living quarters, kitchens, and several very important

View from the Jewish Quarter over El-Aksa mosque at night, with the lights of the Seven Arches Hotel in the background.

synagogues have all been restored. Open Sunday to Thursday from 9 a.m. to 4 p.m.

When Jerusalem was destroyed in AD 70 the rubble was built over and very little remained of what was once a bustling city. One building that survived its encapsulation underground is **The Burnt House**, around the corner from the Cardo. This house is thought to have belonged to a temple priest, and was burnt along with the rest of the city. It was discovered in a fine state of preservation and is now a museum, with a fine slide show, open Sunday to Thursday from 9 a.m. to 5 p.m., on Friday to noon.

More remains found beneath the 1st-century rubble are those of the **Nea**, once the city's second-grandest church. It is open to visitors from 9 a.m. to 5 p.m. but only the foundations are distinct.

One of the most memorable of the Jewish Quarter's sights is the graceful arch of the defunct **Hurva Synagogue**. This was the synagogue of Rabbi Yudah Ha-Hasid, Yudah the Pious One, an 18th-century Ashkenazi spiritual leader. The Hurva has never really had a successful life—it has been destroyed twice, rebuilt fully once but now only the arch and some ruins still remain. The arch is a modern, symbolic addition.

The Western Wall

The Wall lies downhill from the Jewish Quarter, with the plaza often coming into view from various nooks and crannies whilst you're descending. Above the Wall lies the Haram ash-sharif, the Noble Enclosure, or Temple Mount, and offset to one side from the

> **The Kotel**
>
> On 14 June 1967 the way to the Kotel was opened for the first time. Over a quarter of a million Israelis walked from Mount Zion through the bullet-riddled Dung Gate to renew their contact with this potent symbol of Israel and its glorious past.
>
> What you see today is not what Jews have been praying at for centuries. Before the Israeli recapture of the city the Wall lay behind a mass of Arab houses, an extension of the *shuq*. The only access was via a narrow alleyway, with room for only a few hundred worshippers. To make the Kotel into the national monument that it is today, the *shuq* was demolished and an attractive plaza laid in its place.
>
> At the prayer section of the Kotel, grass grows out of the upper cracks. The lower blocks have been stuffed with prayers written on scraps of paper.

Wall lies the golden Dome of the Rock. For Gentiles this Dome is the natural focus; for Jews the focus is the **Western Wall**—Ha-Kotel Ha-Ma'aravi (or simply the Kotel); the Dome disappears and only the bland section of yellow wall has any relevance. Gentiles often call the Western Wall the "Wailing Wall" because the Jews have traditionally come here to bewail the loss of their Temple.

The Kotel is the holiest of Jewish sites, a remnant of the 2nd-century wall that once supported the Temple Mount (and not, as is often believed, a wall from the Temple itself). It is not revered as sacred itself, but rather as the closest it is permissible to get to the ancient Temple. For over 2,000 years, at this place and wherever they have lived in the Diaspora, Jews have mourned the loss of the Temple. "Next year in Jerusalem", a heartfelt phrase said at

The Western Wall is the focus for Jewish worship. Whilst it is not venerated itself, the Wall is the only tangible remains of the destroyed Second Temple.

the end of Passover, meant "next year at the Kotel."

At present, archaeological excavations of the wall's foundations are being carried out and there are daily guided tours of the site. It is necessary to book a place in advance (tel. 02-271333). To see how small the Western Wall would have been in comparison to the immensity of the Temple itself, there is a scale model at **Atara Leyoshna**, 29 Misgav Ladach, Jewish Quarter, Old City, tel. 02-894466. As well as models of the First and Second Temples there is also one of the third—as the Second Temple was the last one standing this "third" is a provocative act of hope by extremely right-wing Jews.

Depending on the time and date of your visit you may see just a few worshippers at the Kotel or thousands. The plaza fills to overflowing during religious holidays. Security is very tight at the Kotel; expect to be thoroughly searched when you enter the plaza.

You should dress modestly if you want to approach the Wall or visit the small synagogue. Head coverings are available for men, and women may borrow shawls and long skirts. Boxes containing these items are situated by the railings at the approach to the wall.

The separate section at the extreme right of the Kotel is reserved for women, who are not allowed at the other section, in keeping with the rules pertaining to sex segregation in synagogues. Services are held here daily; no photography or smoking is permitted on Shabbat.

The Temple Mount and Dome of the Rock

Take the staircase to the right of the Kotel plaza to the Mograbi Gate for the **Temple Mount**. Access is controlled by the Waqf, the Muslim Supreme Religious Council. While one may exit from most of the Temple Mount's nine gates, entrance to non-Muslims is permitted through only two—the Mograbi Gate and the Bab el Hadid, the Iron Gate.

Plan of the ancient Temple of Herod.

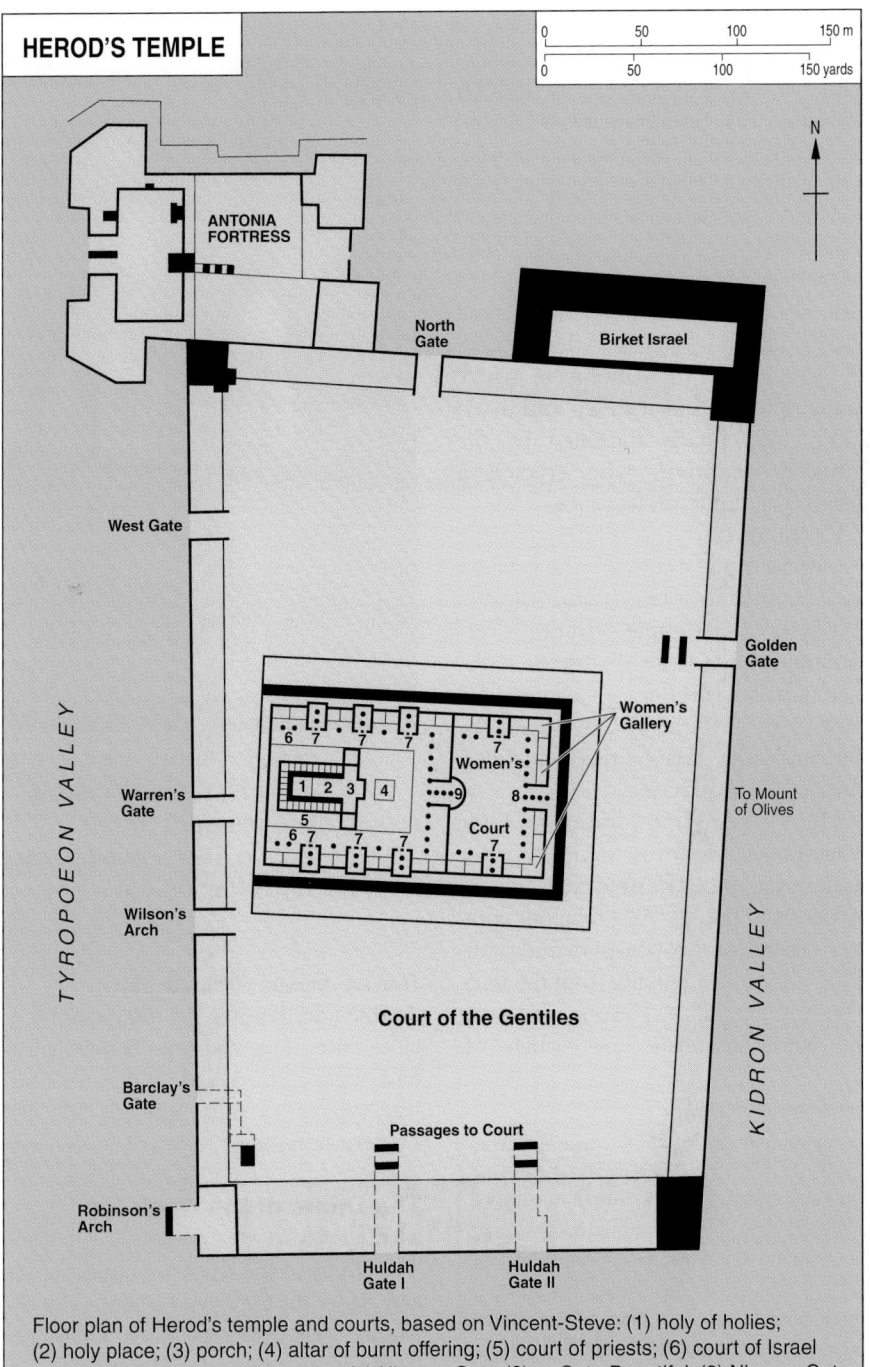

Floor plan of Herod's temple and courts, based on Vincent-Steve: (1) holy of holies; (2) holy place; (3) porch; (4) altar of burnt offering; (5) court of priests; (6) court of Israel (men's court); (7) sanctuary gates; (8) Nicanor Gate (?) or Gate Beautiful; (9) Nicanor Gate.

King David purchased the flat rock on Moriah from Orhan the Jebusite, who had used it as a threshing floor (*II Chronicles 3*). Solomon, David's son, created the First Temple on this site, with building lasting seven years from 964 BC. Nebuchadnezzar destroyed Solomon's creation in 586 BC. The Second Temple was built between 525 and 520 BC, and later much enlarged and beautified by Herod. After the sack of Jerusalem by the Romans in AD 70, the temple was burnt down and in AD 135 it was finally flattened by the Emperor Hadrian, who erected a Temple of Jupiter in its place.

Christian tradition relates that the "pinnacle of the Temple" where Satan took Jesus to tempt him (*Matthew 4:5*) is within the Temple Mount, over-looking the city walls. From the pavement you can certainly get a wonderful view of the Mount of Olives and the Kidron Valley, maybe the view Satan allowed Jesus to have.

The Temple Mount today is a large stone-paved platform, taking up one sixth of the old city's area, surrounded by trees and bushes. As a religious complex it is certainly open-plan and is another oasis of tranquillity from the *shuq*. The Arabs call it the Haram ash-sharif, the Noble Enclosure or Courtyard.

The Haram ash-Sharif is built upon the ruins of the Second Temple. It is a quiet place, ideal for reflecting on life.

Haram means "sacred territory" in Arabic and denotes the area around a cultic site. The Hebrew Temple also had such a courtyard, a feature that was typical to most ancient Middle Eastern religions.

The Dome of the Rock and El-Aksa

The **Dome of the Rock** was built in AD 688–91 by the Omayyad Caliph Abd el-Malik. His motives were as much political as religious. He wanted to acknowledge this site as "the farther-

---

The Temple Mount

Because nobody knows for sure the exact position of the Holy of Holies (the resting place of the Ark of the Covenant, which contained the Ten Commandment stones, and an area only the High Priest was allowed to enter), the Temple Mount is technically out of bounds to Jews. Notices on the ascent to the Mount inform you of this fact.

most mosque" mentioned in the Koran but he also wanted to shift attention away from Mecca, where his political and religious opponent Abdallah Ibn es-Sobair held sway. A third reason for construction was one-upmanship— the Christians had fine shrines in this city, so why not the Muslims? If a shrine were to be built it should be the finest of them all. Indeed, even today the Dome of the Rock is easily Jerusalem's most well-known landmark.

The Old City's most prominent feature is as attractive close-up as it is from far away. The ornate exterior is as attractive as the exquisite interior. Splendid designs decorate the outer surfaces, with white swirling arabesques, taken from the Koran, fighting to outdo the stunning geometric patterns done out in blue, yellow and green tiles. The interior is mostly bare rock, the rock where Abraham was about to sacrifice his son Isaac

*T*he Dome of the Rock is covered in millions of tiny baked tiles, predominantly blue and yellow. Words from the Koran decorate the lintels.

The Holy Rock

According to the Talmud, the Holy Rock inside the Dome of the Rock covers the mouth of an abyss in which the waters of the Flood can still be heard roaring. An esoteric Christian tradition has it that Jesus discovered the great and unspeakable name of God written upon the rock and so, afterwards, was able to work miracles.

Muslims believe the rock to be hovering over the abyss without support and that below the rock is the Bir el-Arwah, or Well of Souls, where the souls of the deceased assemble to pray twice weekly. Other Islamic traditions have it that the rock rests upon a palm watered by a river of paradise; yet others say it is the gate of hell. Religious consensus is rare in this city, even within faiths.

(Ish'mael in Islamic tradition and genealogy). Plush red and green carpets cover what is not rock.

Situated between the Dome of the Rock and El-Aksa is **El-Kas** (the cup)— the fountain where Muslims perform their ritual ablutions before entering the holy places. It is equipped with a circular row of pink marble seats, each with a tap low enough for the feet, hands and face to be washed.

Mohammed never visited the earthly Jerusalem in his lifetime, although the

115

Muslim Relics

As well as a few strands of Mohammed's beard-hair, the Dome of the Rock (Qubbet es-Sakhra in Arabic) also contains Mohammed's footprints, imprinted onto the rock as he ascended to heaven on Buraq, his wonder-steed. Ask also to have the fingerprints of Gabriel (who held down the rock whilst Mohammed ascended), and the footprint of Enoch pointed out.

Koran relates he visited "the farthermost mosque" during his dream-visit to Heaven, and Muslims from early on associated the silver-domed El-Aksa with this farthermost Mosque.

El-Aksa is the main Jerusalem mosque. In religious terms the Dome of the Rock is merely an appendage to El-Aksa. It is hung with chandeliers, decorated with mosaics and the floors are covered with Oriental rugs. At both sites you will have to remove your shoes, leave your bags and be modestly dressed (coverings are available). There is a small admission to both the Dome of the Rock and El-Aksa. Visiting hours are 8.30 to 11 a.m., 12.15 to 3 p.m., and 4 to 5 p.m. On Fridays and Muslim holidays both will be closed. When open, guides will offer to show you around the area. If they have official guide badges they will be very good indeed and well worth the small tip that they require. Haggle beforehand to agree on a price.

After the sumptuous excesses of these two Muslim sites, you can wander around the Temple Mount for a while. When tourists are allowed into the area there is little likelihood of any trouble. Flashpoints are prayer times and Muslim nationalist holidays. At all other times peace will reign and you need have no fear of trouble or molestation (unfortunately, this does not apply to women travelling alone).

South of the Western Wall, near the **Dung Gate** (so named because the area above the wall extending to the gate region was the ancient Jerusalem rubbish dump), is the entrance to the **Ophel Archeological Park** with remains dating from the time of the Book of Kings and the prophecies of Isaiah and Micah. This park is generally very quiet because it is not at the hub of things. It is open Sunday to Thursday from 9 a.m. to 5 p.m., on Friday to 3 p.m. but is closed on the Shabbat.

Mount Zion

The word Zion appears 152 times in the Old Testament as a title of Jerusalem, mostly in the form of prophecies and poems. The hill is synonymous with Jerusalem and with Israel itself. It was the site of the Jebusite city captured by David (*II Samuel 5:6–9*). God dwells on Zion and from here protects the Children of Israel (*Joel 3:16*). Zion is the spiritual centre of God's people.

In the Bible and in popular thought Zion is a mighty mountain. In reality it is little more than a hillock and if it were not for the easily recognizable **Dormiton Abbey** few people would be able to pinpoint the place, despite its importance. According to tradition, this abbey (built

The Dormiton Church stands on Judaism's holy mountain, Mount Zion. It is traditionally one of the sites of the Last Supper.

in 1906) stands on the site where the Virgin Mary died. The Byzantine Hagia Sion was built here but has long since disappeared. The Hagia Sion was considered the place where Jesus washed the disciples' feet, where the Last Supper was held, and where the disciples experienced the outpouring of the Holy Ghost in an Upper Room. Entrance to the grounds is a short walk after passing through Zion Gate. Proceed down a narrow alley bounded by high, stone walls, and turn left to reach **King David's Tomb**. This is open daily, including Shabbat, from 8 a.m. to 6 p.m. (until 2 p.m. on Friday). Cover your head when you enter the room. The tomb is empty and is unlikely to be anything to do with David.

In the cellar of a building near King David's Tomb is the **Chamber of the Holocaust** (tel. 02-715105), an eerie museum lit by candles and dedicated to the memory of the 6 million Jews slain by the Nazis during the Second World War. The chamber is open for visits Sunday to Thursday from 8 a.m. to 5 p.m., on Friday to 1 p.m.; closed Shabbat. Although much smaller and less ambitious than Yad Vashem, the newer Holocaust museum, the Chamber of the Holocaust is still a moving experience.

The Christian Quarter

The Christian Quarter is a quiet mass of wide streets and clean, narrow alleyways. Unlike the Arab Quarter, with its main thoroughfare David Street, the Christian Quarter has no obvious starting point. Generally the most used entry points will be the off-shoot alleyways at **Jaffa Gate**. These bring you round the outside of the Christian Quarter. A more symbolic and meaningful entry point would be to enter via **St Stephen's Gate**, with **St Anne's Church** just inside the gate, on the right. This is a beautiful, 12th-century Crusader church erected in honour of Mary's birthplace. It was built next to the Pool of Bethesda, the site where Jesus healed the cripple.

A couple of minutes walk from St Stephen's Gate is the start of **Via Dolorosa** or the Way of the Cross; the route followed by Jesus from the Praetorium, or the Roman Judgement Hall, to Calvary, scene of the crucifixion. This route is marked out with Stations of the Cross, the last five being within the Church of the Holy Sepulchre. Each Friday at 3 p.m. priests lead a ceremony for Christian pilgrims along the Via Dolorosa and prayers are said at each of the 14 Stations of the Cross. The **Sanctuary of the Condemnation** is the first Station. Many of the other stations are not well marked; look for the Station numbers engraved on walls.

Do not expect the Via Dolorosa to be spectacularly Christian—most of it winds its way past hummous shops, backgammon dens and T-shirt vendors. In places, however, large stone slabs are visible and these are thought to be old enough to have been around when Jesus would have walked this route.

Station 1: Jesus is condemned to death. Station 2: Jesus receives the cross. Station 3: Jesus falls for the first time. Station 4: Jesus meets his mother. Station 5: Simon the Cyrene helps Jesus carry the cross. Station 6: Veronica wipes Jesus' face. Station 7: Jesus falls the second time. Station 8: Jesus consoles the women of Jerusalem. Station 9: Jesus falls the third time.

Within the Holy Sepulchre: Station 10: Jesus is stripped of his garments. Station 11: Jesus is nailed to the cross. Station 12: Jesus dies on the cross. Station 13: Jesus is taken down from the cross and given over to Mary. Station 14: Jesus is laid in the chamber of the Sepulchre.

The **Holy Sepulchre**, which stands on the highest point in the Old City, is not a great beauty from the outside, and is easily missed on any walking tour. Unlike the Dome of the Rock, it is not an obvious landmark. The present structure was built by the Crusaders in the 12th century, although Constantine was the first to build a church on this spot in the 4th century. It was his mother, Queen Helena, who acknowledged the site as Calvary (otherwise known as Golgotha, place of the skull). She even found the True Cross, complete with nails! Two centuries after Constantine, the church was enlarged by Justinian, but it was largely destroyed by fire, earthquakes and the Persians.

If you're looking for peace and tranquillity, the Holy Sepulchre is not the place. Christian goodwill and charity are unknown concepts to the various guardians of the Holy Places. Each and every significant spot in the church is cared for by one or more denominations, and inter-faith rivalries are the norm.

The Holy Sepulchre is five churches in one, and heated disputes between the different denominations are not unknown. Five competing sects—Roman Catholic, Armenian Orthodox, Greek Orthodox, Abyssinian Coptic, and Syrian Orthodox—care for the church. Each denomination has its own

The Church of the Holy Sepulchre does not hold the external visual appeal of the Dome of the Rock, but it is sumptuous inside.

traditions, own beliefs, and its own space—even extending down to lines drawn down the middle of floors and pillars. Even the areas held in common get the rivalry treatment, for instance the Stone of Unction at the entrance has a lamp hanging over it from each denomination.

The architecture within is a heady mix of Byzantine and Crusader styles. To appreciate fully all the intricacies of the various sects and their parts of this church, it would be a good idea to hire the services of an official guide. Or tag onto one of the tour groups being led round the church.

Most of the nuns and monks in the church pay scant attention to tourists, apart from the occasional scowl, but if the church is reasonably empty, a kindly monk may guide you around his section of the church for free (although a donation will be appreciated). You may be shown the **Stone of Unction** where Jesus was anointed, the site of Calvary on the second floor, or the marble tomb in the sepulchre. Armenian monks would show you their part of the True Cross.

Protestants have a Different Calvary

Situated about 5 minutes away from Damascus Gate, the Garden Tomb is a pleasant and civilized spot. It is administered by the Garden Tomb Association of London, England. Surrounded by a very well-cared-for garden is a typical rock-hewn tomb of the 1st century AD, discovered in 1867 by Dr Conrad Schick. The Jewish tomb fits closely the description of the biblical one in which Jesus was interred after his crucifixion, and many Protestants (including General Gordon of Khartoum fame) quickly came to believe this was the true Calvary, despite the fact that Helene's Calvary was not just an idle discovery but a recognition of early traditions.

In the Bible, Calvary is described as outside the city walls—this adds credence to the Garden Tomb, because it and not the Holy Sepulchre lies well clear of the Ottoman walls. However, as Catholics would tell you, the Jerusalem of Jesus' day did not extend as far as Damascus Gate and the site of the Holy Sepulchre then lay outside the city walls. The Garden Tomb gives a better feeling of Calvary—it even has a skull-shaped hillock situated just outside, although you will have to use your imagination to delete the Arab bus station.

East Jerusalem

Walk out of Damascus Gate and you're in another city. With a very distinct Arab feel, East Jerusalem is quite a contrast to both the Old City and West Jerusalem. Many tourists fail to tour East Jerusalem, yet there are a number of interesting sights.

Situated on Sultan Suleiman Street, near Herod's Gate, the **Rockefeller Museum** holds an impressive collection of archaeological artefacts. In the

*T*he Protestant Calvary is at the Garden Tomb, close to the Damascus Gate. It is a peaceful place and very English.

*A*rab *children with an eye for the camera near the* Dome of the Rock.

Palaeolithic section are displayed the bones of Mount Carmel Man, an extinct race combining the characteristics of Neanderthal and Modern Man who lived in Israel about 100,000 years ago. Visiting hours are 10 a.m. to 5 p.m. Sunday to Thursday, to 2 p.m. on Friday, Shabbat, and eves of holidays. Tel. 02-282251.

Between Herod's and Damascus gates lies an entrance leading down under the old city walls into **Zedekiah's Cave**, or Solomon's Quarries, which tradition says was the source of the stones for Solomon's Temple. Jewish and Muslim legends claim that tunnels in these caves extend all the way to Jericho. In 587 BC King Zedekiah was supposed to have fled from the Babylonians through these tunnels, only to be captured near Jericho. You can enter the caves from 9 a.m. to 4.30 p.m., seven days a week. An illuminated path leads you far back into the caves and under the Old City.

Near the meeting of Shivtei Israel-Street, George Street and Nablus Road, an Israeli command post during the 1948 War of Independence is now the **Tourjeman Post Museum** (tel. 02-281278). This is a museum dedicated to the history of a Jerusalem divided (1948–67).

Down the valley and then up again is the lofty university complex on top of **Mount Scopus**. The site of an Arab massacre of Jewish doctors and nurses during the 1948 War, Mount Scopus is a modern-looking development looming high over the Kidron Valley. Meaning Hill of Observation, Mount Scopus is also home to **Hadassah Hospital**. The views of Jerusalem from here are very impressive and tours around the complex are available.

The Mount of Olives

Mount Scopus leads on to the **Mount of Olives**. You reach Mount of Olives Road either by driving north up Saladin Street or by taking a left turn at the Wall, just past the Rockefeller Museum. If you want to go by bus, go to the East Jerusalem bus station and take number 75, the one that goes to the village of Et-Tur. Another bus, number

---

Ancient Burial Caves Discovered

A tractor driver preparing ground for a bird observation point on Mount Scopus in Jerusalem recently came across more than he bargained for: 2,000-year-old burial caves.

The caves, which were carved out of the rock during the Second Temple period (1st century BC to 1st century AD) contained 27 ossuaries (stone boxes to house the bones of the dead). Some of the ossuaries that were found were beautifully decorated, and had names etched on them. The names were Elissar, Joseph Ben Jonathan, Shalom, Jonathan, and Hannah. They were written in a variety of languages, including the Hebrew script of the Second Temple Period, the ancient Hebrew script of the 7th to 8th centuries BC, and Greek. The ossuaries are now on display in The Israel Museum, and a university guide from the Mount Scopus campus will be able to point you to the small caves.

The Arab shuq, *or market, in the Old City is a bustling, heady place, full of exotic sights, sounds and smells.*

42 from the municipal bus depot on Nablus Road, goes through Et-Tur all the way to the Intercontinental Hotel. You can also take a taxi to the top of the Mount of Olives, but very often Israeli taxi drivers are worried about getting stoned as they drive back through the Arab areas. Some will protest they have never heard of such a place as the Mount of Olives and many will tell you the **Haas Promenade** on the **Mount of Evil Counsel** offers better views. Do not listen to them: the view from the top of the Mount of Olives is, without a doubt, the best in Jerusalem. Get here early to see the sunrise from behind you, or come in the evening and see the sun setting behind the Old City. Then you will realize why this city is called Jerusalem the Golden.

On the Mount of Olives itself there are half a dozen churches and the oldest and most sacred Jewish Cemetery in the world. It was this cemetery, once a hill covered with olive trees, that religious Jews had in mind when they came to die in the Holy Land. All await the Messiah, for Jewish tradition declares that on the day of his coming the dead will be resurrected and follow him into Jerusalem through the **Gates of Mercy** (the now-blocked **Golden Gate**). One of the strangest tourist attractions on top of the Mount of Olives is the tomb of publisher Robert Maxwell; for a few

In Jewish folklore, it is on the Mount of Olives that the Messiah will descend to resurrect the dead. Consequently the Mount of Olives is a popular place to be buried.

Many of the graves on the Mount of Olives were damaged by the Jordanian Legion in the period before the 1967 war.

shekels an Arab guide will point out where he lies.

Start down the path on the right and you will come to the **Tomb of the Prophets**, believed to be the burial place of Haggai, Malachi and Zechariah. Since Pharisaic times, Jews have believed the resurrection of the dead will occur on the Mount of Olives, so you can imagine the anguish many Jews felt when the Intercontinental Hotel was built over the easternmost perimeters of the old cemetery, and when the Jordanians incredibly used some of the tombstones in the construction of army barracks and latrines.

Towards the Garden of Gethsemane

Along the main road from the Intercontinental Hotel is a cluster of churches, each of them commemorating one action or another of Jesus. The **Chapel (Mosque) of the Ascension**, marks the spot where it is believed Jesus ascended to heaven. This Christian shrine is under Muslim control. Muslims believe Jesus was a prophet, not a son of God, and believe in the

Dominus Flevit
This Franciscan church, down the path to the right of the Tomb of the Prophets and below the road from the Intercontinental Hotel, marks the spot where Jesus wept as he predicted the destruction of Jerusalem (*Luke 19:41–4*). The fine view through one of the church's windows adorns many postcards.

ascension. It is Jesus, they believe, who will raise Mohammed on Resurrection Day. A footprint of the Risen Christ is displayed under a pane of glass inside the building.

The onion-domed church is the **White Russian Orthodox Church of Mary Magdalene**, built in 1888 by Czar Alexander III in memory of his mother Maria Aleksandrovna. Inside are a number of paintings by such artists as Vereshchagin and Ivanov.

Below this church is The **Garden of Gethsemane**, (aramaic for "oil-press"). Being very small and situated next to the main road, the garden is pretty in its own way but is perhaps not as many Christians imagine it to be. It is an important Christian site, for it was here that Jesus grieved and prayed and was finally arrested by the Roman soldiers on the last night of his life. Some of the gnarled olive trees may date from the time of Jesus. Open from 8.30 a.m. to noon and 3 p.m. to sunset, April to

*T*he Russian Orthodox church of Mary Magdalene, just above the Garden of Gethsemane on the Mount of Olives, is an imposing and unusual sight, with its gold cupolas decorating the skyline.

October; 8.30 a.m. to noon and from 2 p.m. to sunset in winter.

*T**he Church of All Nations lies just above the Garden of Gethsemane on the lower slopes of the Mount of Olives.*

Adjoining Gethsemane is the Basilica of the Agony, or **Church of All Nations**, dating from 1924. It contains the rock at which Jesus is said to have prayed the night before he entered Jerusalem for the Passover supper. The mosaic façade of

*D*own from the Garden
of Gethsemane, in the Valley of
Kidron, is the impressive Tomb of
Zechariah.

the church shows God looking down from heaven over Jesus and the peoples of the world. The Tomb of the Virgin, a deep underground chamber housing the tombs of Mary and Joseph, lies next door.

Below the Church of All Nations, in the **Kidron Valley** ("the dark one"), are three monuments: the conical **Absalom's Pillar**, the pyramid-roofed **Tomb of Zechariah**, and the priestly **Bene Hezir** tombs. They are all thought to date from the 1st century BC, and the first two are believed to have nothing to do with the Biblical figures after whom they are named.

The Gihon Spring

Further down the valley, at the base of Mount Ophel is the **Fountain of the Virgin** (so-called because tradition relates that Mary washed the infant Jesus' clothes here), at the pretty little Arab village of Silwan. This is the **Gihon Spring**, which, as the Hebrew name suggests, "gushes" with water.

*F*urther on from the *Tomb of Zechariah is the equally impressive Tomb of Absalom.*

These gushes come at irregular intervals. The water served as the only water source for ancient Jerusalem and is very possibly the reason why the Canaanites or the Jebusites built a town here in the first place.

In 701 BC, 20 years after the destruction of the northern Kingdom of Israel, Judah was invaded by the Assyrians. Sennacherib, the Assyrian king, laid siege to Jerusalem. Hezekiah, King of Judah, made good his preparations for a long siege. He "built up the wall that was broken down" (*II Chronicles 32*), massive sections of which have been found in the Jewish Quarter—the so-called **Broad Wall**.

Ancient Engineering

In order to protect Jerusalem's water supply, Hezekiah, King of Judah, had workmen construct a tunnel through the rock under the city, diverting the waters of the Gihon Spring to a small reservoir within the city walls.

Teams of workmen dug the tunnel from both ends at once. After months of toil, the two teams connected. How they did it is still not fully understood, because the 533m (1,750ft) tunnel zig-zags its way unpredictably beneath the city. All the Bible says about this incredible feat of engineering is "Hezekiah directed the waters down to the west side of the City of David." The workmen themselves were a bit more forthcoming. In the rock wall of the tunnel they chiselled the so-called *Shiloah* inscription:

"When the tunnel was driven through, the tunnellers hewed the rock, each man towards his fellow, pick-axe against pick-axe. And the water flowed from the spring toward the reservoir for 1,200 cubits."

This inscription was found in the last century by a couple of adventurous Jewish boys who wanted to see for themselves the ghosts who were said to inhabit the tunnel. The block of stone holding the inscription is displayed in a museum in Istanbul, with a copy in the Archaeology Wing of the Israel Museum.

Hezekiah's Tunnel is still extant and the adventurous can wade through its 512m (1,600ft) length to the Pool of Silwan (*Shiloah* in Hebrew), the place where Jesus healed a blind man.

The chisel-marks and 2,700 year-old insulating plaster are very clear along the way, as are the zig-zags near the middle, where the teams began searching for each other by sound.

The water is not very deep, certainly no higher than thigh height on most people. It takes about 40 minutes to walk through; a torch is needed for navigation. Open Sunday to Thursday between 8:30 a.m. and 3 p.m., on Friday and holiday eves until 1 p.m. Entrance is free, but the caretaker should get a tip.

West Jerusalem

This is the New City to the Israelis. Although modern, brash and lively, it is still nowhere near as upbeat as Tel Aviv. West Jerusalem is still growing at a frenetic rate, the outskirts expanding rapidly. These outlying areas are mostly residential and of little interest to travellers. The older and more interesting part of West Jerusalem is that centred around **Zion Square**. Here are most of the hotels, shops and city centre services.

One of the most easily recognized landmarks in the New City is the imposing tower of the **YMCA building**. This complex has a swimming pool, tennis courts, a lecture hall and a gymnasium. Just behind it is a fine football stadium. The YMCA tower and building was designed at the same time and by the same firm as the Empire State Building (Tel. 02-257111).

King David Hotel

Parallel from the YMCA tower is Israel's premier hotel and one of the finest in the Middle East—the **King David**. It was used as the British Military HQ in the Mandate Period and was targeted by the Irgun (Jewish terrorist group) for political demolition. The bombs that blew the place apart in July 1946 were hidden in milk churns. Repeated warnings were given but evacuation did not take place and 91 people

*W*est Jerusalem is the New City, full of life, especially after dark. In the evening this is where to head for.

were killed. This action, superbly recounted in Thurston Clarke's *By Blood and Fire*, hastened the departure of the British from Israel. The entire right wing of the building was destroyed, although it was soon rebuilt and an extra two storeys added. If you ask you can be shown where the bombs were placed (this also gives you a chance to inspect the immaculate kitchens!).

Today the hotel is serene, graceful and a haven of peace. It is wonderfully expensive of course, but well worth it if you like splashing out. If you are not staying as a guest, just pop in and wander around the gorgeous lobby, sit in one of the huge chairs and order refreshments. Try to spot world leaders, diplomats and overseas correspondents. Guests are not ushered away when

M iddle Eastern sweetmeats are delicious. This is a market stall at Mahane Yehuda.

world leaders are staying—this is an everyday occurrence for the King David, and the only change you will notice is that the doorman is that little bit more polite, just in case you are a dignitary too!

Just a few steps down from the King David Hotel is **Herod's Family Tomb**. This burial cave, discovered in the late 19th century, was used as an air-raid shelter during the 1948 war, yet it is believed to be the tomb of some members of Herod's family (possibly his wife Mariamme and his two sons who were killed by Herod himself). It is highly unlikely to be his actual burial site. The tomb is open from 10 a.m. to 1 p.m. Monday to Thursday.

Yemin Moshe

Opposite and down from the King David is a large windmill—this is the focal point of **Yemin Moshe**, the first Jewish settlement outside the secure walls of Jerusalem. The windmill was erected to help feed the new residents of this innovative settlement, first known as Mishkenot Shaananim. Built in 1858–60, this settlement was later renamed Yemin Moshe in recognition of its main benefactor, the British philanthropist Sir Moses Montefiore. During visits to Palestine he was appalled by the ghetto conditions of the Jews in the Old City. Helped with money from the New Orleans philanthropist Judah Touro (the first American Jew to contribute to Israel), Montefiore created a living settlement of stone cottages. Today it is one of the most exclusive residential areas of Jerusalem and certainly one of the most beautiful. An artists "colony" inhabits the lower slopes.

The **windmill**, standing on the upper part of Yemin Moshe, facing the Old City ramparts, was an important observation post during the 1948 War of Independence. It is now a museum dedicated to Montefiore, and may be visited, for free, Sunday to Thursday from 9 a.m. to 4 p.m., until 1 p.m. on Friday, closed Shabbat.

Opposite the windmill, in the **Liberty Bell Garden**, stands an exact replica of the Liberty Bell in Philadelphia. This 2.8ha (7-acre) garden has a picnic area and a large children's playground.

Over the Bethlehem road from the Liberty Bell Garden is the very secular **Cinematheque**, an arty cinema and café combined. Situated on the rise of a hill, but still lower than the surrounding sights, the Cinematheque enjoys stunning views of Mount Zion and **Sultan's Pool** (an ancient reservoir, that is today a venue for open-air pop concerts). Ask for a peek at the visitor's book—the rich and famous have been here before you. Try and see if you can spot the famous actor who can sign his Hebrew name correctly but is rarely thought of as Jewish. As a clue: he's got a dimpled chin, an equally famous son and starred in the movie, *Spartacus.*

The Great Synagogue

Half a mile away and situated much nearer to the centre of the New City is the **Great Synagogue**, the Seat of the Rabbinate, styled along the lines of King Solomon's Temple. It faces the large main park, **Gan Ha-Atzma'ut**, Independence Garden, through which short cuts can take you directly into the centre of West Jerusalem, the New City. Square at the bottom and domed on top, the lofty building offers good views

> **The Windmill of Yemin Moshe**
> A windmill seems an incongruous sight for a Middle Eastern city, although windmills were actually an Arab invention brought to Europe by some impressed Crusaders.

of the New City and beyond from its uppermost balcony. Free tours take place from 9 a.m. to 1 p.m. Sunday to Thursday, until noon on Friday (tel. 02-255361). The same building holds the **Sir Isaac and Lady Edith Wolfson Museum** (tel. 02-635212), with an outstanding collection of Judaica, maps, coins, and the entire interior of an old Italian synagogue.

Museum and Monastery

Israel has many museums, but there are two that should not be missed. The first is the Beth HaTefutsoth in Tel Aviv (*see* page 174) and the second is the **Israel Museum** here in Jerusalem. Visibly the most obvious part of the museum is the white dome-shaped roof which houses the Dead Sea Scrolls. It is situated across from the **Knesset buildings**, on the road to Tel Aviv.

The Museum is split into six departments: the **Bezalel Art Museum**, the **Samuel Bronfman Biblical and Archeological Museum**, the **Shrine of the Book**, the **Children's Museum**, the **DS and JH Gottesmann Centre for Bible Studies** and the **Billy Rose Sculpture Garden**. From modern art to ancient history, the Israel Museum is a varied and stimulating day out.

*T*he Lion fountain is a *focal point in Yemin Moshe.*

Opening times: Sunday, Monday, Wednesday and Thursday 10 a.m. to 5 p.m. The main building is open on Tuesday from 4 to 10 p.m., tel. 02-698211 or 698213. There are daily guided tours in English of individual departments and of the whole museum (tel. 02-708811). Bus numbers 9, 17, 24, and 99 all pass close by.

Below the Israel Museum and the Knesset is the solid-looking **Monastery of the Cross**. It was built by Gregorian monks in the 11th century on the site of a 5th-century church, and it is now maintained by the Greek Orthodox church. According to an early tradition, the monastery is located on the site of the tree from which the Cross was made.

Mahane Yehuda

In eastern Europe, before the Holocaust, Jews lived in *shtetls*, small towns populated with Ashkenazi Jews, as featured in such films as *Yentl* and *Fiddler on the Roof*. For a flavour of what these places must have been like there is no need to shlepp to Latvia: just take a walk west up Jaffa Road and half a mile along you'll come upon Mahane Yehuda, or Camp of Judah. This is a bustling *shtetl*-type produce market and on Thursdays and Fridays is packed out with Ultra-Orthodox Jews stocking up for Shabbat. Cheap fruit, meat and pastries are available in abundance. Much of the market is now covered and just like in the Arab *shuq* there are definite zones of influence, where one food type will dominate.

This is a living market and can be frenetic at times. To survive you will have to be as pushy as everybody else is. Don't be upset by the stall holders ignoring or abusing you—they are not doing this because you are a tourist or do not look

> ### Israeli Parliament
> There are two ways of saying Synagogue in Hebrew—Bet ha-Midrash, House of Study, or Bet ha-Knesset, House of Gathering. The Great Assembly of the Second Temple Period was called the HaKnesset HaGedola. So, the Israeli Parliament is called the **Knesset**—it has 120 members (MKs), just like the 120-member HaKnesset HaGedola.
>
> Today housed in an elegant building opposite the Israel Museum, the Knesset is interesting both because of the political debates you may want to watch and because of the works of art displayed inside. The highlights are the floor mosaics and wall tapestries of Marc Chagall.
>
> Open for guided tours of the building on Sunday and Thursday from 8.30 a.m. to 2.30 p.m. You must have your passport with you. You can attend a session of the Knesset on Monday, Tuesday, or Wednesday from 4–9 p.m. The Knesset recesses during Jewish holidays and in the summer. Tel. 02-753333. Reached by bus 9, 24, 28, or 99.

Jewish; they do this to everybody. Be as rude as you need to get attention.

Mea Shea'rim

To really get the *shtetl* feel you'll have to visit **Mea Shea'rim**, the most famous of the Ultra-Orthodox residential areas. In some parts hereabouts you could easily imagine being in 19th-century Poland rather than modern-day Israel. The *yeshivas* (religious schools), synagogues and tenement buildings all look eastern European and run-down, but the fortress-like appearance of many of the blocks is intentional; when Mea Shea'rim was built in 1875 it was a bit out in the sticks and needed protection from marauders. It has always been an Ultra-Orthodox area.

There are many forms of Ultra-Orthodox Judaism. The Chassidim are most notable for their dress sense, a relic from 18th-century Poland.

The male Ultra-Orthodox inhabitants dress in antiquated Chassidic garb: long black coats (or caftan-type robes), white shirts with no neck-ties, black trousers (or breeches and white knee-length socks), and black broad-rimmed hats (or sometimes flat fur hats, called *shtreimels*). The men will invariably be bearded and have curly side locks (these *payot* become curly through constant twiddling whilst praying or studying). The women will be wearing puritanical dresses that show not an inch of flesh and some sort of head-covering, possibly even a wig. Many married women shave their heads because once safely married, the thinking runs, they have no more use for a good head of hair which might only attract the stares of other men and inspire impure thoughts. If the

women are below the age of forty chances are they will also have a number of children in tow, all of them young and at least one in a push-chair. The Ultra-Orthodox birth rate is far higher than the Israeli average.

Throughout Mea Shea'rim you will see posters disallowing certain codes of dress. It is best to respect these wishes, so dress modestly in clothes that reveal no bare arms or legs. Public shows of affection are also frowned upon.

The Russian Compound

The first turning on the right after Jaffa Road after the central post office leads to the area where the Assyrian army is believed to have camped before attacking Jerusalem in 700 BC. Today it is the **Russian Compound**. The most obvious landmark here is the **Russian Orthodox Church**, an edifice that looks as if it was plucked straight from Russia. The green-domed cathedral and surrounding land long remained the property of the Russian church. In 1965 Israel finally purchased the compound from Russia. In the 1920s this structure was the world's largest "hostel"; it could accommodate 10,000 Russian pilgrims at one time and the whole complex was almost a walled city in its own right.

The Russian Compound is home to Jerusalem's law courts and a police station (you should come here to report any thefts or losses). The **Society for the Protection for Nature in Israel** (SPNI) also have offices and a shop here (13 Heleni Hamalka Street, tel. 02-252357). In the same courtyard is an Agricultural Museum with displays demonstrating agricultural methods from ancient times. The gnarled olive press there is also worthy of attention.

The building itself, the **Sergei Hostel**, is interesting, having been constructed to house Russian Orthodox pilgrims in the days of the czars. The towers were not built as defences, as one would think, but as bath-houses and latrines.

At the back of the compound is the **Hall of Heroism** (tel. 02-233209) which once served as the British Mandate's Jerusalem Central Prison—the cells and execution chambers are part of the exhibits. The museum tells the story of the radical part of the Jewish Underground in the pre-1948 period. Without the patronage of Menahem Begin, the place wouldn't have come into existence and its lack of context will be upsetting to anybody who served in the British Army of the time. Visiting hours are Sunday to Thursday, 9 a.m. to 4 p.m., on Friday until 1 p.m., closed Shabbat.

Near to the entrance of the Russian Compound is an enclosed column 12m (39ft) high, which was probably intended for Herod's Temple but was broken whilst being transported. It is popularly known as the **finger of Og** after the giant who was king of the Ammonites and ruled Bashan at the time of Moses (*Deuteronomy 3:11; Joshua 12:4–5*).

Tombs of Sanhedria

Go up Shmuel Ha-Navi, off Shivtei Israel Street, to north-east Jerusalem's beautiful public gardens of Sanhedria (or take bus number 2 from Jaffa Gate). Called either the **Tombs of Sanhedria** or the Tombs of the Judges, this is where some of the judges of ancient Israel's "Supreme Court" (during the 1st and 2nd centuries) lie buried. The three-storey burial catacomb is carved out of rock, with many intricate features—including rolling stone closures. The gardens are open every day from 9 a.m. to 5 p.m.; the tombs are closed on Shabbat.

The Biblical Zoo

A couple of miles away to the southwest is the **Jerusalem Biblical Zoo** at Malcha. This is a collection of 100 species of animals, 30 birds, and all of the plants mentioned in the Bible. Hours are 8 a.m. until dark; there is a free tour on Sunday at 2 p.m. The zoo is open on Shabbat but buy tickets beforehand at one of the ticket agencies or at the zoo. Tel. 02-430111.

The Holocaust Museum

One of Israel's most sombre "attractions" is **Yad Vashem**, the Holocaust Museum. Adjacent to the monument and museum to the founder of Zionism, Theodor Herzl, is **Har Ha-Zikkaron** (Mount of Remembrance), dedicated to the 6 million Jews murdered by the Nazis and their sympathizers. The **Avenue of the Righteous Gentiles**, lined with trees in tribute to non-Jews who helped save Jewish lives during the Second World War, leads into the central memorial.

Yad Vashem is Israel's saddest monument, the place where all world leaders are brought in order to remind them of the Holocaust. To Jews, Yad Vashem is an expression of the sentiment "never again." As well as a very moving museum, there is a Holocaust Archive collection (the largest in the world), a Hall of Names (giving biographical details on around half of the 6 million dead), a Hall of Mirrors (a monument to the 1 million Jewish children who perished), an art museum

*F*uturistic sculpture opposite the Yad Vashem Memorial and Museum.

(with exhibits from Death Camp inmates) and a Valley of Destroyed Communities (with a colossal wall the shape of Europe bearing the names of 5,000 lost communities). The Hall of Remembrance is the focal point of Yad Vashem, and is a silent and sombre building. Inside burns a perpetual flame, standing over a casket of ashes from the cremation ovens. The flame illuminates a sloped stone floor which has the names of the 21 Nazi Death Camps engraved into it. There are five memorial sculptures in the grounds of

---

Yad Vashem

Yad Vashem means "a monument and a name", from *Isaiah 56:5*, "I will give them in my house and within my walls a monument and a name which shall not perish."

Yad Vashem. Each one of them is intense, brooding and unforgettable. Nador Gild's **Memorial to the Victims of the Death Camps** is particularly moving. It consists of a number of intertwined, emaciated figures, stretched out horizontally, grasping for the sky, representing both barbed wire and death.

Yad Vashem opens from 9 a.m. to 5 p.m. Sunday to Thursday, Friday until 1.45 p.m., closed Shabbat. Buses 13, 18, 20, 23 and 27. Tel. 02-751611.

Outside Jerusalem

Seven kilometres (4.5 miles) south west of Jerusalem lies **Ein Kerem**, Spring of the Vineyard, the birthplace of John the Baptist, and the place where Mary visited Zachariah and Elizabeth before Jesus was born. An ancient spring in the village is called Mary's Well. The **Church of St John** and the **Church of the Visitation** are worth a visit. This second church has a courtyard lined with ceramic tiles bearing Mary's hymn of thanksgiving (the *Magnificat*) in 42 languages. There are some good eating places and interesting art galleries. Bus 17 goes direct.

On a hilltop not far from Ein Kerem stands the largest and most important medical centre in the Middle East, the **Hadassah Hebrew University Medical Centre**. Hadassah is the Women's Zionist Organization of America and was founded in 1951. The synagogue here is famous for Chagall's 12 stained-glass windows, depicting the 12 tribes of Israel. Guided tours in English are given every hour on the hour, Sunday to Friday, and unaccompanied tourists can view the windows between 2 and

3.45 p.m. Sunday to Thursday. Tel. 02-776271/2. Take bus 19 or 27 from Jaffa Gate, Jaffa Road, Agron Street, King George V Street, or Bezalel Street.

Bethany

If you leave Jerusalem via the Arab village of Silwan you'll come to **Bethany** (in Arabic, al-Azariya), the village of Lazarus and his sisters Mary and Martha (*John 11: 17–45*).

A Franciscan church, built in the 1950s, marks the spot where Jesus is supposed to have slept. There are several impressive mosaics in the church, including one of the resurrection of Lazarus and another of the Last Supper. Other churches and monasteries in the vicinity further commemorate Jesus' actions.

Latrun

Half an hour's drive out towards Tel Aviv will bring you to the monastery at **Latrun**. This was the site of fierce fighting during the War of Independence in 1948. Latrun was of immense strategic importance, being located on Jerusalem's vital road link to Tel Aviv. Arab forces closed the only road by which supplies could be brought to the besieged city, and held it against numerous surges. Many Jews were killed in these attacks, some of whom were European Holocaust survivors just arrived in Israel. Eventually the Jews secretly constructed a new road, the Burma Road, outside the range of Arab guns, to bring supplies to West Jerusalem. Latrun remained in Arab hands until the Six-Day War in 1967.

Latrun has long been a mustering point for attacks on Jerusalem: Crusaders, Arabs, Greeks and Romans have all assembled legions hereabouts in preparation for their respective assaults on the Holy City. A display of weaponry can be seen in the Latrun Fort Artillery Museum (tel. 08-255186).

The Monastery of Latrun, built in 1927 by the French Trappist Order on the ruins of a 12th-century Crusader fortress, is said to be the site of the home of one of the thieves crucified at the side of Jesus. The name Latrun comes from the Latin *latro*, "thief".

Near the monastery is the Jewish/Arab village of Neve Shalom, established in 1972, where the two cultures live in an atmosphere of cooperation and equality. There are new tourist accommodation facilities in the village, and half-day visits can be arranged in advance (tel. 02-917160/917412).

In the unique nature reserve of Neot Kedumim, off route 443, the landscape and ecology of the Bible have been recreated. Several trails are marked, and there are guided tours in English on Monday, Thursday and Friday (tel. 08-233840).

Sorek Stalagmite Cave

Nineteen kilometres (12 miles) south west of Jerusalem, next to the village of Nes Harim, lies the **Sorek Stalagmite Cave**, or cave of Avashalom. It contains some amazing stalagmite and stalactite specimens. Drive if possible (or take a tour). Bus 184 or 413 from the central bus station gets to Nes Harim, but there is a 20 minute walk to the cave. Open Sunday to Thursday 8.30 a.m. to 4.30 p.m., Friday 8.30 a.m. to noon (tel. 02-915756).

Latrun Monastery is famous for its wine, olive oil and brandy. At the weekend, it is full of Israelis buying their weekly quota of Christian wine.

The Land of the Patriarchs

The Israelis call it Judea and Samaria, evocative names from the Bible. Everybody else calls it the West Bank. In many ways this is the most important part of Israel—except, of course, that it is not Israel. Travel here can be tough, but very rewarding for those who persevere. There is no longer any kind of tourist infrastructure in the West Bank. Strikes can occur at any moment and curfews mean tourists should be nowhere near the West Bank at night, so a hotel guide would be useless. Most of the towns mentioned here used to have independent tourist information offices—not so anymore. The West Bank is a play-it-by-ear area.

The West Bank

The West Bank is a beautiful region, packed with sites of biblical significance and well worth the discomfort you may face by travelling there. One advantage, or disadvantage, depending on how you look at it, is that there will be few, if any, fellow tourists.

The West Bank is literally the west bank of the River Jordan. It is the part of the British Mandate of Palestine that was occupied by the Jordanian Arab

*P*icturesque Silwan, an Arab village just outside Jerusalem in the West Bank.

Legion in the Israeli War of Independence in 1948 and annexed by Jordan the following year. In the Six Day War of 1967, the area was occupied by Israeli forces as a defence against further aggression from their Arab neighbours. Without this occupation Israel would only be 16km (10 miles) wide in parts and vulnerable to further attack. It has remained under Israeli control ever since, although it has not been formally annexed, an act which would lead to world condemnation. Its status is in political limbo—to the Israelis it is part of the "Administered Territories", to the rest of the world it is part of the "Occupied Territories".

Much in the news, the West Bank is home to Jewish settlers as well as Arabs.

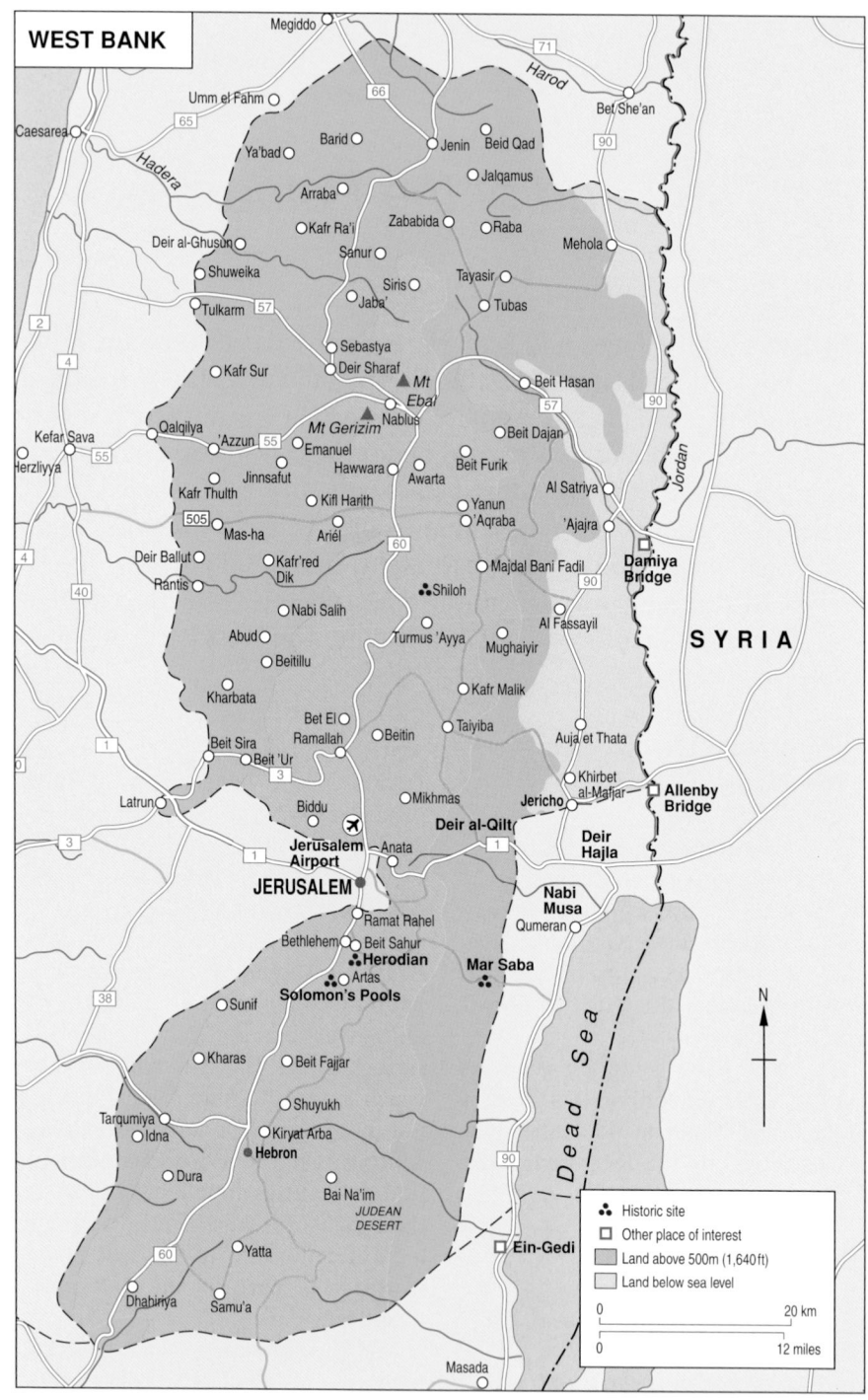

WEST BANK

Megiddo · Harod · 71 · Bet She'an
Umm el-Fahm · 66 · 65
Caesarea · Hadera · Ya'bad · Barid · Jenin · Beid Qad · 90
Arraba · Jalqamus
Kafr Ra'i · Zababida · Raba
Deir al-Ghusun · Sanur · Mehola
Shuweika · Siris · Tayasir
Tulkarm · 57 · Jaba' · Tubas
2 · Sebastya
4 · Kafr Sur · Deir Sharaf · ▲ Mt Ebal · Beit Hasan
Qalqilya · ▲ Mt Gerizim · Nablus · 57 · 90
Kefar Sava · 55 · 'Azzun · 55 · Emanuel · Beit Dajan
Herzliyya · Jinnsafut · Hawwara · Beit Furik
Kafr Thulth · Kifl Harith · Awarta · Al Satriya
505 · Mas-ha · Ariel · Yanun · 'Aqraba · 'Ajajra
4 · Deir Ballut · Kafr'red Dik · 60 · Majdal Bani Fadil · 90 · Damiya Bridge
Rantis · ❖ Shiloh · SYRIA
40 · Nabi Salih · Turmus 'Ayya · Al Fassayil
Abud · Mughaiyir
Beitillu
Kharbata · Kafr Malik
Bet El · Taiyiba · Auja et Thata
Beit Sira · Ramallah · Beitin · Khirbet al-Mafjar · Allenby Bridge
1 · Beit 'Ur · 3 · Mikhmas · Jericho · Deir Hajla
Latrun · Biddu · Deir al-Qilt · 1
3 · ✈ · Anata · Nabi Musa
Jerusalem Airport · Qumeran
1 · **JERUSALEM** ●
Ramat Rahel
Bethlehem · Beit Sahur · ❖ **Herodian** · **Mar Saba**
38 · ❖ Artas · N
Sunif · ❖ **Solomon's Pools**
Kharas · Beit Fajjar
Shuyukh
Tarqumiya · ● **Hebron** · Dead Sea
Idna · Kiryat Arba
Dura
Bai Na'im · *JUDEAN DESERT* · 90 · □ **Ein-Gedi**
60 · Yatta
Dhahiriya · Samu'a
Masada

❖ Historic site
□ Other place of interest
Land above 500m (1,640ft)
Land below sea level

0 — 20 km
0 — 12 miles

The attempted Judaization of the West Bank by the settlers is carried out by means of creating new towns, in direct violation of the Fourth Geneva Convention and the Camp David Accords. There are more than 60,000 Jewish settlers scattered throughout the West Bank, some of them in advanced towns, others in tented villages, waiting for bulldozers to create another concrete statement. The heavily fortified towns and settlements can be seen as you pass through the region.

Travel here is colourful, exciting and mentally stimulating and with its current troubles, the West Bank does not rank as one of the world's most tranquil retreats. Frequent demonstrations are held in support of the Intifada; and are just as frequently crushed by the Israeli Defence Forces. Tourists coming here do so at their own risk. Curfews are strictly imposed and apply to tourists as well as residents. Caution is needed, and a lot of wise planning. Check with the nearest tourist information office, or the Office of Visitor Information of the Civil Administration, 212 Jaffa Road, Jerusalem, on the latest situation.

Three places to check with, especially for information not normally given out by the Israeli authorities, are:
The Jerusalem Visitors, Information
  Bureau
National Palace Hotel
Az-Zahra Street
off Salah al-Din Street
East Jerusalem
Tel. 02-273273

The Alternative Information Centre
14 Koresh Street
Jerusalem
Tel. 02-282834

The Palestine Human Rights
  Information Centre
Tel. 02-287077.

Bear in mind these are very biased against the State of Israel and their comments may reflect this bias, so tread carefully.

Read the newspapers to keep up-to-date with current happenings. Don't get stuck in the West Bank during a general strike—the area grinds to a halt, and violence is much more likely. It is usually best to make day-trips to the West Bank and not to stay overnight; return to Jerusalem, or wherever you are based, every evening.

As a tourist you will not be an intentional target, but you may get caught up in events outside your control. In general Palestinians are warm and welcoming to tourists; after all you are helping to subsidize their fragile sub-economy. However, they do not take kindly to Israelis, so try to look like a tourist: wear obviously western clothes, carry maps, travel in groups, do not speak Hebrew and do not fraternize with Israeli soldiers. If you are Jewish, or look Jewish, think twice before coming here, as anti-Jewish feeling runs high and no amount of protestations will convince a Palestinian mob of your possible sympathies for their cause. Likewise don't wear an Arab head-dress anywhere near the Jewish settlements.

Israeli soldiers are suspicious of any foreigners who stray from the normal

*M*ap of the West Bank.

*P*itched right outside the Inn of the Good Samaritan, this goat-skin tent offers protection from the sun for the local Bedouins.

tourist routes, or enter the West Bank at times of trouble, or who demonstrate a knowledge of Arabic. Don't greet an Israeli soldier with *salaam* instead of *shalom*. The opposite goes for greeting Palestinians; *shalom* will go down like a lead balloon.

Don't call this land Israel. To the Arabs it is Palestine—their maps don't acknowledge the existence of a state called Israel. Jews are infidels, a Dhimmi people. At all times protest your displeasure with the Israeli occupation; you may not feel this way, but it is best not to voice any opinions to the contrary. Similarly, if you do feel any solidarity for their cause, then it

would not be wise to express these feelings to any Israelis you meet in the West Bank. Feelings run high here and animated discussions over who owns what can quickly become more than just heated arguments.

Travel by Israeli buses can be hair-raising, but Arab buses are generally safe from Arab attacks. The Arab *sherutim* or ordinary taxis may be the safest way to get around. Guided tours, when available, should also be relatively safe.

On the whole the Palestinians will be glad you are here, if only so they can tell you the problems they have with their overlords. To the Palestinians, Israel's occupation of their land is seen as a major injustice, reducing them to little more than second-class citizens in a state that they want no part of. To their minds, Israel can have no legitimate claim to a region that has long had a large Arab population and that

Travel by Hire Car

It is not sensible to travel to the West Bank in a hired car. Any vehicle with Israeli number plates risks getting stoned. Hire cars have a green line around the distinctive yellow plates, but stone-throwing youths are not known for their eagle-eyed discrimination. Non-Israeli visitors to the West Bank can go some way towards protecting themselves and their car by having perhaps a prayer mat on the seat, an Arab head-dress on the dashboard or a copy of the Koran placed somewhere that is easily visible.

However, it is possible to hire Palestinian cars with blue West Bank number plates. Of course, you then run the risk of trouble from Israeli settlers who often pick on blue-plated cars when any sort of outrage has been committed on Jews. In East Jerusalem the car hire firm Petra can provide a blue-plated car. It will even come with Arabic writing prominently displayed on the doors and a free *keffiyeh* (Arab head-dress)!

was offered to the still-born Palestinian state under the UN Partition Plan of 1947.

However, Israelis feel that "Judea and Samaria" is an integral part of the State of Israel because it was the historic heartland of ancient Israel. But Israel is a very open and diverse society and not all Israelis feel the need for the settlements and the continued occupation. The Biblical gift of Canaan to the Hebrews means little to them. They can see that permanent Israeli occupation leads to the denial of citizenship for the Palestinians and an abuse of basic human rights. Furthermore, by pure dint of demography, the Arabs will outnumber Jews to such an extent in years to come that no amount of suppression

will keep the lid on Palestinian aspirations for their own state. Because of the influx of millions of Soviet Jews, this demographic argument is not quite as relevant any more, but it still remains that the West Bank is predominantly Arab and unless mass settling or mass Palestinian expulsions take place (and certain extremist Zionist groups advocate both of these abhorrent measures) the West Bank will continue to be Arab, and proud of it.

Politics aside (if, indeed, this is possible) the tourist may want to travel into the West Bank at some point during his or her holiday. Many sites of interest are here—including Jericho and the Dead Sea. More importantly, Judea and Samaria, as the name suggests, is the heartland of the Bible. These hills helped shape three of the world's major religions. The ancient Israelites came here, liked what they saw and under Joshua pillaged and occupied all in their way, in the process amalgamating the Hebrew tribes into a people with a land. The parallels with today are obvious. History is defined by the strong, and written by the winners.

The area will also be very familiar to readers of the New Testament. The villages and areas mentioned by the authors of the New Testament are still here, and largely unchanged. For the archetypal biblical landscape, complete with low-stone buildings, stepped-terraces, olive-tree plantations, and braying donkeys, the West Bank is the place. Using biblical norms, it is possible to define the two regions of the West Bank: the region south of Jerusalem is known as Judea, the area of the Kingdom of Judah, and includes Bethlehem, a town of importance in both the Old and the New Testaments, and Hebron, a city sacred to both Jew and Muslim as the burial place of their mutual ancestor, Abraham.

North of Jerusalem is Samaria, where the breakaway Kingdom of Israel held sway until its inhabitants, the Ten Lost Tribes, were exiled by the Assyrians. Nablus, the biblical Shechem, is the main city. A community of Samaritans, who trace their descent from the Ten Lost Tribes, still live here. This area saw the moulding of the Hebrew tribes, each with their own religious sanctuary, into a single people with a single sanctuary, Jerusalem. For this reason, the area is of great importance. Many of the biblical towns and cultic sanctuaries are little more than dust now and there's often not a great deal to see. But it is the locations that are important, not the amount of ruins.

Apart from visiting the sites of religious significance, there is very little reason to venture into the West Bank. Unlike the rest of Israel, the Occupied Territories are not packed with alternative things to do if you get tired with religion. The only other reason for a visit would be to experience live "politics". Religion is the motivating factor, the chance to visit the exact geographical locations made famous by the Bible.

Bethlehem

Just 11km (7 miles) south from Jerusalem, this small town (which means "house of bread" in Hebrew) nestling in the Judean hills is one of the Holy Land's many religious hot-spots. Palestinians live here; Christians worship

B̲ethlehem, seen here from the air, has a religious significance that transcends its rather lowly appearance.

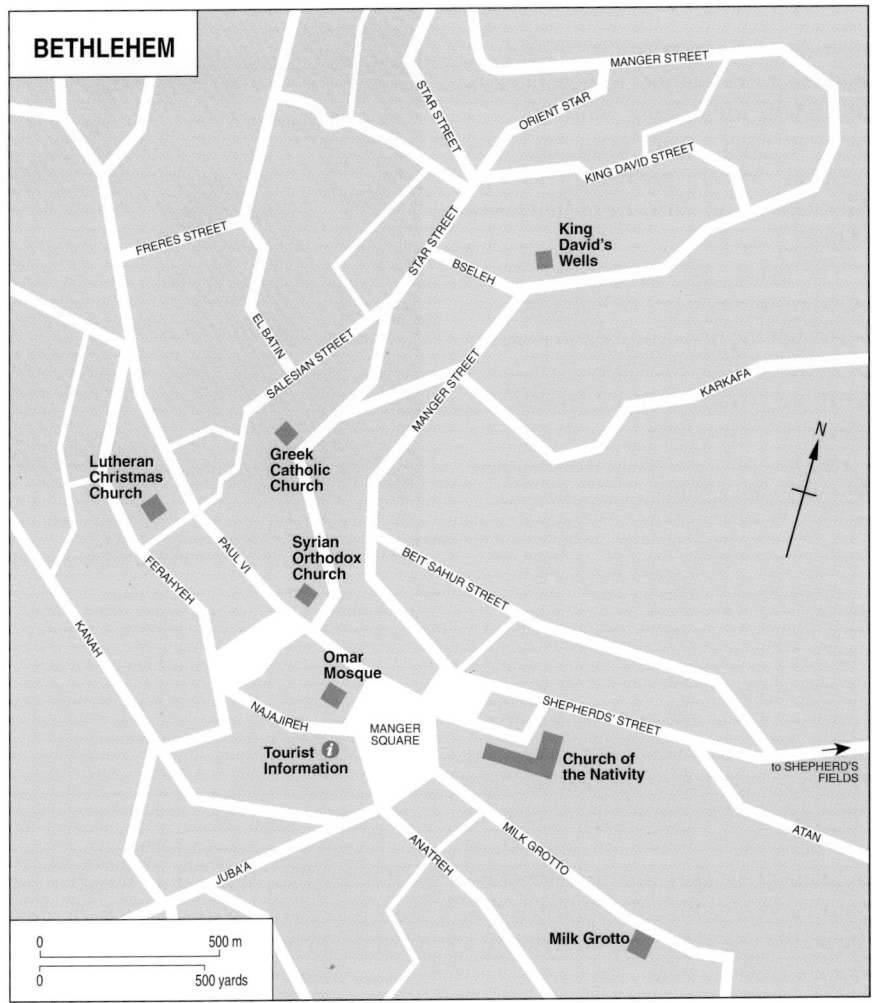

BETHLEHEM

MANGER STREET
STAR STREET
ORIENT STAR
KING DAVID STREET
FRERES STREET
STAR STREET
BSELEH
King David's Wells
EL BATIN
SALESIAN STREET
MANGER STREET
KARKAFA
Lutheran Christmas Church
Greek Catholic Church
FERAHYEH
PAUL VI
Syrian Orthodox Church
BEIT SAHUR STREET
KANAH
Omar Mosque
NAJAJIREH
MANGER SQUARE
SHEPHERDS' STREET
Tourist Information
Church of the Nativity
to SHEPHERD'S FIELDS
JUBAA
ANATREH
MILK GROTTO
ATAN
Milk Grotto

N

0 — 500 m
0 — 500 yards

*M*ap *of Bethlehem.*

here; and Jews trace the line of David from here.

Bethlehem is important to both the Old and the New Testaments. Rachel, the wife of Abraham, died here whilst giving birth to Benjamin and "she was buried on the way to Ephrath (that is, Bethlehem), and Jacob set up a pillar upon her tomb, which is there to this day." (*Genesis 35:19–21*). Ruth, a poor Moabite "gleaner of corn", met and married Boaz, a rich landowner, in Bethlehem in a contractual exchange of kin-redemption (*Ruth 1–4*). From this marriage between convert and Hebrew came a son, Obed, and from Obed came Jesse and from Jesse came David, the shepherd who would become king. From Bethlehem David went out to

149

fight Goliath, the large Philistine warrior; later he was summoned from Bethlehem by Samuel to become king of Judah, after King Saul had displeased God. And even later the prophet Micah predicted that the Messiah would come from Bethlehem (*Micah 5: 2–3*).

The belief that the Messiah would come from this small Judean town was current in the first century and is clearly the reason that the author of Luke, working from existing traditions, placed the Holy family in Bethlehem. "And Joseph ... went up from Galilee, from the city of Nazareth, to Judea, to the city of David, which is called Bethlehem." (*Luke 2:4–5*). Luke states that Joseph and Mary arrived in Bethlehem and Mary gave birth in a manger "as there was no place for them in the inn." (*Luke 2:7*). The stable of the Nativity does not actually appear in the Bible, it is a much later accretion. However, scholars argue that the "stable" would have been in a cave in the back of a house or inn. Many Bethlehem houses are built backing onto rocks. Another possibility is that the stable was the space underneath a *khan*, a traveller's inn.

The Grotto of the Nativity is the West Bank's most visited site and has been for 1,500 years.

The Church of the Nativity

The fortress-like structure of the **Church of the Nativity** dominating the paved expanse of **Manger Square** in Bethlehem, is Justinian's masterwork, not beautiful, but imposing and grand. It is one of the oldest churches in the world, and certainly the oldest in the Holy Land. You enter through a doorway, partially bricked up by the Crusaders, that is so low that you have to bend double to go through it. This was probably to stop men on horseback storming the church.

The basilica of the church is divided into five naves by four rows of pink Corinthian pillars. Each pillar bears the picture of an apostle. Many gilded lamp fixtures hang from the oaken ceiling. The floor is made from stone and wood, with occasional trap-door openings that reveal the original mosaic floor beneath. Up front, beyond an impressive chandelier, is the Altar of the Nativity, very ornate with gold and silver decoration.

As with the Holy Sepulchre in Jerusalem, this church is too religiously important for it to stay in the hands of one sect. Therefore it is divided between the main churches. The Greek Orthodox occupy the area to the right of the altar, the Armenian denomination the left. Armenian, Greek and Franciscan priests are responsible for the upkeep of the church.

To the side of the choir, narrow stone staircases lead down to the grotto of the manger, the birth-cave of Jesus. Lit by an array of hanging lamps, the irregularly-shaped, marble-clad grotto is in the wall of the cave. A blackened 14-pointed silver star marks the site of the birth.

For a more "authentic" cave descend the stairs at the back of the nave in the northern part of the Church. Here is a maze of rock-hewn rooms and chambers which were used as catacombs, and commemorate Herod's martyred innocents. Also beneath the church is a cave-like chapel commemorating a 4th-century Dalmatian priest, St Jerome. Working from the Church of the Nativity, Jerome translated the Bible from Hebrew into Latin, a work known as the *Vulgate*, which was to become the official Bible of the Roman Catholic Church for the next 1,500 years.

The Church stands guard over **Manger Square**, the scene of the televised choir-singing each year. At Christmas it is packed with people, and can look appealing, but during the rest of the year it is just a large open space, used mainly as a car-and coach-park. Souvenir shops and several cafés are all around.

The Milk Grotto

Close to the Church of the Nativity is the **Milk Grotto**, a natural limestone cave that has been a religious site since at least the Iron Age. Christian tradition associates it with the Holy family's flight to Egypt. Whilst preparing to flee, Mary, in hurriedly suckling the infant

Christmas in Bethlehem is special. But which Christmas? Each major denomination of the Church has a different date.

Jesus, is said to have spilt some of her breast milk. This milk promptly turned the red rocks of the cavern chalky white. Christian and Muslim tradition has led to the belief that visits made here by nursing mothers will help their lactation and increase their fertility. From the 7th century onwards there are recorded instances of European pilgrims chipping off bits of this stone as holy relics. Today packets of the powdered stone are sold as souvenirs.

The Shepherd's Fields

Close to Bethlehem, at Beit Sahur, are the **Shepherd's Fields** where 1st-century shepherds saw the angel of the Lord telling them of the birth of the Christ-child. You can easily walk to the fields by heading back toward Jerusalem for a few blocks and turning right along either Shepherds' Street or Beit Sahur Road. Taxis know the way well or you can take one of the local buses (number 52).

Actually, there are two Shepherds' Fields, one of which is maintained by the Roman Catholic church and the other by the Greek Orthodox church. Both are east of Beit Sahur. They have been associated with the angelic visitation since the 7th century. A new Greek church stands over the spot the Greek Orthodox church venerates, and the Franciscan Church of the Angels stands over the cave where the nomadic shepherds were meant to have lived.

King David's Wells

Back in downtown Bethlehem, just off Manger Street, are the three large cisterns, **King David's Wells**. During a campaign between the Israelite army and the Philistines, King David, who was thirsty, asked for a crack team to fetch him some water from the Bethlehem well, as a symbolic gesture of defiance, "O, that some one would give me water to drink from the well of Bethlehem which is by the gate" (*II Samuel 23:13–17*). Three strong men broke through the ranks of the Philistines, who were camped at Bethlehem, and brought back the water. King David sacrificed it to the Lord, saying "Far be it for me, O Lord, that I should do this. Shall I drink the blood of the men who went at the risk of their lives?"

Christmas in Bethlehem

Before the Intifada, Christmas in Bethlehem was always the highlight of the religious year for many Christians. Now the festivities have been curtailed. Events do change, though, so check with the Christian Information Centre, Jaffa Gate (tel. 02-287647) if you think the political temperature is cool enough for masses to begin again.

Christmas in Bethlehem means Midnight mass; Christian processions from Jerusalem; special telephone booths to enable you to phone home Christmas greetings with the bells of Bethlehem ringing in the background; all-night restaurants and cafés; and post office and banks open until midnight. The post office can stamp your passport with a special date mark.

Depending on your religious persuasion, there are a number of alternative dates for a Bethlehem Christmas. Catholics and Protestants hold their services on 24 and 25 December, the Orthodox churches on 6 January, and the Armenians on 17 and 18 January. The main Christmas celebrations are on 25 December, but the other dates often have more colourful processions.

The Tomb of Rachel

Just outside Bethlehem on the road to Jerusalem is the **Tomb of Rachel**, revered by Jews, Muslims and Christians. It is contained in a low rectangular building, set off from the road and watched over by Israeli soldiers on the opposite roof-top. The present structure was built in 1860 by the great Jewish philanthropist, Moses Montefiore.

The outer room is empty, whilst the inner room, the cupola, contains the tomb of Rachel, where normally dozens of Jewish Yeminite women can be seen weeping and praying. Open Sunday to Thursday from 8 a.m. to 5 p.m. (until 6 p.m. in summer), on Friday to 1 p.m.; closed Shabbat.

Arts and Artefacts

If you want Christian religious artefacts, Bethlehem is the place. This small town is packed with stores selling the most diverse of objects—some newly crafted, others antique. The Intifada has disrupted this trade, however, and many once-prosperous merchants are now facing ruin. Bethlehem has a long tradition of craftsmanship—olivewood, mother-of-pearl and coral, and glass have been made into religious souvenirs for many years.

Outside Bethlehem

About 4km (2.5 miles) out of Bethlehem are three rectangular cisterns known as **Solomon's Pools**. These pools collect rain-water and are also fed by springs. The exact origin of the dark-green pools is unknown, but they are unlikely to be anything to do with King Solomon. They appear to date from the time of Herod the Great, who brought the water here by aqueduct from springs

T he West Bank markets offer fruit and vegetables that are as fresh and tasty as those found in more irrigated areas of Israel.

153

near Hebron. However, tradition claims that the pools were part of Solomon's grand scheme for supplying Jerusalem with water. There are claims that the pools' origin can be found in the Book of Ecclesiastes: "I made myself pools from which to water the forest of growing trees." (*Ecclesiastes 2:6–7*).

The spring, **Ein Salah**, in the village of Artas close by, is considered the one referred to by Solomon in the Song of Songs: "A garden locked is my sister, my bride, a garden locked, a fountain sealed." (*Song of Songs 4:12–13*). It certainly inspired Christian building, mainly because this reference clearly points to the virginity of a maiden. A monastery was built here, Hortus Conclusus ("Closed Garden"), to symbolize the virginity of the Virgin Mary.

Whoever first built the pools, it is known that they were an important source of water for the Herodian, Herod's great fortress (*see* below) and more importantly, for Jerusalem. They were brilliantly engineered, with the Lower Aqueduct flowing solely under gravity for the 60km (40 miles) to Jerusalem's Temple Mount; the later Upper Aqueduct involved a siphon system and went via Bethlehem to Jerusalem's Jaffa Gate. They have been used throughout history: the Romans kept the pools and terracotta aqueducts in good repair, the Crusaders built a fort to defend them (Qal'at al-Burak, Castle of the Pools), and the British kept the system in good working order until 1947.

Herodian

For views of both Bethlehem and Jerusalem and for scenery straight out

of the Bible, you must go to Herodian. This is a superbly located hill fort built by Herod the Great. His evils were so great and his enemies potentially so strong, that he devoted much time, effort and money to fortifying desert retreats for himself and any members of his entourage or family in favour with him at the time. The great fortress of Masada (*see* page 255) was heavily improved by Herod but it was a bit too far away for a quick escape from Jerusalem, should his great Antonia Fortress fall.

To commemorate winning a decisive battle, he chose to build a mighty stronghold on the spot. So, on a prominent hill between Jerusalem and Bethlehem he sanctioned a grand building project that was unequalled in the Hellenistic-Roman world of the time. This was no austere hideaway though; Herodium (as it was called) was an extravagant and ambitious palace that just happened to be the strongest fortress around as well; only Masada could have withstood a siege better.

Josephus, the great 2nd-century Jewish historian, goes into great detail about Herodium. It was obviously the Empire State building of its day, a powerful monument to its time and its egomaniacal builder:

"[Herod] having immortalized his family and friends ... did not neglect to make his own memory secure. He built a fortress in the hills facing Arabia and called it Herodium after himself, and seven miles from Jerusalem he gave the same name to an artificial hill, the shape of a woman's breast, adorning it more elaborately than the other.... Round the base he built other royal apartments to accommodate his furniture and his

*E*ven from the air, the fortress-palace of Herodian is an impressive and imposing sight.

friends, so that in its completeness the stronghold was a town, in its compactness a palace." Josephus, *The Jewish War*.

Herodium was built between 24 and 15 BC and after Herod's death in about the year AD 4 it became his mausoleum. He died in Jericho after a failed suicide attempt but was not greatly missed by most people as the last years of his reign had seen a mental and moral degeneration. The biblical story of the Massacre of the Infants (because of the birth of a new king, Jesus) fits in with Herod's wild mood swings and tendency towards vile cruelty, although no other ancient sources mention such a massacre.

As with Masada, Herodium was later captured by the Jewish Zealots during the First Jewish War (AD 66–70) and they used it as a base of operations for their guerrilla attacks on the surrounding area. And also like Masada,

A view from Herodian, a ruin from Hasmonean times, in the West Bank. In the far distance Jerusalem is to the right, Bethlehem to the left.

when facing defeat, the Zealots took their own lives rather than submit to the Romans.

In the Second Jewish War, the Bar-Kokhba Revolt, the Zealots used Herodium as their headquarters (AD 130–5). Bar-Kokhba made many structural changes to the complex. He added more living quarters for his troops and constructed a synagogue for daily worship. After Bar-Kokhba was routed by the Romans, the complex lay dormant until the Byzantine period, when part of it was used as a monastery

by a group of heretical monks. They converted the bath-house into cells and built both a chapel and a bakery. Simple Christian markings can still be seen today. After the Persian and Arab invasions of the area in the early part of the 7th century, the site was abandoned and fell into a state of disrepair.

Later the Crusaders encamped here but were decisively routed by the Muslims. Herodian's alternative name, "The Mountain of the Franks", comes from this period. In Arabic the hill is called Jabel al-Faradis, or Mount of Paradise.

It has been excavated three times since 1962 and there are extensive ruins to see, although of course the palace is long gone and only the truncated walls remain. At the base of the mound excavations have discovered a small reservoir built by Herod, at one time filled with water carried by donkeys and diverted from Solomon's Pools.

Herodian is about 10km (6 miles) south east from Bethlehem. Today it is cared for by the National Parks Authority, and is open daily from 8 a.m. to 5 p.m. (closes at 4 p.m. on Friday). The views from the top of the mound are simply magnificent: Jerusalem to the north, Bethlehem to the west, the bare expanses of the Judean desert and the glistening Dead Sea to the south and east. Herodian can be reached by Arab bus from Bethlehem. Egged bus 38, which goes to the settlement of Tekoah, passes close to the mound's access road. It is a simple drive from Jerusalem.

Mar Saba

Mar Saba monastery hangs precariously to the side of the Kidron Gorge, a few miles off route 398. This desert monastery was founded by St Saba of Cappadocia in the 5th century. In the 7th century Persians, and Arabs ruined the monastery and murdered the monks. After being rebuilt, it suffered further sackings throughout its history, but was entirely rebuilt by the Russian government in 1840. The skulls of monks killed in attacks on the monastery are kept here in a special chapel. The bones of St Saba were taken by the Crusaders to Venice and only returned by Pope Paul VI in 1965, as a gesture of goodwill toward the Greek Orthodox Church.

At its zenith Mar Saba was home to 5,000 monks, most of whom lived in caves dotted around the gorge. Now only a handful of monks are left and they all live within the monastery. A paved road was partially laid to the monastery a few years ago, bringing it closer to the temptations of civilization, although it remains a relatively out-of-the-way destination. Suitably fully clad men are permitted to enter the monastery (pull the chain on the large blue door), but women—and even female animals—are strictly forbidden. There is, however, a special tower to the south of the main annex from which women may look down into the monastery.

Hebron

Twenty-six kilometres (15 miles) from Herodian is the ancient town of **Hebron**, the burial place of the patriarchs and holy to all three of the great religions in this land. But there's nothing holy about Hebron today—it is one of the major flash-points between Palestinians and Jewish settlers. The Arab town (al-Khalil) is next to the more modern settlement of Kiryat Arba, an ultra-zionist settlement. There is almost constant violence between these two groups with frequent serious injury, and even death.

Hebron is a very ancient town; it would already have been old when Abraham came through. Scholars can date it quite accurately because the Bible tells us that "Hebron was built seven years before Zoan", the Hyksos capital. This puts the founding of Hebron some time in the 17th century BC. The original name for the town was Kiryat Arba, "District of the Four", possibly a reference to the four giants who fell from heaven after rebelling against God, or maybe the names of the four Canaanite tribes who lived here before the Hebrew conquest.

Enclosing the Cave of Machpelah (which means "cave over a cave"), it is the existence of the Tombs of the Patriarchs in Hebron that gives Hebron its designation as one of Israel's four "Holy Cities"—the others being Jerusalem, Tiberias and Safed.

To orthodox Jews who can now worship at the sacred Tomb of the Patriarchs, the experience is second only to worshipping at the Western Wall in Jerusalem (*see* page 111). Genesis tells how Abraham bought his family burial cave from Ephron for 400 silver shekels. Modern legend has it that Hebron is thus one of three places in Israel that Jews can claim to have actually purchased—the same claim is made for Mount Moriah in Jerusalem and the Tomb of Joseph in Shechem (modern-day Nablus). The tombs of Abraham, Isaac and Jacob, and their wives are housed in a fortress-like structure in the middle of town. A Muslim legend has it that the massive stones of the exterior wall were laid by Solomon with the help of some friendly spirits, or *jinn*. However, it is more likely that the colossal structure was built by Herod, who was well-known for his grandiose architectural works. The similarities between the great stones used here and those in the Western Wall of Jerusalem, also built by Herod, are striking. Later additions came from the Byzantines (who built a church inside), the Crusaders and the Mamelukes who added the current mosque and the two square minarets.

Inside the walls, a mosque has been built around the tombs. The main basilica is lavishly decorated with inlaid wood, Arabesque and ornate mosaic work. Inscriptions from the Koran run along the walls. In the main section you will see the tombs of Isaac and Rebecca, red and white stone huts with green roofs. Look inside at the embroidered drapes covering the cenotaphs. In an

> **Glass-blowing**
> Hebron is famous for its glass-blowing shops; you can watch glass objects being made, and then buy some for gifts to take home.

adjoining courtyard are the gold-embroidered tapestries covering the cenotaphs of Abraham and Sarah. Just opposite is the tomb of Jacob and Leah. A shrine to Joseph is right next door, but the genuine tomb of Joseph is most probably the one at Nablus (as recorded in *Joshua 24:32*). The actual cave is underground; access is via a trap door but this is kept closed to visitors.

Large parts of the Tombs of the Patriarchs, in Arabic called Haram

T he Arab shuq *of Hebron is a working market-place and has none of the nicities of parts of the sterilized* shuq *in Jerusalem .*

A Muslim holy-man rests in Hebron, a dry and dusty town with an elevation that makes it comfortable to visit in summer.

al-Khalil, have been converted into synagogues so that Jews can reclaim their religious heritage.

The tombs are open between 7.30 and 11.30 a.m. and 1.30–5 p.m. Muslims worship here from 11.30 a.m. to 1.30 p.m. so entrance is forbidden to non-Muslims. No visitors are permitted on Friday, which is the Muslim Sabbath, or on Muslim holidays.

Bet El

The Arab village of Beitin, close to Ramallah (a pleasant enough town in peaceful times, but occasionally dangerous for tourists), is the biblical Bet El or "House of God". This was one of the main Hebrew cultic sites in the period of the Judges, a rival site to the main cultic shrine at Jerusalem. It is one of the key places mentioned in *Genesis 12*. "I will make thee a great nation and I will bless thee, and make thy name great." Abraham passed into Canaan via Shechem, "And he removed from thence unto a mountain on the east of Bethel, and pitched his tent ... and there he builded an altar unto the LORD" (*Genesis 12:1–10*). It was also to Bethel that Abraham and Lot returned from Egypt, "with their flocks and herds and tents." Later, as described in *Genesis 28*, the LORD appeared to Jacob in a dream: "...and behold a ladder set up on the earth, and the top of it reached to heaven: and behold the angels of God ascending and descending it. And, behold, the LORD stood above it, and said, I am the LORD God of Abraham thy father, and the God of Isaac: the land whereon thou liest, to thee will I give it, and unto thy seed."

Jacob was in awe; and called the spot "House of God" (Bet El). Man alone could not find the place for a new cultic sanctuary, it had to be pointed out and sanctioned by God. Jacob set up a stone pillar, a cultic object, at the spot marking the "ladder" (ladder is better translated as stairway or ramp, and signifies the sort of ramp common to temple buildings). The hill today is called **Jacob's Ladder**, but unless you have a guide to point it out, it is difficult to find it.

At **Tel Bet El**, strata have been uncovered ranging from the early Canaanite period to the time of the Second Temple. What is thought to be the cultic temple of Jacob has also been uncovered. There is not a great deal to see here but for students of Bible history this place is important not for its extant remains but for its significance in the development of the Hebrew religion as it started to be centralized, away from the various cultic sites of the tribes, to the main temple at Jerusalem. Even in David's day Jerusalem was not yet the main shrine; each tribe had its own preferred sanctuary, although later Jerusalem was important because it was where the Ark of the Covenant was kept. It wasn't until Solomon built the first Jerusalem temple that the Hebrew cultic sites started to lose ground.

The modern village of **Beitin** is well-kept and neat, with most of the squat houses painted blue and lavender. The mosque here is interesting because it has a minaret with glass windows to keep the chill wind out. This is not normal practice for mosques. When the muezzin calls the faithful to prayer in this extremely breezy village, he simply opens the windows and closes them immediately afterward.

The village is well known for its groves of trees bearing almonds, figs, apples, peaches and olives. However it is better known to Palestinians for the Jewish settlement of Bet El, which houses the headquarters of the Israeli civil administration, which governs the West Bank. Not a place, or a concept, they hold dear to their hearts.

Shiloh

Ancient **Shiloh** is where the Tabernacle and the Ark of the Covenant were housed after Joshua's conquest of Canaan; it was the place of the first central temple of the Hebrew tribes; the first Jerusalem.

"… the whole congregation of Israel assembled at Shiloh, and set up the tent of meeting there; the land lay subdued before them." *Joshua 18:1–2.*

It was also the place where the men of Benjamin's tribe, short of women, carried away the daughters of Shiloh, who were dancing during their annual pilgrimage to the main Hebrew sanctuary.

Valley of Dotan

As the road climbs up towards Nablus the views get increasingly majestic. Stop at the top of **Jebel Batin** and enjoy the whole view. There is a café here serving Turkish coffee. The valley below is the **Valley of Dotan**. This area, in biblical times, was famous for incense production, especially myrrh. This industry still exists and tobacco is also grown here. Between Shiloh and here is the area where Saul met the Philistines, and Eli prophesied doom for Shiloh, then the cultic capital of the land. The territory from Shiloh northward belonged to the tribe of Manasseh. Entering the valley, you'll see many *khans*, some more dilapidated than the others, which would once have served as wayside inns for travellers, housing both animals and men within their walls. They may be reminiscent of the types of dwelling Joseph and the Virgin Mary stayed in at Bethlehem.

The Valley of Dotan was also where Joseph was sold into slavery by his scheming brothers.

Nablus and Shechem

Situated between the important mountains of Gerizim and Ebal, **Nablus** is the largest city on the West Bank outside Jerusalem. This modern Arab town has been completely rebuilt since the earthquake of 1927.

Nablus is close to the biblical **Shechem**, the place where Abraham first entered the land of Canaan. Shechem literally means "neck" because it was built on the neck of land (or ridge) between the mounts of Gerizim and Ebal. It was already a flourishing Canaanite town when Abraham first visited it and it soon became an important cultic sanctuary. Joshua built an altar at Shechem and summoned the tribes together, uniting them in a major covenant ceremony which is considered the beginning of the Israelite nation.

The Samaritans and Mount Gerizim

"Behold, I set before you this day a blessing and a curse: the blessing, if you obey the commandments of the LORD your God, which I command you this day, and the curse, if you do not obey the commandments of the LORD your God, but turn aside from the way which I command you this day, to go after other gods which you have not known. And when the LORD your God brings you into the land which you are entering to take possession of it, you shall set the blessing on Mount Ger'izim and the curse on Mount Ebal." (*Deuteronomy. 11:26–30*).

This passage from Deuteronomy points out the differences between **Mount Gerizim** and **Mount Ebal** (881m [2890ft] and 940m [3084ft] respectively): Gerizim is lush and green, Ebal mostly bare rock. The reasons for these differences are not blatantly supernatural, since Mount Gerizim faces north and is shaded from the sun whilst the south-facing Mount Ebal is more exposed. For Samaritans, Mount Gerizim is a holy mountain: it is believed to be older than the Garden of Eden and its peak was above Noah's Flood. For this reason another name for their mountain is Har HaKedem (the Early Mountain). It was dust from here that was used in the creation of Adam.

The Samaritans are an ancient offshoot not from Judaism but from Israelitism, separated during the Assyrian invasion of Canaan in 722 BC. Shalmane'ser, the king of Assyria, "invaded all the land, and came to Samaria…and he carried the Israelites away to Assyria…" (*II Kings 17:5–6*). Those Israelites who were not carried away into exile, but remained behind in Samaria came to be known as Samaritans.

When the Israelites (now called "Jews" after their home in Judea) returned after 538 BC, the Samaritans offered to help them rebuild the Jerusalem temple. But the Jews refused, and accused the Samaritans of intermarrying with the Assyrians and adopting pagan customs. Yet the Samaritans claimed to be the true adherents of Mosaic Law and rejected that part of the Tanakh (Jewish Bible, roughly corresponding to the order of the "Old Testament") written in exile in Babylon. The animosity between the Samaritans and the Jews was so fierce that Jews on pilgrimage to Jerusalem from the Galilee would go the long way round, via Jericho, rather than pass through "pagan" Samaria. This is one reason why the Samaritan woman was shocked at being addressed by Jesus, a Jewish teacher, at Jacob's Well. The other reason was that she was a woman.

The Samaritan community is a hierarchical one, led by a High Priest. Whilst orthodox Judaism uses the Tanakh as its scripture, the Samaritans recognize only the first five books of the Tanakh and the Book of Joshua. They differ with Judaism on other points too; they maintain that their mountain, rather than Mount Moriah in Jerusalem, was the site of Abraham's near-sacrifice of Isaac and they hold that Gerizim is the site of Joshua's altar (*Joshua 8:30*) rather than Mount Ebal. The Samaritans can also point out altars built by Adam and Noah on Mount Gerizim.

The Samaritans celebrate the most ancient of the Israelite feasts: Pesach, Shavu'ot and Succot in strict accordance with biblical injunctions. The two Samaritan communities spend the entire week of Pesach on the summit of Mount Gerizim. They sacrifice seven lambs on the special altar ("mizbeah", from a Hebrew word meaning "to slaughter"). The lambs are afterwards hoisted onto spits and lowered into a pit, then roasted in the biblical fashion

by being covered with soil and heated with twigs and branches. After the midnight meal, all the remains are burned in the altar depression.

To witness some of this ritual (April or May), it would be best to join one of the tours that bring visitors from Jerusalem and Tel Aviv. About 275 Samaritans live in Nablus today, calling themselves the children of the Tribes of Manasseh, Aaron and Efraim.

Sebastya

The Royal City of **Sebastya** lies 13km (9 miles) north west of Nablus. An extensive complex of ruins in an ideal setting atop a small hill and surrounded by olive groves, it is easily one of the most impressive ruins of the Holy Land. Today Sebastya (also called Samaria, which was later the name given to the whole region) is just a small village but it was once one of the most important towns in Israel, at one point becoming the kingdom's capital, succeeding Shechem and Itzah.

King Omri, the Napoleon of his time, bought the hill of Samaria (in about 880 BC) from Shemer for two talents of silver: "and he fortified the hill, and called the name of the city which he built, Samaria, after the name of Shemer, the owner of the hill". (*I Kings 16:24–25*).

Omri's son Ahab (871–852 BC) continued his father's work with ambitious building projects, and expanded the kingdom through a number of small wars. But "Ahab...did evil in the sight of the LORD more than all that were before him." (*I Kings 16:30*), mainly through the influence of his Sidonese wife, Jezebel. "He took for his wife Jezebel...and went and served Ba'al, and worshipped him." (*I Kings 16:32*).

Worshipping pagan idols was forbidden by Yahweh, who sent Elijah to right the king's ways. Ahab eventually survived the wrath of God by repenting of his various evils, and, as was the custom, by wearing sackcloth instead of his usual finery, but not before his scheming wife had committed a number of wicked deeds. The story of Naboth's vineyard (*I Kings 21:1–16*), where Jezebel conspired to kill Naboth so that Ahab could take possession of his vineyard, is a particularly vivid one. But Elijah was warned of Jezebel's actions and God sent him down to the vineyard before Ahab could annex it completely.

Elijah frightened and shamed Ahab into repentance: "Thus says the LORD: "In the place where dogs licked up the blood of Naboth shall dogs lick up your blood...the dogs shall eat Jezebel within the bounds of Jezreel..." (*I Kings 21:19–24*).

After centuries of decline Samaria was completely refurbished and improved by the greatest instigator of building works the land of Israel has ever seen, Herod the Great. He put the city back on the map, although the map now showed a new name: *Sebaste*, the Greek for Augustus, a tribute to his Roman patron, Caesar Augustus (the Roman governor famous for his census that led to the Holy Family decamping from Nazareth to Bethlehem). It was at Sabastya that Herod committed many of his greatest atrocities such as the murder of his favourite wife and several of his sons.

During the Muslim conquest of Palestine in the 7th century Sebastya again lapsed into obscurity. The Crusaders raised its status during their brief stay by building on top of some of the previous churches, although after their brief period of rule the city fell into decline and all that is left now is a mass of very impressive ruins and the small Arab village of Sebastya.

There are examples of all periods of occupation on view. Sebastya is surrounded by huge walls, thigh-high ruins and free-standing Roman columns. The village square is dominated by the large buttressed walls of the once-magnificent Crusader church, the Church of John the Baptist. It's a 19th-century mosque that stands here today, though, the Mosque of Nabi Yaha (John the Prophet). His birth is celebrated on 25 June each year, and his death on 29 August. In the nave of this church is a small, domed building which has a stairway that leads down into an underground cave, a sort of crypt. Of the six burial niches down here, two are meant to be of the prophets Elisha and Obadiah. Elisha spent much of his life in Samaria and Obadiah is said to have hidden 100 prophets here, feeding them on bread and water.

The site is a large one and it can take the best part of half a day to get round all the different parts. As it is wise to only spend the daylight hours in the West Bank, it would be advisable to come to Samaria in the morning, giving plenty of time for sightseeing. The same goes for the rest of the West Bank. The amount of sites mentioned in this chapter, and this is but a fraction, means you may have to spend up to a week of daytrips to see the region to your satisfaction. Unfortunately this makes the West Bank an inconvenient and expensive place to visit. However, if you have the time, effort and the initiative, it is an extremely exciting destination.

The New York of
the Middle East

A lively mix of concrete and charm, Tel Aviv is the embodiment of urbanized Israel. It is Israel's largest metropolis, built with little planning or control, a hotchpotch of conflicting architectural styles. It may be loud and unco-ordinated but the place has a brash style all of its own, and this is certainly where the action is. Jaffa, right next door, is the perfect antidote to Tel Aviv. It is a haven of quietude.

Over a million souls live within the boundaries of Greater Tel Aviv, yet before 1909, the area on which Tel Aviv now stands was a wasteland, a barren stretch of sand. Today there are pizza parlours and pubs where before there was nothing. The transformation has been fast and the city has grown up alongside the State of Israel, mirroring the State's polyglot background. Tel Aviv is a product of the 20th century and it shows—if you want nightlife and fun, come to Tel Aviv. The same goes for culture, business, haute couture and recreation. Jerusalem is pious and haughty, Tel Aviv is raucous and the "happening" place.

History

A 1905 map drawn for a guidebook to Palestine showed the only features to the beaches around Jaffa were contour lines and sand dunes. By the time of publication in 1906, a new settlement was already in the planning stages. Three years later a group of Jews from Jaffa bought 13 hectares (32 acres) of wasteland and under the leadership of Meir Dizengoff, 60 families staked their claims. A famous photograph shows

*T*el Aviv, a product of
the 20th century, exhibits an
array of architectural styles, from
the modern high-rise apartment
to this surreal gem.

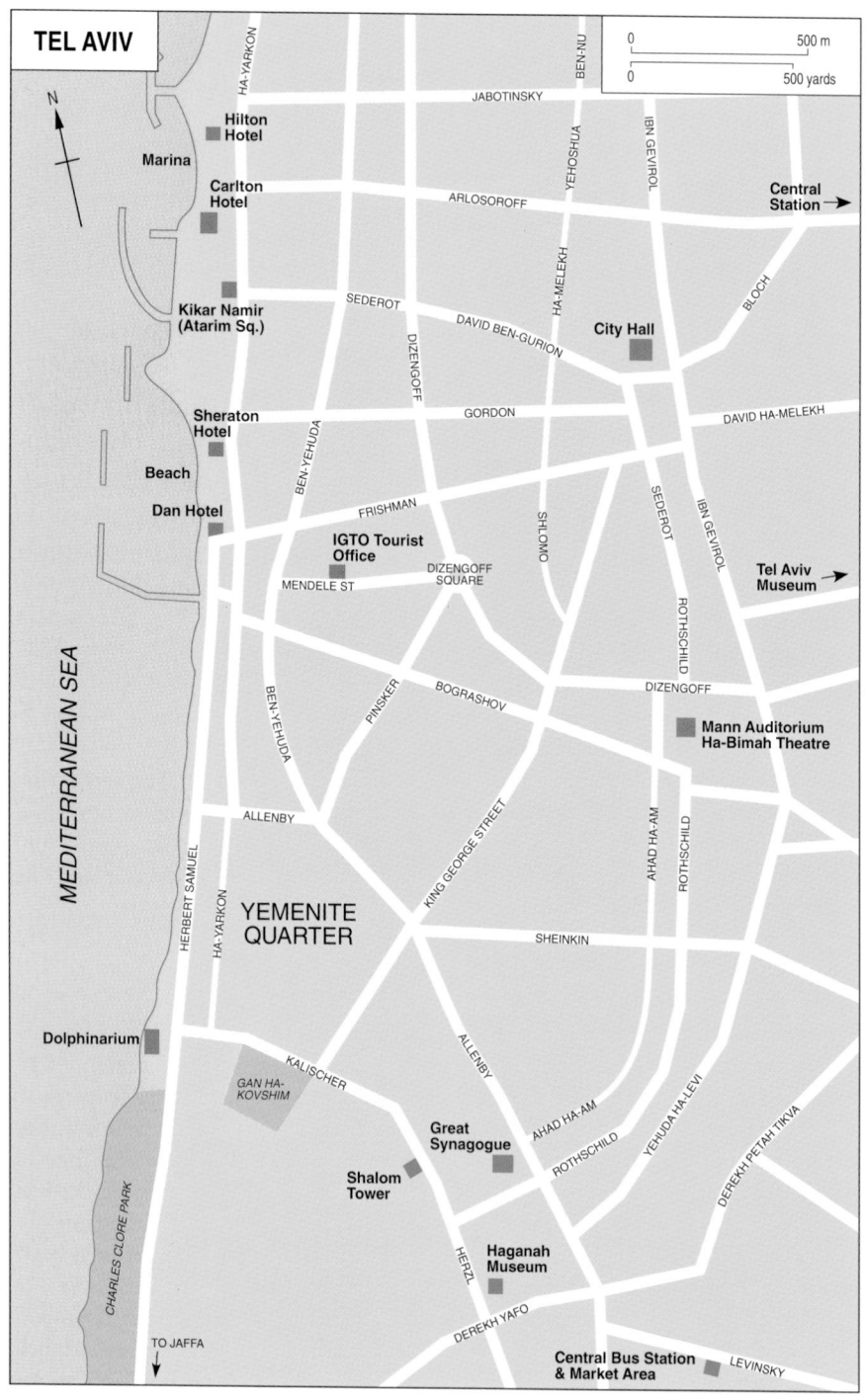

these families posing for posterity, realizing that by their actions history was being made. They were not building a mere garden suburb for noisy, crowded Jaffa but a new Jewish city, the first for 2,000 years.

Makeshift tents turned into cottages and dirt tracks became roads. A fine new school, the Herzliya Gymnasium (Palestine's first high school), was built. The settlers named their new town Ahuzat Bayit (simply, Housing Property). One year later the name was changed to Tel Aviv, Hebrew for the "Hill of Spring", symbolizing hope for a new future to be built on the ruins of the past. Their first thoroughfare they named Herzl Street. Their second and third they called Ahad HaAm Street and Rothschild Boulevard respectively. Three roads with the names of three of the most influential Zionists of the time: two thinkers, one financier.

The town prospered and by 1914, the population of Tel Aviv had already grown to 3,000. The Balfour Declaration launched a wave of immigration, and in 1921 Tel Aviv could no longer be considered a suburb of Jaffa. It had its own mayor, Dizengoff, and it was now home to 15,000 residents. By the outbreak of World War II in 1939, Tel Aviv was a small metropolis of 100,000 people and the capital of the dreamt-of Jewish State. In 1948, with the withdrawal of the British, this dream became reality and the establishment of Israel was officially declared on 15 May from Independence House on Rothschild Boulevard.

*T*own plan of Tel Aviv.

Orientation

For air-travellers, the first view of the Holy Land is usually the northern coast, south of Haifa. However, the clearest view, as the aircraft begins its descent into Ben-Gurion Airport, is of Tel Aviv. You won't be able to get all your bearings from such a swoop, but you should see one or two of the best-known landmarks. At 800kph (500mph) you fly parallel to the major hotels, situated right on the sea front. First the Hilton, then the Carlton (notice the marina), then the Sheraton, then the Dan. Also visible, inland from the hotels, is Moghrabi Square, where Allenby Road meets Ben-Yehuda Street. South of here is Dizengoff Square, the heart of Tel Aviv, where you'll be spending much of your time once you arrive downtown. Perhaps the easiest landmark to recognize is the white, 35-storey Shalom Tower (Migdal Shalom), the highest building in the Middle East. As the aircraft banks to the left and descends you may be able to see Jaffa, partly a preserved old town and partly a sister city to Tel Aviv.

After touchdown take a *sherut*, a bus or hire a car and head for the city. The part you need is the downtown seafront section, extending east only to the thoroughfare of Ibn Gevirol Street. Coming from Ben-Gurion Airport, you'll hit a confluence of several major arteries—Petach Tikva Road, Haifa Road and Arlosoroff Street. If you're in your own car, you can continue to drive along Arlosoroff Street; you will eventually hit the one-way system at the Carlton Hotel. This is HaYarkon Street. This thoroughfare is named after the River Yarkon in northern Tel

Aviv, but it would be far more appropriate to call it the Street of the Hotels, for here are situated most of the major hotels, overlooking the sea front. Turn right for the Tal, the Grand Beach and the Hilton hotels; the others are situated on the left. If you take Bograshov Street, just past the Dan Hotel, you'll be heading in the right direction for central Tel Aviv, the section centering on Dizengoff Square.

So, the most important streets to get to know are Ben Yehuda, which runs parallel to the shoreline, and Dizengoff, which runs from the Mann Auditorium and the café hub of Dizengoff Square down to the River Yarkon and the intersection with Ben Yehuda at the northern tip of the city. These routes are serviced by the number 4 and 5 buses respectively.

Tel Aviv

A *tel* is an artificial mound created on the accumulated debris of the past. Megiddo in northern Israel started out 4,000 years ago on a plain; 20 cities later and it had its own man-made hill. Tel Aviv was not constructed on such a *tel* but it has already started to build on top of itself. The **Shalom Tower** on Herzl Street was erected over the demolished Herzliya Gymnasium in 1959, thus depriving the city of one of its earliest cultural-historical edifices. Only a large

A view of Tel Aviv from Jaffa. It is possible to walk from Jaffa to the main Tel Aviv hotels along the beach.

fresco, by the artist Nahum Gutman, on the wall of the tower, remains of the old building. The tower consists of a large department store, numerous offices, a small amusement park, a **Wax Museum** and an observatory on the 35th floor. The Wax Museum is on the third floor (tel. 03-5177304). It displays a variety of figures such as David Ben-Gurion, Golda Meir and even Nazi war criminal Adolph Eichmann. Modern effigies include Michael Jackson and Israeli pop star Ofra Haza.

The **observatory** can be reached by glass elevator and the view is very much worth the effort. On a clear day you can see the Carmel mountains to the north, the beginnings of the Negev desert to the south, and Jerusalem to the east. To augment the naked eye, telescopes are available. There is also a café up here—

no great gourmet experience, but sipping coffee with much of Israel in view more than makes up for it.

The amusement park, observatory, and wax museum are open Sunday to Thursday, 9 a.m. to 7 p.m., on Friday and holiday eves until 2 p.m.

Behind the Shalom Tower is the **Yemenite Quarter**, Kerem Ha-Teimanim. This is an exotic, Arab-like quarter of bustling winding streets, animated people and some of the best Oriental restaurants in Israel. Close by, where Allenby Road approaches Magen David Square, is the **Carmel Market**,

The marina—a hive of activity, right next door to the Carlton Hotel.

Local Musical Talent
Ofra Haza is one of Israel's more popular exports. Her Yeminite singing is now known worldwide. If you want to buy some representative Haza music, you should try *Shaday* or *Desert Wind*. The song *Im Nin' Alu* was a hit in the UK. For more folksy music try *One to One* by Matti Caspi. Cassettes can be bought in many places but the widest selection can be found at the shops around the central bus station.

or Shuq Ha-Carmel, consisting of a colourful mix of fresh vegetables, fragrant fruit and polished kitchenware. Shoppers are serenaded in rough Hebrew by traders anxious to sell their wares.

The hub of Tel Aviv's cultural life is at the northern end of one of the first three streets in Tel Aviv, Rothschild Boulevard. Here you will find the **Ha-Bimah Theatre** (tel. 03-209888), a youth museum, and the **Mann Auditorium** (03-6415244), home of the Israel Philharmonic Orchestra. Close by, at 6 Tarsat Boulevard, is the **Helena Rubinstein Pavilion** (tel. 03-5287196), which exhibits the works of foreign and Israeli artists. Open Sunday to Thursday from 10 a.m. to 1 p.m. and 5 to 7 p.m., on Shabbat from 10 a.m. to 2 p.m.; closed Friday. Bus 5, 18, 25, or 63.

For a glimpse into modern Israeli history, pop into **Independence Hall**, 16 Rothschild Boulevard (tel. 03-5173942). It was here, in Meir Dizengoff's old residence, that Israel was declared independent. Hours are 9 a.m. to 1 p.m. Sunday to Friday.

The **Haganah Museum** at 23 Rothschild Boulevard (tel. 03-5600809) documents the development and the military cunning of the pre-state Zionist army, the Haganah. Home of Eliyahu Golomb, a former Haganah general, the museum is for many Israelis a proud reminder of a glorious past. On the third floor you can see the various ways the Israelis hid arms inside farm machinery to escape British detection, and how they secretly manufactured hand grenades and Sten guns in clandestine kibbutz workshops.

As many of the explanatory captions next to the exhibits are in Hebrew, English-speaking interpreters and guides can provide assistance. The museum is open Sunday to Thursday, 9 a.m. to 3 p.m., until 12.30 p.m. on Friday; closed Shabbat.

Museums Across the River

The Yarkon River is not exactly the Euphrates, but nevertheless it is an important local landmark. In biblical times it marked the border between the tribes of Dan and Ephraim. Today, where it meets the sea, it is overshadowed by a huge power station. Inland it splits into two and runs through the scenic Exhibition Park, where in summer free concerts are held. You can hire boats and punts in this park and this is certainly a distraction from the usual events Tel Aviv can offer. Across the river are some fascinating museums, one of which, Beth HaTefutsoth, is a "must-see" (*see* page 174).

The **Ha-Aretz Museum Complex** (tel. 03-6415244) lies within a large enclosure that encircles Tel Qasile, an ancient mound in which 12 distinct strata of past civilizations have been discovered. Besides this *tel*, Ha-Aretz has a number of other attractions. The **Kadman Numismatic Pavilion** has various exhibits chronicling the history of money. The

Glass Pavilion has a rare collection of glass vessels spanning 3,000 years of civilization. The **Ceramics Pavilion** is devoted to the history and production of pottery. The **Ethnography and Folklore Pavilion** holds a wealth of Jewish ethnic art and handicrafts. The **Nechushtan Pavmon** delves into the history of mining and metallurgy in biblical times. The **"Man and His Toil" Centre** holds displays, some of them "live", showing how men and women have earned their

The Dizengoff Stroll

Dizengoff Square, with its elevated walkways, is where it's at in Tel Aviv, especially at night. You can't miss the place because right in the middle of it is a huge circular sculpture-fountain by Yaacov Agam named *Water and Fire*. It is not static. Five large concentric metal rings are brightly coloured so that when the rings turn, the painted surfaces produce animated patterns. At the same time, jets of water spurt upwards, and through it all shoots a jet of flame. Music accompanies the whole display in a dynamic show that lasts for about 20 minutes. Beginning at 11 a.m., the shows come around every hour on the hour, continuing until 10 p.m. apart from an 'interlude' between 2 and 3 p.m.

A short walk from *Water and Fire* is Dizengoff Street's famous stretch of sidewalk cafés, one of the best places in Tel Aviv to hang out and watch the world go by. Both business and pleasure is conducted here, usually over a croissant and a cappuccino. The street is busiest, and at its most glamorous, on Friday evenings.

---

*T*he Water and Fire *sculpture fountain by Yaacov Agam in Dizengoff Square.*

daily bread in Israel since ancient times. For astronomy buffs there is the **Lasky Planetarium**. The museums are open daily from 9 a.m. to 1 p.m. and on Tuesday you can also get in from 4 to 7 p.m. They are also open on Shabbat from 10 a.m. to 1 p.m. Take bus 24, 25, 27, or 45.

Beth HaTefutsoth

If you think museums can often be very dry and dull, and more of a chore than a pleasure, then visit **Beth HaTefutsoth**, the Nahum Goldmann Museum of the Jewish Diaspora (tel. 03-646202). Situated on the campus of Tel Aviv University in Ramat Aviv, this museum favours interactive models and reconstruction rather than displays of artefacts decipherable only to experts.

Beth HaTefutsoth was the brainchild of Dr Nahum Goldmann, the founder and first president of the World Jewish Congress. He wished for a museum that could help people understand history by placing it into visual context. The 2,500-year history of the Jewish Diaspora, or Dispersion, was the perfect subject. Photographs, movies, documents, touchable artefacts, maps, and scale models vividly bring to life the communities, synagogues, households, and workshops of Jews living in the Diaspora.

The museum is open Sunday to Thursday from 10 a.m. to 5 p.m. (on Wednesday to 7 p.m.).

Beaches

Tel Aviv is not only a café-city, it is also a seaside resort. The beaches here are good, although normally packed out (especially on Shabbat). Beautiful bodies of both sexes strut and flaunt their stuff, exercising, tanning, swimming or just relaxing. In the early mornings, many of Tel Aviv's more mature residents perform callisthenics before taking a dip in the Mediterranean. At other times of the day you will see activities ranging from pumping iron to windsurfing.

The seashore is a 5-minute walk from Dizengoff Square. A patterned promenade runs the entire length of the beach, and seats and canopies line the route. Most beaches have free showers, facilities for changing clothes and a lifeguard. This last provision is important, as in certain parts that are always well-marked, there are very strong undertows that can trap even the strongest of swimmers. As well as boards telling you not to enter the water, there are also warning flags: black means absolutely no swimming in the area; red warns you to be especially cautious; white indicates that the water is safe.

The cleanest beach is the one at **Clore Park**. The quietest beach is likely to be the one opposite the Tal Hotel, just east of the junction of Ben Yehuda and Dizengoff. Facing the Hilton Hotel and Namir Square is the **Hof Hadarim** (Orange Beach), also known as the Hilton Beach. Use of changing rooms is free and you can rent lockers and deck chairs. The Tel Aviv

> *Matzkot*
> If you want to blend into beach society, get yourself a couple of wooden bats and a suitable projectile. Paddle ball, in Hebrew *matzkot*, is a national obsession. If you don't want to blend into the sand, get yourself some armour plating because paddle-ball players are no respecters of individual space!

marina is close by. The beach at the suburb of **Bat Yam** 5km (3 miles) south of Tel Aviv, is wide and sandy and never really gets as crowded as the main Tel Aviv stretch. The best beach is at **Kefar Shmariyahu**, north of Herzliya, which is about half an hour away by bus or car.

Take care of your valuables whilst on the beach, as opportunist thieves roam around and can strike quickly.

The **Tel Aviv Sailing Club** in Marina Atarim (PO Box 16285; tel. 03-5272257/27) is good for a wander. It lies between the Carlton and Hilton hotels. You can rent a sailboat here by the hour, with or without a skipper. Hiring a windsurf board and sail is cheaper and instruction is available. The marina is open from 9 a.m. to 5 p.m. daily.

Jaffa

Jaffa is one of the oldest cities in the world, and is almost certainly the oldest still-functioning port in the world. It has had an eventful, and mythical, history. It was from here that Jonah boarded the ship for Tarshish, in his attempt to flee the instructions of God (*Jonah: 1, 3*). The famous cedars of Lebanon were shipped through Jaffa to be used in the building of Solomon's great Temple in Jerusalem. The healing of Tabitha was performed by the

Apostle Peter when he stayed at the Jaffa house of Simon the Tanner (*Acts 9: 36–42*). Greek mythology has it that Andromeda, the beautiful daughter of the King of Jaffa, was chained to a rock just outside Jaffa's harbour to appease a great sea monster. She was subsequently dramatically rescued by Perseus on his winged white horse.

Half an hour's walk from downtown Tel Aviv will take you to the old part of Jaffa (Yafo in Hebrew—the etymology is confused but probably comes from the Hebrew word *yafah*, which means "beautiful"). The **Old Port** area is picturesque, and is just a tiny suburb of Tel Aviv. This was not the case, when one hundred years ago it was the main port of Palestine, and Tel Aviv was still only a dream. With the

*B*oxes of Jaffa oranges being unloaded for Israeli consumption. Jaffa oranges are famous throughout the world.

British decision to convert Haifa into the main Mediterranean port, the town lost its *raison d'être* and started to decline.

Greater Jaffa is just as sprawling as Tel Aviv, but the old town is more compact and inviting. Often used as a movie backdrop, the place is quiet, and for those with a taste for the sea it has some amazingly good fish restaurants, most of them having fine views over the old part of town and the sea.

Jaffa has long interested the great powers and it has been besieged, crushed and rebuilt by a succession of conquerors. Egyptians, Philistines, Israelites, Persians, Greeks, Syrians, Romans, Idumeans, Muslims, Crusaders, Mamelukes, the French and the Turks have all passed through, first destroying and then rebuilding. The British eventually took over from the Ottoman Turks at the end of World War I. Jaffa came under Israeli control during the War of Independence in 1948.

Old Jaffa was refurbished and improved in 1963, and today it contains one of the best artists' colonies in the country, as well as various tourist shops, seafood restaurants and nightclubs.

The harbour area shows Jaffa to be a working port, with smelly boats daily landing freshly caught fish. Above the harbour nestles Old Jaffa, with its haphazard, golden buildings and a red-and-white-striped lighthouse. The Old City starts at the **Clock Tower** on Yefet Street, built in 1906. The tower's stained-glass windows each portray a different chapter in the town's history (wait here at 9.30 a.m. on a Wednesday for a free walking tour of the city). Opposite the tower is a large inner courtyard, once the Armenian Hostel which used to be a main stopping-off point for travellers. Just past the police station is the **el-Mahmoudia Mosque**, built in 1812 and named after the Jaffa's Turkish governor (entrance is forbidden to non-Muslims).

Continue one block south past Yefet Street, turn left and you'll come to the **Jaffa Flea Market**, easily one of the best of its kind in Israel. Available here will be an eclectic selection of goods from Persian carpets to leather goods; and brassware to hubbly-bubbly pipes. There are plenty of unusual items on sale, but if you don't haggle you're not doing it right. If you feel peckish after bargain-hunting, you can stave off those hunger pangs by popping into one of the bakeries near the flea market. As well as various types of spiced bread, you could also try the bread baked with feta-like cheese and egg, mushrooms or even spinach.

Sunsets can be spectacular the world over, but in the Holy Land they seem to be particularly special. Here we see the sunset over the Jaffa port area.

The Rock of Andromeda

Any tourists that get shown the Rock of Andromeda are following in a long tradition: one historian notes that as far back as 58 BC, tourists were being shown the alleged broken chains that bound Andromeda and also the skeleton of the great marine monster that would have killed her had it not been for Perseus.

*T*he area around Saint Peter's Church, seen here, has often been used in films, most notably an Agatha Christie murder-mystery in which Peter Ustinov played Hercule Poirot. The monastery associated with the church has played host to crusaders, pilgrims and even the Emperor Napoleon.

At the **Jaffa Museum of Antiquities** at 10 Mifratz Shlomo Street (tel. 03-825375), there are numerous archaeological exhibits to do with the history of Jaffa. Erected in the 18th century, the building used to be the notorious local prison. Later, it won acclaim throughout the Middle East as the soap factory of the Greek Orthodox Damiani family.

Next door is the Franciscan **Saint Peter's Church**. The Saint Louis Monastery in the courtyard was named after the French Crusader king who stayed here in 1147. The monastery later served as a hostel for pilgrims on their way to to Jerusalem (Jaffa was always known as "the port of Jerusalem") and Napoleon also relaxed here after conquering Jaffa.

Just past the grassy **HaPisgah Gardens**, that contain a modern amphitheatre and the ruins of an 18th-century BC Hyksos town, the Horoscope Path begins to crawl its way through the Jaffa Wall. It goes past houses, galleries and artists' studios on its way to the lighthouse at the southern entrance of the wall. Close to this lighthouse is the **House of Simon the Tanner** (tel. 03-836792), open 8 a.m. to 11.45 a.m. and 2 to 4 p.m. (until 6.30 p.m. in summertime) every day.

At the centre of the renovated section is **Kedumin Square**, in which the Jaffa excavations present a reconstruction of the city's multi-layered history; this is also one of Tel Aviv's most tranquil evening spots.

Overlooking the bay and the whole of Tel Aviv is an outdoor sculpture garden with some pretty weird and wonderful exhibits. Some of these are symbolic others merely good looking.

*J*affa is well known for
its impressive sculpture garden.

A visit to Jaffa would
not be complete without a sunset.

Sea, Sand and Sunsets

Away from the minarets and the golden domes, away from the ruins and the biblical watering holes, Israel is also known for its beaches and the resorts that service them. Whilst Israel is normally thought of as a pilgrimage centre and historical wonderland, it is becoming clear that an increasing percentage of tourists are coming to Israel for the coastline, a glorious strip of sand, surf and beautiful people. Yet Israel's Mediterranean coastline is not all a playground. This is the Holy Land after all, and even the beaches have archaeological ruins.

The resort towns that have grown up to look after these tourists stretch 190km (118 miles) from the Gaza Strip in the south to Rosh Hanikra in the north. Yet about a third of this coastline, including some of the most beautiful beaches in Israel, is army land, and kept out-of-bounds. South of Tel Aviv, the Israeli Defence Force hold sway over 50 per cent of the beaches, and another 15km (9 miles) of beach are occupied by technical installations such as power stations and ports. Despite this, the Israeli coast-line is stunningly attractive—the sunset over Caesarea or the night-time strolls on the Netanya promenade make for memorable holidays.

The Israeli coast can be divided into two sections: north and south. The northern section begins in the Lebanon, and it is characterized by bays, capes, valleys, islands and peninsulas. The mountain ranges in this region extend to the coast, dipping their lower reaches into the sea. The hidden inlets and the peninsulas of the northern coast made for convenient anchorages for ships and seafarers down through the ages. It was from here that the Phoenicians, the greatest sea-faring nation of the ancient Mediterranean, set forth. The small town of Dor was their southernmost city.

Even if you cannot afford to buy, you are welcome to browse and dream at the Diamond Jewelry Center in Netanya.

COASTAL STRIP

N

MEDITERRANEAN SEA

Hadera
Givat Hayyim
Netanya
Shekhem
Tulkarm
Kefar Sava
Shekhem
Herzliya
TEL AVIV
Petah Tiqiva
Bat Yam
Lod
Rishon le-Zion
Ramla
Modi im
Rehovot
Yavne
Latrun Monastery
Ashdod
Eshta'ol
Bet-Shemesh
Zor'a
Ashkelon
Guvrin
Qiryat Gat
Bet-Guvrin
GAZA STRIP
Shiqma
Gaza
Netivot
Gerar
Hevron

WEST BANK

Bethany
JERUSALEM
HEBRON
Arugot

Legend:
- Historic site
- Land above 500m (1,640 ft)

0 — 10 km
0 — 6 miles

*N*ahsholim, a kibbutz by the Mediterranean, offers splendid bathing and holiday accommodation in individual chalets just a few kilometres north of Caesarea.

South of Caesarea the coastline changes radically, becoming totally straight. There are no bays and as we continue southwards, sand dunes become more common. In the southern part of the country, these can even penetrate inland for up to 50km (31 miles).

No invading army has ever landed on the coast of Israel south of the Carmel without first capturing the interior of the country. Even the Philistines, a great nation of warrior seafarers, had to conquer from land, fighting their way

*I*srael's coastal strip.

through Egypt. Alexander the Great, Pompey, and Napoleon all took land routes, either from Egypt or from Asia Minor. The Crusaders, the scourge of Muslims and Jews everywhere, arrived overland, this time from Akko and Tyre. Richard the Lion-Heart arrived in Palestine at the head of a mighty army, and went on to conquer all of the coastal fortresses in the Third Crusade, yet he did so from the direction of Mount Carmel. The Crusader naval fleet, one of the largest ever to approach the coast of Palestine, was used only to land provisions.

The southern coast, with its lack of natural harbours, failed to produce any great seafaring nations. Rather it was home to farmers and land-traders. Only a very few anchorages were created, accommodating ships that were passing through.

According to the Bible, God informed Moses: "You will have the Great Sea for a border; this will be your

*T*he ruins of Caesarea are the most extensive and impressive in Israel. This is a Crusader archway.

western border" (*Numbers 34:6*). The Great Sea—the Mediterranean—was the final border. It was the point beyond which man could continue no further. The tribes of Israel looked eastward, with the sea behind them, hence the other biblical designation for the Mediterranean, "the Back sea".

Three of the Israelite tribes received territories near the sea. The southernmost was occupied by the tribe of Dan. Out of Dan came the great long-haired hero, Samson. During the time of Deborah the Judge, the tribe still lived on the coast. Deborah asked: "Why did Dan remain in ships?" (*Judges 5:17*). The Philistines answered this question as they squashed the Dan into the sand, driving them northwards, to Laish, in the Hula Valley.

The southern coast's lack of natural harbours did not worry the great constructor Herod, hundreds of years after the Philistines. He ordered an artificial port to be built at Caesarea. This port, now mostly submerged, is one of the many highlights along the coast. Like the rest of the country, the coastal strip contrasts new with old in a typically Israeli fashion. Right next door to that pre-biblical ruin is a hot-dog stall (kosher, of course); and where galleons used to float, tourists and Israelis now swim, dive, boat, ski and surf.

The sun shines here continuously (well, almost) and the beaches are packed with people from every walk of life. At any one time there are likely to be 150,000 individuals on the beaches of Israel. Israel's southern coastline is not indented with any hidden coves or harbours, so the beaches near the resort towns are not havens of solitude, they are hives of activity.

South of Tel Aviv

Ashkelon

This is the southernmost resort town, and a place of great antiquity. Indeed, as it is depicted on the Temple of Karnak in Egypt, it would appear to be more than 4,000 years old. During its heyday it was one of the five Philistine city-states (the others were Gath, Gaza, Ekron and Ashdod). It was here that Samson got his famous haircut from Delilah (although it was in Gaza where he subsequently brought down the temple.)

Modern Ashkelon is a spacious and attractive town, with most of the amenities based in the part of town called Afridar. The **Afridar Centre**, with its large Clock Tower, is the place to head for. Here you'll find the Tourist Information Office (tel. 07-732412), and most of the banks, shops, restaurants, and cafés. Also a cinema and a small museum.

Many Israelis feel that Ashkelon has the perfect climate: cooled by soft breezes from the sea, but warmed by the dryness of the desert winds. The resulting climate is just about right and the 12km (7.5 miles) of beautiful beaches surrounding Ashkelon is the perfect place to experience heat tempered by a breeze.

Just north of the Shulamit Gardens Hotel, on the beach, is a family tomb called the **Painted Tomb**, thought to date from the 3rd century AD. With a number of after-life themes, including a very populous paradise, the tomb is in a good state of preservation and well worth a look. Open daily from 9 a.m. to 3 p.m.

The **National Antiquities Park**, not far from the Painted Tomb, is the site of ancient Ashkelon; a mass of pillars, columns and broken-down walls.

Access is officially restricted to certain times, but as the entrance from the beach is not blocked, in practice you can walk round here anytime.

Most of the ruins are of the Philistine port and the Roman reconstructions. Some of the finds from the scanty excavations that have been conducted around here can be seen in the **Sculpture Corner** inside the park.

Beaches

Ashkelon has several public beaches, one of which, the **Bar Kockba**, is reserved for the religiously observant. Men and women should not swim together or show too much flesh. The most popular spot is **Delilah's beach**, which has three small islands a swimmable distance away. However, because of the undercurrents around here it would be advisable to swim only where the flags tell you to and when a lifeguard is present.

The Weizmann Institute and the Gedera Museum

One visit to the **Weizmann Institute of Science** (tel. 08-483393) will convince anyone that Israel is no technological back-water. The Institute is Israel's foremost scientific establishment; and the phrase "high-tech" seems a poor description for the work that is done here.

Founded in 1949 in honour of the first president of Israel (an important organic chemist and inventor of the mass-production of acetone), the institute grew out of the Daniel Sieff Research Institute, established in 1934 and funded by money from the Marks and Spencer dynasty. Conducting both fundamental and applied research, the Weizmann Institute also has a graduate school.

Set in exquisite grounds, the institute holds the Wix Library, where there is an exhibition on Dr Weizmann's life, and the **Wix Auditorium**, where audio-visual shows on the Institute's activities are shown at 11 a.m. and 3.15 p.m. daily (except Friday, held at 11 a.m. only). Weizmann's tomb is also here.

The Gedera Museum is 10km from the Weizmann Institute on the road to Be'er Sheva. It is on the site of the only Israeli settlement founded by members of the Jewish Bilu movement, who emmigrated from Russia in the 19th century. Artefacts and photographs illustrating the harsh life in the early

Sunset over the Mediterranean. The slipway is for launching boats.

settlement are displayed in a house built by the Biluim in 1924. The museum is open Sunday to Friday (tel. 08-5993316).

Rishon-le-Zion

Rishon-le-Zion is the home of Israel's wine industry. The free tours of the wine cellars, interesting in their own right, are concluded with samples of the local stock. Don't, however, drink and drive as Israeli police clamp down hard on offenders.

Rishon-le-Zion was also one of the first Jewish settlements in Israel. Started in 1882 by a group of idealistic Russian Jews escaping pogroms in Russia, Rishon-le-Zion had a tough time of it in the early days. The settlers suffered from agricultural inexperience, Arab bandits, malaria and low morale. In desperation, they sent a deputation to Baron de

Ancient Glass Factory Discovered

A large, ancient factory for the manufacture of raw glass was recently discovered in the town of Hadera, half-way between Tel Aviv and Haifa on the coast. The factory, dating back to the 7th century AD, is the first of its kind and size to be excavated in the world.

Various globs of glass and rubbish from glass manufacturing from Byzantine times had been found in the Beit Eliezer neighbourhood of Hadera many years ago. However, the erosion caused by recent torrential rains, and plans to build a road on the site, led to an emergency excavation financed by the Ministry of Housing. The dig was particularly difficult, since the earth was covered with heavy silt and almost had to be chiselled out, but the astounding finds more than compensated for the hard labour.

A large factory for the manufacture of raw glass was uncovered, with some 20 facilities for producing the globs of glass (known as *bullos*), in such colours as turquoise, olive green and brown, from which glass utensils were later fashioned. In the ancient glass industry, the factories producing raw glass were separated from the process of manufacturing glass utensils and were usually located away from the towns because of the attendant extreme heat and smoke. They required three basic physical conditions: material for burning, raw material for manufacturing and proximity to trade routes. The site at Beit Eliezer met all these.

Adjacent to each of the glass-producing facilities was an oven facing west. The north-westerly winds from the sea raised the temperature to 700°–1,000°C (1,290°–1,830°F), fusing the raw materials into tons of glass.

While it seems that the factory was in use for only a short time, it produced hundreds of tons of glass. A museum for the finds has recently opened.

Rothschild in France. The financier and philanthropist came to their rescue by dispatching agricultural experts to help the settlers find water and transplant young French vines. The vines, from Beaujolais, Bordeaux, and Burgundy took hold, and in 1887 the Israeli wine industry was born, under the name Carmel Oriental (or Carmel-Mitzrahi). Today these wines are exported all over the world. (Zichron-Yaakov, south of Haifa, is also a leading wine centre.)

Bat Yam

"Daughter of the Sea" says the Hebrew. Bat Yam is fast becoming a very popular resort town. Its beaches are particularly fine, uncrowded and within easy reach of Tel Aviv. Cars will get here very easily. For buses, take numbers 10, 18, 25, and 26.

This town can be used as a good base for the Tel Aviv area, as there are many good hotels around, but it's a bit out in the sticks and Tel Aviv is much more lively. However, if it is peace and quiet you want, in a modern setting, with plenty of amenities, then Bat Yam may fit the bill.

North of Tel Aviv

Herzliya

Herzliya is named after the founder of modern Zionism, Theodore Herzl. It was founded in 1924 as a farming settlement, but has now become Israel's most exclusive seaside resort, the haunt of the wealthy, good looking and smart. In fact, Israel's version of Monte Carlo. None of the hotels here have "budget" printed on their in-house

stationery. If you stay here you'll be staying in luxury hotels only. Food and drink is consequently more expensive than elsewhere in Israel.

The entire waterfront area is packed with fine hotels, gourmet restaurants and plush ice-cream parlours. The beaches here are lovely, but those you have to pay for are very expensive for what you get. The finest are the **Zebulun-Daniel**, near the Daniel Hotel; the **Sharon**, next to the Sharon Hotel; and the **Accadia**, next to the hotel of the same name. The **Shefayim** beach is noted for being one of the only nudist beaches in Israel. As a useful counter to this there is also the **Separate Beach** for the religious.

As in some other coastal places in Israel, there is a powerful undertow at Herzliya, so only swim where the signs say it is safe and when there is a lifeguard on duty.

Not far from Herzliya is the ancient *tel* of **Arshaf**, a port of the Canaanites, named after Reshef, the Canaanite god of war, and later called Apollonia by the Greeks. Nothing much remains today except a tantalizing glimpse of the jetty as it peeps out of the sea. A 12th-century Crusader fort lies ruined nearby. Like all of the Crusader coastal forts, this one was obliterated by the Mamelukes, who were fearful of this "sea people" ever coming back. The desolation of the south Israeli coast is a result of this widespread despoilation.

In the evening, the modern amphitheatre in Netanya is often used for classical concerts and theatre productions (previous page).

Netanya

Netanya is the centre of Israel's diamond industry and also the capital of the Sharon Plain, a rich and fertile citrus grove area stretching north from Tel Aviv to Caesarea. The town was founded in 1929 as an agricultural centre, although in the last few years it has become first and foremost a resort town. The beaches are particularly fine and most of them are clean. There is a fine park parallel to the beaches and the coast and cliffs are attractive.

There's a large expatriate English community here, made up of English Jews who made *aliyah* (emigrated to Israel). Consequently it has come to be the epitome of a middle-class English seaside town. If Herzliya is Monte Carlo, then Netanya must be Brighton.

In the winter, Netanya is almost lifeless, but in summer the place comes into its own, with July and August being very busy. Each week, in the amphitheatre of **Gan Ha-Melekh** park, there are community sing-songs and free screenings of international movies. There are also occasional renditions of classical music. Ha-Atzma'ut Square offers entertainment by top Israeli singers and folklore groups. Also in the square are regular programmes for children with magicians, clowns and puppet shows in the Gan Ha-Melekh in July. A one-week art exhibition takes place on Ha-Atzma'ut Square (Sunday to Thursday from 5.30 to 11 p.m.; closed Friday; on Shabbat from 8.30 p.m. to midnight). A chess tournament is held annually during May and June, and every two years there is a match for international contestants. The games start at 3.30 p.m. and last until 10 p.m.

Diamond Factories

Israel is a major world centre for cutting and polishing diamonds. Netanya is the main location for this industry, with two large factories. Even if you are not interested in buying any diamonds, a visit to the Netanya Diamond Centre, 31 Benjamin Boulevard (tel. 09-642770) is well worth while. Apart from being able to see the diamonds being cut, polished and finally cleaned, there are a number of interesting exhibits, such as a model of a South African diamond mine (complete with a working model railway), a gem museum, and a short film telling the story of the diamonds as they proceed from the South African mines to the potential buyer.

The best part of the visit has to be the showroom. Once inside this treasure house, it seems as though all the baubles in the world are winking at you. Of course, the guides would like you to buy his company's wares, but they exert no pressure and browsers are the norm rather than the exception. Open: 8 a.m. to 7 p.m. daily, on Friday until 3 p.m.; closed Shabbat.

Netanya's other diamond factory is Diamimon, located near the beach in Ha-Atzma'ut Square, 2 Gad Machnes Street (tel. 09-341725). Although smaller and not so well-geared to the tourist (there are no fancy exhibits and definitely no toy trains), there's a real Aladdin's cave of a showroom and you are allowed to dream as much as you want. Diamimon does have one exhibit of note: the Yeminite clothing display. This is up a flight of stairs to the small café, which also happens to have some lovely sea views. Open in summer from 8 a.m. to 10 p.m. Sunday to Friday, on Shabbat from 6 to 10 p.m. Winter hours are until 7.30 p.m. every day, except Friday when it closes at 2 p.m.

Caesarea

The Israeli Government Tourist Office likes posters. It uses them at travel fairs, on billboards and as adverts in the press. When the main picture is not of the Dome of the Rock in Jerusalem, it is often of the ruins of **Caesarea**. And no wonder; Caesarea is a truly beautiful place in an ideal location, washed by the clear, blue waters of the Mediterranean and terribly romantic.

After a while in Israel you may start to tire of ruins, no matter how grandiose. Biblical references start to flow in one ear and out of the other. You get the sudden urge to be in a metropolis once more; places like Tel Aviv start to appeal. Your brain deadens and the word "culture" takes on a sinister meaning.

Then you come to Caesarea and all is forgotten. Caesarea captures your attention like no other set of ruins in Israel. Other sites may be of greater significance historically, religiously and socially, but Caesarea transcends all this simply because it is so beautiful, and so extensive. You even start to like Herod the Great; he can't have been such a bad fellow if he was responsible for a town like this.

Caesarea was the Tel Aviv of its day—loud, rumbustious, licentious even; the place where everything happened. Caesarea lived life to the full. Today Caesarea is a large archaeological site, with impressive Roman and Crusader ruins. As well as the ruins, the site contains souvenir shops, cafés and even a nightclub. The amphitheatre here plays host to the annual Israel Festival, where the Roman ruins come alive to classical music concerts, operas and ballets.

Many of the ruins of Caesarea are submerged in 15m (50ft) of water so that the place has a City of Atlantis feel to it. The coast of Israel "slipped" 2,500 years ago due to tectonic activity. Ports like Caesarea, Ashkelon and Gaza disappeared. Buildings standing proud one day vanished the next. This is possibly one explanation of the familiar Samson story, when the mighty Danite pushed down the amphitheatre at Gaza.

On this site before Herod's city was a Phoenician harbour called *Stratonas Pyrgos* (Straton's Tower), but this would have been a mere village compared with the later construction. The land was given to Herod by Caesar Augustus after the Roman defeat of the Hasmonean Jewish empire.

Caesarea, the city that took just 12 years to complete (22–10 BC), was Herod's attempt to equal the splendour and pomp of Athens, the main port of the age. He dedicated his magnificent port to his benefactor and overlord, Augustus Caesar. Caesarea soon became the largest city in Judea, the chief port, the governor's residence, and, later, the home of the infamous Pontius Pilate.

Caesarea is mentioned in the New Testament as the place where the Holy Ghost was first given to the Gentiles (*Acts 10 and 11*). An extremely significant event in the development of Christianity, it was now a religion apart from Judaism. The city also figures prominently in the story of the apostle Paul, who was here warned not to go to Jerusalem; he ignored the advice, and returned in fetters to stand trial for heresy. After his imprisonment and subsequent trial in Caesarea, it was from this port that he was sent to Rome to stand trial again (*Acts 21:8–14; Acts 23:23–25;* and *Acts 25 and 26.*)

It was at Caesarea that the massacre of 20,000 Jews led to the First Jewish War (AD 66–70) and the eventual destruction of Jerusalem. It was also at Caesarea that 2,500 Jews were slaughtered by wild animals in the name of sport, a sport later extended to Christians too.

Despite its violent excesses, Caesarea was a rich, lively, cosmopolitan city. Its grandeur lasted for over 300 years, during which time it saw the fall of Rome and the rise of Christianity. Many churches were built here, and the Christian community flourished before ultimately the Arabs took the town from the Byzantines in the year AD 639.

Four hundred years later, the Crusaders reconquered Caesarea, and among the treasures they found after their extensive sacking was what was reputed to be the Holy Grail, the green crystal vessel from the Last Supper. It was taken to Italy, where it is preserved in the Cathedral of San Lorenzo in Genoa.

Sultan Salid captured Caesarea in 1187 and razed the place, leaving it deserted and unloved. True to the continuous game of Muslim-Christian swings-and-roundabouts, Richard the

Caesarea has many extant ruins. Some of the best are those from the Crusader period.

Just outside Caesarea are two aqueducts; one is Roman, the other Greek. This is the Roman version.

Lion-Heart moved into the town and later still the Crusader king Louis IX built a fortress here; most of the Crusader remains seen here today date from his time. When Muslim armies again took the city (in 1265 and 1291), they pillaged and destroyed in a deliberate policy of "scorched earth" proportions. Caesarea faded from history, submerged under water from one side and sand from the other. In the 18th century El-Jazzar, the Ottoman governor of the province, reclaimed much of Caesarea's marble, decorative pedestals and finely carved capitals for use in the reconstruction and beautification of his provincial capital at Akko.

Excavations after World War II revealed the city once more and a programme of restoration was started. The ruins visible today are but a fraction of the original city. A map available at the entrance to the site puts ancient Caesarea into context. The extant remains include the massive Roman aqueduct, Roman hippodrome and amphitheatre, a 4th-century synagogue, a Crusader cathedral and a Crusader city. The site is open daily from 8 a.m. to 4 p.m., to 3 p.m. on Friday and eves of holidays.

Modern Caesarea is made up of a fine town, many archaeological digs, a luxury hotel, a golf course (the first and only in Israel) and a Country Club.

Dor

Close to Caesarea is **kibbutz Nahsholim** and **Moshav Dor**, both famous for being located near one of Israel's most beautiful beaches: **Nof Dor.** An excellent sandy beach, Nof Dor is ideal for bathing and is enhanced by some natural lagoons.

Close by is Tel Dor, site of an ancient city settled since the Bronze Age. Dor was featured in ancient Egyptian text as being "a site of magnificence". It has been inhabited by Phoenicians, Israelites, Greeks and Romans. The ruins of a massive Graeco-Roman temple

The ruins of Caesarea attract tourists from all over the world. These are budding Dutch historians being told the history of Caesarea by a guide in the Roman amphitheatre.

dedicated to Zeus and Astarte are impressive. In kibbutz Nachsholim is the Hamizgaga museum. It houses objects such as sacrificial figures and jewelery excavated from Tel Dor, and there are displays of underwater finds, including anchors and navigational tools, which attest to the level of activity in the Port of Dor in earlier times. The museum is open all week (tel. 06-390950).

A ruined Crusader fortress, Castle Merle, stands nearby but is more under water than above. At the modern town of Dor is an unusual set of caves, eroded by the encroaching sea to form a natural tunnel at the water's edge.

195

Green Hills, Golden Domes and Giant Waves

Viewed from the sea, the most striking image of Haifa is the Baha'i Shrine halfway up Mount Carmel. A golden dome is given a perfect green backdrop: a whole hillside of gardens and trees. Further along the coast, Akko still echoes to the sounds of the Crusaders, with some of the best preserved Crusader buildings in the world.

The Sharon Plain is packed with orange groves and Mount Carmel is packed with pine trees. The change between the two occurs as you drive along the main road between Tel Aviv and Haifa. The plain becomes squeezed between the Mediterranean on the left and the Carmel mountains on the right. You are now entering haTzafon, the north.

This road is not the most interesting in Israel—a four-lane highway crossing

*O*nce a thriving hub of activity, Akko port was eclipsed by Haifa early in this century. The port area has retained its charm, and is now a very pleasant attraction in its own right.

a flat landscape. Only when Haifa is within sight does the road become pleasant and the scenery interesting. Yet, radiating out from this road are a number of attractions—the caves of prehistoric Carmel Man, the wine town of Zichron Ya'akov, and various kibbutzim and moshavim.

Haifa

Haifa is Israel's third-largest city. It lies on and below Mount Carmel. The place is consequently very hilly. There are three distinct tiers of development—the first tier is the port area; the business district Hadar, higher up, is the second; and the residential Carmel district, partially covered with pine trees, is the third.

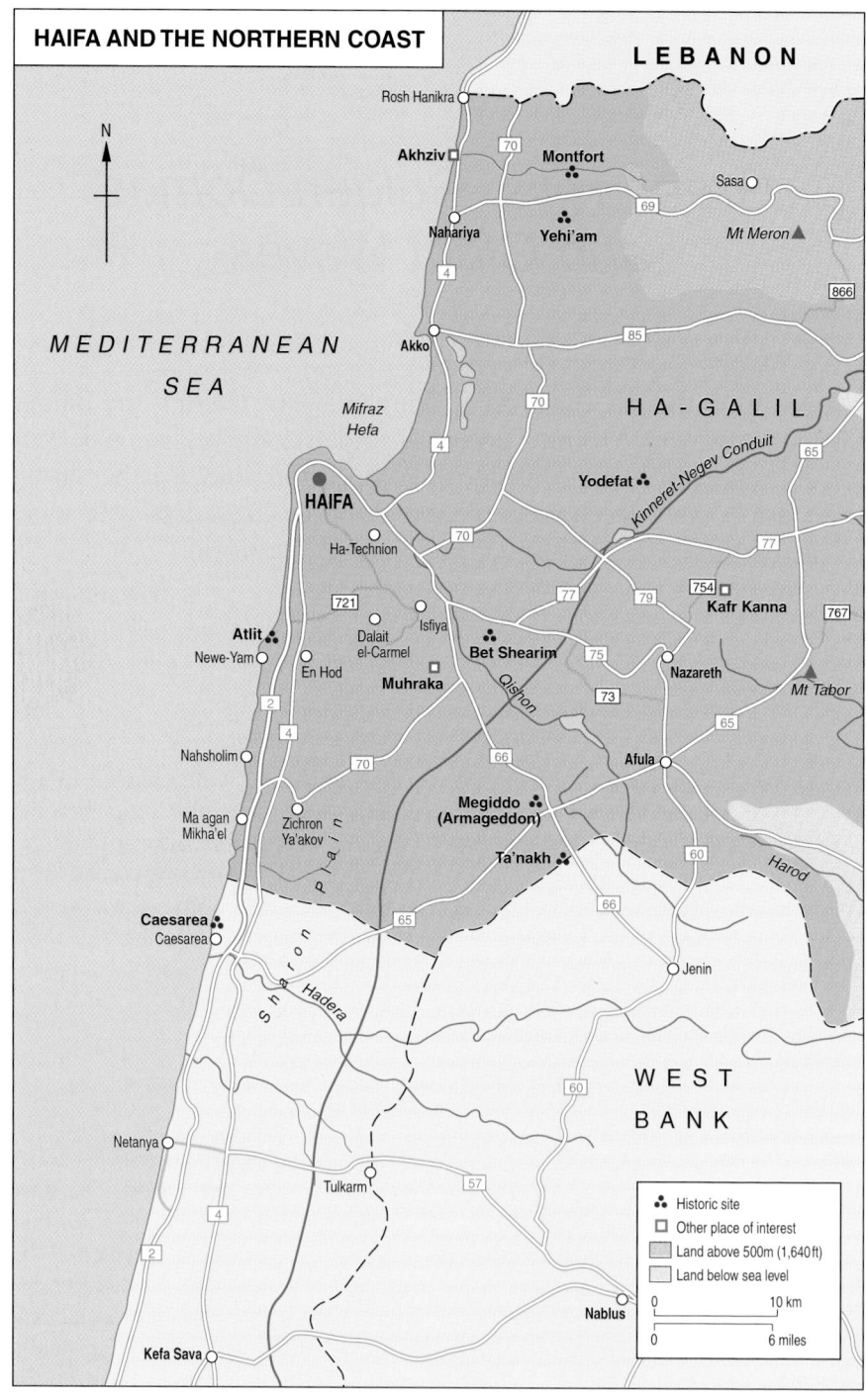

HAIFA AND THE NORTHERN COAST

LEBANON

N

Rosh Hanikra

Akhziv □   70   **Montfort**

Sasa ○

69

Nahariya   **Yehi'am**   Mt Meron ▲

4   866

Akko   85

MEDITERRANEAN
SEA

70   **HA-GALIL**

Mifraz
Hefa

Kinneret-Negev Conduit   65

Yodefat   ●

HAIFA

Ha-Technion   70   77   77

721   79   754 □
Kafr Kanna   767

Atlit   Isfiya   77
Newe-Yam   Dalait
el-Carmel   **Bet Shearim**   75   Nazareth
En Hod   73
2   **Muhraka**   Qishon   Mt Tabor ▲

4   Nahsholim   66
70   **Afula**   65

Ma agan
Mikha'el   Zichron
Ya'akov   **Megiddo**
(Armageddon)   60   Harod

Ta'nakh   66

Caesarea   65
Caesarea ○   Jenin ○

Hadera

WEST

BANK

Netanya ○   60

Tulkarm   57

4

2

Nablus   ●○○ Historic site
□ Other place of interest
☐ Land above 500m (1,640 ft)
☐ Land below sea level
0   10 km
Kefa Sava ○   0   6 miles

198

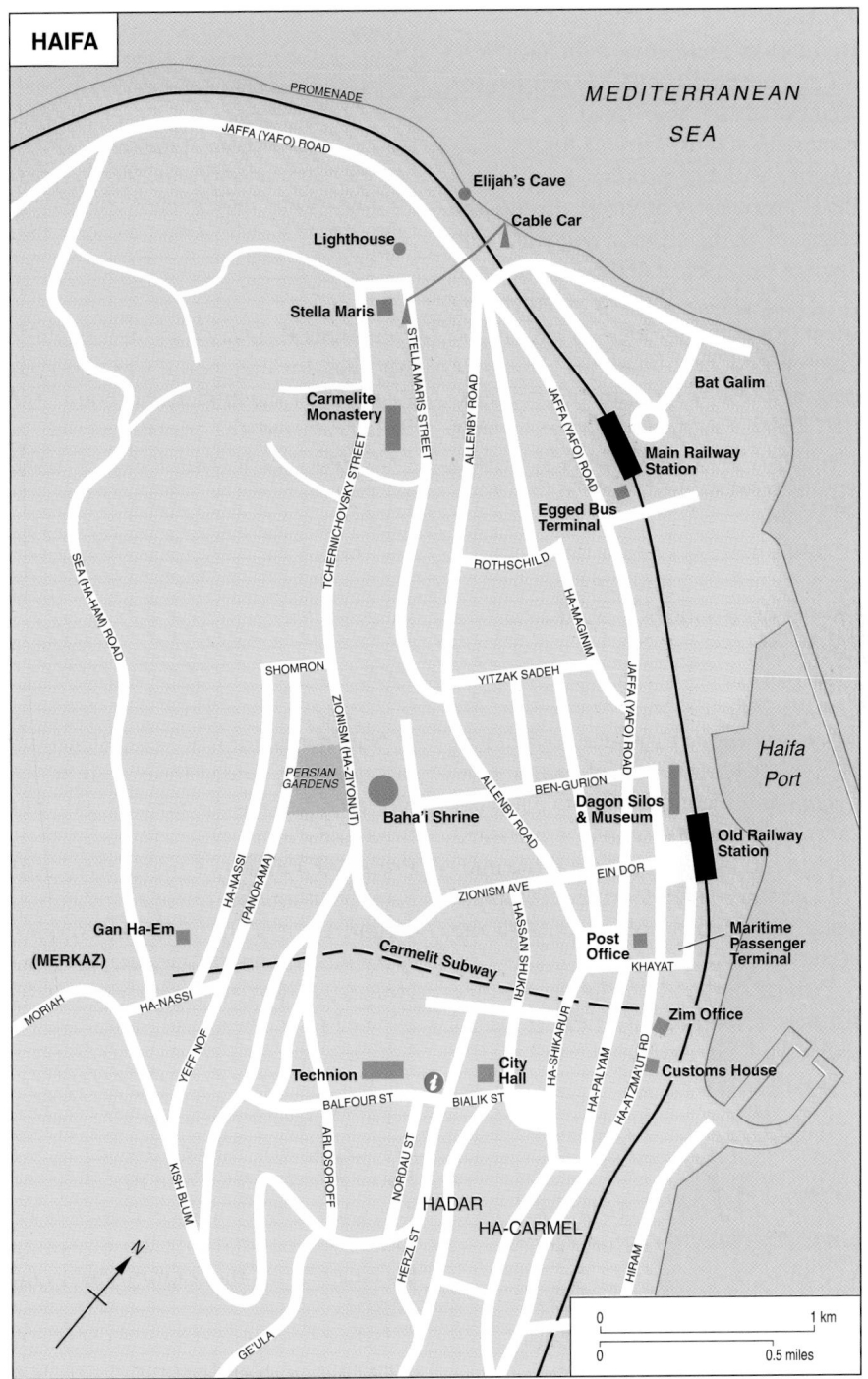

History

Remains of prehistoric man have been found on Carmel (which is Hebrew for "Vineyard of the Lord") but the mountain is most famous for its associations with the prophet Elijah. This fiery prophet, who lived during the reign of King Ahab and his wife Jezebel, disposed of 450 priests of Ba'al (*I Kings 18:19-40*) by challenging them to a religious duel—Yahweh, the Hebrew god, beat Ba'al, the Canaanite god, in a test of spontaneous combustion. Elijah's sacrificial bull was divinely consumed by fire and the 450 hapless priests were executed down at the brook of Kishon.

Haifa itself has had a fairly nondescript history and until this century was always overshadowed by the port of Akko, across the bay. In the early Christian era it was a centre of the purple-dye industry, but Haifa was destroyed when the Crusaders sacked it in 1099. After centuries of being conquered and reconquered, the place became little more than an impoverished village and lay dormant until the mid-19th century when German Templars began to build a colony outside the cramped old city.

Zionist settlers later in the century further developed the new parts of town. The real development of Haifa, however, started when the Haifa–

*M*ap of Haifa and the northern coastal region (page 198).

*T*own plan of Haifa (page 199).

> **Haifa**
>
> Haifa is a very busy place—indeed, there is a Hebrew saying: *Jerusalem studies, Tel Aviv dances, Haifa works!* From its early days Haifa has been at the centre of the Israeli heavy industries and the city is the birthplace and traditional stronghold of the main Israeli labour union, the *Histradrut.*

Damascus Railway was built in 1905. Another turning point was the construction of the modern harbour—the British started the transformation in 1929 and had it completed by 1934. Thereupon Haifa became the vital trading and communications centre it is today, taking on major importance as a shipping base, naval centre and terminal point for oil pipelines.

In 1939 a British government White Paper restricted Jewish immigration into Palestine—and this was at a time of Nazi persecution of Jews. Blockade-busting ships landed thousands of immigrants who were now illegal, but thousands more failed to reach their Promised Land and many were sent back to mainland Europe to face uncertain futures. In 1942 the *Struma*, carrying Romanian Jews escaping the Holocaust, was told it would not be allowed to berth at Haifa and the ship subsequently sank, causing a great loss of life.

On 21 April 1948, Haifa became the first major city to be controlled by the Jews after the end of the British Mandate and the UN Partition Plan in 1947. The city expanded rapidly, becoming the backbone of the country's heavy industries.

Urban transport is good in Haifa (it even runs on Shabbat) but it can be a difficult city to get around, especially on foot. Few routes, aside from downtown, are flat and straight. Most switch back up **Mount Carmel**, giving increasingly wonderful views as they go. The sites are well spread apart and so the first thing to do is study the street maps in order to work out the most energy-effective routes.

The **Carmelit subway** is both a transport system and a tourist attraction. This very steep Metro line is a fast, cheap and efficient means of getting up and down Haifa's various levels. The terminal station is located on Jaffa Road, a few blocks north of the port entrance and not far from the old railway station. It goes direct, every 10 minutes, misses out all of the switchbacks and is faster than a *sherut* or a bus. There are six stops in all:

1. Place de Paris (lower terminus, port area).
2. Solel Boneh (Hassan Shukri Street).
3. Ha-Nevi'im (Hadar business district, tourist office).
4. Masada (Masada Street).
5. Eliezer Golomb (Eliezer Golomb Street).
6. Gan Ha-Em (Central Carmel, upper terminus).

Hadar

Hadar Ha-Carmel, the Glory of Carmel, is the commercial part of town, located halfway between the port and the Central Carmel residential section.

Herzl Street in Hadar is good for just strolling and window-shopping. Street vendors sell a variety of refreshments (depending on the season). Freshly boiled corn on the cob can be combined with a freshly squeezed fruit cocktail—and all for just a few shekels.

Further up the hill from the Haifa Baha'i Gardens, on Zionism Avenue, is the lovely **Mitzpe Ha-Shalom** (Peace View Park), that contains the Ursula Malbin Sculpture Garden. Amid the pleasant surroundings of trees, shrubs and lawns there are 18 bronze sculptures by Ursula Malbin depicting men, women, children and animals at play. The view from here is a truly magnificent one. On a clear day you can see all of Haifa, Akko, Nahariya and sometimes north all the way to Rosh Hanikra at the Lebanese border, plus the mountains all around.

Central Carmel

Haifa boasts Israel's largest national park—**Carmel National Park** (or "Little Switzerland" to the locals), 10,100 hectares (25,000 acres) of pine, eucalyptus and cypress forest. It covers much of the Carmel mountain range, and is well, endowed with picnic areas and playgrounds. Take bus 92 from the central bus station.

HaTechnion, the Israel Institute of Technology, is a 120 hectares (300 acre) university campus in the Carmel hills. The views of the city, the bay, the coastline clear to Lebanon and the snow-topped Syrian mountains can be stunning. Since this campus is on the tourist trail, a **Visitor Centre** (tel. 04-294464 or 294446) has been established to give out information. There's a free 25-minute film shown at 9 a.m., 11 a.m. and 1 p.m., showing the different kinds of modern technology being researched and taught here. To reach the Ha Technion, take bus 17 from the Central Bus Station, bus 31 from Central Carmel, or bus 19 from Hadar at Daniel Street.

The Baha'i Shrine and Gardens

Haifa's most obvious and most impressive sightseeing attraction is the golden-domed Baha'i Shrine and Gardens, reached from Zionism Avenue (bus 22 from the port, or bus 23 or 25 from Hadar). Haifa is the international headquarters for the Baha'i faith, considered by its followers to be one of the world's major religions, despite being a mere baby in comparison to the others. Baha'i leaders claim their faith has some 4 million adherents, and because of its universalism, this figure is rising fast (for details of Baha'i history *see* pages 73–4).

The Baha'i gardens, with their stone peacocks and eagles and delicately manicured cypress trees, are peaceful and very pleasing to the eye. In the centre of these gardens, the domed shrine entombs the remains of the Bab, the forerunner to the founder of the Baha'i movement, Baha'u'llah. Complete with ornamental goldwork, the shrine is open to visitors from 9 a.m. to noon daily; shoes must be removed before entering and you must be modestly dressed. The gardens are open until 5 p.m.

On a higher hilltop stands the Baha'i International Archives building, modelled after the Parthenon in Athens, and the Seat of the Universal House of Justice, with 58 marble columns and hanging gardens behind. These are administrative buildings, not open to tourists. They, and the shrine of the Bab, all face toward Akko, the burial place of Baha'u'llah.

The Baha'is have plans to erect more buildings on this site with the new ones likely to be just as ornate as the present ones. However, the original architect of one of these (the eventual House of Worship) has since ceased to be a Baha'i so his grand plans will probably have to be changed now.

Baha'is try to come on pilgrimage to Haifa at least once during their lifetime; if they can't they donate money instead.

Shrine of Baha'u'llah and the gardens at Bahji just outside Akko.

The stunning golden-domed Baha'i Shrine contains the remains of Bab, the forerunner to the founder of the Baha'i movement.

The Shrine and gardens are funded by Baha'i donations from around the world. Non-Baha'is are not allowed to donate cash for the Shrine's upkeep.

To get to the Shrine and gardens take bus 22 from the central bus station, or numbers 23, 25, or 32 from HaNevi'im Street.

A few kilometres away another Baha'i monument can be visited, with yet more gardens. This is Bahji, the place of delight, just outside Akko, the mansion where Baha'u'llah lived during the last years of his life. Over the entrance to this mansion is an Arabic inscription, engraved into marble, which was written in 1870 just before Baha'u'llah came:

"Greetings and salutations rest upon this mansion, which increaseth in splendour through the passage of time.

Manifold wonders and marvels are found therein, and pens are baffled in attempting to describe them."

Baha'is take this to mean that Baha'u'llah's stay in the Mansion was in

The seat of the Universal House of Justice in Haifa.

some way foretold. He is buried near to the mansion in a relatively simple one storey tomb that, according to Baha'i literature "has not yet received the magnificent embellishment destined for it." It is the most important place of pilgrimage for Baha'is, more important than the Shrine of the Bab on Carmel.

The gardens at Bahji are impressive. Radiating from a circle, many pebbled paths converge upon central edifices, forming large quadrants. One of the gardens is terraced and has been likened to the hanging gardens of Babylon.

The gardens (tel. 04-812763) are open daily from 9 a.m. to 5 p.m. They are easily reached by car; drive for about 10 minutes along the Akko–Nahariya road. Or take bus 271 from Akko and alight when you see the sign Shammerat.

*T*he Jezreel Valley from Mount Carmel. This was the site of many Old Testament battles and is said to be the site of the final battle at the end of time: Armageddon.

The **Stella Maris French Carmelite church**, monastery, and hospice (PO Box 9047; tel. 04-337758) is situated on Stella Maris Road, across the street from the Old Lighthouse. The monastery served as a hospital for Napoleon's soldiers during his unsuccessful siege of Akko in 1799. The pyramid in front of the church entrance stands as a memorial to these soldiers, bearing the inscription "How are the mighty fallen in battle," from King David's lamentation over Saul and Jonathan (*Kings II, Samuel 1*).

The church, open daily from 8.30 a.m. to 1.30 p.m. and again from 3–6 p.m., is notable mainly for the cave situated below the altar which is believed to have been inhabited by Elijah.

Port Area

Opposite the *Af-Al-Pi* ship (*see* below) is the lower terminal of the **Haifa Aerial Cable Car** (tel. 04-510509). It rides from the beach at the western end of Bat Galim up to the tip of Mount Carmel, the site of the Old Lighthouse and Stella Maris. The round aerial cars, imported from the Alps, are equipped with recorded information about what you can see as you fly along. The cars run daily from 9 a.m. to 11 p.m. in winter, until midnight in summer (closed on Shabbat). Buses serving the cable car: 26, 28 and 31 to the top terminal; buses 40, 41, 42 and 44 to the bottom terminal.

The large ship on display on Haganah Boulevard is the blockade-busting **Af-Al-Pi** ("In spite of"). After its sterling service during the British Mandate years, it is now a memorial commemorating all the ships that defied the British blockade to smuggle immigrants into Israel. Here also is the **Clandestine Immigration and Naval Museum**, a look at an exciting but desperate attempt at human-smuggling. Open Sunday and Tuesday from 9 a.m. to 4 p.m., on Monday, Wednesday and Thursday to 3 p.m., on Friday until 1 p.m., closed Shabbat. Buses 3, 5, 43, 44 and 45.

From the *Af-Al-Pi*, it's just a short walk up to **Elijah's Cave** (tel. 04-527430), below the Stella Maris lighthouse and the Carmelite Monastery. Tradition has it that Elijah hid here when fleeing the wrath of King Ahab and his infamous wife, Jezebel. In common with many biblical sites in Israel, a Christian tradition attempts to link New Testament characters historically to the Old: the cave is also said to be one of the places where the Holy Family found shelter for a night on their return from Egypt. The cave is holy to Jews, Christians, Muslims and Druse, all of whom venerate Elijah. To Muslims Elijah is the ecologically-sound, forest-living, "Green Prophet". Open in summer Sunday to Thursday from 8 a.m. to 6 p.m., in winter until 5 p.m., Friday hours are 8 a.m. to 1 p.m. all year round, closed Shabbat. Dress modestly. Buses: 43, 44 and 45.

Museums

Next to the old Mercaz railroad station in Bat Galim is one of the most unusual museums in Israel, the **Dagon Grain Silo**, otherwise known as the Archaeological Museum of Grain Handling in Israel. On display are earthen storage jars, mosaics and various exhibits showing the development of one of man's oldest industries—the cultivation, handling, storage and distribution of grain. Far more fascinating than it sounds, the museum is free and there's a free tour of the plant itself daily (except Shabbat) at 10.30 a.m.; tel. 04-664221 for reservations. The public is admitted only at the time of the tour, or by appointment. Take one of the following buses: 10, 12, or 22.

The **Haifa Museum complex** at 26 Shabtai Levi Street (tel. 04-523255), not far from the Ha-Nevi'im Carmelit station in Hadar, contains several museums of interest. The **Museum of Ancient Art** displays archaeological collections of Mediterranean cultures from the beginning of history until the Islamic conquest in the 7th century. The **Museum of Modern Art** holds some unusual modern works of art. Various lectures, art films, and slide presentations are held in the evenings. The **Museum of Music and Ethnology** has displays of ancient Jewish origin plus African, Asian and American Indian tribal art. Hours are 10 a.m. to 1 p.m. daily except Friday, on Tuesday,

> **Beaches**
>
> Haifa has many good beaches, some of which are so good you have to pay to enter. The *Carmel Beach* (Hof Ha-Carmel) can be reached by buses 3, 44 or 45 from Shapiro Street. *Hof haShaket*, a pay-beach in the harbour area of Bat Galim. is open with a lifeguard all year round, and can be reached by buses 40, 41, or 42. *Bat Galun* swimming pool and sea beach is on the opposite side of the small Bat Galim promontory, but is not as nice as the above. The free *Municipal Beach* is next door. There's also a public beach at *Kiryat Haim*, a Haifa suburb reached by bus 51.
>
> South of town, heading toward Tel Aviv, are a number of other good public beaches, including *Hof Zamur* and *Hof Dado*. Most of the beaches are made up of fine white sand, and are generally very clean.

Thursday and Saturday there are extra hours, from 6–9 p.m. Buses 10, 12 and 22.

The **Reuben and Edith Hecht Museum of the Archaeology of the Land of Israel**, Hebrew University (tel. 04-257733), contains many unique archaeological items illustrating the theme of "The People of Israel in the Land of Israel." Buses 24 and 37will get you there.

Haifa's **Railway Museum** (tel. 04-564293) in the port area has a number of large exhibits of interest to the train-buff. There are also displays of photographs, timetables, tickets and other memorabilia. Hours are 10 a.m. to 1 p.m., Sunday to Thursday. Take buses 17, 42 and 93.

Grouped together at 124 Ha-Tishbi Street, on the north-west edge of Gan Ha-Em Park in Central Carmel, are the **Museum of Prehistory** (tel. 04-337833), the **Zoo**, (tel. 04-371833/372886), and the **Biological Institute**. Visiting hours for the museums are 8 a.m. to 2 p.m. Sunday to Thursday, and 10 a.m. to 2 p.m. on Shabbat, closed Friday. Zoo hours are Sunday to Thursday from 8 a.m. to 4 p.m., on Friday until 1 p.m., on Shabbat from 9 a.m. to 4 p.m. Take buses 22, 23 and 31, and the Carmelit subway (Central Carmel stop).

The **National Maritime Museum**, 198 Allenby Road, not far from the *Af-Al-Pi* (tel. 04-536622), covers 5,000 years of seafaring on the Mediterranean and the Red Sea. Opening hours are Sunday to Thursday from 10 a.m. to 4 p.m., on Shabbat to 1 p.m., closed Friday. Take buses 3, 5, 43, 44 and 45.

The **Israel Edible Oil Museum** (tel. 04-670491) is another unusual Haifa museum. It is situated in the Shemen Oil Factory in the industrial section of Haifa. Many fascinating items connected with the oil industry in Israel, from 2,000 years ago up to the present, are housed in the original, old stone factory building. Edible oil museums are not common in this world so it gets full marks for originality! Hours are Sunday to Thursday from 9 a.m. to noon, closed Friday and Saturday. Take bus 2.

Near Haifa

Haifa is the most natural base for touring around the north of Israel. Nowhere in Israel is that far away; after all you can drive the entire length of the country in about 10 hours.

The two Druse villages of **Dalait el-Carmel** and **Isfiya** are located a 20-minute drive from Haifa. Both villages are lively, interesting places. Souvenir-hunting is very good here with lots of bargains, but more importantly you should find many unusual gifts or mementoes which you won't find elsewhere in Israel. The hand-crafted items, new or antique, are the choicest items. Bear in mind that the markets will be closed on Friday, the Druse Sabbath. Buses 92 and 93 take about half an hour from Haifa's central station.

A 5-minute drive south of Daliat-el-Carmel is the monastery at **Muhraka**, the place where Elijah got the better of the prophets of Ba'al (bus 92). As well as an imposing statue of Elijah, there is a tranquil Carmelite monastery, open daily from 8 a.m to noon, closed for lunch, then open until 5 p.m. (on Friday until noon only). The view, like just about everywhere else on Mount Carmel, is terrific.

Akko

Akko (Acre to English-speakers) is within sight of Haifa, just across the bay. It has a sprawling new town but is far better known for its 200-year-old Arab town, ancient Turkish fortifications, and vast, subterranean Crusader city. This airy, underground city is unique. It lies directly beneath old Akko and predates it by approximately 600 years. The Crusaders first came here in 1140, but Akko has a much longer history than that. It was originally a Phoenician port and was assigned to the Israelite tribe of Asher (although they failed to conquer it—see *Judges 1:31*). Akko was one of the busiest commercial ports of its day and was much prized both for its port and for its strategic location on the coastal road linking Egypt and the Lebanon. Consequently it was much conquered, and, to last the many sieges, it became much fortified.

Today's old city was built by an Albanian adventurer, Ahmed, who became the Turkish pasha El-Jazzar ("the butcher"). The city, in its many heydays, had plenty of important visitors—Julius Caesar, St Paul, Francis of Assisi and Marco Polo all passed through.

Akko is a city for walking round: absorb the atmosphere, tour the Crusader city, walk alongside the Ottoman fortifications, and buy from the Arab *shuq*; or you may want to take a boat trip and see the walls from the water.

*A*kko continues to echo to the sound of the Crusaders—the port that they built still stands, 800 years after they were first here.

The **Mosque of El-Jazzar** is the third-largest mosque in Israel, and the most important one outside Jerusalem. It dominates this grandiose city with its large green dome and piercing minaret and was built in 1781 on what is believed to have been the site of San Croce, the original Christian cathedral of Akko.

Opposite the Mosque is the entrance to the **subterranean Crusader city**. Only the area that was originally known as the "Hospitaller's Quarter" is open to tourists, but this is enough to feel the immense scale of the place. Excavations have been halted because of the danger of collapse. This complex of buildings was once above ground, but the place was buried by El-Jazzar who built his citadel above the city rather than have to dismantle the very secure fortifications and foundations. Its main sites include:

The **Entrance Hall**. Three huge pillars guard an enormous entrance hall, a hall worthy of any great European cathedral. The frescoes on the pillars are mainly Crusader in origin; the arabesques date from the Ottoman period.

The **Crypt of St John**. The hiding place and escape route of the Crusader knights, later adapted by El-Jazzar to serve as a means of escape if Napoleon, who laid siege to the place in 1799, broke though his defences.

Yehi'am, a ruined Crusader Fort, was used by the Crusaders as a protection and as an early-warning beacon.

*T*he walls of Akko port have witnessed many attackers—repelling most, surrendering to the rest. The fortifications were rebuilt by Arab rulers after the Crusaders.

The **Municipal Museum**. This is excellent on local archaeology, Crusader weaponry and folklore, and Islamic art and culture. There are regular guided tours and film presentations in English.

The Crusader city is open from Saturday to Thursday 9 a.m. to 4.30 p.m., Friday 9 a.m. to 2 p.m. A short, instructive film, *3,000 Years: The History of Akko*, can be seen at the Crusader city and is useful for placing the town within its historical context.

Like its counterparts throughout Israel, the Akko *shuq* is noisy, smelly and pure pleasure. Of particular interest apart from the standard stalls are several *khans*; quadrangular inns with large inner courts where travellers and their caravans camped in days gone by. The best among them is **Khan el-Umdan** (Inn of Pillars), just past the Isnan Pasha mosque. It is possible to climb the old clock tower for a lofty view of the city. Near this *khan* is the **Akko Marina**. During the summer months, Arab fishermen take tourists out in boats for tours of the sea walls or you can hire boats (motor or pedal) without an accompanying guide.

The **Museum of Heroism** (tel. 04-913900), a monument to the Jewish resistance during the fight against the British after the Second World War, is situated in the imposing Citadel, 10 Haganah Road. This stronghold, with a very large inner courtyard, was used as the central prison by the British, (and by the Turks before them who imprisoned the founder of the Baha'i faith, Baha'u'llah, here). It was the setting, in 1947, for a spectacular prison break of 49 Jewish prisoners (29 escaped, 9 were killed, and 11 were recaptured). Open Sunday to Thursday 9.30 a.m. to 5 p.m., Friday 9.30 a.m. to noon, Shabbat 9.30 a.m. to 4 p.m.

The imposing Crusader bastion **Burj el-Kommander** (Commander's Fortress), at the northern corner of the city, is one of the best places to view the extensive battlements and bastions built by El-Jazzar. To enter the watchtower, climb the steps that begin where Weizmann Street crosses the wall. Akko has historically been known as one of the most impregnable ports in the East. The view from Burj el-Kommander will confirm this. The city walls originally stretched around the entire port, but all that remains of the harbour walls today is the ruined Tower of the Flies, the site of the original lighthouse. The original fortifications were destroyed by an earthquake in 1837.

When you have had your fill of history, head down to what some say is the finest beach in the country, **Hof Argaman** (Purple Beach). Follow Yonatan HaHashmonai Street from the Land Gate south along the coast for about 5 minutes, taking the route around the naval school. The beach is in front of two large hotels. You have to pay for the privilege of entering, but the added attractions of a gym, a sauna and other leisure activities soften the blow somewhat. The beach is owned by the Palm Beach hotel who operate a Country Club from here. Strictly speaking, only hotel guests and Country Club members can gain access, but usually tourists can pay a day-use fee. In the peak summer season, numbers allowed onto the beach can be restricted so it may be wise to ring ahead and check. Tel. 04-916691.

Kibbutz Lohamei HaGheta'ot

This kibbutz, on the way from Akko towards Nahariya, was founded by Death Camp and Warsaw Ghetto survivors. A museum, **The Ghetto Fighters' House** (tel. 04-820412) is dedicated to the "fighters of the ghettos", in Hebrew *lohamei haGheta'ot*. The museum displays the rich and vital cultural life of the Warsaw Ghetto as well as paintings, drawings, sculptures and prints by both prisoners and survivors. The work of Yitzhak Katznelson, a poet who perished in Auschwitz, is chronicled here.

The museum open from Sunday to Thursday 9 a.m. to 4 p.m., Friday 9 a.m. to 1 p.m., Shabbat 10 a.m. to 5 p.m. Bus 271 from Akko.

Nes Ammim

Nes Ammim is a Christian kibbutz situated between Lohamei and Nahariya, founded in the 1960s to show Christian solidarity with the Jewish state and to improve Jewish–Christian understanding. There are usually about 120 residents from various European countries who combine agricultural work in the kibbutz with study programmes on

Jewish life and history, and the rich cultural heritage of all groups within Israel. Day visitors are given a guided tour, and can stay for longer in the guest house or hostel, set in beautiful grounds with a swimming pool (tel. 04-825522).

Nahariya

Nahariya, the northernmost town on Israel's coast, is a lively beach town with fine white sands and many leisure amenities. There are many good cafés, pubs and discos and the place is especially busy at weekends. At Lag Ba'Omer, Nahariya is packed with Israeli honeymooners, because this is the only available day for Jews to get married in a six-week period stretching from Pesach to Shavu'ot.

The town was founded in 1934 by German Jews hoping to make their living by agriculture. However, this area's greatest natural resource was soon realized to be its beach—a holiday resort was developed, and from early on it became a honeymooners' town. Horse-drawn carriage rides are available but are very expensive, although the carriages can take up to ten people.

On a hill near the town's shore, a small Canaanite temple of the 18th–17th centuries BC was discovered in 1947. Aside from this, there is no real history to Nahariya and it is rather more of a pleasant place to stay in between imbibing the culture around and about this part of the north. It is also a useful stopping off point for the sea caves of Rosh Hanikra.

As Nahariya is a resort town there are many hotels, but as the tourist trade is seasonal, prices can increase by an amazing amount if you come here at peak periods.

Rosh Hanikra

Famous for its sea grottoes, Rosh Hanikra is the most northerly point on Israel's Mediterranean cost. The Lebanon frontier post is also here and Beirut is only an hour's drive away. The sea-carved **grottoes**, embedded in the white chalk cliffs, are reached via a small cable-car. The crashing of the waves against the interior of the cliffs is the main attraction and the worse the weather, the better the effect. It is best to visit the caves early in the morning because the queue for the cable-car, which takes you down to the first platform, can often get very long in the afternoon.

The waters around here can be treacherous but powerful swimmers do risk them.

Christianity's Inland Sea and Mysticism's Most Revered Green Hills

The Galilee is mountainous and green, easily Israel's lushest region, an area of great natural beauty. With its grassy slopes, fertile valleys, rolling hills and majestic mountains, it is a fine touring area. Also the region is packed with sites of special significance and interest—especially to Christians.

The Galilee

First and foremost the Galilee (in Hebrew, HaGalil) is known for its association with the earthly Jesus. He based his short ministry in this area and performed eight of his eleven most famous miracles on and around the Sea of Galilee (Lake Kinneret). The Galilee region is also important for its connection with learning and mysticism: Safed, Peki'in and Mount Meron being sites of Jewish pilgrimage.

T he beautiful Italian Church on the Mount of the Beatitudes, built with help from Mussolini where Jesus gave the Sermon on the Mount.

The area is not all cerebral, however, but is also an outdoor lover's paradise. Adventure sports and hiking are both very popular; if you have the energy after touring the more obvious sites you could receive instruction in such pastimes such as climbing, mountain biking, horse-riding, gliding, or white-water rafting. There are also many parks, nature reserves and animal sanctuaries, where diverse flora and fauna can be found in natural settings. More than 400 species of bird make their migratory path over the Galilee on the journey from Africa to Europe, stopping off for a breather at the Hula Nature Reserve and the fish ponds of the Jezreel Valley. Consequently, ornithological holidays are often based in the Galilee.

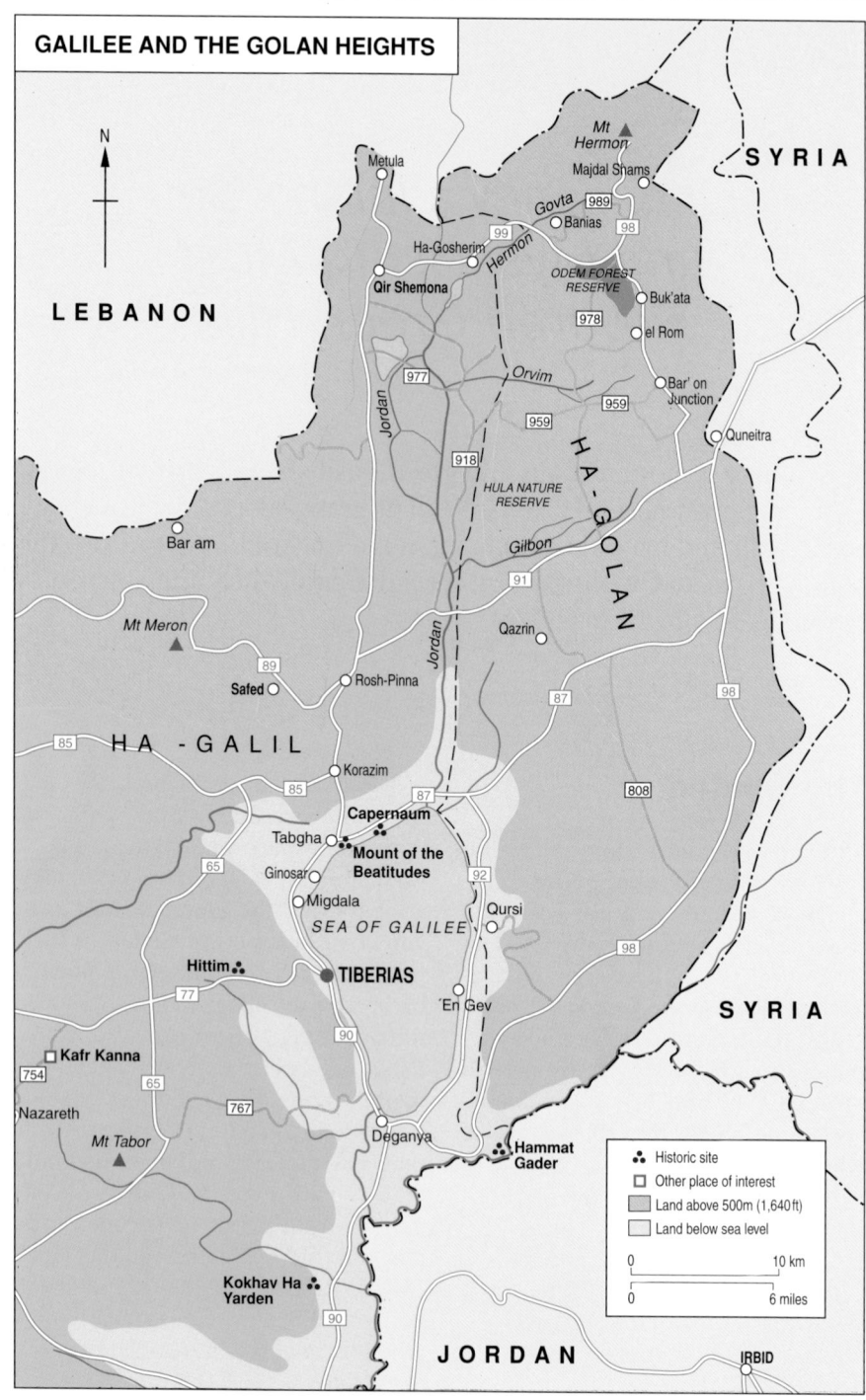

GALILEE AND THE GOLAN HEIGHTS

N

SYRIA

Mt Hermon

Metula

Majdal Shams

Govta

989

Banias

98

LEBANON

99

Ha-Gosherim

Hermon

Qir Shemona

ODEM FOREST RESERVE

Buk'ata

978

el Rom

Jordan

977

Orvim

Bar' on Junction

959

959

Quneitra

918

HULA NATURE RESERVE

HA-GOLAN

Bar am

Gilbon

91

Mt Meron

Jordan

Qazrin

89

Safed

Rosh-Pinna

87

98

HA - GALIL

85

Korazim

85

87

808

Capernaum

Tabgha

Mount of the Beatitudes

65

Ginosar

92

Migdala

Qursi

SEA OF GALILEE

98

Hittim

TIBERIAS

77

'En Gev

SYRIA

Kafr Kanna

90

754

65

767

Nazareth

Deganya

Mt Tabor

Hammat Gader

Kokhav Ha Yarden

90

JORDAN

IRBID

∴	Historic site
☐	Other place of interest
▨	Land above 500m (1,640 ft)
▨	Land below sea level

0 _____ 10 km

0 _____ 6 miles

*V*iew over the ruined temple area at Megiddo. The round platform made up of stones in the foreground was for sacrifices—it was a "ba'ma", a biblical High Place.

The Galilee region stretches northwards from Haifa and eastwards to Nazareth and the Sea of Galilee. It is bordered by Lebanon, Syria, Jordan and the West Bank. There is a basic geographical subdivision: firstly, the Upper Galilee, a rugged area of lush vegetation and fertile valleys, including

*T*he region of the Galilee and the Golan Heights.

the lofty towns of Safed and Rosh Pinna; and secondly, the Lower Galilee, typically Mediterranean in look and feel, with rolling hills and fertile plains, including the towns of Nazareth and Megiddo.

Since 1948, the Galilee has known much conflict and the area has been bitterly contested by Israel and her neighbours. This fighting is nothing new, as the many ancient walled towns and fortresses illustrate.

Megiddo

Kibbutz Megiddo, on route 66, looks fairly insignificant, but the *tel* of Megiddo looms large in Christian Apocalyptic thinking. Har-Megiddo, as the place was known in biblical times, is said to be the location of the "battle of last things"—the Armageddon. The ancient town was destroyed so many times and by so many different conquerors that its name became synonymous with all-out war and total destruction. The Revelation of John in the New Testament (*Revelations 16:16*) picked up on this tradition and predicts earthquakes and great hailstones "heavy as a hundredweight" for the area at the end of time.

Megiddo lies in a strategic position overlooking the Jezreel Valley and has been militarily important since ancient times. Thutmose III (1504–1450 BC) of Egypt remarked that "the capture of Megiddo is the capture of 1,000 towns." Today there are 20 layers of mostly unreconstructed ruins.

The long tunnel burrowing from inside the old city to the spring outside the walls is reminiscent of Hezekiah's Tunnel in Jerusalem and was built around about 600 BC. It is still accessible today. There is a small museum near the entrance of the site containing exhibits and models that help to explain the layers of excavations (at one point 21m [70ft] deep) and the long history of the *tel.*

Today Megiddo is a designated national park. The **Megiddo Archaeological Excavations** are open Sunday to Thursday 8 a.m. to 4 p.m., Friday 8 a.m. to 3 p.m. A car is advisable to get you here, but bus 823 leaves Nazareth for Megiddo every hour during the morning, and every 30 minutes from noon to 7.30 p.m.

Nazareth

Nazareth, the home town of Jesus, is today populated predominantly by Christian Arabs. It is a sprawling, dusty town that is much visited because of its holy associations. It is dotted with

Nazareth from the air, with the Basilica of the Annunciation in the centre.

> **Reader at the Synagogue**
> Jesus' local synagogue was in Nazareth, and he used to read here as recounted in *Luke*. "…Jesus returned in the power of the Spirit into Galilee...And he came to Nazareth, where he had been brought up; and he went to the synagogue, as his custom was, on the sabbath day. And he stood up to read." *Luke 4:14–17*.

the churches, convents and monasteries that have been built here since the 6th century. Situated in the Lower Galilee on a slight elevation north of the Jezreel Valley, it is made up of two "towns" forming a sort of natural amphitheatre. The first is the old **Arab Town**, where the Christian sites are located; and the second is the thriving Jewish town of **Natzeret Illit** (Upper Nazareth).

Nazareth is dominated by churches. The **Franciscan Basilica of the Annunciation**, the most visually arresting of them, is a complex of two churches built in 1966 over the remains of earlier structures. It covers the traditional site of the Virgin Mary's house, the **Virgin's cave**, where the archangel Gabriel appeared to Mary to herald the birth of Jesus (*Luke 1: 26–31*). It is a very modern-looking church, with some stunning internal murals. Open Monday to Friday 8.30 a.m. to noon and 2 to 6 p.m., Sunday and feast-days 2 to 6 p.m.

Across the square is **St Joseph's Church**, where you can look down on the cave thought to be Joseph's house. Remnants of an older church lie beneath, and stairs lead down to caves where grain and oil were once stored. The Greek-Catholic Church in the centre of the animated *shuq* is the site of the synagogue where Jesus is said to have preached as a young man.

Uphill from the bus station, on Paul VI Street, you come to **Mary's Well**, the water of which is said to heal all ailments. Bearing left from the well and continuing uphill, you come to the **St Gabriel Greek Orthodox Church**, which stands over the town's original water source. The original church was erected in AD 356 over the spring where Mary drew water and where the Greek Orthodox believe Gabriel appeared to Mary. The present church, built in the 18th century, has some exquisite paintings, wall-hangings and tiled mosaics.

Nazareth today is a large town, much different to the tiny hamlet it would have been in the first century (indeed, it never gets a mention in the Old Testament). The traditions surrounding most of the holy sites are comparatively late and you won't get much of a feeling of the town as it was. After so many years of imagining Christian sites, pilgrims are often disappointed with the reality. Huge, ornately decorated churches cover the traditional sites of miracles, births, deaths and so on. They are often a far cry from the simple biblical sites of the imagination.

Kfar Kanna

Kfar Kanna, the New Testament **Cana**, a village to the north of Nazareth, is where Jesus rebuked his mother for pre-empting his calling, but then turned the water into wine anyway. "This, the first of his signs, Jesus did at Cana in Galilee, and manifested his glory." (*John 2:1–11*). Pretty undistinguished today, the village at least has a religious feud: the Franciscans believe their 19th-century church stands over

the spot where the miracle occurred; the Greek Orthodox posit their own church. Modern experts refute both claims: Kfar Kanna is not the biblical Cana at all. They prefer Khirbet Kana, 10km (6 miles) away.

The Franciscan church, which is the one with the white towers, is worth a visit. Direct buses leave for Kfar Kanna every 45 minutes from Nazareth, or take the number 431 to Tiberias and alight at the village.

Mount Tabor

In the ancient Middle Eastern religions, mountains were often considered holy; they reached up to the heavens and were thought to be the residence of the gods. For instance, Mount Sinai was the home of the weather god, wrapped in clouds, who later became Yahweh, the single Hebrew God; and, of course, Mount Zion in Jerusalem was the home of Yahweh too. The Old Testament expressly teaches that these two mountains are the only holy mountains of the Hebrews, but when the Hebrews moved into Canaan, they came into contact with other holy mountains and other gods. They could either destroy these other cults (for instance Elijah winning Carmel from the priests of Ba'al) or absorb them into the Hebrew

T he Basilica of the Annunciation in Nazareth was consecrated in 1969, and built on ancient foundations over the spot where the Angel Gabriel is supposed to have told Mary of the birth of Jesus.

religion. For the most part the other mountains were absorbed. Mount Tabor was one of them.

Mount Tabor, 35km (21 miles) south east from Nazareth, was an important cultic mountain from early times. Sacrifices were offered here and esoteric cults are also hinted at in the Bible (*Hosea 5:1*). However, Tabor, which stands on the edge of the Jezreel Valley is more famous for two events—firstly the rout of the Canaanites by Deborah and secondly the Transfiguration of Jesus. Deborah, one of the biblical Judges, saved the Israelites after they "again did what was evil in the sight of the Lord." Here she led the 10,000 Israelite soldiers into a victory over the Canaanite army of King Jenin. As was the biblical wont, she slaughtered her foes, "...all the army of Sisera fell by the edge of the sword; not a man was left", and General Sisera had a tent peg hammered into his temple, "until it went into the ground, as he was lying asleep from weariness." (*Judges 4–5*).

In the Bible, the Transfiguration of Jesus, "the appearance of his countenance was altered, and his raiment became dazzling white..." (*Luke 9: 28–36*) takes place on an unnamed mountain, but a 4th-century Christian tradition has Mount Tabor as the spot. During the Transfiguration, Jesus talked with Moses and Elijah, a device to show the ascendancy of Jesus over the great Hebrew prophets. God announced his approval and the validation of Jesus by saying, "This is my beloved Son, with whom I am well pleased."

Today, two churches, the ruins of a 13th-century Arab fortress and a monastery sit on the top of Mount

Tabor. The **Basilica of the Transfiguration** looks old, but was in fact built in 1924. Inside, above the altar, is a golden mosaic depicting the Transfiguration.

The top of the mountain is reached after a 3km (2-mile) ride along a dirt road. Cars can manage the ascent, but it would be more authentic to walk. Site open daily, 8 a.m. to noon and 3 p.m. to sunset.

Nearby is the **Toledot Ha'Yshove Museum**. It has impressive exhibitions on life in the region before the First World War and on the Jewish and Arab settlers who came to live here in the 19th century.

Tel Bet She'an and Environs

Despite having some very impressive Roman remains, **Tel Bet She'an** is not visited all that much (after all, the Galilee has much else to occupy the curious). However, the Roman amphitheatre, built in the 2nd century to accommodate 8,000 spectators, is superbly preserved and well worth a visit. It is probably the finest Roman building in Israel, and certainly the largest. Open Shabbat to Thursday 8 a.m. to 5 p.m., Friday 8 a.m. to 4 p.m. (tel. 06-488045). Buses 415 and 412 from Afula.

The Byzantine **Monastery of the Noble Lady Maria**, north of the *tel*, has been abandoned since about AD 614. Today surrounded by grimy buildings, it has some wonderfully ornate 6th-century mosaic floors.

Five kilometres (3 miles) north west of Bet She'an, at the foot of **Mount Gilboa** is the lovely and very popular park of **Gan HaShlosha** (known locally as the Sakne, which is Arabic for "warm", a reference to the warm waters which bubble up into the pools). It dates back to Roman times and there are waterfalls, exotic flowers and swimming holes full of the most welcoming water. There is also an underwater cave that can be easily reached. Shallow areas have been created that are suitable for children. Changing rooms are available and there is a restaurant and a café on site. Open daily 7 a.m. to 5.30 p.m.

Tiberias

Tiberias is a thriving resort town with a lively nightlife and plenty of daytime attractions. However, during summer the place can be extremely humid due to its location 200m (330ft) below sea level.

Founded in AD 18 as a spa-centre, it was built by Herod Antipas (the son of Herod the Great) and named in honour of the Roman Emperor Tiberius. After the Roman destruction of the city and temple of Jerusalem, Tiberias became the centre of Jewish life in the Holy Land.

It was here, in about the 3rd century, that the Mishnah (edicts of Jewish law) was codified and the "Jerusalem" Talmud edited. The Sanhedrin, the great court of scholars and rabbis, met here. Rabbi Moses Maimonides, known as Rambam, the mediaeval doctor, sage and philosopher lived here; his poorly signposted tomb is on Y Ben Zakkai Street. Tombs of other great rabbis are dotted around Tiberias. Along with Jerusalem, Hebron and Safed, Tiberias gained the title of one of Israel's holy cities.

Tiberias is justly famous for its curative hot springs. One lies a short distance out of town, but there are two in the downtown area. All are well signposted and easy to find. Also well worth a visit is the Galilee Experience on the waterfront, which unfolds the history of the region every hour (tel. 06-723620).

*S*pring flowers in the hills near Tiberias, overlooking the Sea of Galilee.

*W*ines from the Galilee are exported all over the world—those "Kosher for Pesach" are unique.

The Sea of Galilee (Lake of Kinneret)

The **Sea of Galilee** is surprisingly small, its circumference being only 58km (36 miles), but for Christians it is hugely important as it is here that Jesus performed four of his major miracles. Its sheer beauty, and the fact that it is relatively unspoilt, means it is no disappointment. Boat trips leave regularly from Tiberias and other points on the lake, or you could take an evening cruise with musical accompaniment.

Travel around the Kinneret is easy with a car (you will probably want to make frequent stops) but is much more difficult by bus.

The Sea of Galilee: a Circumnavigation by Road

The old village of Magdala, 3km (2 miles) north of Tiberias, is the birthplace of Mary Magdalene. Apart from the white houses and tall eucalyptus trees, there's not a lot to visit but the view from the road is worth a 5-minute halt.

A little farther on, amongst the banana plantations, is the Kibbutz Ginossar (tel. 06-792161). The kibbutz museum has a fisherman's boat, preserved from Jesus' time, found when the water level in the Kinneret was terribly low. There is also a fine kibbutz guesthouse, Nof Ginnosar (tel. 06-792161), which as well as providing good four-star accommodation hires out kayaks, pedal boats and windsurf boards for use from its private Kinneret beach.

North from Ginossar is the modern **Church of the Multiplication of the Loaves and Fish** (tel. 06-721061) at Tabgha. Search out the fine mosaic floor. The rock inside the church is the rock upon which Jesus is said to have placed the bread and fish when he fed the 5,000 (*Mark 6:30*). It was used as the altar in a church erected over the spot in the 4th century. The present church, built upon Byzantine foundations, was erected in 1980–1982.

Carrying on around the lakeside, signposts will direct you to the **Mount of the Beatitudes**. It was on this high hill, just beyond Tabgha, that Jesus gave his famous Sermon on the Mount (*Matthew 5–7:29*). Today, a beautiful Italian church stands on the spot where Jesus preached to the multitude. It was built with the help and encouragement of Benito Mussolini. The views from here are unbeatable. The church is open daily 8 a.m. to noon and 2.30 to 5 p.m.

On from the Mount of the Beatitudes and down by the lakeside is **Capernaum**. In the days of Jesus, Capernaum was a large border town between the kingdoms of Antipas and Philippas. It was the home town of Peter the fisherman, and perhaps four more of Jesus' original disciples. It figures largely in the New Testament and much of Jesus' ministry revolves around the town. At the excavated ruins, Peter's House (or what could have been Peter's House, and it certainly can't be disproved) can be explored, and there is a 2nd- or 3rd-century synagogue, which may stand on the site of the synagogue of Jesus' day. The site is open daily from 8.30 a.m. to 4.15 p.m.

Near where the Jordan River flows out of the Sea of Galilee, about 8km (5 miles) from Tiberias, is the oldest kibbutz in Israel. Founded in 1910, **Deganya Alef**, known as *em hakvutzot* ("mother of the collective settlements") is the birthplace of the great military leader and amateur archaeologist, Moshe Dayan. It was attacked in the 1948 War and a burnt-out Syrian tank, which was stopped by a homemade grenade, symbolically reposes on the kibbutz lawn. Today Deganya Alef is a prosperous community, with a thriving diamond tool factory and a museum, Beit Gordon. This is split into two parts: "Regional Settlement from Prehistoric Times to the Present" and "Flora, Fauna and Minerals."

Beit Gordon is open Sunday to Thursday 9 a.m. to 4 p.m., Friday 8.30 a.m. to 2 p.m., Shabbat and holidays 9.30 a.m. to noon.

View from the Sea of Galilee up to the Mount of the Beatitudes.

Church of the Multiplication of the Loaves and Fishes at Tabgha. Inside is the rock on which Jesus is said to have placed the loaves and fishes when he fed the 5,000.

*T*he Sea of Galilee in the distance is surrounded by green fields, most of them owned and worked by the many kibbutzim in this area.

There is an all-day ticket, the Minus 200, available from Egged Tours (tel: 06-791080/725306). This offers you the advantage of being able to get on and off all day long for one set price, and the ticket includes site and restaurant discounts. However, the buses do not come round very frequently and it can be an annoyance waiting for the next scheduled service. For the young-at-heart, an excellent way of slowly circumnavigating the Kinneret is by bicycle. In Tiberias, bicycles are available for hire from the Aviv hostel on HaGalil Street (tel. 06-720007) and Cal Gal at the central bus station (tel. 06-736278). Protect yourself from the sun

(especially your head) and drink plenty of water. Shorts may be fine for cycling, but you will need long clothing for entry into the various churches en route.

A short distance south east from Kibbutz Deganya on the Galilee are the hot baths of **Hammat Gader**, close to the Jordanian border. These baths were well known in Roman times. The Roman ruins here are impressive, with several large bathing areas and a smaller pool that was set aside solely for lepers. At the south-west corner of the complex is the hottest spring in the area, at 51°C (120°F). It was named *Ma'ayan HaGehinom* in Hebrew, meaning "the Pool of Hell". Today the waters have been diverted to a modern pool and bath-house. They are very much worth a visit, especially to smear on some of the sticky, black Tiberias mud, but it can get crowded. The 18 radioactive sulphur springs are claimed to alleviate certain skin conditions, but are also great for just relaxing in.

Hammat Gader is becoming famous for its alligator farm. The original beasts were specially imported from Florida and today can be seen gliding ominously through their pools. **Kibbutz Ha'on**, not that far away, has an ostrich farm.

Hammat Gader is a short drive from Tiberias or take bus number 24. Bear in mind that the last bus back is at 2.15 p.m. on weekdays and 12.15 p.m. on Fridays.

Peki'in

Peki'in is the place where Rabbi Shimon Bar Yohai and his son, Eliezer, fled after the 2nd-century Bar Kokhba revolt and a Roman decree prohibiting Jews from studying the Torah. For over 10 years, the learned pair hid in a small cave in the hillside, sustained by the miraculous gushing of a nearby spring and the fruiting of a carob tree. During their sojourn they are traditionally supposed to have composed the Zohar, the seminal work of Kabbalah (Jewish mysticism, from the Hebrew word meaning "revelation", a revealing to the select of great secrets). However, scholars now agree that the work was in fact very European and that it was typical of ideas current in the 13th-century Jewish communities of Spain. It is believed that it was probably composed by the person who claimed to be the work's discoverer, Moses de Leon of Granada.

Despite the claim of forgery, or at least deception (a claim current at the time), the Zohar and its esoteric teachings spread like wildfire through the European Diaspora. A spiritual gap had been found in Judaism, a faith which is not, in essence, a mystical

---

Castle in a Natural Setting

Another Crusader castle, 10km (6 miles) south of Montfort, and on the road from Nahariya to Safed, is the little-visited Yehi'am. The kibbutz here has bed-and-breakfast places and is a pleasant and relaxing spot to spend some time—with exploration of the castle then being an unhurried affair. Whilst neither as grand nor as imposing as Montfort, Yehi'am has some extensive ruins, most of which are easily accessible. There is good access for disabled people. When the ruins are lit up on a clear night they can be seen from Nahariya.

The castle itself was built by the Order of the Templars at the end of the 12th century AD and they called it the Fortress of Judin. It was destroyed in 1265 by the Mamelukes in preparation for a siege on Montfort. Not until 500 years later, in the 1760s, did restoration take place when the ruins were incorporated into a palatial stronghold of an influential Sheikh, Dahar el-Amr.

Today the site is administered by the National Parks Authority and there is an admission charge.

The kibbutz on the castle's doorstep has been awarded national prizes for its contribution to nature tourism—a fact borne out by the name of the tourist part of the kibbutz, Teva Yehi'am—Nature of Yehi'am. Tel. 04-856057/856058.

---

religion. Earlier forms of Jewish mysticism had been concerned with finding God through the experience of ecstatically visualizing Elijah's chariot as it ascended to Heaven. The Kabbalah went much further and the Zohar became the second Torah (the mystics claimed that the Zohar, as an oral tradition, was given to Moses at the same time as the Torah, but that it was only passed down through a select few).

Safed

High in the Galilean hills, built on three slopes and the home to scholars and artists, is Safed (also Tzfat, Tsfat, Sefat or Zefat). This holy city is a place of overwhelming beauty—tranquil, pious and good-looking. In the summertime it is cooler than the plains below and becomes a favourite Israeli escape from the heat.

Aside from its very obvious physical attractions, Safed is also spiritually important; the Jewish cemetery hereabouts contains the graves of some of Judaism's most important and influential rabbis. In the 16th century, it was made the centre of the Kabbalah, a town of great learning. Today it is still mainly populated by religiously orthodox Jews.

Safed, along with Hebron, Tiberias and Jerusalem, is one of the four holy cities of Judaism. The Chassidim believe that the Messiah (note that Jews do not believe Jesus was the Messiah, they are not waiting for a Second Coming but still wish for the First) will travel from Mount Meron to Safed before ushering in the New Age at Jerusalem.

Originally built by the Canaanites and then settled by Jews during the time of the Second Temple, Safed was not an economically important town until the time of the Crusades (it is never mentioned in the Bible). The Crusaders built the citadel that you can still see today. With the influx of Jewish refugees from the Spanish Inquisition, Safed grew in importance, and by the 17th century possessed 18 schools, 21 synagogues and a large religious seminary with 20 teachers. In 1759 a deadly combination of earthquake and epidemic put an end to further growth, and by 1764 only 60 families were left. However, just over 10 years later Safed was bolstered by the arrival of 300 Chassidic Jews from eastern Europe. By the late 19th century, Safed had become predominantly Arab, and in the 1948 War of Independence, the town was bitterly fought over because of its commanding position in the centre of the northern Galilee. Pockmarked buildings, the police station especially, stand as evidence of the ferocity of the gun-battles. All 12,000 Arab residents fled when Israeli forces stormed the town.

Today Safed is a peaceful resort, ideally located in a beautiful setting and a natural home not only for the pious but also for the many artists who live, work and sell from studios spread throughout the town. The city can be divided into three sections: the Park Area, at the top of the hill (bounded by Jerusalem Street); the Artists' Quarter, down at the bottom of the hill; and the Old City, to the north of the Artists' Quarter.

Just off HaPalmah Street is the **Shem va Ever Cave**, one of the many sacred caves in the locality. It is believed to be

Chassid at prayer.

Jew wearing a prayer shawl.

where Noah's son, Shem, and great-grandson, Ever, studied the Torah (although as the Torah was supposed to have been written by Moses many generations after these two biblical figures lived, no logic can explain how they could have studied a Holy Book that did not exist). When the cave is locked, ask the caretaker in the nearby synagogue if he will open it for you.

The **Artists' Quarter** lies to the south west of town and is full of a variety of studios and galleries. Many are coach-party orientated and sell unimaginative prints and watercolours. However, diligent searching will turn up much of merit: the avant-garde work can be stunning. Prices, do of course, rise dramatically the more original the artist. The **General Exhibition Hall**, housed in an old mosque, gives a good representation of what is available. Head down from Jerusalem and Arlosov streets. Opening hours for the quarter vary but are generally l0 a.m. to l p.m. and 4 to 7 p.m.

The **Old City** (also called the **Synagogue Quarter**) is a maze of tiny cobbled streets and dark alleyways. Your best bet for navigation is to buy a map or get the free street-plan from the tourist office at 23 Jerusalem Street. Of the many synagogues in the quarter, there are two worthy of closer examination, the **Caro Synagogue** and the **Ha'Ari Synagogue**.

In the 16th century, Yosef Caro penned The Shulkan Arukh, the seminal work on Jewish daily ritual, within the walls of the synagogue that now bears his name. The Ha'Ari Synagogue is famous for its association with Rabbi Isaac Larry, who introduced the Kabbalat Shabbat, the Kabbalistic preparation for the Sabbath.

Close to the Caro synagogue is the **Ethiopian Folk Art Centre** which displays and sells the beautiful and unusual artwork of Ethiopian Jews. In the late 1970s and early 1980s the Israeli airlift, Operation Moses, secretly transplanted Ethiopian Jews out of Ethiopia and into Israel, to save them from religious persecution and starvation. Today the Ethiopian community is gradually integrating into normative society.

The Chassidic community that lives here today is made up of a number of sects—each one of which can differ widely from the rest, the religious rivalry often being intense. The sects are Bratslaver, Lithuanian Mitnagid and Habad. Despite this rivalry, most of which will be invisible to the casual observer, the Chassids come together for special occasions—the festival of Purim is the most visually appealing. Safed at the time of Purim is a special place.

As you walk around Safed notice the preponderance of two colours: blue mainly, but also lots of green. As with much Kabbalistic thinking, the world is perceived through symbols. Blue symbolizes *malkhut* ("God's reign as king of the world"), and green symbolizes *tsmihat hage'ulah* ("the growth of redemption"). Blue-topped tombs lie, higgledy-

piggledy, in the cemeteries on the western side of the Old City. You can't miss them, and the sloping ground, fantastic light and scenic tombs are a photographer's delight. At most times of the day there will be Chassidic Jews tending the tombs or praying, and this adds to the charm.

According to a local legend, seven Jewish brothers, whose torture is recorded in the *Fourth Book of Maccabees*, are associated with Safed. The *Book of Maccabees* is part of the *Apocrypha*, a compilation of 14 Jewish books not included in the standard Bible (although included in the New English Bible). The tortures inflicted upon the brothers by their Syrian opponents are very graphically described, but the details are given in order to show the power of faith over bodily passions. The brothers refused to eat meat that was not Kosher and all died violent deaths. Their mother, later given the name of Hannah, did not flinch. She too preferred keeping the Holy Laws rather than saving her offspring (*4 Maccabees 15:1–4*). According to Jewish Rabbinical Law, you can transgress most laws if a life is threatened (murder, incest and idolatry count among the exceptions). Hannah and her sons are meant to be buried somewhere hereabouts; legend says you will know where by a sudden feeling of empathy and fatigue. However, Antioch, in Syria is the more likely place for their burial.

Various legends and stories can be gleaned as you walk around the place but for the complete picture, a 2-hour walking tour offered by a commercial organization (opposite the City Hall on 2 Jerusalem Street, tel. 06-930012) is worth while if only for the trivia.

The tourist information office (tel. 06-920633) also gives daily tours of the Old City leaving from the office on Jerusalem Street.

The Zohar can best be described as an encyclopaedia of occultism and meditations on God, the universe and science. These mystic elements were a way out of the rigorous logic and immutable laws of the Talmud. Kabbalah tried to experience truth and religion by intuition; the Talmud searched with the aid of reason. Kabbalah was a return to an earlier form of religion, a return to "mythology" in which truth and religion could be symbolized and explained. In myth the persecuted Jews could find an escape from the indignities of mediaeval life. The Kabbalah gave them the feeling that they could control their own destiny. They could influence the coming of the Messiah rather than waiting for him helplessly. It was a strong anti-authoritarian message, but one that took Judaism in a vice-like grip. By the 16th and 17th centuries, it was a major force and the Galilee had become the major centre.

You are not meant to study Kabbalah until you've reached the age of forty, just to make sure of your intellectual maturity; so any visitors to Peki'in of forty or over can safely expand their knowledge of this wonderfully esoteric branch of Judaism by visiting the small museum situated in the synagogue near the cave. Youngsters will just have to wait!

Peki'in is a non-Muslim Arab village with a mixed Druse and Christian population. It is also noted for being the only place in Israel where Jews have resided continuously since Roman times. Today it is well known for simple Druse cafés that serve fragrant Turkish coffee and pitta-sandwiches made from very thin bread brushed

> **Marks of Respect**
> The stones and rocks you may see on the surface of the tombs in any Jewish cemetery are marks of respect for the occupants within, and not security against them rising again!

with olive oil, *za'ata* (a tangy ground herb) and *labaneh* (sour cheese). The pitta bread is usually baked in front of you and is much thinner than the normal Arab "pouch-bread".

Bus number 44 from Netanya will get you here, but a car would make the trip a lot easier.

Montfort

Montfort is a lonely fortress, ruined but imposing, clinging to the side of a steep, wooded gorge near the town of Mi'ilya. It was built in the 12th century to protect and administer the domains of the lords of the manor at Mi'ilya. Unlike other forts and defensive citadels, Montfort had no other strategic purpose other than this protection, a relatively minor role for a Holy Land fort. Once constructed, however, it became its own reason for existing.

Lost to the Muslims in 1187, it was regained by the Crusaders in 1192, and in 1228 was sold to the Order of the Teutonic Knights of St Mary. They improved the fortifications, translated its French name to Starkenberg, and were so impressed by it that they transplanted their whole headquarters here from Akko.

A good path leads down to the gorge, and you reach the fortress from its south side, which is its most dramatic angle. It is very scenic around here and the view of the fortress and the woods makes an ideal picnic spot.

The Hula Valley

In the early part of this century, the **Hula Valley** was a swamp: stagnant and malaria-ridden. The early Zionist settlers, after great effort and much loss of life, drained the swamps and created farmland; a modern miracle worthy of many in the Bible. Amongst the fields, certain areas have been set aside as nature reserves. The finest of these, the **Hula Nature Reserve** (tel. 06-937069), is situated south of Kiryat Shmona, the travel-hub of north Galilee. It is rich in flora and fauna—pelicans, heron, wild boar and water buffalo have all made their home here. Migratory birds are especially populous and the best way to see them is to go to the observation tower in the middle of the reserve.

Buses 841 or 511 leave hourly from Kiryat Shmona and will get you close to the reserve. It is open Sunday to Thursday 8 a.m. to 4 p.m., Friday 8 a.m. to 3 p.m. The visitors' centre has static exhibits and a 15-minute film show to help you identify the animals and plants on the reserve (or, as is more likely, this is a chance to see the animals you missed, because of their innate shyness!). Other reserves close by include Ayun, Hurshat Tal and Tel Dan. Contact Nature Reserves Authority, 78 Yirmeyahu Street, Jerusalem (tel. 02-513253).

With a small waterfall and pleasant walks, the **Ayun** reserve is a worthwhile detour into the far north of the country. Metulla, the nearest town, is the northernmost town in Israel.

Hurshat Tal National Park is famous for its ancient oak trees, some of which may date from the 1st century and the time of Jesus. The Dan River, a tributary of the Jordan, passes through the valley, collecting in a large man-made pool, where you can swim. The park is open from 8 a.m. to 4 p.m. daily (tel. 06-942360).

Tel Dan

Tel Dan was a thriving Canaanite town when Joshua led the Israelites here over 3,000 years ago. In fact Dan was the northern limit of the Promised Land (the southern limit was Be'er Sheva). Today the *tel* is part of the **Tel Dan Nature Reserve**. Many cold-water springs gush right up from the ground here, forming the Dan River, one of the three principal sources of the Jordan River. In fact "Jordan" is a contraction of the Hebrew term *Yored Dan*, "descending from Dan". This river descends indeed—all the way down to the lowest point on earth, the Dead Sea 265km (165 miles) away. Open daily 8 a.m. to 4 p.m., until 3 p.m. on Friday (tel. 06-951579).

In the nearby Kibbutz Dan is a nature museum, **Bet Ussishkin** (tel. 06-941704), covering the flora, fauna, geology, topography and history of the region. Open Sunday to Thursday 8.30 a.m. to 3.30 p.m., on Friday until 2 p.m.

The Jordan River

This holy river, so well known from the stories of the Bible, is not exactly the size of the Nile, but is just as impressive in parts. The largest and most important water source in the country, it has three tributaries: Nahal Hermon (Banias), starting as a spring at the foot of Mount Hermon; Nahal Dan, originating in springs flowing at the foot of Tel Dan; and Nahal Senir (Hatzbani), originating in the Hatzbani Springs in Lebanon. The three of them come together south of Tel Dan, near Sde Nehemia, and, after flowing through the Hula Valley, they join to form the Jordan. The three of them bring to the Jordan 500 million cubic meters (100 billion gallons) of water a year.

The Jordan flows into the northern part of the Sea of Galilee, in the Beit Tzida (Betucha) Valley, and is its main water source. In the winter, the Sea of Galilee receives more water from streams that flow into it from the east and west. Salt springs, some of them hot, bubble up from the sea-bed.

Pollution and Problems

The Sea of Galilee provides a quarter of Israel's water. It is therefore of vital importance for it to be kept unpolluted, but there is a conflict between the need to provide water and the desire to retain its quality. Two million tourists a year, the saline springs on the sea-bed, the peat from the Hula Lake that comes after flood run-offs, and the sewage of 120,000 inhabitants in the vicinity all affect the water.

Rising levels of pollution and falling water levels due to droughts could leave the Sea of Galilee severely depleted and contaminated within 20 years. In fact in the summer of 1990, the water fell to its lowest ever level, just 45cm (18in) above the so-called "red-line". If the water falls below the line, increased concentration of salts, phosphorous and algae in the sea could render it unusable.

Conflict over water is a recurring theme in this land. The Syrians and the Jordanians are planning to build the Unity Dam to shore up water from the Yarmuk River. This water is vital to all three countries for human consumption and agriculture. The three rivals (the word rival comes from the Latin *rivalis,* "one sharing the same stream as another") may end up fighting not over oil but over water. Water is life; oil a mere luxury.

The Golan Heights

Mountains with commanding views over plains and valleys have always had a strategic importance for the military. **The Golan Heights** have been fought over since Roman times.

Before the Six-Day War in 1967, Syrian heavy artillery based in the Golan, as the area is simply known, intermittently pounded the kibbutzim in the Hula Valley below. After various losses and gains Israel formally annexed the Golan in 1981. The United Nations does not recognize this annexation and the Golan Heights are officially known as Occupied Territories. A UN buffer zone exists to separate Syria from Israel at this point. Independent touring in the Golan is very difficult, scheduled buses are infrequent and a car is the best option.

Stock up with food and water as eateries are few and far between, and also away from the few kibbutzim and settlements, there is not a lot of human activity. Don't be tempted to leave the paved roads, because not all Syrian land mines have been cleared. Contact the Golan Field School for information on hikes and walks (tel. 06-961234). To save time and trouble you could book yourself onto an organized tour. Egged offers full-day tours of the region from Tiberias on Tuesdays, Thursdays and Shabbat. By far the best tours are the camping trips organized by the Society for the Protection of Nature in Israel. They last two or four days and visit otherwise inaccessible spots, and often include special treats like white-water rafting on the Jordan River.

Banias

Situated scenically on the southern slope of Mount Hermon, **Banias** used to

be a strategically important place, mainly because it lies on the ancient trade route from Akko to Damascus. It is also famous for being one of the main sources of the River Jordan; a very fine waterfall lies close to the actual spring.

The ancient world venerated the forces of nature before they developed the concept of independent gods: special stones, trees and springs were all thought to contain a sacred force, or spirits. For instance, the concept of the altar comes originally from the veneration of standing stones, and both the Ka'aba in Mecca (the main shrine of Islam, said to be the stone of Abraham), and the tablets of stone brought down from Mount Sinai by Moses, were cultic objects long before their later incarnations. Springs, being sources of water, which is itself a sacred element, were similarly considered cultically powerful. The Spring of Banias was venerated from a very early time.

Today the **Cave-Temple of Pan** is the only extant evidence of this veneration. Pan was the Greek god of nature.

Banias is one of the three sources of the Jordan, near the New Testament town of Caesarea Philippi. It was dedicated to local deities in ancient times, and to Pan under Greek influence.

Cultic niches in this cave would have once contained statues of the god. Greek inscriptions of dedication are still visible. The Greek town Paneas which grew up near the cave became Banias through transliteration into Arabic. The Muslims took over the veneration of the Spring and in the place of Pan put their own cultic figure, the prophet Elijah, (also called el-Khadar, "the green one"). The place is also associated with St George, the Dragon Slayer, and is sacred to the Alauwy, an Islamic sect whose members live on the banks of the nearby Hatzbani River.

King Herod the Great built a pagan temple here dedicated to Augustus

Caesar. Herod's son, Philip, expanded the town into a small city and changed its name from Banias to Caesarea Philippi. Jesus came here (*Matthew 16:13*), when it was known by its new name. And, in response to the question "And who do you say I am?", Simon Peter confessed the true nature of Christ, a turning-point in Jesus' ministry, "You are then Christ, the Son of the living God."

Many authorities believe that Jesus may have deliberately selected the heartland of paganism for this unveiling of his true authority; certainly in Jesus' day the place would have been well-known as a hotbed of immorality and "false religion". A small **Greek Orthodox church** nearby commemorates the event. The Crusaders had a town here, too, and some scant remains can still be seen, but little is left of earlier periods. To compensate for this, take a swim in one of the large pools to be found near the Spring.

Close to Banias is an impressive hill-fortress, **Nimrod's Castle**. The present structure was built in the 12th century by the Crusaders, but local legends relate that the structure was constructed by the biblical Nimrod, "...the first on earth to be a mighty man." (*Genesis 10:8*). A plaque above one of the formidable gates reads, in Arabic: "God gave him the power to build this castle with his own strength."

The legend also says that, as well as building the Tower of Babel (which is the next story on in the Bible, *Genesis 11:1–10*), Nimrod built this huge fortress high enough to shoot his arrows up to God. The arrows wouldn't have to go far as the fortress is in a commanding position; there is a very impressive view of the whole region from the top. On a clear day you can see Mount Hermon to the north and the Hula Valley to the south east. Below you can make out small villages populated by Druse. The Druse village of **Majdal Shams** is the highest settlement in the country.

Before the time of the Crusades, Nimrod's Castle was home to members of the Hashishi brotherhood, an extremist Muslim sect originating from Persia that used political killings to further its own ends. Its name may be derived from the fact that its followers smoked hashish as a means of inducing ecstatic visions of paradise before setting out to kill. The Crusaders were impressed by the Hashishi methods of cut-throat negotiation and the word "assassin" entered the English language. Marco Polo, the 13th-century Italian explorer, wrote of being captured by the Hashishi and held "somewhere between Damascus and Jaffa", quite a geographically wide area, but possibly meaning Nimrod's Castle. Marco Polo started the stories, unconfirmed by Hashishi sources, of lush gardens being used to generate a foretaste of the paradise-to-come for the drugged devotees.

After various other owners, including the Crusaders and the Mamelukes Turks, the fort was abandoned and became a sheep and cattle pen used by local villagers. Despite this rather inglorious end, the castle is well preserved and in better condition than most other Crusader forts.

In the Six-Day War, the Syrians used Nimrod as an observation post and mortar position, utilizing the castle's obvious strategic advantage. Modern legend has it that the Israelis did not want

Alternative Guidebooks

The Bible is the best ancient guidebook to the Holy Land, but another excellent tome is *The Jewish War* by the 2nd-century historian and general Josephus. It records the various Roman campaigns against the Jews of 1st-century Palestine and in places makes for graphic reading.

to destroy such a wonderful castle, so they attacked it gently (if such a thing is possible). The Syrians were routed and the Israelis turned the castle into their own observation post. The castle is now a national park and is open daily from 8 a.m. to 4 p.m., and on Friday until 2 p.m.

Gamala

As well as Israel's highest waterfall, **Gamala** is also the site of a mass suicide by Jews, reminiscent of and contemporary to the more famous incident at Masada. During the First Jewish Revolt against the Romans of AD 66–70, the Jews of the cliff-town of Gamala became trapped and, "despairing of escape and hemmed in every way ... flung their wives and children and themselves into the immensely deep artificial ravine that yawned under the citadel." (*Josephus, Book IV, ch.1*).

Today the ruins of Gamala are not up to much, but the location is dramatic, and it needs no great imagination to conjure up images of desperate people jumping to their sure death from the sheer-sided cliffs.

Past the ruins at Gamala, you will reach a look-out point over the **Gamala waterfall**. The falls are more impressive than the ruins. Allow at least 3 hours for the hike and sightseeing to Gamala and the waterfall.

Mount Hermon and Neve Ativ

Snow-capped **Mount Hermon** rises majestically over the surrounding plains and it is easy to see why, from the earliest times, it has been associated with the gods, and later the one God. Its name has two possible sources. Firstly, it could mean "forbidden place", a pointer to its cultic significance. Secondly it may come from the Arabic word *haram*, which means a "sacred enclosure", usually of a temple. A main temple, believed to be quite ancient, has been found on the summit, and various lesser ones, dating from the 2nd century AD, have been identified with Greek gods.

The southern slopes of this mountain today form Israel's version of an alpine ski resort. The summit (2,814m/ 9,232ft) is actually in Syrian territory, so mountain exploration is not to be recommended. The highest Israeli elevation on Mount Hermon is at **Ketet HaHermon** (The Shoulder of Hermon) which rises to 2,220m (7,200ft). Snow caps the mountain all year round, but only in winter can you actually ski.

The moshav of **Neve Ativ** (tel. 06-981341) is the actual "resort village" and here you can hire ski equipment, try a bit of après-ski, and look out onto a tangled web of borders and military no-go areas. As snow can often block the road, making it impassable, it would be prudent to phone ahead to check on conditions.

Basic accommodation is also available; tel. 06-981333. It is best to drive here, but for the intrepid, bus 55 leaves Kiryat Shmona twice a day. The ski season lasts from late December to about mid-April. On Shabbat the slopes can get very crowded.

Salt Pillars and Scorched Earth

Desolate and steaming, the Dead Sea area has fascinated visitors for thousands of years. Wild legends grew up to explain the strange natural phenomena. Another area stimulating awe was the desert wilderness surrounding the Dead Sea. This wilderness has been revered for centuries as a place for cleansing the soul and purging impure thoughts. Today much of the area has been made to bloom, and with Eilat, is one of Israel's best natural playgrounds.

Judean Desert

No visit to Israel would be complete without a float in the Dead Sea. The feeling will be nothing new to an astronaut, but for we lesser mortals the experience is well worth going out of the way for. And the Dead Sea is very much out of the way. Situated on the border between Israel and Jordan, and lying at the lowest point on earth, the Dead Sea is in the middle of a desert:

*D*uring the 2nd century BC the Nabateans built a town in the Negev desert, but how a large population was fed in such a dry place is still a mystery. The ruins can still be seen at Avdat.

the Judean Desert. The same desert that Joshua and the Hebrews entered to start their conquest of Canaan; the same desert to which Jesus retired for his forty days and forty nights in the wilderness; and the same desert of the Good Samaritan.

Today there are tourists and resort villages here. In the past there have been just monasteries, desert dugouts and religious hideaways—both Zealots and hermits being drawn to lives of meditative solitude in the desert cliff-face caves and impenetrable canyons. At the junction of the desert and the Dead Sea is the retreat of the Qumran sect, the Essenes, and the caves where their scrolls, known as the Dead Sea Scrolls, were hidden. To the south is Masada where, in the 1st century, the Jewish

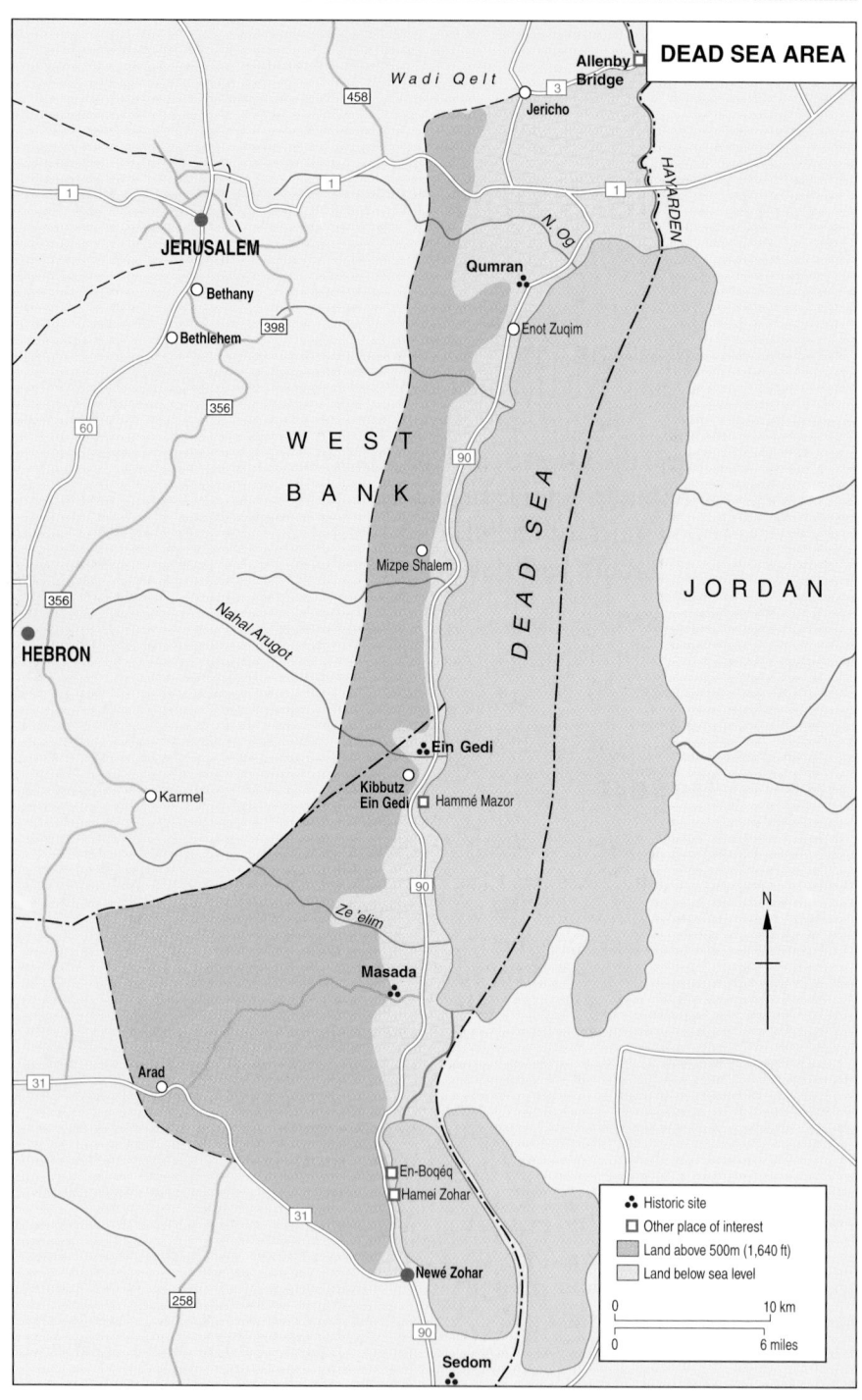

DEAD SEA AREA

Wadi Qelt

Allenby Bridge

458

3

Jericho

1

1

HAYARDEN

JERUSALEM

N. Og

Bethany

Qumran

398

Bethlehem

Enot Zuqim

356

W E S T

B A N K

60

90

D E A D   S E A

JORDAN

356

Mizpe Shalem

Nahal Arugot

HEBRON

Ein Gedi

Kibbutz Ein Gedi

Hammé Mazor

Karmel

Ze'elim

90

N

Masada

Arad

31

En-Boqéq

Hamei Zohar

31

Newé Zohar

258

90

Sedom

Historic site

Other place of interest

Land above 500m (1,640 ft)

Land below sea level

0   10 km

0   6 miles

Zealots took their own lives rather than face defeat at the hands of the Romans. South from Jerusalem, and extending westwards over to Jericho and the Dead Sea, the Judean desert eventually merges into the Negev desert, and down to where Israel gets narrowest is the desert resort of Eilat, surrounded by hazy mountains and watered by the Red Sea.

The Dead Sea and the Red Sea, crossing-point for the Children of Israel, are gouged out of the Syrian-African Rift Valley. This valley extends from Turkey right the way through to southern Africa, one of the longest depressions in the rock crust of the planet. Trekking in the Judean and Negev deserts is a tough but unforgettable experience (*see* pages 276 and 283 for trekking and adventure travel).

Though it makes up two-thirds of the area of pre-1967 Israel, the Negev has only 6 per cent of the population, many of them pioneers in desert reclamation projects. Water from the north has helped to create pockets of productive land: the desert, as they say, has bloomed. The desert can be split up into distinct areas, each with its own particular attractions.

The northern Negev is a region of low sandstone hills, steppes and fertile plains, abounding in canyons and *wadis* (dried-up river beds) in which winter rains often produce flash floods. Be'er Sheva, city of the Patriarchs, has thrived since 1948, its population exploding from 5,000 to over 100,000 today. Other towns have sprung up, Dimona in par-

A French walking party negotiates a small wadi, or dried-up river-bed, near the Dead Sea.

*M*ap of the Dead Sea area.

ticular, famous for its association with Israel's suspected nuclear weapons capability. In 1987 Mordechai Vanunu, a former technician at the Dimona Atomic Research Station, told the world, via the London *Sunday Times*, that Israel was producing nuclear weapons. The hapless Vanunu was lured to Italy by a female *Mossad* (Israeli secret service) agent and shipped back to Israel where he is currently serving a very long prison sentence for treason. This, despite

the fact that the knowledge that Israel had nuclear weapons was useful; Arab armies would think twice before engaging Israel in a fight to the bitter end. Of course, Dimona has no tourist amenities but for followers of modern history a visit to the town and the "facility" just outside can be instructive.

The northern Negev desert is home to thousands of Jewish desert pioneers but its most visibly unusual occupants are the Bedouins. Their black-tented camps grow more sparse as you proceed farther south. Roughly 32,000 Bedouin roam Israel's deserts and hills, an estimated 27,000 in the Negev (with about 5,000 in the Galilee mountains). Until recently they haven't respected border lines very much, but many are now settling down in the development towns.

In the Central Negev to the south, the mountains are higher and the climate drier; it is a tract of bare rocky peaks, craters and lofty mountain plateau. Mitspe Ramon, perched opposite the crest of Mount Ramon (1,035m/ 3,395ft), is still the only town. The craters here are unique to Israel. Quite startling to look at, they are even more impressive to traverse. Specialist desert-trekking companies will guide you through by jeep, camel or foot.

The Arava is an extremely parched stretch of desert between the Dead and Red Seas. It has an average annual rainfall of less than one inch, and summer temperatures are extremely high. On its flatlands, new villages have de-veloped sophisticated winter farming techniques and produce vegetables, mainly for export.

The Eilat Mountains form the southern tip of the Negev triangle. Sharp pinnacles of grey and red granite, broken by dry gorges and sheer cliffs, the brilliant layers of sand glow under the fierce desert sun.

Eilat itself is a modern city of hedonistic delights, Israel's winter playground. Popular with Israelis and tourists alike, Eilat is a fun place to stay, as deeply unreligious as it is brash. It's also a deep-sea port, and is Israel's outlet to Africa and Asia, the terminal of the land-bridge and oil pipeline for Europe and the Mediterranean. To the north of Eilat, the biblical Eloth, are the copper mines of Timna, where Solomon's slaves and workers would once have mined.

There are two basic options for getting to Eilat. The first is to leave from Jerusalem and travel via the Judean Desert and the Dead Sea. The second is to travel from either Jerusalem or Tel Aviv via Be'er Sheva. Both routes have their merits. The most popular for tourists is probably the former because of the higher attractions per square mile.

From Jerusalem to Jericho

The 30-minute drive eastward from Jerusalem to Jericho is easily the best descent in Israel. Starting at 800m (2,615ft) above sea level in Jerusalem, the road careers down through a stark but beautiful desert landscape to the oasis of Jericho at 250m (820ft) below sea level, the lowest city on earth. The black shapes and strips of corrugated iron on either side of the road are small Bedouin encampments. The next time you

The sun sets over another successful day walking through the Judean Desert.

pass they may have moved on to another site. The white shapes and the barbed wire are Zionist settlements. The next time you pass they will not have moved on to another site.

Note: a modern road has been built to bypass **Bethany** and the other Arab towns on the descent to the Dead Sea so that Jews in cars and buses, especially the settlers, can pass without fear of attack. The road described here is the old route, much more scenic, but also a bit more dangerous.

The Inn of the Good Samaritan

Despite the fact that it was a parable (*Luke 10:30–36*) there is still a tradition marking out the spot where the Good Samaritan took pity on the injured traveller and took him to a nearby inn. Today this spot is on the right-hand side of the road as you travel from Jerusalem, roughly 10km (6 miles) from the Mount of Olives. There is a sign telling you where to pull over but if you're doing anything over 15kph (10mph) you will miss it. Set your mileometer instead. (Buses do not stop here.)

The inn is no longer here (and, as this is part of the ancient route from Jericho to Jerusalem, there is no doubt that a inn of some sort would have existed here in the 1st century) but in its stead is a 16th-century Turkish *khan*. The location is more inspiring than the actual building. Beyond the khan, the road descends into the **Valley of the Pomegranates** (Wadi al Rummaneh). A little further along and you will see a sign pointing out that you're now at sea level, which is odd considering how far you still have to descend.

The early morning or at dusk is the best time to watch and photograph the changing colours of the desert. Here dusk sharpens the desert shadows.

Just before the final descent into the Jordan Valley, a right turn off the road leads to **Nabi Musa**. This, according to Muslim belief, is where Moses is buried. There are a number of desert-brown tombs here (Muslims feel that the burial place of a prophet is an excellent spot for their own burial) and a simple mosque.

The views of the desert, the Jordan Valley and the hills of Moab in the distance to the east from the minaret are superb from here.

oasis town can be considered the birthplace of civilization—it was the growth of "cities" that led to states, countries, nations and empires. Subsistence agriculture slowly changed into cropping agriculture which developed surpluses; men could divert their attention away from tending the fields and could expand their horizons. Man has never looked back—we can blame Jericho for starting the trend.

Jericho today is a resort town with a balmy winter climate (September–April are the best months as in summer the temperature often soars into the 40s°C

Jericho

Claimed to be the oldest city in the world, **Jericho,** the "City of Palms", is a fascinating place to spend a day. However, since it is part of the West Bank it is advisable to find accommodation further along at some of the Dead Sea resorts, or climb back up to Jerusalem. In many ways this small

A view of modern Jericho that shows well its title of "City of Palm Trees". The view here is looking east towards Jordan, the direction from which Joshua probably came to conquer the town.

[over 100° F]). It used to be very popular with the Arab world, although since 1967 Arab tourists have all but dried up. The historical sites are good here but even more importantly the restaurants and cafés in Jericho are some of the best in the West Bank, excellent for Arab delicacies and especially good for fresh fruit and vegetables.

The name Jericho probably derives from the Hebrew word for "moon", *yereah*, because the town was once the main cultic site of an ancient moon religion. Jericho's importance as an oasis town derived from its perennial spring, **Ein al-Sultan** (Elisha's Spring), which would have enticed mesolithic nomadic hunters to settle down here. The oldest of some 23 successive settlements excavated here dates back to around 8000 BC; settlements known elsewhere are almost 2,000 years younger, and the pyramids were constructed 4,000 years later!

Around 1200 BC, Joshua and the invading Israelites destroyed Jericho, then a Canaanite city of great strength. Only through the actions of a seven-day "religious" siege and the fortuitous sounding of ram's horn trumpets did the wall "fall down flat" (*Joshua 6–7*). Later in the Bible, King Ahab refortified the city, and Elisha purified the water of the spring with a sprinkling of holy salt (*II Kings 2:19–22*). Jericho was visited by Jesus several times; here, he restored the sight of a blind beggar (*Luke 18:34–43*) and on the Mount of Temptation, he spent forty days and forty nights contemplating his calling.

In the Byzantine period, the centre of population shifted from the site of the old city, Tel al-Sultan, to the site of the present town. A magnificent palace was

Wadi Qelt
This valley, a walker's paradise should you care to spend a day or so without the car, stretches all the way from Jerusalem to Jericho. Monks have inhabited this spectacular valley since the beginnings of Christianity, initially in caves, later building monasteries and hermitages throughout the area. Of the many that once existed here, just the **Monastery of St George of Koziba** remains. It was built into the rockface and hangs over the side of the wadi like some fairy-tale castle. There are about ten monks here today and visits to the chapel can be arranged by just appearing and asking. Don't ask on a Sunday, however.

To see the monastery park your car near the orange signpost, some 6km (4 miles) from the Settlement of **Ma'ale Adumim**, and walk down the stepped track for about fifteen minutes. Another route exists from **Mitspe Jericho** (in Hebrew this means "look-out over Jericho" and sure enough the views are excellent). The monks survived on water from perennial springs, one of which you can see from this last route. **Ain Qelt** is an amazing torrent of water pouring out of the limestone rock. Fed by the winter rains from around Jerusalem, the water collects in underground pockets in the rock and eventually pours out through a fault into the wadi. Wintertime is the best time to see it at full gush. You can't drink the water but it is safe to swim here.

All around are remains of ancient aqueducts from the Hasmonean, Herodian and Roman periods. Some of these still have water coursing through them and again there's a chance for a swim or at least a paddle.

A waterfall in Wadi Qelt turns the desert green.

*V*iewed from on high, Tel Jericho stands out in sharp relief despite its age.

built here in AD 724 by the Ummayad Sultan Hisham Ibn Abd al-Malik. His hunting palace at **Khirbet al-Mafjar** is a wonderful example of the Islamic architecture of the period. The Crusaders renamed the place "New Jericho" and erected a church in commemoration of the Temptation of Christ on the Mount of Temptation.

Although it may not be much to look at, basically a few mounds of earth, **Tel Jericho** (or Tel al-Sultan) is important for its location and history rather than its visible remains. As you come into Jericho look for the soft, brown mounds situated to the north west of the modern town, a short distance from the centre.

Only since the 1950s has Jericho been considered the oldest city in the world. Yet today the archaeological impor-

tance of the site is unquestionable. T[] is due to the British archaeologist Da[] Kathleen Kenyon, who discovered t[] remains of 23 cities and who first p[] forward the claim that Jericho provid[] evidence of the human transition fr[] hunter-gatherer to settled farm[] Amongst the dirt and rubble the m[] important archaeological discovery[] the remains of a 7m- (23ft-) high stor[] age tower which dates from arou[] 7000 BC and would have provided t[] city with an excellent defence against [] tackers; it's certainly the most impre[] sive fortification of its time. To t[] north of this tower lay the cultic shri[] thought to be the earliest structure [] the site.

The city walls that have been unco[] ered are of a much later period, prob[] bly the Early Bronze Age (2600 B[] These may be the walls which fell dow[] when the seven Israelite priests ble[] their rams' horns. Proof for this is i[] possible to find but there is evidence f[] a break in the occupation of the []] around the 13th century BC and th[]

could tally with Joshua's conquest. Open daily 7 a.m. to 6 p.m. in summer, 8 a.m. to 5 p.m. in winter.

At **Hisham's Winter Palace** (or Khirbet al-Mafjar) there are more ruins, this time of more easily recognizable nature. Not much remains of the palace but the impressive ruins make it easy to imagine how splendid this palace would once have been. One of the finest examples of Ummayad architecture in the country, the palace was originally a hunting lodge used by the Ummayad princes in the late 7th and early 8th centuries AD. A small museum, to the right of the entrance, houses a collection of pottery found on the site. The bath-house contains a very fine mosaic, said to be the largest ancient mosaic to have survived intact anywhere. Open Saturday to Thursday 8 a.m. to 5 p.m., Friday 8 a.m. to 4 p.m.

A great slab of mountain looms over Jericho. On the top of this slab is a Greek Orthodox monastery, the **Monastery of the Temptation**, the traditional spot of Jesus' temptation by the devil. To reach the monastery follow the signposts north west out of town and once at the base of the mount 20 minutes of reasonably tough walking will see you to the summit. As with so many hill-tops and vantage points in Israel, the views are superb: the whole Jordan Valley, Jericho included, lies beneath you. The Arabic name of the mountain, Quruntul, derives from the Latin *Mons Quaranta*, meaning "Mountain of the Forty". This is what the Crusaders called it in commemoration of the forty days and forty nights Jesus spent here fasting, when he was tempted by the Devil to end his hunger. Today's monastery, full of some very impressive icons, was built in 1874 around a rock on which Jesus reputedly sat during the temptation. Above the monastery is the ruined Maccabean fortress of Dok. It was here that the Hasmonean leader, Simon Maccabaeus, was murdered by his son-in-law Ptolemy.

A short distance south of the **Allenby Bridge** (the border crossing between Israel and Jordan) is the **Jordan Baptismal Site**, one of the sites where John the Baptist is believed to have baptized Jesus in the Jordan River (*Matthew 3:13–17*). The area is out of bounds now for military reasons and there are alternative sites for the baptism, especially where the Jordan flows out of the Sea of Galilee.

Food in Jericho

Jericho is justly famous for its food, drink and outdoor restaurants. As well as the obvious hummous and falafel stalls there are many fine cafés and restaurants serving a variety of locally grown fresh vegetables and seasonal fruit. Most of the restaurants are found along Ein al-Sultan Street between the centre of town and the tel and offer live music, some of which can be very good as Jericho attracts Palestinian musicians from miles around. Fridays are the best days for music. Many Jericho restaurants offer "all-that-you-can-eat" menus.

Freshly squeezed fruit juices can be found all over Jericho, although the best juices in town can be had from Khalil Walaji at the tel. Apart from the customary orange and grapefruit juices, you can also ask for date, apricot, almond, and walnut juices, or maybe even a mixture. These exotic juices cost at least twice as much as the standard ones but are very different and very refreshing.

Dead Sea

The Dead Sea is the lowest point, the most saline body of water and the area most rich in oxygen on earth. In winter the weather is lovely: warm and balmy. In summer, however, the contrast with Jerusalem is much more severe. The Dead Sea lies deep down in the great Rift Valley and the build-up of heat can be intense. This area is one of the hottest in the country. Indeed the heat hits you like a wall around about **Qumran**. The Dead Sea has no outlet at its southern end so the water evaporates: this leaves behind strangely shaped salt formations and creates an uncomfortable haze with up to 25cm (1in) of water evaporating every 24 hours during summer.

Despite the physical discomfort, the Dead Sea is worth a visit at any time of the year. The area is popular with Israelis, Palestinians and tourists. The public beaches here are just about the only places in Israel where all three get along just fine. The pay-beaches, attached to hotels, campsites and spas, are cleaner and well worth the expense.

The Dead Sea is famous for its high mineral content (up to 30 per cent). There's no animal life as such in the water and you float easily; in fact it is impossible to sink. For these two reasons it would be an ideal dip for a non-swimmer. Strong swimmers can forget front crawl; as soon as they try, they flip over and bounce backwards. Reading a newspaper is the most obvious visual cliché, but there's not a lot else you can do. Just lie back and enjoy it.

The high concentration of minerals is said to be good for curing cuts and bruises, but open cuts will sting as soon as you enter the water. Similarly it would be best to keep your eyes well clear of any splashes or you'll soon find yourself with a sharp stinging sensation and temporary blindness. Also, try to wear sandals and a hat—the sandals protect your feet against sharp stones and hot sand and the hat prevents your head from frying. The water has a very bitter, oily taste should you accidentally get a mouthful. Once you leave the water a white film of mineral residue will form on your body as the sun dries the moisture out. For an irritation-free day rinse this off at the many showers available along the shoreline. The locals leave it on until bedtime. They say it's healthy and good for the skin.

While floating in the Dead Sea, it is possible to read a newspaper once your body is partially submerged; only experts can keep the paper dry!

The Dead Sea Scrolls and Qumran

In 1947 a young Bedouin shepherd was searching for lost goats in the caves above the Dead Sea, at Qumran. To save crawling into one of the caves, he threw a stone in to see if he could flush his animals out, but instead of a goat he heard the breaking of pottery. On investigation he discovered in the back of the cave fifty cylindrical jars containing a mass of scrolls dating from the 1st century BC. These scrolls, many of them containing the earliest known

The narrow caves and niches around Qumran were largely moisture free, and leather and parchment scrolls were, in effect, "preserved" ready for their discovery in 1947.

examples of biblical texts, were a revolutionary find, of immense importance to modern biblical scholarship. In the 1950s, as the text started to be deciphered, the popular press ran sensationalistic stories about the scrolls—maybe here would be proof of the existence of Jesus Christ.

However, the wide-eyed were to be disappointed, for the scrolls were written and stored away not by early Christians, as was first thought, but by the "philosophical" group, the Essenes, described by the contemporary historian Josephus. The Essenes were a sectarian Jewish group who had separated themselves from the Pharisees and Sadducees, and who relied heavily on ritual purity and strict observance of the Jewish law. This group withdrew into the desert after their original leader, the Teacher of Righteousness, rebelled against the perceived religious laxity and Hellenizing tendencies of the Maccabean Temple priests. Whilst still believing in the Temple cult, the Essenes adopted the simple monastic life. This involved abstention from defiling practices (for instance, as they believed firmly in the sanctity of the Sabbath

The canyons around Qumran are dotted with caves and openings in which the Dead Sea scrolls were hidden.

they refrained from relieving themselves on this day), and any contact with the outside world. They had very strict rules concerning religious observance and everyday practice. As a punishment for any transgression, the Essenes (who were all male, although they could sleep with "pure" wives in order to produce offspring) were banished from the community for set periods and had their already meagre rations reduced by a quarter. So, for instance, "Anyone who laughs foolishly with a loud voice shall be punished with thirty days."

The Essenes withdrew into their pure communities around 150 BC and Qumran was the Essene's main religious centre until their destruction in the First Jewish War in AD 68. They believed in the imminent arrival of the Messiah, and saw the end of the world as a battle between the Sons of Darkness and the Sons of Light. They identified themselves with the Sons of Light, and only they possessed the true knowledge of the meaning of the Torah. Many commentators have linked John the Baptist with Essene groups, although similar attempts to link Essene ideas to Jesus have so far proved unsatisfactory.

Qumran today is a right turn off the road from the direction of Jericho. The caves and Essene settlement are close to this turn-off. There's plenty to view but everything is quite low key. There are the remains of a tower, a dining hall, a kitchen and a writing room where the scrolls may have been copied down. It is open Sunday to Thursday from 8 a.m. to 5 p.m. If you're interested in the scrolls themselves, many can be seen at the Israel Museum in Jerusalem, or contact Kiboutz Almog for a film and explanation of the scrolls (tel. 02-945201).

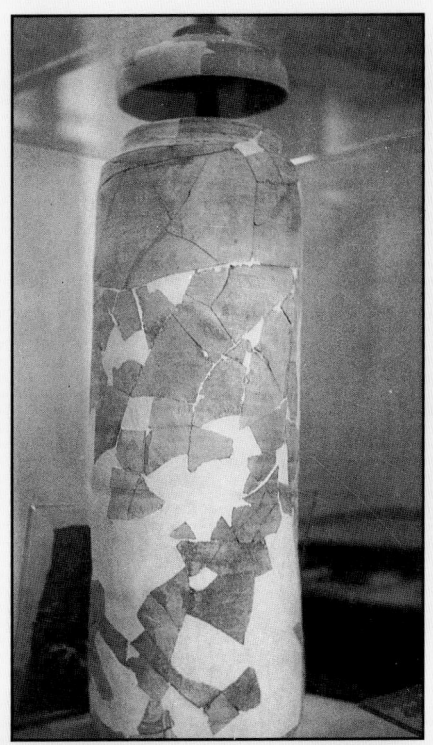

Right: *a restored pot that once held some of the Dead Sea scrolls.*

Below: *example of a Dead Sea scroll.*

*D*ead Sea mud is said to have curative powers and can be purchased all over the world. Here it is free, just dig it out and smear it on!

On some of the beaches you can dig through the shale into the grey, slimy clay and try to find some Dead Sea mud. Watch the locals as they know where the best deposits can be found. Smear it on all over, wait for it to dry and then immerse yourself in the water again. This, also, is meant to be very good for the skin. Psoriasis sufferers come from all over the world for this treatment, which is meted out at the resort hotels and spas all along the Dead Sea coast. However, it's much more fun to find it yourself.

Ein Gedi, or Goat's Spring, is a desert oasis, situated right next to the shores of the Dead Sea. Although now a na-

ture reserve, it has been known as a tranquil spot since biblical times (and most probably before this too). In the *Song of Songs*, King Solomon used the oasis as a metaphor for great beauty: "My beloved is to me a cluster of henna blossoms in the vineyards of En-gedi" (*Song of Songs 1:14–15*).

It was here that David hid in a cave from the wrath of Saul. **David's Spring**, the Ein Gedi waterfall, is still here and is a remarkable sight in the midst of a desert landscape. The spring and the *nahal* (Hebrew for "river-valley") water a thin strip of land that forms the oasis. Animal life is rich here and you should definitely spot ibex and hyraxes (small badger-like creatures). Further into the nahal there are thirteen leopards roaming free. Signs tell you of their presence, but they are said to be a good deal more frightened by your presence

---

Was Qumran the Paris of Palestine?
An interesting new theory has it that Qumran was not an isolated, monastic settlement at all. It was a factory, and it was not Essenes who lived and worked here, say some archaeologists, but perfume makers. The upper storey "dining hall", which once looked out to the Dead Sea was not an austere room of silence but a lively 1st-century works cafeteria.

These views have yet to gain wide acceptance, and at the modern site Qumran is still portrayed as an Essene monastery. But consider this: would an early monastic order really choose to site itself next to a busy highway, only two hours walk away from Jericho, a bustling metropolis? The Dead Sea area was famous for its perfumes in ancient times and Qumran may turn out to be much more secular than is commonly thought.

*K*ing David's waterfall in the lush surroundings of Ein Gedi. Standing beneath the torrent is a truly invigorating experience.

than you will be by theirs. Very few people have seen them, and for a long time they were believed not to exist here at all. Israeli scientists have tracked them down, however, and some of the leopards are electronically tagged so that their whereabouts and habits can be monitored.

This trip into a natural wonderland could very possibly be the highlight of your visit to Israel, as the luxurious growth and cool, clear waters are certainly memorable. As well as natural formations, there are also various excavations and ruins spread throughout the valley. Most are hard to get to and

therefore rewarding for the intrepid. If you're hiking across the Judean Desert you can get into the reserve through the "back door", and then the waterfalls and natural pools seem ten times more wonderful.

However, as the waterfall is easy to get to from the "front" there are many visitors wandering about—watch out for the groups of boisterous Israeli schoolchildren—and only when the place is relatively empty will it feel like paradise. If you get here too early in the morning it won't be hot enough for you to brave the ice-cold water of the falls. Try and come mid-week, spend some time here and definitely go off on a short hike. All of the routes are well waymarked; just follow the rocks with colour-coordinated paint stripes on them. These colours tally up with the ones on large scale Israeli maps (available from the SPNI, 13 Heleni HaMalka Street tel. 02-252793).

The **Nahal Arugot** route takes about six hours to complete. In winter it would be wise to check at the Ein Gedi kibbutz to see if any flash floods are likely. The **Ein Gedi Nature Reserve** is open from 8 a.m. to 3.30 or 4 p.m.

Masada

This imposing hill-top fortress, where Jewish Zealots martyred themselves and their families rather than give in to the Romans, has become a symbol of Israeli pride symbolic of the fact that Jews will fight to the death rather than submit. Every Israeli schoolchild has made the climb up to **Masada** and army recruits often get sworn in here. Masada has a long history. The caves here-abouts were home to neolithic man and the plateau top of Masada itself was inhabited from about 1000–700 BC. The first fortifications here were built by the Maccabees in the 2nd century BC. King Herod the Great improved on these fortifications and built for himself a magnificent, and very safe, palace and fortress sometime around AD 40. He furnished the luxurious palace with every known comfort and laid in storehouses of food and arms, in case he should ever have to flee from his many enemies.

In succeeding years a small Roman garrison occupied the mount. However, during the Jewish revolt against the Romans in AD 66, an army of Jewish Zealots led by Eleazar took over the fortress by surprise. These *Sicarii* (or daggermen, as the Zealots were also known) brought with them their wives and families. 960 Zealots lived off the vast storehouses of food cached here by Herod, and had more than enough arms with which to defend themselves.

The weapons were even put to use in raids on Jerusalem.

Finally, in AD 70, two years after the fall of Jerusalem, the Romans became so incensed with the Zealots sitting well-fed and safe on top of their inaccessible mountain that they decided to lay siege to Masada. However, the plentiful food and huge cisterns full of water meant that the Zealots could not be starved into submission, so Flavius Silva and the Tenth Legion constructed an amazingly ambitious ramp to reach the walls of the fortress. This ramp, still very visible today, is one of the most impressive sights in Israel. The Roman camp, now no more than scratches in the ground, is also visible from on high.

T he Snake Pass to the hill-top fort of Masada. The cable car is quicker and easier but not so much of an achievement.

As soon as the ramp was high enough to reach the walls of Masada, siege engines, flaming torches, rock bombardments, and battering rams took their toll—and the Romans succeeded in breaching the Zealot defences. Eleazar decided he and his men should die honourably; so they decided to kill themselves. From this night of mass suicide two women and five children survived, hiding in one of the water conduits. The Romans, who had expected to fight their way in, were astonished at the lack of resistance and "When they came upon the rows of dead bodies, they did not exult over them as enemies but admired the nobility of their resolve and the way in which so many had shown an utter contempt of death in carrying it out without a tremor." Josephus, *The Jewish War, Book VII, 390.*

At Masada today you can either ride to the summit in a cable car or walk up via the **Snake Path** (so-called because it winds its way up the hill, and not because of the prevalence of any actual snakes). If you climb, especially in the summer months, start early and go gently as the heat can be overpowering. Wear a hat, carry a canteen of water and drink from it regularly. The walk should not take much more than 40 minutes (much less if you're fit) but once at the top there's still a lot of ground to cover.

For an easier route you can also walk up from the Arad side of the mountain, but the views are not so good. This path is called **The Battery**, after the ramp the Romans built here to storm the Zealot stronghold. Walking to the top will take only 15 to 30 minutes. The paths open at 4.30 a.m. and close at 3.30 p.m., and you must start down by then just to get to the bottom before dark.

The lazy can take the cable car, although this is over-priced and you don't feel as if you have worked to get to the top, despite having to manage the last 75 steps by yourself. Why not hike up and ride down? Cable cars operate from 8 a.m. to 4 p.m. on Friday and eves of holidays from 8 a.m. to 2 p.m. (also operates on Shabbat).

Try to see the **Sound and Light** show held on the Arad side of the mountain every Tuesday and Thursday evenings, at 9 and 10 p.m. Tel. 057-958144.

Excavations at Masada have unearthed perhaps the most exciting ruins in the entire country, and certainly the most dramatically positioned. Indeed, many of the extant remains have now authenticated much of what was told in story form by Josephus. You can actually climb into the water cisterns (watch for the rays of sunlight streaming in through the roof). The palace walls can still be seen and even the modern-day toilets are built into ancient structures. Some Israelis believe the synagogue up here may be the oldest one in Israel, although this has yet to be verified.

A very useful guidebook is available at the entrance and as this site is so large it is well worth the few shekels. The black lines painted on the ruins denote the level of the unreconstructed walls.

A short drive from Masada are the **Zohar Springs** (tel. 07-584331/584161), which have naturally hot waters with even more minerals per gram than the Dead Sea. Psoriasis sufferers claim great things for these waters, and for non-sufferers, at the very least a soak here is relaxing. The spa (and hotel) is luxurious,

*T*he ramp that the Romans built to break the siege at Masada was massive and is still impressive today.

expensive and totally self-indulgent. To escape the hot humid air of the real outdoors the spa is equipped with a powerful air-conditioning system, excellent facilities in the sulphur baths and pools, mud baths, vibration and electro-galvanized baths, underwater massages, and cosmetic treatments. The baths are open every day of the week from 7 a.m. to 3 p.m.

Arad

The modern desert town of Arad, a 45-minute climb from the Dead Sea by car, is said to have the cleanest and driest air in Israel (and possibly the world). Consequently it has become a favourite resort town for those suffering from respiratory problems such as asthma or hay fever (the air is also pollen-free). A local bye-law exists forbidding the cultivation of plants which may cause allergies, or factories which may cause pollution.

Arad is not an Alpine village; it looks new, as though it dates from the sixties. Despite this it has a soul, the people are very open and friendly and the village is a surprisingly nice place to stay. Arad is the logical place to find accommodation if you're coming east from Be'er Sheva and you don't want to pay the exorbitant prices of the spa hotels down on the shores of the Dead Sea.

Tel Arad is the main sight in and around Arad, a partially reconstructed 5,000 year-old Canaanite town. Open Sunday to Thursday from 8 a.m. to 4 p.m. October to March, until 5 p.m. the rest of the year.

Driving on the desert road out towards Eilat you will come across the site of a big mineral extraction plant on the thinning-out shores of the Dead Sea. On Israeli maps the city of Sodom is marked here, yet the place hasn't existed since Patriarchal times. In Abraham's time, Sodom was a city that was one of a confederation of five cities: the others being Gomorrah, Admah, Zeboiim and Bela (*Genesis 14:2–3*, and *10, 19*). Sodom lay in the Valley of Siddim ("the Salt Sea", meaning the Dead Sea). The inhabitants of Sodom were considered "wicked and sinners before the Lord exceedingly" (*Genesis 13:13*). The names of Sodom and Gomorrah are often linked: "They commit adultery, and walk in lies: they strengthen the hand of the evil doers, that none doth return from his wickedness: they are all of them unto me as Sodom, and the inhabitants thereof as Gomorrah" (*Jeremiah 23: 14*). Another quotation reads: "For their vine is of the vine of Sodom, and of the fields of Gomorrah: their grapes are grapes of gall, their clusters are bitter: their wine is the poison of dragons, and the cruel venom of asps." (*Deuteronomy 32: 32–3*). Male homosexuality (sodomy) was one of the sins practised here according to the Bible.

Both towns were destroyed by God with brimstone and fire (scientists claim the destruction did indeed occur and say it would have been some sort of volcanic eruption—which actually fits in with the biblical account). Lot was told by angels to escape from the town before its destruction, but he was warned not to look back on the devastation. Lot's wife ignored this warning and she was turned into a pillar of salt. She can still be seen to this day, as a human-shaped pillar is close by to the mineral works.

The landscape hereabouts is weird to say the least. It looks tortured and torn. Clusters of white foam, a solid brine, cling to the dried plants. The smell of sulphur hangs in the air, and some of the trees next to the sea are petrified, with crystals of gypsum and bitumen hanging from them in strange, unusual shapes.

*T*own plan of
Be'er Sheva.

Negev Desert

Deserts are not always rolling vistas of sand dunes. In fact the majority of the world's deserts are rock-deserts, as is the Negev. It has a savage beauty, packed with sites of natural and human interest.

The main town in the Negev is **Be'er Sheva**, famous for being the birthplace of Isaac and Jacob. The name means "Well of the Seven", a reference to the seven lambs that Abraham gave to Abimelech (*Genesis 21:25–34*) as part of their peace settlement. Apart from **Tel Be'er Sheva,** a short distance north east of the town, and the Bedouin market held every Thursday morning, Be'er Sheva is not exciting, and is more of a transit town than an ideal stopover point. You should, however, visit the nearby **Jo Alon Bedouin Centre**, a museum that illustrates the rapidly disappearing way of life of these nomadic people (tel. 07-919889).

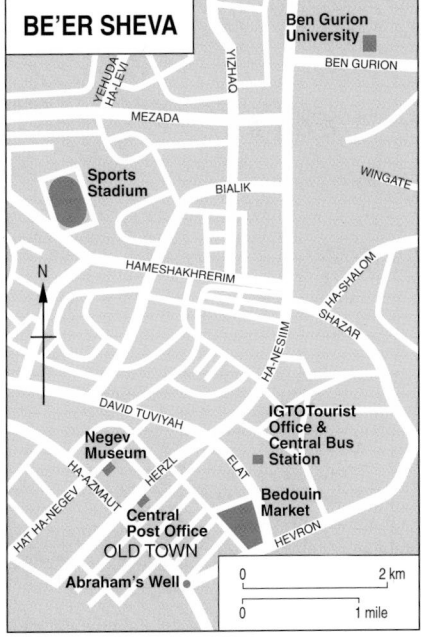

259

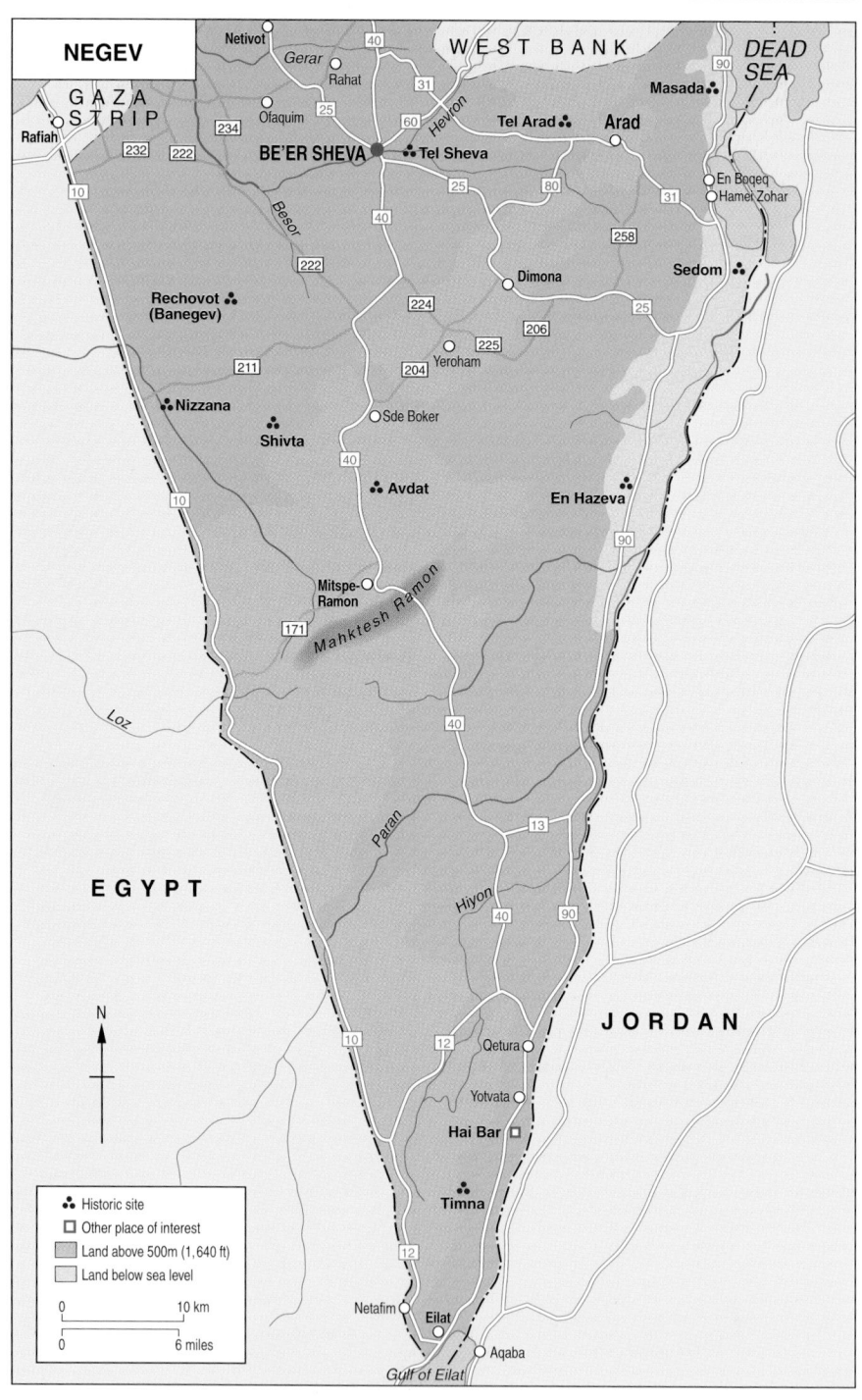

The market is held on the southern fringes of the old city by the junction of the roads to Eilat and Hebron. If you want to buy a camel, a kilo of *baklava* sweetmeats or a case-load of incense, this is the place to come. When trying to buy gifts or souvenirs, such as Arabic brassware or leather products, haggle for all you're worth; don't accept the first price given to you—reduce it by 75 per cent and then work upwards until both you and the vendor can agree on a reasonable price.

A short and sparse drive out from Be'er Sheva will bring you to **Shivta**. The Nabateans, the great desert-dwellers who once ruled this part of the world and who had their capital in Petra, now in Jordan, constructed a way station here in the 1st century BC. Shivta's real heyday, though, came during the time of Justinian the Great when Byzantine wealth and power were at their height. Caravans laden with merchandise and pilgrims seeking out the Holy Land made their way through this town.

Besides this commercial wealth, Shivta's ingenious citizens built an elaborate irrigation system that allowed them to farm the barren soil. However, Shivta's location on major trade routes proved its undoing. When the invading Arab armies, fired by the new and violent religion of Islam, burst out of

Sde Boker and the Home of Ben-Gurion

Deep in the desert is Sde Boker, once home to one of Israel's founding fathers, David Ben-Gurion. His tomb is here and the kibbutz is an Israeli pilgrimage site. Ben-Gurion was Israel's first Prime Minister and he lived at Sde Boker because of its desolation and the fact that from desert was being created farmland—an incredible achievement.

Orchards and green fields sprout from nowhere as you cross the desert. Sde Boker was founded in 1952, at the Prime Minister's instigation, when the country was first encouraging settlers to populate the Negev. His words, "If the State does not put an end to the desert, the desert may put an end to the State," provided the inspiration. He then provided the example by becoming a member of the kibbutz a year later; he lived and worked here till his death in 1973, at the age of 87. He and his wife, Paula, are both buried here. A memorial and small museum exists here today, the Paula and David Ben-Gurion Hut (tel. 07-558444). Open Sunday to Thursday from 8.30 a.m. to 3.30 p.m., on Friday and Shabbat, holidays, and holiday eves from 9 a.m. to 1 p.m.

Arabia in their mission to convert the world—by sword if necessary—Shivta was overrun, and the trade routes moved elsewhere. Shivta stagnated and by the time of the Crusades it was nothing but a ghost town. This was fortuitous because the town wasn't raided by builders for ready-cut stone—its very inaccessibility, away from the new trade routes, meant it stayed largely intact, and today the "ruins" are well preserved and impressive. Buildings include three churches, a mosque, a *khan*, and a number of houses.

*B*e'er Sheva is part modern and part Middle Eastern marketplace. This is Independence Square in the centre of the modern town.

Cut-out metal sculptures of foraging goats at Avdat—one of several such unusual pieces of sculpture to be found here.

Without a car you will get nowhere near Shivta. With a car it can still be a tough drive and you have to skirt a sensitive military area. The rewards, however, are enormous and you may be the only visitors around.

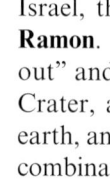

On the old trade route from Gaz to Petra (in modern-day Jordan) the town of **Avdat** was carved out of the forbidding desert during the 2nd century BC by the Nabateans, initially being a mere staging post. The remains of an extensive irrigation system have been found here and Israeli scientists are trying to learn how the Nabateans could feed a comparatively large population in the midst of what is today a desert. Monks used Avdat as a meditative retreat during the Byzantine period. The Byzantine bath-house is one of the best preserved in Israel. The site is open daily and the views over the Negev are superb.

In the middle of the Negev are some of the strangest topographic features in Israel, the largest of which is **Mitspe Ramon**. *Mitspe* is Hebrew for "lookout" and Ramon refers to the Ramon Crater, a huge bowl gouged into the earth, and peculiar to the Negev. It is a combination of the Grand Canyon and the surface of the moon—a wild mix of multicoloured patterns, rock formations and sparse desert vistas. In addition to its fascinating scenery, the crater area contains many types of vegetation and wildlife, as well as sites of ancient habitation. The region has recently been designated a national park, called **Park Ramon**, Israel's largest nature reserve, with visitors' centre, hiking trails, and observation points around the crater (tel. 07-588691).

Forty kilometres (24 miles) to the east of Mitspe Ramon is **Kadesh-Barnea**, noted not for any supreme archaeological remains or superb views but because of its biblical associations. Kadesh-Barnea served as a centre for the confederation of tribes that wandered in the Negev and the Sinai during the time of Abraham; it was also called Enmishpat at that time (*Genesis 14:1–11*). Most of the biblical references to it, however, are connected with the

The Mitspe Ramon is a huge, enclosed crater, teeming with hard-to-spot wildlife.

time of the Israelite sojourn in the desert under Moses. The Bible says they "abode in Kadesh many days" (*Deuteronomy 1:46*); it was from Kadesh that Moses sent 12 men to spy out the land of Canaan (*Numbers 13:26*), and messengers to the king of Edom to request passage through his territory (*Numbers 20:14*). It was also at Kadesh that Moses smote the rock and got water (*Numbers 20:11*), and here that his sister, Miriam, died and was buried (*Numbers 20:1*).

Excavations have unearthed three fortresses built one on top of the other,

guarding the southern border of the kingdom of Judea, the earliest dating from the early 10th century BC, the latest existing up until it met its fate at the time of the destruction of the First Temple in 586 BC. The land here, therefore, is the land of the Bible and the views you see today will have changed very little from the days of the Patriarchs. On the coastal Sharon Plain there were forests in the time of the Patriarchs, and Abraham and his tribe would have great trouble recognizing their hills and valleys, but the landscape here just hasn't changed in thousands of years. It's a humbling thought.

Nevertheless, there has been one change—in days gone by the area would have been teeming with wildlife. Not so today; the best you'll find is at the **Hai Bar Wildlife Reserve**. This reserve is 3,240 hectares (8,000 acres) of safari park. Situated some 40km (24 miles) north of Eilat, its purpose is to save any rare and endangered desert animals mentioned in the Bible and breed them for eventual release into the wild. Among the 450 animals wandering wild here are the Nubian ibex, the Dorcas gazelle, the addax antelope, the Persian onager, the Arabian gazelle, as well as wolves, hyenas, foxes, desert cats, cheetahs, leopards and wild donkeys. There are also many ostriches, and various species of snakes and lizards. If you have sharp eyes, many of these are visible from the road to Eilat.

This breadth of fauna may be one of the reasons why early man could survive in the harsh desert landscape. Up until just a hundred years ago many of these animals were still indigenous to the area. Bedouin hunters, afraid for their domesticated animals, killed off many of the species that you see here today. You can ride around the Reserve in your car (no open-topped jeeps) or see many of the 450 in the enclosed "zoo-area". Open daily from 8.30 a.m. to 1.30 p.m.

Just before you get to Eilat there are the ancient copper mines of **Timna**, once worked by the Egyptians and later by King Solomon's slaves. Today the area is a national park, and the mines consist of sandstone arches, underground mining shafts and various galleries. There are also strange rock formations here, including **Solomon's Pillars**, two weirdly shaped red sandstone columns, and the "The Mushroom" a huge boulder resting on a column of sandstone, both formed by the action of desert erosion. Solomon's Pillars are also famous for their Egyptian rock carvings, and the small temple dedicated to the Egyptian goddess Hathor. The temple is from the 14th century BC and although there's not much left to see the location is impressive.

Various tours are led here from Eilat, but it is an easy place to discover by yourself. A car is vital both for actually getting to the reserve in the first place and for seeing the sites, most of which are spread well apart (tel. 07-356215).

For the more adventurous, activities available in the Negev desert region include camel trekking, hiking, jeep touring and visits to Bedouin camps (*see* pages 276 and 283).

Eilat

Eilat is not the Hebrew word for fun, but it ought to be. Plenty of sun, sea and sand make Eilat an ideal resort town and along with the vibrant nightlife, this is the fun capital of the south of Israel. Of course, as everywhere else

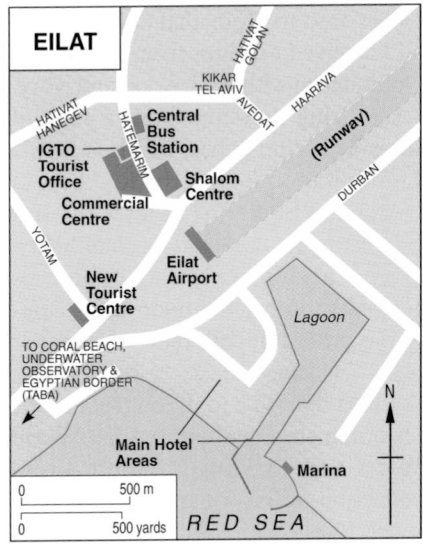

T own plan of Eilat.

in Israel, Eilat also has historical and archaeological attractions but these alone would not make you travel the 312km (194 miles) south from Jerusalem or the 354km (220 miles) from Tel Aviv.

Situated at the southern tip of the Negev Desert and lying parallel to the Jordanian resort of Aqaba (in fact the border is only a 15-minute walk from downtown), Eilat has sunshine just about every day of the year, rainfall is slight and the word "cold" is unknown. It is also a young city—less than fifty years old itself and with a population with an average age of only 26. Many of the young Israelis are here on army duty, protecting the port of Eilat, Israel's Red Sea lifeline, from possible attack from Jordan across the bay, Saudi Arabia, approximately 20km (12 miles) south of Aqaba, and Egypt a very short distance to the west (the Sinai desert).

Historically, Eilat was a one-horse town for a very long time. Its only claim to fame was that it was from Etzion-Geber, next to Eloth, that Solomon sent and received his ships from the land of Ophir, laden with gold, wood and ivory. "And King Solomon built a fleet of ships at Etzion-geber, which is beside Eloth on the shore of the Red Sea, in the land of Edom." (*I Kings 9:26*). It is also probable that the Queen of Sheba landed at Eilat when she came to Jerusalem to see Solomon and "commune with him all that was in her heart." (*I Kings 10:3*).

From that time to the collapse of the Ottoman empire after the First World War (1914–18), Eilat lay dormant, a collection of fisherman's huts and not much else. Lawrence of Arabia came

this way, but didn't stay long before heading off to Wadi Rum, a short distance away in Jordan. It was the founding of the State of Israel that made Eilat into a boom town, a Red Sea port was important for trade and as a lifeline. A concrete city sprung up overnight, trees were planted and lawns laid down. Today Eilat is still a concrete city but it has a soul, and the place is as busy as it is attractive.

Direct flights from Europe land here laden with holiday-makers—especially from Britain and Sweden, and on the surface Eilat is just like any Mediterranean seaside resort. However, Eilat is on the Red Sea, and has more style than most of the similar holiday resorts.

Eilat is made up of three distinct areas: the town itself, built on gentle hills rolling down toward the sea; **Coral Beach**, about 6km (3½ miles) from town on the western shore of the bustling harbour; and North Beach, a ten-minute walk from the centre of town on the eastern shore of the harbour. A fourth area, Taba, a strip of sand and a hotel south of Coral Beach is now in Egyptian territory following years of disputes. You can still get in though, and it's worth the extra effort because the beach is excellent. **North Beach** is where the major beach activities are concentrated, where the best hotels and the public beach are located. This is also the site of a complex marina system which started with the building of a u-shaped lagoon, cutting a short distance inland and making room for more hotels and clubs.

The best way to get your Eilati bearings is to step into the tiny Tourist Office (tel. 07-334353) in the Commercial Centre, next door to the

Egged Bus Station, and pick up a free map on which everything is clearly marked. The three-dimensional map is most useful. A small magazine *Events in Eilat* will also be available here, telling you all the events in the month ahead.

Activities, Tours and Sights

Eilat is a lively place full of activity. You would find it very difficult to get bored here. The Red Sea is the main attraction; its waters are clear and blue and beneath the waves lie some of the best coral reefs in the world. Eliat's location also makes it the perfect base for trips to Sinai, Egypt and Jordan.

> **Underwater Safaris**
> One of the most popular tourist attractions in Eilat, and one of the newest, is the Yellow Submarine berthed at Coral World. It seats 48 and submerges to a depth of 25m (80ft). The sub weighs 100 tonnes and is free to wander around the Coral World reserve —although, obviously it steers well clear of the border between Israeli waters and Jordanian ones!

Boats for Hire, Snorkelling, Scuba-diving

The North Beach marina and lagoon is the place for hiring boats for water-skiing, water parascending and fishing. Paddleboats, sailboards, kayaks and motorboats are also available. Rides in glass-bottomed boats can be a fun introduction to the underwater delights of the Red Sea. You can find one opposite the Neptune hotel or at the jetty just north of Coral Beach. Tour Yam Ltd. (tel. 07-332325) and Israel Yam (tel. 07-373988) are the specialists in such boats and trips lasting nearly two hours are reasonably priced.

Snorkelling and scuba-diving fans should head to Aqua Sport, (PO Box 300; tel. 07-334404). This is opposite the Caravan Sun Club Hotel on Coral Beach, and hires out all the necessary equipment. It also operates diving lessons, and diving tours. For more information *see* pages 279–281.

Coral World is a fascinating underwater observatory situated just south of

During the summer months, this lifeguard station on the Red Sea at Eilat will be constantly manned.

Coral Beach. It's an unusual looking complex, pretty much unmistakable, especially with its observatory linked to the main building by a long pier, which has been sunk into position 90m (300 ft) out to sea in that part of the coral reef known as the Japanese Gardens. Brightly coloured fish swim by and the experience is just like scuba-diving except that you don't get wet! Just in case you miss the most exotic fishes the observatory also has an aquarium. There are also large outdoor observation pools: one for sharks, another for sea turtles and rays. Open daily from 8.30 a.m. to 4.30 p.m., until 3 p.m. on Friday (tel. 07-376829).

Sunbathing and Swimming

You have two basic choices—downtown or further out. Sunbathing and splashing about is good on the sand beach in front of the Moriah Hotel. For a bit more adventure and a lot more quiet Coral Beach and the **Coral Beach Nature Reserve** (tel. 07-372724) are the best places to go. Snorkels, masks and flippers can be hired for those who don't want the expense of full-blown scuba diving. The beach is more stony but it is always less crowded than the main public beach. The coral reef is very impressive here and there are tropical fish to be chased if you have the energy. The water is very warm close to

*T*he futuristic shape of *the Underwater Observatory is a trademark of Eilat. The 48-seater Yellow Submarine plies the waves beneath it, giving wonderful views of the coral reefs.*

the shoreline but once you swim further out, a shelf falls away and all of a sudden the water temperature drops. Eilat is usually hot enough for this cold onrush of water to be bearable.

Remember that the sun can burn your back and neck while you are snorkelling on the surface of the water—it actually concentrates the rays and if you're not careful in applying waterproof sunscreens you may end up badly frazzled because the cold water makes you think your back is nice and cool. Also, protect your feet from the sharp coral and spiny sea-urchins by wearing sandals. Flip-flops are no good; they will just float away. Leather sandals will not react well to sea-water submersion so use a plastic pair. These can be bought cheaply in Israel.

The corals and shells you will see are protected by law; it is strictly forbidden to remove them from the water or collect them from the beaches, so leave them behind for other people to see.

Birdwatching

Because of its prime location on the migration path for birds going between Europe and Africa, Eilat is one of the best places on earth for birdwatching, a twitcher's delight. Migration times are twice a year: from September through November the birds head south to Africa, and from March through May they head back north to Europe.

Specialist tours can bring you to Eilat from your home country or you can arrange a few days birdwatching whilst you're here. Eilat's Birdwatching Centre, PO Box 774, Eilat (tel. 07-374276), with an office in the King Solomon Palace Hotel, is the place to visit for all your information.

More than Meets the Eye

There is far more to do in Israel than visit sites of religious significance. Israelis are passionate about sport—*matzkot* and basketball in particular—and their enthusiasm means there are good facilities for many sports easily available. Whether you fancy a round of golf, a game of tennis, an excursion on a mountain bike or a day by the pool, Israel will provide. Nature lovers will be happy roaming through Israel's many reserves and national parks, while those who prefer cerebral exercise to purely physical pursuits are catered for with museums, classical concerts and even the occasional lecture. Finally, those who live for the nightlife will find theatres, cinemas, cafés and much more besides in the big cities.

Sports

Sports-mad individuals will find Israel a veritable paradise. Gorgeous weather (most of the time) means outdoor sports are very popular. Grounds, stadia, athletics tracks, swimming pools and other such attractions can be found all over the country.

*W*indsurfing is popular all along the Mediterranean coast and down on the Dead Sea at Eilat. This surfer is in the marina at Tel Aviv.

Indoor sports are also well catered for—so, for instance, basketball is practically the national game. Israeli teams have taken on the best in the world and beaten them, although this may have something to do with the fact that tall, black non-Jewish American stars have been coaxed out to Israel with cash and then given quickie religious conversions. There has been much debate amongst the Orthodox about such conversions. Secular Israelis don't mind—so long as the recent converts play their socks off!

The Mediterranean shoreline and the Sea of Galilee are ideal for water sports: swimming, surfing, sailing, kayaking and water skiing. Parts of the river Jordan are even used for white-water rafting.

The Tel Aviv Marina offers yachting as well as sailing. Most of the large hotels have swimming pools and there are municipal or private pools all over the country. Fishing equipment, both angling and underwater, can be hired along the Mediterranean and the Red Sea, though the latter is a protected area, with fishing permitted only in certain places.

Tennis courts are available at a number of hotels and at the Tennis Centre at Ramat HaSharon, near Tel Aviv. Israel's only golf-course is at Caesarea. You can find horse-back riding clubs in Arad, Be'er Sheva, Caesarea, Eilat, Netanya, Vered Hagalil and other places. Bicycles can be rented in most cities and cycling tours of the country can be arranged. During the winter, there is skiing on the slopes of Mt Hermon. Marches, races, and swimming competitions are organized by the HaPo'el and Maccabi sports organizations. A programme of events is published monthly and can be obtained from:
Israeli National Sports Association
5 Rehov Warburger
Tel Aviv
Tel. 03-296387

Golf
Caesarea Golf Club
PO Box 1010
30660 Caesarea
Tel. 063-61174/2

Squash
HaCarmel
Tel. 040-539160

Herzliya
Tel. 09-557877

Ramal Can
Kfar Hamaccabiah
Sport Center
Ramat Chen
Tel. 03-6715715

Tennis
Israel Tennis Center
Ramat HaSharon
Tel. 03-6487222

For further information, contact:
Israel Tennis Association
79 Rehov Maze
67137 Tel Aviv
Tel. 03-613911

Skiing
Israel's only snow skiing resort is located on Mount Hermon, in the Upper Galilee. Hermon's highest peak offers a stunning panoramic view of the Golan Heights, Upper Galilee, the Hulah Valley, the Birket Ram Lake, the Qalat Nimrod Crusader Fortress and the Banias Spring. The skiing season begins in December or January and ends in mid-April. The heavy and wet snow ranges from 2–3m (6½–10ft) on the highest slope to 1m (3ft) at base level. There may be days when the roads are closed due to drifting snow. Skiers may phone the ski site between 9.00 a.m. and 3.00 p.m. or Moshav Neve Ativ, the holiday village which runs the ski site, throughout the day. The site is open daily from 8.30 a.m. until 3.30 p.m., subject to the weather. The last ride on the chair-lifts is at 3.30 p. m. Runs are available for all levels of skiers, with the longest run being about 2km (1 mile) long.

For further information, contact:
Hermon Ski Site
Tel. 06-981341

Moshav Neve Ativ
12010, MP Ramat Hagolan
Tel. 06-981531

Israel Ski Club
PO Box 211
Givatayim

Horse Riding

For those wishing to explore, there are riding stables that specialize in trail riding. Among the larger riding stables are:

Caesarea
Herod's Stables
Dan Caesarea Golf Hotel
Tel. 06-361181

Eilat
Sunbay Hotel
Lagoon Beach
Tel. 07-373105

Jerusalem
Havat Amir
Atarot
Tel. 02-352190

Nahariya
Bacall's Riding School
Sderot Ben Zvi
Tel. 04-920534

Tiberias
Vered Hagalil Ranch
Mobile Post Korazim
Tel. 06-935785

Cycling

Israel is a fantastic country for cycling: distances are not that great between sites, towns and amenities; views are wonderful; the weather is ideal and people react very well to cyclists. For mountain-bikers the above is true, but even more so! Israel is crisscrossed with plenty of off-road routes. The Judean desert and the Negev desert are especially good. The army may restrict your movements if you stray onto firing ranges or security zones but mostly you'll be free to cycle where you like.

As cycling is an active sport and as Israel can be a very hot country it is imperative that you drink plenty of water. Don't just rely on cafés and roadside taps. Take jerry-cans or water bottles with you. Use a good sun-screen and wear a hat and a pair of sunglasses. Don't over-exert yourself until you're totally acclimatized.

*T*he beach game matzkot *can be played with one bat or two. This Tel Aviv resident favours the two-bat approach.*

Bike navigation is easy as Israeli maps are extremely detailed. Buy the large-scale Hebrew maps and learn the Hebrew alphabet. Large-scale maps, which come already protected with plastic and which often have flora and fauna information on the reverse, are available from the shops of the Society for the Protection of Nature in Israel (SPNI). These are located at:

13 Rehov Helene Hamalka
Jerusalem
Tel. 02-252793

4 Rehov Hashfela
Tel Aviv
Tel. 03-375063.

Bikes can be hired throughout the country. The Jerusalem Cyclists Club will be able to advise on this.
JCC
PO Box 7281
Jerusalem
Tel. 02-344452

Organized tours are very worthwhile. Ayala Tours in Jerusalem organize cycle-tours on standard touring bikes and on mountain bikes, although off-road touring is not covered. Contact them at:
Ayala Tours
13 Hazvi Street
(behind the central bus station).
Jerusalem
Tel. 02-381233.

Also in Jerusalem, for touring and rental, contact Kif Ofanyim (tel. 02-519570) or Quality Biking (tel. 02-345603); in Haifa, contact Beyond Biking (tel. 04-679796); and for information in the UK on cycling tours in Israel, contact Classic Tours (tel. 071 613 4441).

The Israel Cyclists Touring Club organizes various tours between the months of March and October.
ICTC
PO Box 339
Kefar Saba 44102
Tel. 052-23716.

Hiking

Israelis are great hikers. The main reason for this is that Israel is great for hiking. Scenic pastoral walks, in areas such as the Galilee, can be completed as well as rough, tough desert hikes in say the Judean or Negev deserts. On many of the desert trails, walking is often the only way to get through. Steep, rocky ascents and dried-up river beds, *wadis*, make for exciting trekking. Gentler walks are also available.

Most trails are waymarked in some way—usually with a small splash of whitewash and a thin coloured stripe. These markings will correspond to the coloured dotted lines on your maps. Getting lost is hard. Walks are graded and unless you are fully equipped with water, provisions, ropes and stout boots, it would be foolhardy to attempt the tougher routes.

Walking independently is possible, but there are many Israeli guides only too happy to show you their country. There are also many large travel companies who can take you off the beaten track: Walk Ways in Jerusalem (tel. 02-344452); Neot Hakikar in Tel Aviv (tel. 03-5228161) and Eliat (tel. 07-330425/6);

*H*iking through wadis of the Judean desert is popular, but watch out for flash floods.

Geographical Tours in Jerusalem and Tel Aviv (tel. 02-253846); Etgar in Tel Aviv (tel. 03-5244121); Field School Ein Gedi (tel. 07-584350); the National Park Authority (tel. 02-387471); and Classic Tours in London (tel. 071 613 4441).

The Society for the Protection of Nature in Israel (SPNI) offers some fascinating tours which combine unique learning experiences in natural settings with hiking and swimming. Experienced guides explain the natural and human history of the region and often point out hidden places of beauty and interest.

SPNI Offices
Jerusalem
13 Rehov Helene Hamalka
Tel. 02-252793

Tel Aviv
4 Rehov Hashfela
Tel. 03-375063

Hang Gliding
The Agur Hang Gliding School in Bat Yam, Tel Aviv, offers courses in hang gliding for beginners. The duration of the course is 18 hours spread over 5 lessons. Equipment can be rented from the company for a fee and upon presentation of an authorized hang gliding certificate.

Agur Hang Gliding School and Club
124 Rehov Balfour
Bat Yam
Tel. 03-580144

Water Sports
Water-skiing and wind-surfing (board surfing) are available at the following centres:

After a dip in the sea, you can rinse off the salt water in one of the many freshwater showers along the beach at Tel Aviv.

Eilat
Aqua-Sport Red Sea Diving Center
Coral Beach
PO Box 300
Tel. 07-334404

Netanya
Blue Bay
37 Rehov Hamelachim
Tel. 09-603603

Tel Aviv
Aquamarine International Diving
  Club
23 Rehov Hissin
Tel. 03-5271009

Swimming
Israel's superb climate allows year-round swimming in the Mediterranean, the Gulf of Eilat, the Dead Sea and the Sea of Galilee. The Mediterranean is safe for bathing except at designated places where there is a strong potential undertow. Flags, warning symbols and lifeguards will make sure you only swim in safe areas. The larger hotels normally have pools, all of which will have a lifeguard on duty. If you are staying somewhere without a pool it is usually possible to pay to get into another hotel's pool.

Municipal pools in main cities include:
Gordon Swimming Pool
Kikar Atarim
Tel Aviv
Tel. 03-5271555

Jerusalem Swimming Pool
13 Emek Refaim
Tel. 02-632092

Galei Hadar Pool
11 Rehov Hapoel
Haifa
Tel. 04-667854

Scuba Diving in the Mediterranean
The Mediterranean has two particularly good diving seasons—autumn (September to December) and spring (March to May), although there are also fine periods during the summer and winter when diving is possible. Visibility on

*L*ooking like a David Hockney print, this swimming pool is on a terrace of the King Solomon Hotel in Jerusalem.

good days averages 10m (33ft), with calm waters. Tides are never a problem as their average fluctuation is only about 40cm (1½ feet) even on rough days. Water temperatures range from 16°C (61°F) in February to 29°C (84°F) in August.

Scuba Diving in the Gulf of Eilat
The Gulf is one of the more impressive diving centres in the world, containing an underwater nature reserve with especially exquisite coral reefs. Diving can be carried out every day of the

279

year. The area is usually free of large and strong waves; currents and tides are moderate, with variations of up to only 80cm (2½ft) between high and low tides. These variations do not in any way affect the diver's movement. Visibility is generally excellent, ranging from 15–40m (50–130ft) and sometimes even more. Water temperatures are pleasantly high and range from 21°C (70°F) in February to 27°C (80°F) in August.

Diving in the Red Sea is immensely popular. Eilat is the closest resort to Europe offering genuine tropical waters. The Red Sea at Eilat, and all the way down the Sinai coast, is one of the richest areas for tropical fish and corals in the world.

Scuba-diving can be taught by specialist schools, or for licensed divers, equipment can be hired from a number of diving centres and shops.

Ahziv Scuba Diving Center
Regional Council Sulam Zor
MP Western Galilee
Tel. 04-823671/820146

Aqua Sport
Red Sea Diving Center
Coral Beach
Eilat
Tel. 07-334404

Red Sea Divers
Caravan Hotel
Eilat
Tel. 07-376569

Skin Diving Center
Galei Galil Beach
Nahariya
Tel. 04-820540

Archaeological Holidays

History is never far away from the surface (literally) in Israel and if you want to go and delve after hidden treasure (such as broken pottery) then this can be arranged.

However, any budding Indiana Jones needs to be prepared to spend a couple of weeks in Israel, slaving away in often spartan conditions. The rewards are great (the self-satisfaction at helping to excavate in the Holy Land), but normally only the young can stand the hard labour. Bookings should be made as far in advance as possible from:

Department of Antiquities and Museums
Ministry of Education and Culture
PO Box 586
Jerusalem
Tel. 02-387505/307926.

Amateur archaeologists with only hours to spare, and who would prefer not to rough it for too long, can contact:

Dig for a Day
11 Shonai Halachot Street
Jaffa Gate
Jerusalem
Tel. 02-2735515; fax 02-222660.

As well as a pertinent lecture on history and basic techniques you will be given a trowel for a day, then, under supervision, you can dig to your hearts content.

If all you want is a tour of the major sites then there is a cheaper way of going about it if you are travelling independently. The National Parks Authority will sell you a 14-day pass:

National Parks Authority
3 Het Street
HaKirya
Tel Aviv
Tel. 03-252281.

Tel Aviv
Aquamarine International
    Diving Club
23 Rehov Hissin
Tel. 03-5271009

For diving with a difference, try one of the underwater archaeology or photography courses. One of the largest companies offering diving holidays and assistance is:
Aqua Sport
PO Box 300
Coral Beach
Eilat
Tel. 07-334404

More information is available from:
The Federation for Underwater
    Activities in Israel
PO Box 611
61060 Tel Aviv
Tel. 03-5236436.

Back to Nature

Nature Reserves

Although Israel is a very compact country, it has an impressive range of different landscapes and natural phenomena. Thanks to its geographic location and its particular topographical structure, Israel is a climatic meeting place. There are more than 3,000 different species of plants, 350 species of birds, 100 mammals and 100 reptiles. To preserve some of these landscapes, habitats and species there are over 160 Nature Reserves in Israel.

Israel caters very well for wildlife lovers. Numerous companies sell holidays which involve animal spotting.

T he holy orchid photographed in April near Tiberias.

Ornithology is one of the most popular, and you can obtain information on holidays catering for "twitchers" from: the Raptor Centre (tel. 02-932383/4), the Ornithology Centre (tel. 06-396266) and from holiday operator, Noam Michel (tel. 02-524982; fax 02-526170).

Season tickets are available for entry into all of the reserves. Details from:

Nature Reserve Authority
78 Rehov Yirmiyahu
94467 Jerusalem
Tel. 02-536271.

*E*in Gedi Nature
Reserve, one of over 160 reserves
spread across the country.

National Parks

Visitors to sites and parks can buy a ticket for multiple entrance at the site or park, permitting them to visit all of the sites or parks within a period of 14 days. In the case of groups the ticket can be used for 21 days. It can also be purchased from the National Parks Authority. The national parks range from sites of special natural interest to archaeological ruins. For further information, contact:

National Parks Authority
4 Rehov Aluf M Makleff
Hakirya
61070 Tel Aviv
Tel. 03-252281.

Adventure Travel

Action-minded individuals can get to see Israel at close quarters: on foot, horse-back, camel-back, white-water raft or on the saddle of a bicycle. You could bring your own equipment (impractical if it's a horse or camel) or you can hire once out in Israel. Package deals often come with hire included in the price.

Many companies exist to furnish your desire for excitement. Most of the guides and instructors are genuine experts in their respective disciplines. Israelis are great lovers of the outdoor life and their enthusiasm for this land is deeply engrained.

The following companies are involved in adventure holidays:

The Society for the Protection of Nature in Israel
4 Hashefela Street
Tel Aviv
Tel. 03-375063

SPNI run hundreds of different tours, ranging from flower-spotting to tough (very tough!) desert hikes. Many of the tours are specially for tourists but for a real experience join one of the Israeli-only tours. There will always be somebody who can speak English and you can be sure you'll get off the beaten track this way. The Israeli tours have the added advantage that they are usually cheaper!

Neot Hakikar
Jerusalem
Tel. 07-330425

Tel Aviv
Tel. 03-5228161

The specialist in desert tours, this company has been around for a long time and is very experienced.

Johnny's Desert Tours
Box 261 Eilat
Tel. 07-376777
Negev tours by camel, foot and jeep.

Metzoke Dragot
DN Bikat Yericho
Tel. 02-964501
A desert adventure "village", a useful stepping-off point and/or base for the Judean or Negev deserts.

Tracks
Head Office:
10 Caplan Street
Tel Aviv, 64734
Tel. 03-6916103

Regional Office:
Mount Kamoun Ranch
Carmiel
Galilee
Tel. 04-885603

Broad-ranging adventure specialist. Based in both the Galilee (horse-riding, trekking, white-water rafting, kayaking, cycling) and at the Shacharut Desert Adventure Centre in the Negev (camel-riding, abseiling and climbing, sand-buggy riding, mountain biking). They can arrange "soft" or "hard" action holidays. As well as the adventure aspects, Tracks can accommodate other activities into its programmes—including educational visits, political seminars and archaeological explorations. Tracks is a new concern, but was formed by real experts and is becoming one of the most versatile and exciting of all the tour companies.

Also offering adventure travel are Walk Ways (tel. 02-344452), Classic Tours in London (tel. 071 613 4441), David Choen (tel. 07-588890) and Kef O Fun (tel. 07-91442). For trips to Bedouin camps, contact Farchan Shlbi (tel. 07-113330) or Amir Abo Sian (tel. 07-918263).

Entertainment and Nightlife

Jerusalem

Jerusalem may not be as lively as Tel Aviv when it comes to all-night discos and the like but it is no entertainment black-spot—theatres, cinemas, bars, club and pubs are in great supply. Apart from these, there are often special events of interest. For this sort of information read the entertainment supplement in Friday's *Jerusalem Post*, the various pamphlets supplied by the Tourist Office, and the posters pasted up on street corners. Don't expect too many events on Friday night itself, Jerusalem tends to shut down during Shabbat. Many Israelis take a sherut to Tel Aviv for the real action.

Most tourists prefer to wind down by just sitting and watching the world go by as they sip coffee and nibble at *falafel*—a common Israeli practice too. The best place for this—and you can't miss it because this is the hub of Jerusalem's night-life—is the pedestrian

One of the pleasures of hiking through the Judean desert is to happen upon a hidden desert pool.

portion of Ben Yehuda, the **Midrahov**. As well as cafés, falafel stands and ice-cream parlours there are also street musicians and local artists displaying their wares.

If it is culture you want the place you need is **Binyanei HaUma** which is opposite the main station at the top of Jaffa Road. This is a concert hall and hosts classical music concerts and other events (tel. 02-252481).

The **Jerusalem Theatre** on David Marcus and Chopin Street (tel. 02-617167) is home to the Jerusalem Symphony Orchestra. There are also numerous plays, dances, and lectures held here—some of them are given in English.

The **Hebrew University** campuses at both Mt Scopus and Givat Ram often have cultural events and English-language lectures.

The **Gerard Bakhar Center** (tel. 02-242157), at 11 Bezalel Street hosts a variety of concerts, not all of which will be classical.

Across from the railway station in Remez Square is the **Khan Theatre** (tel. 02-718281). This small complex contains the tiny theatre, an art gallery and a nightclub (open until 2 a.m.).

For live rock music outside of Tel Aviv the only place big enough to stage international acts is **Sultan's Pool**, which occasionally attracts big-name singers and groups. This outdoor amphitheatre is situated opposite the Cinematheque, near Mt Zion and was once an ancient water supply for Jerusalem.

The **International Cultural Center for Youth** (ICCY), at 12a Emek Refa'im Street offers dancing most Saturday and Tuesday evenings at 9 p.m. (tel. 02-664144).

Israeli cinemas are boisterous places and Tel Aviv generally has a better selection of films. The **Orion Cinema**, at 13 Hillel Street (tel. 02-252914) usually has subtitled Hollywood films.

The **Jerusalem Cinematheque** (tel. 02-724131), screens art films and old favourites. The café here is one of the only places in West Jerusalem that opens on Friday evenings.

The Jerusalem nightclub scene is all but non-existent. Two which are popular with Jerusalemites more for their rarity value than their quality are **The Underground**, at 8 Yoel Solomon Street just off Zion Square, and **Lalo's Pub**, at 27 Jaffa Road, which has a small dance floor (tel. 02-254500).

Next door to The Underground are Jerusalem's best pubs, serving Israeli and English beers at inflated prices.

Tel Aviv

Tel Aviv comes alive at night and there is no shortage of things to do, see and hear. The simplest night out will be a stroll along the various promenades, finished off with a cappuccino. For the more adventurous the options are simply endless.

Cultural Events

The fullest listing of cultural events appears in the Hebrew press but the next best thing is the Friday edition of the *Jerusalem Post* (not just a regional newspaper). *Events in the Tel Aviv Region* produced by the IGTO is also useful.

Contemporary theatre can be seen at a number of locations: the most controversial is usually the **Ha-bimah Theatre**, Kikar Habimah (tel. 03-296071/209888). If the play is a particularly

*T*he street entertainment in Israel will normally be in Hebrew, but the art of busking is the same the world over.

interesting one there will be simultaneous translations from the Hebrew into English. Other venues include **Tzavta**, 30 Ibn Gvirol Street (tel. 03-6956222) and **Beit Leissin**, 34 Weizmann Boulevard (tel. 03-264594/6950156).

Classical music buffs will need the **Mann Auditorium**, Hubermann Street (tel. 03-289163); **ZOA** (Zionist Organisation of America) **House**, 1 Frisch Street (tel. 03-6959341) and the **Tel Aviv Museum**, 27 King Sha'ul Street (tel. 03-257361). If you visit Tel Aviv in May and early June, you will catch the Israel Festival, when a number of major international orchestras and musicians perform in the festival's four main centres: Tel Aviv, Jerusalem, and the restored Roman theatres in Beit She'an and Caesarea.

Danceniks should know about the Israel Ballet Company, which performs regularly at the **Ha-bimah Theatre**; The Israel Contemporary Dance Company; and The Batsheva Dance Company (tel. 03 652479).

Cinemas

There are many cinemas available, all of which will show foreign films undubbed into Hebrew. The area around Ben Yehuda, Dizengoff, and King George Street has the highest concentration of cinemas.

Popular Music

Big bands command big audiences, so a section of **HaYarkon Park** is often cordoned off and bands play under the stars. Most weeks will have something going on. Other live music venues include **Kolnoa Dan Disco**, 61 HaYarkon: a popular venue for local bands and the smaller international bands. At **Cassibar** on 7 Mendele Street, New Wave bands perform on Friday evenings. **The Rock Cafe** at 92 Herbert Samuel offers live music on Mondays and Wednesdays. **Penguin**, found at 43 Yehuda Halevi Street has Israeli rock music. Two jazz clubs are at **Dixieland**, 270 HaYarkon and **Shablul**, in the Dizengoff Centre.

Nightclubs

The Israeli nightclub scene, especially on Friday nights, is far from staid. There are many exotic locations, all of which play loud Western music well into the small hours. The selection may be a trifle dated, but the beautiful people don't seem to notice. **Coliseum** on Kikar Namir is upbeat and trendy, but expensive. Drinks are astronomically expensive, mainly because Israelis are not great drinkers of alcohol. **Liquid** at 18 Montefiore Street favours New Wave music. A standard disco is **Studio 73** at 73 HaYarkon Street. So to is **Gordon** located on Namir Square. This is nothing special but the drinks are cheap. Finally, there is **Soweto**, on HaYarkon Street which favours reggae music to the exclusion of everything else.

There are also many nightspots in Old Jaffa, usually catering specifically to tourists with "ethnic" folklore renditions. **The Cave** on Kedumim Square in Old Jaffa is typical of the breed, although there are many more.

Haifa

Haifa has a good nightlife, although Tel Aviv will always be livelier. Nightclubs are fairly well attended and there are many bars and late-night eateries in the downtown area.

Snacking on falafel whilst strolling is very popular.

Call the 24-hour telephone hotline for *What's On in Haifa* (tel. 04-640840), or check with any of the Tourist Information Offices to find out about special events.

For concerts, dances, and exhibits, the **James de Rothschild** Centre, Bet Rothschild, next to **Haifa Auditorium** at 142 Ha-Nasi Boulevard (tel. 04-382749), always has something going on. For classical music concerts and dance shows get along to the **Haifa Auditorium** (tel. 04-380013). The **Haifa Municipal Theatre** (tel. 04-670956) boasts many fine productions in an exceptionally good theatre; some are in English. Many modern plays are critical of the Israeli state, or at least certain aspects of it, and the theatre is considered very controversial.

For film-goers there is the **Cinematheque** at 104 HaNassi Boulevard, Carmel (tel. 04-383424), showing arty and foreign films.

Clubs and pubs in Haifa change with an amazing regularity—either going out

On leaving the Timna mines in the south near Eilat you will come upon this sign: "Shalom and come again". Hopefully you will have enjoyed your stay enough to do just that.

of business completely or changing their names. For the most-up-to-date listing of the best places contact:

The Haifa Tourism Development
    Association
10 Ahad Ha-Am Street
Tel. 04-666521.

Places worthy of mention, which have been around some time, include **Davka** on Jerusalem Street, **Rodeo** at 23 Balfour Street and **Studio 46** at 46 Pevsner Street.

Most of the bigger hotels have acceptable bars: the 5-star Dan Carmel Hotel, 87 Ha-Nasi Boulevard in Central Carmel (tel. 04-386211), has Palache's Pub, which has a bar with definite potential for dancing. The Hotel Carmelia, 35 Herzliya Street in Hadar (tel. 04-521278), has a 1960s disco every Friday night. Both the terminals of the Aerial Cable Car can be fine places to spend an evening, with restaurants, bars and dancing; you can ride the cable car until 11 p.m. most of the year, until midnight in summer.

Possibly the liveliest place in town, especially on Saturday nights is **Club 120** (tel. 04-382979) at 120 Panorama (Yefe Nof) Road, near the Hotel Dvir. Although it is a private disco club, tourists are welcome. Other nightclubs include **Sunset** on HaNassi Boulevard and **Little Haifa**, 4 Sha'ar HaLevanon Street.

The Israeli night-time ritual is sitting at outdoor cafés and watching the world go by. For this sort of action and a number of lively bars, the place to be is the area around Arlosoff and Herzl streets, in Hadar; a lot more respectable than the port area.

The **Al Pasha**, Hammam el-Pasha Street (tel. 04-671309), in the Old City area downtown, is a folksy-type club with live music, light meals and a varied selection of drinks that includes many imported lagers. Close by is **The Khan**, which has a similar character. **London Pride**, 85 HaAtzma'ut Road in the downtown area, is a bar and disco, plastic like the rest but quite lively. The name is a bit of a misnomer.

On Mt Carmel there's a European style club, **HaMo'adon** (The Club), 130 Hatishbi Street (tel. 04-373844). As well as live entertainment it offers dancing and a disco.

Listings and a 24-hour "What's On" service (tel. 04-640840) will keep you informed.

Eilat

Just like any other popular resort Eilat has a lively night-life, most of which is based around the major hotels. The larger hotels have extremely good restaurants, nightclubs and piano bars. The best include the smart **Disco-Americano** at the Americano Hotel and the **Club Inn** at the Coral Beach.

The New Tourist Centre also has a lot going on in the evening, with several pubs, clubs and outdoor cafés plying for trade. The food available here is unadventurous and "fast". You can get a burger at MacDavids or at Miss Lucy, but for more nutritional snacks head up to the top of **HaTmarim Boulevard** where the various stalls serve a mean falafel.

Cinema Eilat screens films in English at the Philip Murray Cultural Centre (tel. 07-373357), at the corner of HaTmarim Boulevard and Hativat HaNegev.

Language Guide

Hello/goodbye (also means "peace")	shalom
How are you?	ma shlomkha (m)/ shlomekh (f)
Fine/OK	beseder
See you	l'hitra'ot
Let's go	yalla (from Arabic)
Good morning	boker tov
Good evening	erev tov
Good night	lyla tov
Yes	ken
No	lo
Thank you (very much)	todah (rabah)
Please	be'vakasha
You are welcome	al low davaar
Sorry	slikha
Excuse me	slikha
Never mind	ain davar
I	ani
You	ata
He	hoo
She	hee
We	annaknoo
There is	yesh
There isn't	ain
Little	m'aat
A little	ktset
Much	harbeh
Very	me'od
So-so	kacha-kacha
Good	tov
Bad	rah
Hot	chaam
Cold	car

What's your name?	aikh korim lakha (m)/ lakh (f)
Friend(s)	chavare/ chaverim
I speak English.	ani m'deber anglit
Do you speak Hebrew?	ata'm deber ivrit
I don't speak Hebrew.	ani lo m'deber ivrit
Do you speak English?	ata m'deber anglit
What's that in Hebrew?	ma zeh be-ivrit
Yesterday	etmohl
Right (correct)	nachon
Too much	yotair meedie
Bless you!	lab-re-oot
Cheers!	l'chaim
Patience	savlanoot
Hands off!	blee yahdieim
I want . . .	ani rotzeh (m)/ rotzah (f)
Where is?	eifo yesh
What?	mah
Why?	lama
How?	aych
When?	mahtiee
Today	ha-yom
Tomorrow	machar
Movie	cinema (also kolnoah)
House	bait
White	lahvaahn
Black	shachor
Synagogue	bait knesset
School	bait sayfer
Newspaper	eetahn
Healthy	baree
Sick	choleh

Pretty/nice	**yoffee**
Well done (*literally "power to your glory"*)	**kola kavod**

Hotel

Hotel	**mehlon**
Room	**cheder**
Key	**maftayach**
Balcony	**meerpeseth**
Toilet	**bait keysay nochi yoot sherooteem**
Water	**myim**
Dining room	**cheder ohchel**
Bill	**cheshbon**
Money	**kessef**
Bank	**bank**
Mr (*sir*)	**adonee**
Mrs (*madam*)	**g'veret**
Where is?	**eifo**
Manager	**minahhel/ ba'al ah-bayit**
Accommodation	**makom**

Local Travel

Station	**tachanah**
Railway	**rahkehvet**
Airport	**sde t'ufah**
Bus	**autoboos**
Bus stop	**tachanaht ha autoboos**
Which bus goes to...?	**ehzeh autoboos nosayah le**
Taxi	**taxi**
Taxi (sherut)	**shayroot**
Stop here	**ahtsor kahn**
Wait	**reggah**
To the right	**yehmeanah**
To the left	**smolah**

Straight ahead	**yashar**
North	**tsafon**
South	**darom**
East	**mizrach**
West	**m'arav**
Far	**rahchok**
Near	**karov**
From	**may**
To	**le**
Central	**meerkazith**
Street	**rechov**
Store	**chanoot**
How much is it?	**kamah zeh ohleh?**
Do you have...	**yesh lekha**
Expensive	**yakar**
Cheap	**zol**
Doctor	**rowfeh**
Pharmacy	**bait merkahchat**
Appointment	**p'geeshah**
Dentist	**rowfeh shineyeyim**
Hairdresser	**mahspehrah**
Shampoo	**hafeefah**

Food and Restaurants

Restaurant	**missahdah**
Café	**cafe**
Breakfast	**ahroochat boker**
Lunch	**ahroochat tsaharyeim**
Dinner	**ahroochat erev**
Menu	**tafreef**
Waiter	**meltsar**
Food	**ochel**
Meat	**bahsahr**
Chicken	**tarnegolet**
Fish	**dag**

Egg	baytsa
Vegetables	yehrahkoht
Tomatoes	agvoneeoat
Cucumber	mahlafefon
To eat	le-ehchol
Tea	tay
Coffee	cafe
Milk	chalav
Wine	yahyin
Ice	kerach
To drink	lishtoth
Fruit	payrote
Pepper	pilpel
Salt	melach
Sugar	suecar
Bread	lechhem
Butter	chemah
Cheese	g'veenah
Soup	marock
Salad	salat
Omelette	chavitah
Ice cream	gleedah
Sour	chamuts
Sweet	mahtok
Pleasant	nahim
Excellent	metsooyan
Hungry	ra'ev

Post Office

Post office	doughare
Letter	miktav
Stamp(s)	bool(im)
Envelopes	maatafoth
Postcard	glooyah
Telegram	mivrock

Airmail	doughare ahveer

The Countryside

Trip	teeyule
Road	derech
Mountain	har
Hill	givah
Valley	ehmek
Stream/river valley	nahal
Dried-up river bed	wadi (from Arabic)
Forest	yahare
Desert/wilderness	midbar
Sand	chol
Sea	yaam
Village	k'far
Farm	meshekh
Spring/well	ayn/ain/en/ein

Days and Time

Saturday	yom shabbat, shabbat
Sunday	yom reeshon
Monday	yom shaynee
Tuesday	yom shleeshee
Wednesday	yom rehvee-ee
Thursday	yom chamee shee
Friday	yom sheeshee
What time is it?	ma ha'sha'ah
Minute	dakah
Hour	sha'ah
Day	yom
Week	shavooah
Month	chodesh
Year	shanah
Seven o'clock	hashaah shayva

292

Numbers

1	ehhad
2	shtayim
3	shalosh
4	arbah
5	chamaysh
6	shaysh
7	shevvah
8	shmoneh
9	tayshah
10	esser
11	ehhad essray
12	shtaym essray
13 etc...	(essray = teen)
20	essreem
21	essreem v'ehhad
30	shlosh eem
50	chameesh eem
100	mayah
200	matayeem
300	shlosh mayoat
500	chamaysh mayoat
1,000	elef
3,000	shloshet elefeem
5,000	chamayshet elefeem

Arabic Expressions

Hello	ahalan, mahrhaba
Goodbye	salaam aleichem, maahsalameh
Do you speak English?	techkee Ingleesi
How much is this?	ahdesh hadah
Please	min fadlach
Thank you	shookhraan
Pardon?	samechnee
Yes	aywah
No	la
Left	shemal
Right	yemine
Straight	dooree
Scram/Beat it!	rooch minhon!
Coffee	kahwah
1	wahad
2	tinen
3	talatay
4	arbaha
5	chamesh
6	sitteh
7	sabah
8	tamanyeh
9	taisah
10	ahsharah

USEFUL NUMBERS AND ADDRESSES

Jerusalem

Bus Services

West Jerusalem
Egged Bus Station
224 Jaffa Road (Romema District)
Tel. 02-3045555 or 304444
   West up Jaffa Road, past Mahane Yehuda.

Beit Tannous
Jaffa Gate terminal
Tel. 02-304774

Egged Tours
44a Jaffa Road (Zion Square)
Tel. 02-253454
Reservations centre (Bus 99)
11a HaMeasef Street
Tel. 02-247783

East Jerusalem
Suleiman Street Bus Station (in between Herod's and Damascus Gate) operates routes to the south (Hebron, Bethlehem, Jericho).

Nablus Road Bus Station operates the northern routes (Ramallah, Nablus).

Camp Sites
There are three camp sites situated close to Jerusalem. All of them are full-facility sites, often in superb natural locations.

Aqua Bella
Ein Hemed
Tel. 02-342741

Bet Zayit
Tel. 02-332239 or 346217

Ramat Rachel
Tel. 02-702555

Car Rental Companies
Ar Car
6 Pines Street
Tel. 02-384889

Avis
22 King David Street
Tel. 02-249001

and

19 Salah al-Din
Tel. 02-281020

Budget
14 King David Street
Tel. 02-248991

Eldan
36 Keren Hayesod
Tel. 02-385515

Europcar
68 Jaffa Road
Tel. 02-248464

Eurotour
36 Keren Hayesod
Tel. 02-661749/663392

Visa Car
23 Hillel Street
Tel. 02-223440/227117

Yourent
5 Pines Street
Tel. 02-383943/383883

Christian Hospices and Hostels

Details from:
The Christian Information Centre
Jaffa Gate
Tel. 02-272692

Churches

Details from:
The Christian Information Centre
Jaffa Gate
Tel. 02-287647

Consulates

British
Sheikh Jarrah Quarter
Mount of Olives Road
East Jerusalem
Tel. 02-828644

US

Near the YMCA Aelia Capitolina Hotel; intersection of Nablus Road (Derech Shechem) and Pikud Ha-Merkaz Street, East Jerusalem.
Tel. 02-734635

and

18 Agron Street, just down the hill from the Jerusalem Plaza Hotel
West Jerusalem
Tel. 02-253888

Dentists

Department of Dentistry
Ministry of Health
20 King David Street
Tel. 02-247471
There are several private clinics at the bottom of Salah al-Din Street.

Emergency dental treatment is available at weekends and on holidays from the Magen David Adom (tel. 101, or in East Jerusalem 02-911288). Hadassah Hospital at Ein Kerem has an emergency room, open daily 4 to 10 p.m.

Emergencies

Ambulance 101
Fire 102
Police 100
First Aid from Magen David Adom (tel. 101) or in East Jerusalem at Dung Gate (tel. 02-911288)

Hospitals

Hadassah Hospital
Mount Scopus
Tel. 02-818111

or

Ein Karem
Tel. 02-427427

Natural History Information

Society for the Protection of Nature in Israel (SPNI)
13 Rehov Helene Hamalka
Jerusalem
Tel: 02-252793

Post Offices

Central Post Office
23 Jaffa Road
(near the intersection with Shlomzion HaMalka Street)

Sun.–Thurs. 7 a.m. to 7 p.m.; Fri. 8 a.m. to 1 p.m.

Telephone and telegraph services are open nights and on Shabbat.
East Jerusalem Main Office
Salah al-Din Street
(opposite Herod's Gate)

Old City post office is next to Christ Church Hospice and opposite the entrance to the Tower.

Sport

YMCA
opposite King David Hotel
Tel. 02-894271

The East Jerusalem YMCA
Nablus Road
Tel. 02-282375/6

Swimming

Aside from hotel pools there's a municipal pool at Brekhat Yerushalayim in the German Colony (buses 4 or 13); a municipal pool in Kiryat Hayovel (bus 18); a religious pool (with separate bathing days for men and women) in the Jerusalem forest at Kfar Hanofesh (buses 13, 18, 20, 23 and 27). Three pools which lie in settlements just outside Jerusalem are worth a visit purely because of their positions: Ma'ale Hakhamishah, Shoresh and Bet Zayit all have buses going past them; ask at the Central Bus Station.

Synagogues

Jerusalem has many synagogues. A list and times of their services are available from the IGTO. The Great Synagogue (Hakal shlomo), at 58 King George Street is one of the most popular for the Shabbat service, and is within walking distance of downtown hotels.

Telephones

Information 144
Speaking clock 155
Overseas information 195
Overseas collect calls 03-622881
Overseas operator 188
Telegrams 171
Auto alarm 174
24-hour daily fax and telex service; tel. 02-244737

International telephone office
1 Koresh Street
Jaffa Road
(behind the main post office)

West Bank

Bethlehem Tourist Information Office
Manger Square
Bethlehem
Tel. 02-741581

Tel Aviv

Airport

Ben-Gurion Airport flight information
Tel. 03-381111

Buses

Egged (InterUrban Bus Lines)
Tel. 03-304555

Dan (Urban Bus Lines)
Tel. 03-7543400
Central bus station off Neve Shaanan Street and Petach Tikva road.

As well as buses and sherutim Tel Aviv is also blessed with little white vans. These 9-seater mini-buses follow the number 4 bus route (parallel to coast from Central Bus Station, and along Allenby and Ben Yehuda). They operate more like taxis than buses and can be stopped anywhere along their designated route.

Car Rental
Most of the car hire firms in Tel Aviv have central offices on HaYarkon Street, near the large sea-front hotels.

Avis (tel. 03-5271752)
Budget (tel. 03-5623111)
Hertz (tel. 03-562221)
Eldan (tel. 03-5271166)

All these firms are also well represented at Ben-Gurion Airport.

Embassies
British
192 HaYarkon Street
Tel. 03-5249171
Open Mon.–Fri. 8 to 11 a.m. Closed Israeli holidays.

US
71 HaYarkon Street
Tel. 03-5174338 or 5174338
Open Monday to Friday 8 to 11 a.m.

Egyptian
(for visas to Egypt)
54 Basel Street
just off Ibn Gevirol Street
Tel. 03-376882
Visa section open Sunday through Thursday 9 to 11 a.m. Bring your passport and two current photos. Get there early as the embassy can get very crowded. Passports and visas can be collected at 2 p.m.

Ferries
Tickets for ferries to Athens, Rhodes and Cyprus are sold by the following two companies:

Mano Passenger Lines
60 Ben Yehuda Street
Tel. 03-2821 21

and

J Kassas Agency
1 Ben Yehuda Street
Tel. 03-664902

Medical Services
Emergencies requiring hospitalization, dial 102.

Magen David Adom has a mobile intensive-care unit tel. 03-5460111 on call 24 hours a day.

Dental Association
Emergency clinic
49 Bar Kokhba Street
Tel. 03-5284649

Open Fri. 6 p.m. to midnight and on Shabbat 10 a.m. to 2 p.m. and 8 to 10 p.m.

Natural History Information
4 Rehov Hashfela
Tel Aviv
Tel. 03-375063

Sherut taxis
To suburbs, Haifa and Jerusalem: Solomon Street, opposite the central bus station.

Other cities: Allenby Road and Kikkar HaMoshavots.

Telephones

Bezek
13 Frischmann Street
Open Sun.–Thurs. 9 a.m. to 11 p.m.,
Fri. 8 a.m. to 2.30 p.m. To make international calls from outside the phone
office dial 18. For reverse charge calls
dial 03-622881.

Tourist Information

Government Tourist Information
Office (IGTO)
7 Mendele Street
off Ben Yehuda, parallel to Frisch-
mann.
Tel. 03-660259
Open Sun–Thurs. 8.30 a.m. to 6 p.m.,
Fri. 8.30 a.m. to 2.30 p.m.

Coastal Strip

Bus Stations

Ashkelon
Ben Gurion Street
Tel. 051-22911
Buses to major cities every hour.

Netanya
3 Binyamin Boulevard
Tel. 053-33 70 52
Buses to Tel Aviv every 10 minutes.

Car Rental

Ashkelon
Eldan
Herzl Street
Tel. 07-722724

Netanya
Avis
1 Ussishkin Street
Tel. 09-623233

Hertz
8 Ha'Atzma'ut Square
Tel. 053-288 90

First Aid

Ashkelon and **Netanya**
Emergency tel. 101

Information

Ashkelon
Tel. 051-233 33

Netanya
Tel. 053-233 33

Post Office

Ashkelon
18 Herzl Street
Tel. 051-225 02 in Migdal.
Open Sun.–Tues. and Thurs. 8 a.m. to
12.30 p.m. and 3.30 to 7 p.m., Wed. and
Fri. 8 a.m. to noon. International tele-
phones and Poste Restante here.
Branch office in Afridar Centre.

Netanya
59 Herzl Street
Tel. 053-34 11 09.
Poste Restante here.

Branch also on
8 Ha'Atzma'ut Square
Tel. 053-34 21 05
Open Sun.–Tues. and Thurs. 8 a.m.
12.30 p.m. and 3.30 to 6 p.m., Wed.
8 a.m. to 1.30 p.m., Fri. 8 a.m. to noon.

Tourist Information

Ashkelon
Afridar Centre
Tel. 051-32412
Open Sun., Mon. and Wed.–Thurs.
8.30 a.m. to 1 p.m., Tues. 8.30 a.m. to
12.30 p.m.

Netanya
Ha'Atzma'ut Square
Tel. 053-272 86.
Open Sun.–Thurs. 8.30 a.m. to 3 p.m.
and 4 to 6 p.m., Fri. 8.30 a.m. to
12.30 p.m.

Taxis

Ashkelon
Yael Daroma
Tzahal Street
Tel. 07-750334
Operates sherutim to Tel Aviv.

Private Taxis
Keren Kayemet Street
Shimshon
Tel. 07-750266

Bet HaMishpat Street
Barnea
Tel. 07-755555

Directly opposite the central bus
station.
Tel. 07-733077

Netanya
Hashahar
1 HaMeyasdim Street
Tel. 09-347777

2 Smilansky Street
corner of Herzl Street
Tel. 09-823838

8 Raziel Street
Tel. 09-344443

Haifa

Buses
Central Bus Station
Yafo Street
Tel. 04-5945555
From 5 a.m. to 11.30 p.m. Sun. to
Thurs.; on Fri., till 4.30 p.m. Shabbat
9 a.m. to midnight.
Information; tel. 04-515221.

Ferries
Terminal at the port, next to the train
station. Departures for Cyprus, Crete,
and mainland Greece, Sun. and Thurs.
8 p.m. Buy tickets at:
Kaspi Travel
67 Ha'Atzma'ut Street
Tel. 04-6744444

Multitour
55 HaNamai Street
Tel. 04-663570

Mano Shipping
39/41 HaMeginnim Street
Tel: 04-531631

Hospitals
Carmel Hospital
7 Michal Street
Tel. 04-250211

Rambam Hospital
Bat Galim
Tel. 04-543111

Medical Services
Emergency 101 for Magen David
Adom first aid services. Emergencies requiring hospitalization 102. Mobile intensive-care unit; tel. 04-512233.

Post Office

Haifa's Central Post Office
19 Ha-Palyam Street (in port area)

and

Shabtei Levi and HaNevi'im Street
Hadar district.

Rental Cars

Budget
145 Jaffa Road
Tel. 04-538558

Eldan
117 HaNassi Boulevard
Tel. 04-375303

Europcar
3 Allenby Street
Tel. 04-571842

Sherut Taxis

Tel Aviv/Jerusalem
10 Nordau Street
or
157 Jaffa Street

Acre/Nahariya
16 HaNeviim Street in the Hadar or
Plumer Square downtown.

Druse villages
Eliyahu Street
Sun.–Fri. 6 a.m. to 6 p.m. On Shabbat
from corner of Schmeriyahu Levin
Street and Herzl Street.

Taxis

Kavei HaGalil
1 HaHalutz
Tel. 04-664422

Mercaz Mitspe
7 Balfour Street
Tel. 04-662525

Tourist Information

IGTO
16 Herzl Street
Tel. 04-666521

A branch office at the port is open for
arriving ferries
Port building 12
Tel. 04-663988

Haifa Tourism Development
  Association
10 Archad Ha'am Street
Tel. 04-671645. Ask for the "Discover
Haifa by Yourself" pamphlet.

The Galilee

Bus Stations

Tiberias
HaYarden Street; tel. 06-791080
To Jerusalem every 30–45 min. 6 a.m. to
6 p.m.
To Tel Aviv every hour, 5.30 a.m. to
8 p.m.
To Haifa every 20–45 min. 5.40 a.m. to
8.30 p.m.

Nazareth
Paul Vl Street
(Opposite Mashbir department store).
Egged Information Office
Paul Vl Street
Open daily from 6 a.m. to 6.30 p.m.
Bus 431 comes from Haifa and contin-
ues to Tiberias. Buses 823 and 824 run
frequently to Afula, the bus travel-hub
of the region.

Safed
Ha'Atzma'ut Square
Tel. 06-931122
Bus 459 travels between Tiberias and Safed every 1–2 hr.

All buses to Kiryat Shmona from Jerusalem and Tel Aviv stop at Rosh Pinna, where you can transfer for a bus to Safed. There is a direct bus, 964, to Jerusalem daily at 7.30 a.m. Buses 361 and 362 travel to and from Haifa through Akko every 20 min. Last bus Sun. through Thurs. 9 p.m., Fri. 4.45 p.m.

First Aid
Nazareth
Tel. 06-720111 or 06-791011
Open 24 hours.

Safed
Tel. 06-930333.

Hospital
Nazareth Hospital
Tel. 06-571501/2

Police
Emergency 100
Nazareth: 06-574444
Tiberias: 06-792444
Safed: 06-930444 or 972444

Post Office
Tiberias
HaYarden Street
Tel. 06-722432
Open Sun.–Tues. and Thurs. 8 a.m. to 12.30 p.m. and 3.30 to 6 p.m., Wed. 8 a.m. to 1.30 p.m., Fri. 8 a.m. to noon.

Nazareth
Near Mary's Well, off Paul Vl Street.
Tel. 06-554019

Safed
HaPalmah Street
Tel. 06-930405
Next to a radar dish visible from the corner of HaPalmah Street at Aliyah Bet.
Branch office
Jerusalem Street
(Near tourist information office).

Taxis
Tiberias
Sherutim and private taxis can be found on the stretch of HaYarden Street running from the bus station to the lake.
For reservations tel. 06-720098.

Nazareth
Mu'ayan, on Paul Vl Street
Tel. 06-555l05
Along Paul Vl Street.

Safed
Sherutim
Tel. 06-970707
Near the central bus station. Inter-city rides also available from:
19 Jerusalem Street
Tel. 06-972272 or 06-972987

Tourist Information Offices
Tiberias
8 Alhadef Street
Tel. 06-720992
Right as you leave the bus station onto HaYarden Street. Turn left on Alhadef Street. Open Sun.–Thurs. 8.30 a.m. to 5 p.m., Fri. 8.30 a.m. to 2 p.m.

Nazareth
Casa Nova Street
Tel. 06-573003 or 06-570555
Open Mon.–Fri. 8 a.m. to 5 p.m., Sat. 8 a.m. to 2 p.m.

Safed
23 Jerusalem Street
Tel. 06-920633
Open Sun.–Thurs. 9 a.m.to 6 p.m., Fri.
9 a.m.–noon: in winter Sun.–Thurs.
8.30 a.m. to 12.45 p.m. and 4 to 6 p.m.,
Fri. 9 a.m. to noon.

Nazareth
Casa Nova Street
(Near intersection with Paul Vl Street).
Tel. 06-573003 or 06-570555
Open Mon.–Fri. 8 a.m. to 5 p.m., Sat.
8 a.m. to 2 p.m.

Eilat

Airlines
Arkia
Shalom Plaza Centre
Tel. 07-376102

El Al
Shalom Plaza Centre
Tel. 07-331515

Car Rental
All the major international companies
are represented on HaTmarim Boulevard.

Eldan Rent a Car
HaArava Street
Shalom Plaza Centre
Tel. 07-374027

Europa Car
HaArava Street
Tel. 07-374014

Egyptian Consulate
34 Dror Street
Tel. 07-376882
Open Sun.–Thurs.
Visa issued on day of application de-
pending on nationality.

Emergencies
Police 100
Ambulance 101
First-aid posts on Hatmanlr Boulevard
and on the beaches.

Hospital
Yoseftal Hospital
Yotam Road
Tel. 07-372301 or 373151

Post Office
Main post office
Commercial Centre
facing HaTmarim Boulevard
Open Sun., Tues. and Thurs. 7.45 a.m.
to 12.30 p.m. and 4 to 6.30 p.m., Mon.
and Wed. 7.45 a.m to 2 p.m., Fri. 7.45
a.m. to 1 p.m.

Reverse charge (collect) calls can also
be made from the public telephones at
the front of the post office.

International phone calls can be
made at "Bezek" in the Commercial
Centre (Sun.–Thurs. 8 a.m. to 2 pm.
and 7 to 10 p.m., Fri. 8 a.m. to 1.30
p.m.).

Tours
Egged Bus Station
HaTmarim Boulevard
Tel. 07-375161

United Tours
New Tourist Centre
Tel. 07-374217

Johnny Desert Tours
Shalom Centre
Tel. 07-376777

Ne'ot HaKikar
Commercial Centre
(facing HaTmarim Boulevard)
Tel. 07-330425/6

Dan United
Tel. 07-374217

Galilee Tours
Neptune Hotel
Tel. 07-374720

Geographical Tours Ltd
Moriah Hotel
North Beach
Tel. 07-372151

Good Value Hotels and Places to Eat and Drink in the Holy Land

Hotels

Accommodation in Israel varies enormously, and every kind of traveller should find genial surroundings to suit their personality and their pocket. Do remember to check availability of hotel rooms during times of religious festivals. Due to the erratic exchange rates, the price bands are given in pounds sterling. They indicate the price of a double room for one night. Facilities in the rooms will vary with the grade of hotel.

▯	less than £30
▯▯	£30–70
▯▯▯	more than £70

Akko

The Argaman Motel ▯▯
Acre Beach 24101
Tel. 04-916691

The Palm Beach Hotel and ▯▯▯
Country Club
Acre Beach 24101
Tel. 04-815815
Exclusive retreat.

The Dead Sea

Bet Sara Youth Hostel ▯
Mobile Post
Dead Sea 86980
Tel. 057-84165
Clean but spartan.

Kibbutz Ein Gedi Guesthouse ▯▯▯
Mobile Post
Dead Sea 86980
Tel. 057-84757
Luxury by the Dead Sea.

Nof Arad Hotel ▯▯▯
Moav Street
Arad 80750
Tel. 057-957056
This hotel has a fully equipped clinic for the climatic treatment of asthma. There is a swimming pool here, too.

Eilat

Americana Eilat ▯▯
North Beach
Tel. 07-333777
Good swimming pools and a "happening" atmosphere— one of Eilat's best nightclubs is based at the Americana.

The Carlton Coral Sea Hotel ▯▯▯
Coral Beach
Tel. 07-379555
A neat 4-star luxury hotel with a Bedouin tent and camel in the grounds for entertainment.

King Solomon's Palace ▯▯▯
North Beach Lagoon
Tel. 07-334111
Luxurious. Also very good for the activities available to guests.

The Neptune ▯▯
North Beach
Tel. 07-369369
Good water facilities.

The Orchid ▯▯▯
South Beach
Tel. 07-360360
This is a luxury "resort village" directly opposite the Coral Beach observatory and is now the best accommodation in Eilat. The rooms are in wooden, air-conditioned chalets. A complex of swimming pools is connected by waterfalls.

Red Rock ▯▯
North Beach
Tel. 07-373171
Plush hotel on the beachfront.

Haifa

Hotels in Haifa are found either in Hadar or at the top of Mount Carmel. The views from many of them are superb. The hotels on Mount Carmel will have rooms which can either look out over Haifa Bay or over the greenery of Mount Carmel itself.

Carmelite Pilgrim's Hospice ▯
Stella Maris
Mount Carmel
PO Box 9047
Tel. 04-332084
Christian retreat in the style of a country inn.

Dan Carmel ▯▯▯
87 Sederot Hanassi
Tel. 04-386211
Located on Mount Carmel, with a spectacular view of the bay. Good restaurant, great bar, swimming pool in lovely grounds and a small health club.

Dan Panorama ▯▯▯
107 Sederot Hanassi
Tel. 04-352222
The Panorama is very tall and many of the rooms have spectacular views.

Dvir ▯▯
124 Panorama Road
Yefe Nof Street
Tel. 04-389131
Excellent location on Mount Carmel. Ask for a front-facing room and avoid the annexe. The service here is very good as many of the staff are still in training and are aiming to please. Nice view of the bay and the Baha'i dome.

German Hospice ▯
105 Jaffa Road
Tel. 04-523705
Simple, clean accommodation.

International Tourist Hostel │
40 HaGefen Street
Tel. 04-521110
Standard hostel-type rooms.

Nesher │
53 Herzl Street
Tel. 04-620644
Reasonably well located, in the Hadar section. Pension-type rooms.

Nof Hotel │││
101 Sederot Hanassi
Tel. 04-354311
All of the rooms have stunning bay vistas.

Talpiot │
61 Herzl Street
Tel. 04-673753
Another Hadar mid-town location. Very basic rooms.

Jerusalem

In the peak periods finding a suitable place to stay in Jerusalem can be difficult despite the many different accommodation options. The most crowded periods, for which pre-booking would be essential are Christmas, Easter and *Pesach* (March or April). The peak season runs from March to May and from late-September through to October.

Jerusalem has 98 "official" hotels, with 8,598 rooms. This is the largest concentration of hotels and rooms in Israel, exceeding Tel Aviv's accommodation by 25 per cent and it has twice the number of rooms as Eilat. The following is a small selection from these 98.

American Colony Hotel │││
Nablus Road
PO Box 19215
East Jerusalem
Tel. 02-285171
Well located for the Old City and East Jerusalem. The 19th-century stone building gives a feel of Jerusalem in days gone by. Arab-run hotel with excellent service. Formally the home of a Turkish pasha. Archaeological finds are displayed in glass cases in the lobby and the rooms are decorated with antiques. Worth paying the price for a good room as there are rooms available which are quite ordinary.

Beit Shmuel │
13 King David Street
Jerusalem
Tel. 02-203466
A guest house and cultural centre, sponsored by the World Union for Progressive Judaism. The large,

modern complex has good views of the Old City, terraces and court-yards, and a friendly ambience.

The Capitol Hotel │││
17 Saladin Street
East Jerusalem
Tel. 02-282561
Moderate luxury at moderate prices.

Commodore Hotel │
Mount of Olives Road
East Jerusalem
Tel. 02-284845
Tidy hotel with imposing lobby.

Eilon Tower Hotel │││
Migdal Ha'ir Building
34 Ben Yehuda Street
West Jerusalem
Tel. 02-252161
Good downtown location. All rooms have good views of the New City.

Eyal Hotel │││
21 Shammai Street
West Jerusalem
Tel. 02-234161
Central 3-star hotel, located one block behind Zion Square. Rooms are comfortable and include refrigerators.

Holyland East Hotel │
6 Harun er-Rasheed Street
PO Box 19700
East Jerusalem
Tel. 02-271538
Most of the rooms have a view of the Mount of Olives.

King David │││
23 King David Street
West Jerusalem
Tel. 02-221111
The best hotel in Israel—top marks for style, charm and décor. Has much more personality than any other hotel and certainly has more history. Very expensive, but worth at least one or two nights for even cost-conscious tourists.

King Solomon ││││
32 King David Street
West Jerusalem
Tel. 02-241433
Religiously observant hotel that is quiet and low-key, a welcome change from the hustle and bustle of touring Jerusalem. Has the advantages of being the cheapest and smallest of the 5-star luxury hotels. The tiny swimming pool on a roof-terrace is under-used and has fine views over to the Judean desert.

Moriah Plaza Jerusalem Hotel │││
39 Keren Hayessod Street
West Jerusalem 94101
Tel. 02-361111 or toll free 800-221-0203
Located around the corner from the King David Hotel, close to Liberty Bell Park, Yemen Moshe, and the Cinematheque, a walk or a quick bus-ride to Jaffa Road, the Moriah Plaza offers comfortable 5-star accommodation and a rooftop swimming pool.

Mount Scopus Hotel │
Nablus Road
Sheikh Jarrah
East Jerusalem
Tel. 02-282891
Very good views, from an unusual position over the Old City. A car is a must.

Mount Zion Hotel │││
17 Hebron Road
Jerusalem 94356
Tel. 02-724222
The hotel's terraces, sprawling wings, hidden gardens, and swimming pool offer views of the Old City that rival those of the King David Hotel.

National Palace Hotel │││
4 Al-Zahara Street
East Jerusalem
Tel. 02-273273
Well positioned for the Old City and East Jerusalem, with a fine Oriental restaurant on the roof.

Notre Dame Guest House │││
PO Box 20531
West Jerusalem
Tel. 02-894 511
Located in a beautifully restored landmark just steps away from both sides of the city. The Notre Dame complex is a centre for Roman Catholic institutions and pilgrim groups, but all travellers are welcome. Public areas are spacious and the rooms are simple but comfortable. Many share a balcony.

Palatin Hotel │││
4 Agrippas Street
West Jerusalem 94301
Tel. 02-231141
Quiet 2-star hotel a few steps off King George V Avenue. Good position and very peaceful. Small rooms but comfortable.

St Andrews Hospice   I
PO Box 14216
West Jerusalem
Tel. 02-716809
Situated on a small hill, surrounded by a garden with panoramic views of Mount Zion and the Old City. In the homely lounge, guests will find a fine portrait of General Allenby, who captured the city from the Ottomans in World War I.

St George's Hotel   I
20 Nablus Road
PO Box 19018
East Jerusalem
Tel. 02-283302
An Anglican guest house with an English garden. Accommodation is old-fashioned and comfortable.

Sheraton Jerusalem Plaza   III
47 King George Street
West Jerusalem
Tel. 02-259111
Centrally situated, 414 mod-con rooms. Guest activities, including free walking tours, are very good.

Pilgrims Palace Hotel   I
Sultan Suleiman Street
PO Box 19066
East Jerusalem
Tel. 02-284831
This hotel is near the East Jerusalem bus station, which means it tends to be noisy. Fine views of the Old City walls.

Windmill Hotel   II
3 Mendle Street
West Jerusalem
Tel. 02-284883
Good location. Reasonable rates. Nice coffee shop.

YMCA (West)   I
26 King David Street
West Jerusalem
Tel. 02-257111
Rooms are clean and airy. Bell tower can be climbed for stunning views. The terrace bar serves good food. In a pleasant location, but view of the Old City is blocked by the King David Hotel. Sports enthusiasts would appreciate the YMCA the most.

Budget Accommodation

There are many very cheap hotels in and around the Old City. Prices are rock-bottom but facilities are limited and the buildings can be very run-down. Most are Arab-run and un-listed by the IGTO. They have the advantage of being wonderfully lo-cated inside the Ottoman walls. A list would be pointless as there are many of the same class. Conditions in some of them are prone to dete-rioration. Wander around the alleys inside Jaffa Gate and you'll soon find you're spoilt for choice.

Kibbutz Guest Houses

If you don't mind travelling to and from Jerusalem, there are a number of kibbutz guest houses dotted throughout the Judean Hills. Most are no more than a 15-minute drive away. They are more peaceful than Jerusalem and often have very good facilities such as a swimming pool. There are two of special merit.

Mitzpe Rachel   II
Tel. 02-702555; fax 02-733155
Overlooks Bethlehem and the Judean Hills and is about 10 min-utes from downtown Jerusalem.

Neve Ilan   II
Tel. 02-341241
Has many first-class amenities.

Nahariya

Carlton   III
23 Ga'aton Boulevard
Tel. 04-922211
Fine heated pool.

Kalman
27 Jabotinsky Street
Tel. 04-920355
Nicest of the smaller, cheaper hotels.

Kibbutz Loheme Ha-Geteot   I
Off Route 4
Tel. 04-858711
Excellent bed-and-breakfast accommodation on a hard-working, fascinating kibbutz. As well as the Warsaw Ghetto Museum, there is a small farm and a vegetarian food factory which exports its extremely tasty products all around the world.

Kibbutz Yehi'am   I
Yehi'am
Tel. 04 856058
A 15-minute drive from Nahariya, this small kibbutz nestles among the hills and is a perfect rural retreat. Neat, tidy and simple bed-and-

breakfast accommodation available. A Crusader castle and a swimming pool are added attractions.

Panorama   III
6 Hama'apilim Street
Tel. 04-920555
Lives up to its name.

Nazareth

The choice of hotels is not exactly wide, but with this being a Christian town there are many hospices of-fering basic accommodation.

Galilee Hotel   II
Paul VI Street
Tel. 06-571311
Good value for money.

Grand New Hotel   II
St Joseph Street
Tel. 06-576281
Modern, with good views.

The Nazareth Hotel   II
Paul VI Street
PO Box 291
Nazareth 16000
Tel. 06-577777
Reasonable, but not very central.

Hospices

The Casa Nova Pilgrims House   I
(Franciscan)
PO Box 198
Tel. 06-571367
Often fully booked.

Christian Encounter Centre   I
(Greek Catholic)
PO Box 1548
Tel. 06-571367
Simple accommodation.

Franciscaines de Marie   I
(Roman Catholic)
PO Box 41
Tel. 06-554071

Freres de Betharramm (Catholic)   I
PO Box 22
Tel. 06-570046

St Joseph Theological Seminary   I
(Greek Catholic)
PO Box 99
Tel. 06-570540

Convent of the Sisters of Nazareth (Roman Catholic)   I
Casa Nova Street
PO Box 274
Tel. 06-554304

Netanya

Hotel Ginot Yam ▌▌
9 King David Street
Netanya 42264
Tel. 053-41007
All mod-cons, clean and pleasant.

Hotel Goldar ▌▌▌
1 Ussishkin Street
PO Box 1150
Netanya 42272
Tel. 09-338188
Some nice views.

King David Palace ▌▌
4 King David Street
PO Box 1060
Netanya 42264
Tel. 09-342151
Excellent views of the park and the sea.

Maxim Hotel ▌
8 King David Street
Netanya 42264
Tel. 09-621062
Good value for money.

Safed

Due to its elevation, Safed is a pleasant resort town during the hot summers—consequently prices of hotel rooms are raised. The hotels are situated in two sections: on Mount Canaan above the town and in Safed itself.

Bet Benyamin Youth Hostel ▌
1 Lohamei Ha-Getaot Street
Tel. 06-931086
Central location.

Central Hotel ▌▌
Jerusalem Street
Tel. 06-972666
Good position.

David Hotel ▌
Mount Canaan
Tel. 06-920062
Cheap and cheerful.

Nof Hagalil ▌
Mount Canaan
Tel. 06-931595
Excellent views.

Rimon Inn ▌▌
Artists' Colony
Tel. 06-920665
Very old, graceful and quite cheap for its class, yet still the best hotel in Safed.

Ron ▌▌
Hativat Yiftach Street
Tel. 06-972590/1
Splendid location.

Ruckenstein ▌
Mount Canaan
Tel. 06-920060
Good value for money.

Tzameret Canaan ▌
Mount Canaan
Tel. 06-920914
Value for money.

Hotel Yair ▌
59 Jerusalem Street
Tel. 06-920245
Good location and cheap.

Guest House Moshav Amirim ▌▌
14 km (9 miles) out of Safed
towards Akko
Tel. 06-987365
Perfect for vegetarians.

Sea of Galilee

Guest Houses

Nof Ginnosar ▌▌
9 km (6 miles) north of Tiberias
Tel. 06-792161/3
Great location on the Sea of Galilee, with a private beach and its own museum. Lectures on kibbutz life and on the kibbutz itself are available.

Ein Gev Holiday Village ▌
Tel. 06-758027/8
Accommodation is in self-sufficient air-conditioned caravans or bungalows.

Kibbutz Lavi ▌▌
10 km (6 miles) west of Tiberias
Tel. 06-799450
Good for sports.

Kinar ▌
Situated on the north-east shore of the lake
Tel. 06-732670
Civilized and respectable pension-type rooms.

Poriya Youth Hostel ▌
PO Box 232
Tiberias
Tel. 06-750050
Basic accommodation 5 km (3 miles) south of Tiberias.

Vered Hagalil ▌
18 km (11 miles) north of Tiberias
Tel. 06-935785.
American-style ranch.

Tel Aviv

Hotels in Tel Aviv, like in the rest of Israel, range from deluxe to plain horrible. Most are located opposite the beach along HaYarkon Street or in that area. The Hilton and the Carlton are a touch too far away from downtown, but the rest are ideally situated right in the centre of things, close to both the cafés and the beach. Another popular location is the beach of Herzliya, north of Tel Aviv, where the hotels tend to be all-in entertainment and sporting complexes. Of course as these two areas are in premium sections of town the prices charged are also premium. Bargain-hunters should head away from the beach and find somewhere a bit more peripheral. Allenby and Ben Yehuda Streets have a number of cheaper hotels worthy of mention. Those with hired cars can pick a hotel away from downtown altogether. This way you avoid the chronic congestion, annoying one-way systems and terrible lack of parking spaces. The Herzliya hotels spring to mind—but they can be expensive.

Hotels can get fully booked by mid-afternoon in the summertime, so reservations are recommended. These can be arranged through the IGTO in Tel Aviv or at Ben-Gurion Airport on arrival. As Tel Aviv has a year-round season there are no fluctuations in price as in many other parts of Israel. Tel Aviv hotels are, however, slightly more expensive than those in Jerusalem.

Hotel Armon Ha-Yarkon ▌▌
268 Ha-Yarkon Street
Tel Aviv
Tel. 03-5522424
A block away from the beach and close to good restaurants and nightlife.

B'Nei Dan Youth Hostel ▌
32 B'nei Dan Street
Tel Aviv
Tel. 03-5441748
Air conditioned, and a cut above normal youth hostels.

Carlton ▌▌▌
HaYarkon Street
Tel Aviv
Tel. 03-5201818
Overlooks the Tel Aviv marina and has a wonderfully scenic swimming pool on the roof. Rooms are standard but the restaurant is very good despite its name, the Yum-Yum. Breakfast is charged as extra.

Dan Accadia ‖‖‖
Herzliya Pituach
Tel Aviv
Tel. 052-556677
All mod-cons beach hotel. Sports facilities are good.

Dan Panorama ‖‖‖
10 Y Kaufman Street
Tel Aviv
Tel. 03-5190190
Close to Jaffa, but quite a way from the main hotel district and downtown. A very tall hotel with excellent views over the rest of town and Jaffa.

Dan Tel Aviv ‖‖‖
99 HaYarkon Street
Tel Aviv
Tel. 03-5202525
The oldest of Tel Aviv's deluxe hotels, with the bar area straight out of the 1970s. The enclosed pool is good and the location is one of the best.

Daniel ‖‖‖
Herzliya Pituach
Tel Aviv
Tel. 09-5444444
Hotel with spa and healthclub and some fine, healthy restaurants.

Dizengoff Square ‖
2 Zamenhof Street
just off Dizengoff Square
Tel Aviv
Tel. 03-296181
Well situated and clean.

Mandarin ‖‖
North Tel Aviv
Tel. 03-6902777
Very good value-for-money hotel, but a little too far removed for those without transport.

Migdal David ‖
8 Allenby Street
Tel Aviv
Tel. 03-5103868
Clean rooms, good location, friendly staff.

Moriah Plaza ‖‖‖
155 HaYarkon Street
Tel Aviv
Tel. 03-5271515
Located on the beach, overlooking Atarim Square, the Moriah offers great value. It is in a good location, close to the heart of the HaYarkon Street restaurant district.

Moss Hotel ‖
6 Nes Ziona Street
Tel Aviv
Tel. 03-5171655
Good location. Comfortable.

Ora ‖
35 Ben Yehuda Street
Tel Aviv
Tel. 03-5170941
Small hotel with good access to café society.

Sheraton ‖‖‖
115 HaYarkon Street
Tel Aviv
Tel. 03-286222
Plush and friendly.

Shalom Hotel ‖
216 HaYarkon Street
Tel Aviv
Tel. 03-5243277
Good views of the Mediterranean and Independence Park.

Sinai ‖‖
11 Trumpeldor Street
Tel Aviv
Tel. 03-5172621
A relatively luxurious hotel in a reasonable location.

Tadmor ‖‖
38 Basel Street
Herzliya
Tel Aviv
Tel. 09-572321
Like the Dvir hotel in Haifa, the Tadmor is a hotel training school so the service is very good.

Tel Aviv Sheraton Hotels & Towers ‖‖‖
115 HaYarkon Street
Tel Aviv
Tel. 03-5286222
Located on Gordon Beach, the Sheraton is in an excellent position by the HaYarkon Street restaurant and café district and the art galleries of the Gordon Street area.

Tiberias

Tiberias is very pleasant in winter and high season is generally April to May (the Spring *Pesach*/Easter season) and September to October. Most hotel rates increase significantly during this high season.

Ariston ‖‖
19 Sederot Herzl
Tel. 06-790244/6
Quiet, mid-range hotel.

Astoria ‖
13 Ohel Ya'akov Street
Tel. 06-722351
On the main Nazareth–Haifa road.

Dafna ‖
PO Box 52
Tel. 06-792261/3
Reasonable views.

Galei Kinneret ‖‖‖
Kaplan Avenue
Tel. 06-792331
The best of the Tiberias hotels. Grounds are very nice and the location is good.

Ganei Hammat ‖‖
(Holiday Inn)
HaBanim Street
Tel. 06-792890
Plush hotel next to the Tiberias Hot Springs spa.

Ganei Menora ‖‖
3 km (2 miles) south of town
Tel. 06-792770
Peaceful, with its own extensive grounds.

Golan Hotel ‖‖
14 Achad Ha'am Street
Tel. 06-791901/4
Good views of the Sea of Galilee and a nightclub on the premises.

Kibbutz Hakuk ‖‖
MP Hevel Korazim 12355
Tel. 06-799811
Pleasant bed-and-breakfast accommodation 20 minutes from Tiberias by car in a very peaceful rural setting. Good hiking area, but no views over the Sea of Galilee. The small fortress here was built by the first kibbutzniks, and there are only two others like it in the whole country.

Neve Kayit ‖
Migdal
Tel. 06-721654
Vacation apartments and bed-and-breakfast rooms overlooking the Sea of Galilee, 10 minutes from Tiberias by car.

Quiet Beach ‖‖
Gedud Barak Road
Tel. 06-790125
Very good location.

Ron Beach ‖‖
PO Box 17
Tel. 06-791350
Great location, right on the water's edge.

Tiberias Plaza ‖‖‖
PO Box 375
Tel. 06-792233
Modern hotel with many leisure activities.

Tzameret Inn ‖
PO Box 200
Tel. 06-794951/3
Very good views.

Hospices

Church of Scotland Center
(Presbyterian)
PO Box 104
Tel. 06-790144

Terra Sancta
(Franciscan, Catholic)
PO Box 179
Tel. 06-727955

YMCA Peniel-by-Galilee
(Protestant)
PO Box 192
Tel. 06-720685

Restaurants

Israel as a whole has a very wide choice of places to eat and drink—from eastern European to Oriental (this word may have connotations of Chinese food but is in fact a literal translation of a Hebrew word. A more wordy, and therefore unwieldy, equivalent would be Middle Eastern); and from French cuisine to Vietnamese. Some of the best food in Israel can be found in the cafés at bus stations. Quality depends on a fluctuating management, so only a few have been mentioned below.

The price bands should give an indication of the cost of a three-course meal for two people. This does not include wine as Israelis tend not to drink it with their meals, and a bottle can add a considerable amount to the bill. Prices are given, again, in pounds sterling.

I	less than £20
II	£20–30
III	more than £30

Akko

There are many restaurants and cafés in Akko. The main thoroughfare, Ben Ami Street, has the usual assortment of pizza shops, cafés and *falafel* stands.

Abu Cristo　　　　II
Akko harbour
Tel. 04 910 065
Serves very good seafood.

Monte Carlo　　　　I
Saladin Street
Akko
Tel. 04 916 173
Next to the El-Jazzar mosque. Good mix between Oriental and European food.

Eilat

Much is made of the Eilati restaurant scene which is good for seafood, but also renowned for its high-class French cuisine.

La Barracuda　　　　III
Coral Beach
Tel. 07-373442
French and seafood menu.

La Boheme　　　　III
Coral Beach
Tel. 07-374222
Seafood.

La Brasserie　　　　III
King Solomon's Palace Hotel
French cuisine.

La Coquille　　　　III
North Beach
Tel. 07-373461
One of the country's best French restaurants.

Fisherman's House　　　　I
Coral Beach
Tel. 07-379830
Fish and salads, and an all-you-can-eat menu.

Galletino　　　　III
174 Eilot Street
Tel. 07-373578
Nouvelle cuisine in exquisite and arty surroundings.

Maradonna　　　　II
New Tourist Centre
Tel. 07-371649
Good value oriental dishes.

New York, New York　　　　I
99 HaAlmogim Street
Another all-you-can-eat menu, mostly eastern European food.

Pago Pago　　　　II
North Beach Lagoon
Tel. 07-376660
Fish and seafood in a floating restaurant (and a bar open until 3 a.m.).

The Last Refuge　　　　II
Coral Beach
Tel. 07-373627
Seafood in an elegant setting.

Haifa

There are many snack bars throughout the city serving staples such as *falafel*. (The best area, in Hadar, is at the junction of HaHalutz and HaNevi'im Streets.)

Bagel Nash　　　　I
135 HaNassi Boulevard
Serving fresh bagels with a variety of fillings.

MacDavids　　　　I
131 HaNassi Boulevard.
Fast-food, Israeli style.

Gourmet restaurants are mostly found on the top of Mount Carmel, where all the affluent neighbourhoods and hotels are located. Some of these restaurants have very fine views over Haifa Bay or the Carmel.

Amado　　　　II
5 Hamishtara Street
Tel. 04-511092
Well-respected seafood restaurant.

The Caféteria　　　　II
Dan Panorama Hotel
107 Hanassi Boulevard
Tel. 04-352222
The views are good and the food is better than the name suggests.

La Chaumiere　　　　III
40A Ben-Gurion Boulevard
Tel. 04-538563
In an old Arab house. Exclusive French menu.

Chin Lung　　　　I
126 Hanassi Boulevard
Tel. 04-381308
On Mount Carmel. Chinese food.

The Four Seasons　　　　II
116 HaNassi Boulevard
Tel 04-338366
Good for Oriental dishes and eastern European specialities.

El Gaucho　　　　II
25 Tchernichovsky Street
French Carmel
Tel. 04 338837/8
Argentinean restaurant in the Ahuza Club.

Rondo　　　　II
Dan Carmel Hotel
87 Hanassi Boulevard
Tel. 04-242205
Go for the views alone.

Zvi Fish Restaurant　　　　II
2 Paris Square
Tel. 04-668596
Good-value fish dishes.

Jerusalem

Jerusalem is one of the better places in the country for eating and drinking. The Oriental restaurants and cafés in East Jerusalem are easily among the best in Israel. The simple cafés that serve *hummous* and nothing else (for instance, the renowned Abu Shukri on the Via Dolorosa in the Old City) are simply unforgettable. What they lack in hygiene and décor they make up for in making the best *hummous* imaginable.

Abu Shukri |
63 Al Wad Road, Old City
Tel. 02-271538
The best hummous in Jerusalem.

Alumah |
8 Ya'avetz Street
Tel. 02-225014
Wholesome vegetarian food.

American Colony Hotel ||
off Nablus Road
Tel. 02-285171
Excellent. Buffets in fine setting.

Artists' House Café |
12 Shmuel Ha-Nagid Street
Tel. 02-232920
Bar food.

The Café Atara |
7 Ben-Yehuda Street
Tel. 02-225008
Light meals and good selection of pastries.

The Cinematheque ||
Hebron Road
Tel. 02-724131
Continental Cuisine with fine views of Mount Zion and Sultan's Pools.

Cheese Cake |
23 Yoel Salomon Mall
Tel. 02-245082
An amazing range of American cheesecakes and desserts.

The Coffee Shop |
Jaffa Gate
Tel. 02-286812
Good salad bar.

The Cow on the Roof |||
Sheraton Plaza Hotel
47 King George V Avenue
Tel. 02-228133
An excellent reputation; possibly Jerusalem's finest eatery. Famous for its French nouvelle cuisine.

The Family Restaurant |
3 Ha-ma'alot Street
Tel. 02-231590
Moroccan and east European cuisine.

Fonte Bella ||
Rabbi Akiva Street
Tel. 02-248408
Kosher Italian food.

Gilly's ||
33 Hillel Street
Tel. 02-255955
Good value-for-money meat dishes.

Golda's |||
Moriah Plaza Hotel
39 Keren Hayessod Street
Tel. 02-232232
Traditional Jewish eastern European food.

Hachoma ||
128 Jewish Quarter Road
Tel. 02-271332
Once the most exclusive restaurant in the Old City.

Kamin ||
4 Rabbi Akiva Street
Tel. 02-256428
Continental cuisine that includes meat and vegetarian dishes.

King David Hotel Coffee Shop ||
King David Street
Tel. 02-221111
Expensive, but worth it for the ambience.

Mamma Mia |
18 Rabbi Akiva
Tel. 02-248080
Kosher vegetarian Italian menu.

The Marrakesh |||
King David Street
Tel. 02-227577
Very good Moroccan dishes.

Off the Square ||
6 Salomon Street (just off Zion Square)
Tel. 02-242549
Glatt-kosher dairy restaurant. Pleasant surroundings.

Off the Square Meat Restaurant ||
17 Salomon Street
Tel. 02-257719
Kosher meat restaurant.

The Philadelphia Restaurant ||
9 Az-Zahra Street
Tel. 02-289770
Middle Eastern food.

The Pie House, or HaZtrif ||
5 Hyrcanos Street
Tel. 02-242478
A pie shop with many pie combinations.

La Rotisserie |||
Notre Dame Center
opposite the New Gate
Tel. 02-894511
French cuisine with a touch of Middle Eastern taste.

Tavlin Restaurant ||
16 Solomon Street
Tel. 02-243847
Kosher dairy menu. Vegetarian dishes.

Yo Si Peking ||
5 Shimon Ben Shetah Street
Tel. 02-250817
Kosher Chinese food.

Cafés and snackbars are everywhere. Ben Yehuda has many of these places as well as a plethora of coffee-shops and salad-bars. The views—of the world walking past your table—are more important than the food and drink. The Midrahov (Ben Yehuda pedestrian mall) is where to go, and you can easily spend whole evenings here just sitting, watching, sipping and nibbling.

For snacks on the run, when you're not going to be spending hours on the Midrahov, there are a number of places on and just off King George Street and Jaffa Road. Pizza places are sprouting up everywhere. The best are on King George Street. Out-of-the-way eating places include the many Oriental restaurants around Mahane Yehuda, and several of the expensive restaurants in Ein Kerem, a few kilometres outside of Jerusalem but worth the effort.

Nahariya

Ga'aton Boulevard, the main Nahariya drag, is lined with cafés and restaurants. There are also some recently opened restaurants on the new shoreside promenade.

Hollandische Konditorei |
31 HaGa'aton
Tel. 04-922502
Good pastries.

Singapore ||
Ha-Meyasdim
Tel. 04-929209
Chinese food. Excellent desserts.

Nazareth

Nazareth is an Arab town and Oriental food is available everywhere, especially from street-stalls. The bus station is good for *falafel*. Only in the hotels and the hospices is western food the norm. Most restaurants can be found near the intersection of Paul VI and Casa Nova Streets, although few can be recommended.

Astoria ▌▌
Casa Nova Street
Tel. 06-577 965
Middle Eastern cuisine. Curious wall mural of scenes from a German river valley.

Netanya

Renaissance ▌▌
Ha-Atzma'ut Square
Tel. 09-957653
Nice setting, simple food.

Conditory Espresso Ugati ▌
1 Herzl Street
Tel. 053-22604
European food.

Ha-Nasi President ▌▌
5 Herzl Street
Tel. 053-22952
Wholesome Oriental/European fare.

Safed

Bus Station Caféteria ▌
Kikkar Ha-Atzma'ut
Tel. 06-921112
Whilst hardly high cuisine, the food here is plain, simple and good. Self-service.

HaMifgash ▌
75 Rehov Yerushalyim
Tel. 06-930510
Good, wholesome Israeli food— with falafel *stands in the front and behind the restaurant serving some excellent soups.*

Pinati ▌
81 Rehov Yerushalyim
Tel. 06-920855
Hearty portions of Israeli and European food. This is the only restaurant open in Safed during Shabbat.

Tel Aviv

Whatever your tastes, Tel Aviv, with its amazingly broad range of eateries, will be able to satisfy. The best restaurants in Israel are in Tel Aviv, and even the hotels seem to serve up a much better class of fare than in the rest of the country. Restaurants come in all price categories and range from simple Oriental cafés to sophisticated French restaurants serving *haute cuisine* with style. Jaffa is considered to have the cream— plus the views on most evenings are superb. Cheap eats can be found everywhere. There's a large supermarket on Ben Yehuda near the Carlton Hotel if you want to picnic on the beach, or choose from the various *falafel* stands dotted on every street corner. Tel Aviv is a café society so the pastries available are very good. You can easily imagine yourself in a Viennese coffee shop rather than in the tumultuous Middle East.

Alhambra ▌▌▌
30 Jerusalem Boulevard
Jaffa
Tel. 03-6834453
Don't be put off by the less than salubrious location; this restaurant is one of the best in Israel.

The Banana Natural Foods Restaurant ▌▌
334 Dizengoff
Tel Aviv
Tel. 03-6057491
Varied menu of vegetarian food.

Beriozka ▌▌
77 Ben Yehuda Street
Tel Aviv
Tel. 03-5223355
Russian cuisine and live entertainment.

Bukarest ▌▌▌
52 Chen Boulevard
Tel Aviv
Tel. 03-6962922
Rumanian menu and live music.

Fisherman's Restaurant ▌▌
12 Jaffa Port
Tel Aviv
Tel. 03-6813870
Excellent fish specialities.

Genesis ▌▌
Sheriton Hotel
115 HaYarkon Street
Tel Aviv
Tel. 03-5286222
Vegetarian food.

Hippopotam ▌▌
12 Yirmiyahu Street
Tel Aviv
Tel. 03-6048729
The gourmet French cooking is extremely good.

Keton ▌▌
145 Dizengoff Street
Tel Aviv
Tel. 03-5342798
All the Jewish favourites—gefilte fish, chicken soup, blintzes.

Kum Kum ▌▌▌
Sheraton Hotel
115 Ha-Yarkon Street
Tel. 03-5286222
Sumptuous Middle Eastern buffet.

Maganda ▌▌
26 Rav Meir Street
Yemenite Quarter
Tel Aviv
Tel. 03-659990
Yemenite menu, spicy and filling.

Naturalist ▌▌
59 Ben Yehuda
Tel Aviv
Wholly vegetarian. Some good Oriental dishes.

Yin Yang ▌▌
64 Rothschild Boulevard
Tel. 03-621833
Kosher Chinese food.

Panorama/Second Floor ▌▌▌
Astor Hotel
105 HaYarkon Street
Tel Aviv
Tel. 03 5238913
The Second Floor specializes in vegetarian dishes and the Panorama in meat and poultry.

The Pink Ladle ▌▌▌
15 Balfour Street
Tel Aviv
Tel. 03-6418295
Cosy restaurant with an Israeli-inspired menu.

Toutonne ▌▌▌
1 Simtat Mazal Dagime
Old Jaffa
Tel Aviv
Tel. 03-6820693
French food in a fantastic setting, especially in summer when the rooftop terrace is used.

Restaurant Yamit ▌▌
16 Kidar Kedumim
Tel Aviv
Tel. 03-5332695
Middle Eastern cuisine with a menu to suit all price ranges.

Budget

There are lots of budget eateries ranging from burger joints to pizza places. *Falafel* stalls are everywhere, the best being either at the Central Bus Station or at the so-called Falafel market which is off Tchernykovsky Street.

Baobob
43 Ahad Ha-Am Street
Tel Aviv
Tel. 03-203331
Mixture of exciting cooking, situated away from the busy hotel areas.

Cherry
166 Dizengoff Street
Tel Aviv
Tel. 03-5240134
Wide-ranging dairy restaurant.

Eternity
60 Ben Yehuda
Tel Aviv
Tel 03-203151
Tel Aviv's only vegan restaurant. Run by Black Hebrews. The menu is broad-ranging.

Hungarian Blintzes
35 Yirmiyahu Street
Tel Aviv
Tel. 03-6050674
Heavy crêpes.

Maganda Restaurant
26 Rabbi Meir Street
Tel Aviv
Tel. 03-5179990
Yemenite cuisine, strictly Kosher.

Nes Ziona
8a Nes Ziona Street
Tel Aviv
Tel. 03-5172855
Authentic Hungarian cuisine.

Peninat Hakerem
Hakovshim Street
Tel Aviv
Tel. 03-5178779
Yemenite food.

TIV Restaurant
130 Allenby Street
Tel Aviv
Jewish cooking.

Cafés and Snackbars

Most cafés serve light meals, and they are usually good value for money.

Apropos
4 Tarsat Boulevard
Tel Aviv
Tel. 03-5269288
Situated in the Mann Auditorium garden. Cheap and stylish.

Kapulsky
166 Dizengoff Street
Tel Aviv
Excellent pastries and cream cakes.

Kassit
117 Dizengoff Street
Tel Aviv
A traditionally arty place with plenty of style.

Piltz
81 HaYarkon Street
Tel Aviv
Overlooks the beach. Live entertainment.

The White Gallery
2 Kikar Habimah Square
Tel Aviv
Vegetarian café and bookshop.

Tiberias

The Sea of Galilee is famous for its St Peter's Fish, which you will be offered everywhere in Tiberias and its environs. This fish will win no beauty contests but it's very tasty—the marks beside its gills were traditionally left by the Saint's fingers when he picked it up. Although the fish is a native of the Sea of Galilee, most of those that end up on plates are from local fish farms.

Café Hayam Eli Abadi
Waterfront Promenade
Tel. 06-720048
Grilled meats and fish, including St Peter's Fish.

Guy Restaurant
Rehov Ha-Galil
Tel. 06-721973
Oriental dishes with a homely taste.

Kafkas
Nr the Great Mosque
Tel. 06-723074
Very filling Russian-style food made by new Russian immigrants to Israel.

Karamba
Waterfront Promenade
Tel. 06-791546
Mainly vegetarian menu, with some seafood dishes.

Kibbutz En Gev Fish Restaurant
Tel. 06-758035/6

Nof Kenneret
Waterfront Promenade
Tel. 06-720310
Grilled meats and fish, including St Peter's Fish. This restaurant is a boat trip away from Tiberias, but worth it for the grilled St Peter's Fish and the chance to laze on the private beach. By car it would take less than 15 minutes to get to Kibbutz En Gev from downtown Tiberias.

Index

References to illustrations are in *italic*; those in **bold** refer to main entries; those with an asterisk refer to maps.

Abraham's Well 96
accidents *see* emergencies
accommodation 20–5, 34, 294
adventure travel 283, 284
Afula 96
Ain Qelt 83, 89, 246, *247*
air travel
    baggage services 19–20
    internal 16–17
    international 16, 90
airlines 302
airports 11, 16–17, 296
    transport from 11
    transport to 19, 300
Akko 79–80, *196*, *208–9*, **208–12**, *211*
    Burj el-Kommander 212
    Crypt of St John 210
    Hof Argaman 212
    Khan el-Umdan 211
    Marina 211
    Mosque of El-Jazzar 210
    Municipal Museum 211
    Museum of Heroism 211–12
    subterranean Crusader city 92, 210–11
Al-Hijra 62
Allenby Bridge 12, 249
Arad 258–9
    Tel Arad 258
archaeological holidays 280
Armenian Remembrance Day 75
Arshaf 190

arts 37–41
Ashkelon 93, **185–6**
    Afridar Centre 185
    Bar Kockba 185
    Delilah's beach 185
    National Antiquities Park 185
    Painted Tomb 185
    Sculpture Corner 185
    useful numbers and addresses 298–9
    Weizmann Institute of Science 185–6
    Wix Auditorium 186
Automobile and Touring Club 20
Avdat *44*, *238*, 264, *264–5*

baggage services 19–20
Baha'i 69–70, 202–4
Banias 88, *235*, **235–7**
    Cave-Temple of Pan 235
    Greek Orthodox church 236
banks 11, 13
Bat Yam 187
beaches 174–5, 185, 190, 194, 206
Beatitudes, Mount of the 81, 87, *214*, 224, *224*
bed and breakfast 22
Be'er Sheva 52, 93, 241, 259, 259*, *261*, *262*, 263
    Tel Be'er Sheva 259
Bet El 159–60
    Beitin 160
    Jacob's Ladder 160
    Tel Bet El 160
Bet Shearim 93
Bethany **140**, 244
Bethlehem 148–53, 149*
    Christmas celebrations *151*, 152
    Church of the Nativity 150–1
    King David's Wells 152

Manger Square 151
Milk Grotto *150*, 151–2
Shepherd's Fields 152
Tomb of Rachel 153
birdwatching 215, 271, 281
boat trips 269
buses 18, 294, 296, 298, 299, 301

Caesarea 59, 79, **191-4**, *192*, *194*, *195*, 274, 275
calendars 57
camping 25, 294
Cana 96, 219, 221
Capernaum 82, 92, 224
Carmel, Mount 201
Carmel-Oriental Wine Company 91, 187
Carmel Park 95
cars
    Automobile and Touring Club 20
    breakdowns 20
    rental companies 90, 294–5, 297, 298, 300, 302
    rented 12, 18, 28
    see also driving
Channukah 73
Chassidim *13*, *65*, 137, *137*, 229, *229*, 231
children 27–8
Christian holidays 75
Christian Hospices and Hospitals 22, 295
Christian houses 22
Christianity 66–9
Christmas Day 75
churches 295
cinemas and film 59, 134, 286, 287, 288, 289
climate 9–10
clothing
    recommended 41–3
    religious requirements 42–3, 112, 137
Coastal Strip **181–95**, 182*, 298–9

communications *see* mail;
telephone service
consulates 295, 302
costs 34, 36
credit cards 13, 14
cruises 11
Crusaders 48, 50, 55
arches *184*, *192*
ruins 79–80, 80*
statues *51*
cuisine *see* food
currency 13
foreign currency 12–13
customs 12–13
cycling 275–6

Dalait el-Carmel 207
Dan *see* Tel Dan
dance 37, 59, 285, 287,
288
Dead Sea *16*, 47, 88–9,
89*, 239, 240*, *250*, **250**,
254, *254*
Dead Sea scrolls 251–3,
253
Deganya Alef 224
dentists 295, 297
desert *see* Judean desert;
Negev
desert car-safari 95–6
diamond factories *180*,
190, 191
Dimona 241, 243
disabled visitors 32–4
documents, entry *see*
passports; visas
Dor 194–5
Dotan, Valley of 160–1
drink 30, 46, 249
driving 12, 17–18, 186
desert car-safari 95–6
in the Golan Heights
234
in the West Bank 147
see also cars
driving licences 18
Druse 71
duty-free allowances 12

Easter 75
Ebal, Mount 161
Egypt
entry from 12
visas 12, 20, 297, 302
visits to 12, 20
Eid al-Fitr 75
Eilat 9, 243, **267–71**, 267*,
269
Cinema Eilat 289
Club Inn 289
Coral Beach 93, 268
Coral Beach Nature
Reserve 271
Coral World (underwater
observatory) 93, 269,
270, 271
Disco-Americano 289
entertainment 289
HaTmarim Boulevard
289
North Beach 268, 269
Red Sea 269
useful numbers and
addresses 275, 278,
280, 281, 302–3
Water Festival 59
Yellow Submarine 93,
269
Ein Gedi 90, 93, **254–5**,
282
David's Spring 254, *255*
Nahal Arugot 255
Ein Gev 82
Music Festival 59
Ein Kerem 139
Church of St John 139
Church of the Visitation
139
Ein Salah 154
electricity supply 43
embassies 297
emergencies
motoring 20
telephone numbers 27,
295, 297, 298, 299,
301, 302
En Fashkha 89–90

entertainment 285–9
see also festivals
entry documents *see*
passports; visas
Evil Counsel, Mount of
125
Haas Promenade 125

ferries 297, 299, 300
Festival of Music and
Drama 59
festivals 59
first aid *see* emergencies
food 30, 32, 34–5, 232
kosher 21, 33
vegetarian 33

Galilee, Sea of *47*, 223,
223, 227, *227*, 234
Galilee, the 81–2, 81*, 87–
8, 88*, **215–37**, 216*
useful numbers and
addresses 301–2
Gamala 237
waterfall 237
geography 46–7
Gerizim, Mount 161, 162
Gethsemane, Garden of
87, **127–8**
Church of All Nations
128–9, *128–9*
Gilboa, Mount 222
Gan HaShlosha 222
Ginnosar 81, 224
glass factory, ancient 187
Golan Heights 47, 55, 56,
216*, **234**
golf 274
Government Tourist
Information Office
(IGTO) 11, 298, 300
guide-driven limousines
19

Hadassah Hebrew
University Medical
Centre 139–40
Hadera 187

Hai Bar Wildlife Reserve 93, **266-7**
Haifa 58, **197-207**, 198*, 199*
  aerial cable car 205
  Af-Al-Pi (ship) 205
  Al Pasha 289
  Auditorium 288
  Baha'i Shrine and Gardens 202, *203*, 204, *204*
  Bat Galun 206
  beaches 206
  Biological Institute 207
  Carmel Beach 206
  Carmel National park 201
  Carmelite subway 201
  Central Carmel 201, 205
  Cinematheque 288
  Clandestine Immigration and Naval Museum 205-6
  Club 120, 289
  Dagon Grain Silo 206
  Davka 289
  Elijah's Cave 206
  entertainment 287-9
  Hadar Ha-Carmel 197, 201, 274
  HaMo'adon 289
  HaTechnion Visitor Centre 201
  history 200-1
  Hof Dado 206
  Hof haShaket 206
  Hof Zamur 206
  Israel Edible Oil Museum 207
  James de Rothschild Centre 288
  The Khan 289
  Kiryat Haim 206
  Little Haifa 289
  London Pride 289
  Mitzpe Ha-Shalom 201
  Mount Carmel 201
  Municipal Theatre 288
  Museum complex 206
  Museum of Ancient Art 206
  Museum of Modern Art 206
  Museum of Music and Ethnology 206-7
  Museum of Prehistory 207
  National Maritime Museum 207
  Port area 205-6
  Primordial Man Museum 95
  Railway Museum 207
  Reuben and Edith Hecht Museum of the Archeology of the Land of Israel 207
  Rodeo 289
  Stella Maris French Carmelite church 205
  Studio 46, 289
  Sunset 289
  useful numbers and addresses 299-300
  Zoo 207
Hammat Gader 82, 227-8
handicapped visitors 32-4
hang gliding 278
Ha'on 228
Happy Name Day 75
Hebrew 62
Hebron 157-9, *158, 159*
  Tombs of the Patriarchs 157, 158-9
Hermon, Mount 237, 274
  Ketet HaHermon 237
  Neve Ativ 88, 237
Herodian 154-6, *155, 156*
Herzliya 187, 190, 274
  Accadia 190
  Arshaf 190
  Separate Beach 190
  Sharon 190
  Shefayim 190
  Zebulun-Daniel 190
hiking 276, *277*, 278
hire cars *see under* cars
history 45-6, 48-57, 49*, 52*
holidays 25, 57-9
Holocaust Memorial Day 74
horse riding 275
hospitals 122, 295, 299, 301, 302
hotels 20-1, 27, 28
Hula Valley 233
  Ayun reserve 233
  Hurshat Tal National Park 88, 233
  Nature Reserve 87-8, 92, 233, *233*

IGTO *see* Government Tourist Information Office
Independence Day (Yom HaAtzmaut) 25, 74
information, tourist 11, 145, 231, 268-9, 288, 298-9, 300, 302
Inn of the Good Samaritan *67*, 89, 92, 244
insurance
  damage and accident 18
  flight 14
  travel 14
International Harp Contest 59
International Music Festival 59
Isfiya 207
Islam 69
Israel 8*
Israel Festival 287
Israel Independence Day 61
Israel Museum 134, 136
Israeli year 72-5
  Christian holidays 75
  Jewish year 72-4
  Muslim holidays 75

Israelis 60–2

Jaffa *40–1*, 94, *175*, **175–8**, *179*
  Clock Tower 177
  el-Mahmoudia Mosque 177
  Flea Market 177
  haPisgah Gardens 178
  House of Simon the Tanner 178
  Kedumin Square 178
  Museum of Antiquities 178
  Old Port area 175, *176*, 177
  Rock of Andromeda 177
  Saint Peter's Church 178, *178*
Jebel Batin 161
Jericho 52, *53*, *245*, **245–9**
  Ein al-Sultan 246
  Hisham's Winter Palace 249
  Khirbet al-Mafjar 248
  Monastery of the Temptation 83–4, 249
  Tel Jericho 248–9, *248*
Jerusalem 9, 19, 72, 75, **99–139**, 100*, *101*
  Absalom's Tomb 87, 129, *130*
  Agricultural Museum 137
  ancient burial caves 122
  Arab Quarter (Old City) *35*, 85, 102, *123*
  Armenian Quarter (Old City) 84, 102, **108–9**
  Atara Leyoshna 112
  Avenue of the Righteous Gentiles 138
  Ben Yehuda *36*, 94
  Bene Hezir 87, 129
  Bezalal Art Museum 134

Biblical Zoo 138
Billy Rose Sculpture Garden 134
Binyanei HaUma 285
Broad Wall 131
Burnt House 84, 111
Cardo 84, 102, 110
Chamber of the Holocaust 118
Chapel (Mosque) of the Ascension 126–7
Children's Museum 134
Christian Quarter (Old City) 102, **118–20**
Church of All Nations 128–9, *128–9*
Church of the Holy Archangels 108
Church of the Holy Sepulchre 109
Cinematheque 59, 134, 286
City Museum 105
city walls 104, 105*, 108
Damascus Gate *10*, 86, 104, *104*, 108
David Street 84, 108–9
Dome of the Rock 41, *71*, 86, *98*, 102, 111, *114*, **114–15**, *115*, 116
Dominus Flevit 127
Dormiton Abbey 87, 116, *116*, 117
DS and JH Gottesmann centre for Bible Studies 134
Dung Gate 87, 108, 116
East 75, 100, **120–31**, *122*
Edward Mardigian Museum of Armenian Art and History 108
El-Aksa 43, *110*, 116
El-Kas 115
entertainment 285–6
finger of Og 138
Fountain of the Virgin 131

Gan Ha-Atzma'ut 134
Garden of Gethsemane 87, **127–8**
Garden Tomb 86, 120, *120*
Gate of the Chain 109
Gates of Mercy 125
Gerard Bakhar Center 285
Gihon Spring 131
Golden Gate 108, 125
Great Synagogue 134, 296
Gulbenkian Public Library 108
Hadassah Hospital 122
Hall of Heroism 138
Har Ha-Zikkaron 138
Haram ash-sharif *70*, 86, 111, 114, *114*
Hebrew University 285
Herod's Family Tomb 133
Herod's Gate 108
Hezekiah's Tunnel 131
history 54, 55, 100–2
Holocaust Museum (Yad Vashem) *37*, 43, 138–9, *139*
Holy Sepulchre 75, 86, 119, *119*
Hurva synagogue 111
International Cultural Centre for Youth 285
Israel Museum 134, 136
Jaffa Gate 84, 104, 108, 118
Jerusalem Theatre 285
Jewish Quarter (Old City) 84–5, 93, 102, **109–11**, 109*
Kidron Valley 122, 129
King David Hotel 21, *21*, 55, 132–3
King David's Tomb 118
King David's Tower *50*, 84, 104–5, *107*

Knesset 60, 134, 136
Kotel (Western Wall)
    67, 84, 85–6, 93,
    111–12, *112*
Lalo's Pub 286
Liberty Bell Garden *26*,
    134
Library of Manuscripts
    108
Mahane Yehuda *133*,
    136
Mary Magdalene
    Russian Orthodox
    Church 127, *127*
Mea Shea'rim 42–3,
    136–7
Memorial to the Victims
    of the Death Camps
    139
Midrahov *30–1*, 94, 285
Monastery of the Cross
    136
Mount of Olives *15*, 87,
    122, *124–5*, 125–6, *126*
Mount Zion 87, 116,
    118
Mount Scopus 122
Nea 111
New Gate 108
Old City 84–7, 85*,
    100, 102, **104–20**,
    106*, 108, 280
Old Yishuv Court
    Museum 110–11
Ophel Archeological
    Park 84, 116
orientation 103–4
Orion Cinema 286
Ramparts Walk 104
Rockefeller Museum
    120, 122
Russian Compound
    137–8
Russian Orthodox
    church 137
St Anne's Church 86,
    118
St James Cathedral 108

St Stephen's Gate 108,
    118
Samuel Bronfman
    Biblical and Archeo-
    logical Museum 134
Sanctuary of
    Condemnation 118
Sergei Hostel 138
Shrine of the Book 134
Sir Isaac and Lady
    Edith Wolfson
    Museum 134
Sound and Light Show
    105
Stone of Unction 119,
    120
Sultan's Pool 134, 285
Temple Mount *70*, 86,
    111, 114, *114*
Temple of Herod 113*,
    114
Tomb of the Prophets
    126
Tomb of Zechariah 87,
    129, *129*
Tombs of Sanhedria
    138
Tourjeman Post
    Museum 122
The Underground 286
useful numbers and
    addresses 275, 276,
    278, 280, 294–6
Via Dolorosa 62, 86,
    118–19
West 100, *132*, **132–9**
Western Wall (Kotel)
    63, 84, 85–6, 93,
    111–12, *112*
windmill 133, 134
Yad Vashem
    (Holocaust Museum)
    37, 43, 138–9, *139*
Yemin Moshe 41,
    133–4, *135*
YMCA Building *103*,
    132
Zedekiah's Cave 122

Zion Gate 84, 87, 108,
    108
Zion Square 94, 132
Jerusalem Day 75
Jerusalem International
    Film Festival 59
Jewish sites 93
Jewish year 72–4
Jezreel Valley 92, *205*
Johnny's Desert Tours
    283, 303
Jordan
    entry and exit laws 12
Jordan Baptismal Site
    249
Jordan (river) 233–4
Judaism 63–6
Judea 49*
Judean desert **239–45**,
    240*, *244*, 275, 276, *277*

Kabri Springs 80, 92
Kadesh-Barnea 265–6
Kfar Kanna 96, 219, 221
Karmeil Dance Festival 59
kibbutz guest houses 21
kibbutzim 24
Kidron Valley 122, 129
    Absalom's Tomb 87,
    129, *130*
    Bene Hezir 87, 129
    Tomb of Zechariah 87,
    129, *129*
Kinneret, Lake of *see*
    Galilee, Sea of
Knesset 64, 134, 136
Kursi 82

LA Meyer Memorial
    Institute for Islamic Art
    41
Lag Ba'Omer 61
language 66
    guide 290–3
    place names 48
Latrun 140
    Fort Artillery Museum
    29, 56

Monastery 83, 92, 140, *141*
less able visitors 32–4
Lohamei HaGheta'ot 92, 212
  Ghetto Fighter's House 212

Ma'ale Adumim 246
magazines 36–7
mail service 25
  see also post offices
Majdal Shams 236
Makhtesh Ramon (Ramon Crater) *17*, 93, 96, 264, *266*
Mar Saba 83, 156–7
Masada *18*, 54, 93, **255–7**, *258*
  The Battery 257
  Snake Pass *256*, 257
  Sound and Light Show 257
  Zohar Springs 257–8
matzkot 11, 174, *275*
Mawlid an-Nabi 75
medical services *see* dentists; emergencies; hospitals
Megiddo 46, 92, 97, *217*, **217–18**
  Archaeological Excavations 218
Meron, Mount 47, 93-4
Metzoke Dragot 283
Migdal 81
Mimouna 58
mini-buses 19, 296–7
Mitspe Jericho (Mitzpe Yeriho) 89, 92, 246
Mitspe Ramon 93, 96, 243, 264
monasteries 82–4, 82*
money 12–14
Montfort 80, 92, 232
moshavim 24
Mount of the Beatitudes *see* Beatitudes, Mount of

Mount of Olives *see* Olives, Mount of
Mount Zion *see* Zion, Mount
Muhraka 207
music 59, 287
  classical 37, 59, 285, 287, 288
  popular 171, 287
  rock 285, 287
Muslim holidays 75

Nabi Musa 245
Nablus 161
Nahal Arugot 90
Nahariya 92, 212–13, 275, 280
Nahsholim *183*, 194
national parks 282
natural history information 295, 297
nature reserves 87–90, 95, 271, 281–2
  see also Ein Gedi; Hai Bar Wildlife Reserve; Hula Valley; Meron, Mount; Tel Dan
Nazareth 96, *218*, **218–19**
  Arab Town 219
  Franciscan Basilica of the Annunciation 219, *220*
  Mary's Well 219
  Natzeret Illit 219
  St Gabriel Greek Orthodox Church 219
  St Joseph's Church 219
  useful numbers and addresses 301, 302
  Virgin's cave 219
Negev 241, 243, **259–71**, 260*, 275, 276, 283
Neot Hakikar 283
Netanya 59, 190–1
  diamond factories *180*, 190, 191

Gan Ha-Melekh amphitheatre *188-9*, 190
  useful numbers and addresses 278, 298–9
Neve Ativ 88, 237, 274, 275
newspapers 36
nightclubs 286, 287, 289
Nimrod's Castle 236–7

Occupied Territories 46–7, 57, 234
Olives, Mount of *15*, 75, 87, 122, *124–5*, **125–7**, *126*
  Chapel (Mosque) of the Ascension 126–7
  Dominus Flevit 127
  Mary Magdalene Russian Orthodox Church 127, *127*
  Tomb of the Prophets 126
ornithology 215, 271, 281

Park Ramon 264
passports 10
Peki'in 228, 232
periodicals 36–7
Pesach 73–4, 162
pilgrimages 15
place names 48
police 27, 137, 295, 301, 302
political structures 60
Pomegranates, Valley of the 244
population 60–2
post offices 11, 25, 295–6, 298, 300, 301, 303
prices 34–5
public holidays *see* holidays
public toilets 27
Purim 73, 231

Qumran 82, 250, *251*, *252*, 253, 254

Dead Sea scrolls 251–3, *253*

radio stations 37
rail service 17
Ramadan 25, 62
Ramon Crater *see*
   Makhtesh Ramon
religion 62–71
restaurants 30, 32, 34, 35, 46, 249
Rishon-le-Zion 186–7, 275
Rosh Hanikra 92, 213
   grottoes 213
Rosh Hashanah 25, 59

Safed 93, **229–31**
   Artists' Quarter 230
   Caro Synagogue 231
   Ethiopian Folk Art Centre 231
   General Exhibition Hall 230
   Ha'Ari Synagogue 231
   Old City (Synagogue Quarter) 230–1
   Shem va Ever Cave 229–30
   useful numbers and addresses 301, 302
sailing 175
St Theodosius monastery 83
Samaritan Passover 74
Samaritans 70, 161–2
Scopus, Mount 122
   ancient burial caves 122
   Hadassah Hospital 122
scuba diving 269, 279–81
Sde Boker 263
Sebastya 162–4
security 16
service charges 27
Shabbat 58, 59
Shavu'ot 25, 74, 162
Shechem 161
Shiloh 160

Shivta 263–4
shops and shopping 34, 263
   costs 34–5
   shuqs 34, 108–9
Sigd, the 60
Simhat Torah 25, 72
skiing 237, 274–5
snorkelling 269
Society for the Protection of Nature in Israel (SPNI) 137, 276, 278, 283, 295
Solomon's Pools 153–4
Sorek Stalagmite cave 140
sports **273–81**, 296
squash 274
student travel 14
Sukkot 72–3, 162
summer camps, children's 28
swimming 279, 296
synagogues 296

Tabgha 92
   Church of the Multiplication of the Loaves and Fish 81, 224, *226*
Tabor, Mount 221–2
   Basilica of the Transfiguration 222
taxis 11, 19, 27, 125, 146, 299, 300, 301–2
   sherutim 11, 19, 27, 146, 297, 299, 300, 301–2
Tel Aviv 9, 19, 58, 59, *164*, **165–75**, 166*, *168–9, 170, 270*, 274, *278*
   Bat Yam 175
   beaches 174–5
   Beit Leissin 287
   Beth HaTefutsoth 174
   Carmel Market 171
   Cassibar 287
   The Cave 287

   Ceramic Pavilion 172
   Clore Park 174
   Coliseum 287
   Dixieland 287
   Dizengoff Square 172, *172–3*
   Dizengoff Street 94
   entertainment 286–7
   Ethnography and Folklore Pavilion 172
   Glass Pavilion 172
   Gordon 287
   Ha-Arets Museum Complex 171
   Ha-bimah Theatre 171, 286–7
   Haganah Museum 171
   HaYarkon Park 287
   Helena Rubinstein Pavilion 171
   history 165, 167
   Hof Hadarim 174–5
   Independence Hall 171
   Kadman Numismatic Pavilion 171–2
   Kefar Shmariyahu 175
   Kolnoa Dan Disco 287
   Lasky Planetarium 174
   Liquid 287
   Man and His Toil Centre 172, 174
   Mann Auditorium 171, 287
   museums 171–2, 174
   Nechushtan Pavmon 172
   observatory 170
   orientation 167–8
   Penguin 287
   The Rock Café 287

   Sailing Club 175
   sculpture fountain 172, *172–3*
   Shablul 287
   Shalom Tower 168, 170
   Soweto 287

Studio 69, 287
Tel Aviv Museum 287
Tzavta 287
useful numbers and
  addresses 278, 279,
  280, 281, 283, 296–8
Wax Museum 170
Yemenite Quarter 170
ZOA 287
Tel Bet She'an 222
Monastery of the Noble
  Lady Maria 222
Tel Dan 233
Bet Ussishkin 233
Nature Reserve 88, 233
telephone service 25, 27,
  296, 298, 303
useful numbers 27, 295,
  296
television 37
temperatures, average 9
tennis 274
theatre 39, 285, 286–7,
  288
Tiberias 81, 87, 93, **222**,
  281
useful numbers and
  addresses 275, 301,
  302
time 10
Timna 267
Mines 93, 243
Solomon's Pillars 267

tipping 13, 27
Tisha B'Av 74
toilets, public 27
tourist information *see*
  information, tourist
tours 17–18
for the disabled 32–3
themed routes 79–97
tour companies 283,
  285, 303
Tracks 283, 285
trains 17
transport 139, 140, 146,
  201
see also buses; ferries;
  guide-driven
  limousines; mini-
  buses; taxis; trains
travel
in Israel 16–20
to Israel 11–12
see also cars; driving
traveller's cheques 14
Tu bi'shvat 73

vaccinations 14
Vered HaGalil 87
visas 10, 12, 20, 297, 302
volunteer work 24

Wadi Qelt 246
Ain Qelt 83, 89, 246,
  247

Monastery of St George
  of Koziba 6, *68–9*,
  83, 92, 246
water-skiing 278–9
watersports 59, 175, 269,
  278–81
weather 9–10
West Bank 25, 46–7, 55,
  75, **143–64**, 144*, 296
when to go 10
wind-surfing 175, *272*,
  278–9
wine industry 186, 187
work, volunteer 24

Yad HaNah *23*
Yavne 54, 93
Yehi'am 80, 92, *210*, 228
Yom Ha'Atzma'ut 25, 61
Yom Kippur 25, 59
youth hostels 22, 132

Zichron Ya'akov 91
Zimriya 59
Zion, Mount 87, 116, 118
Chamber of the
  Holocaust 118
Dormiton Abbey 87,
  116, *116*, 117
King David's Tomb
  118
Zohar Springs 257–8

029/410 LUD